GLOBETROTTER™

Safari Guide

KENYA

NEW
HOLLAND

Safari Guide
KENYA
Dave and Val Richards

CONTENTS

CHAPTER ONE:
Part One: Planning your trip   8
    Types of safari – special safaris   9
    Sites of historical or cultural interest   14
    Accommodation   16
    What to pack   17
Part Two: Eco issues and climate   18
    Kenya's safari code   18
    Climate   19
    The world's greatest wildlife spectacle   20

CHAPTER TWO:
Nairobi, Ol Doinyo Sabuk and Amboseli   24

CHAPTER THREE:
Chyulu Hills, Tsavo East and Tsavo West   40

CHAPTER FOUR:
Shimba Hills, Mwalanganje and Tana River   50

CHAPTER FIVE:
Rohole, Kora and Meru   56

CHAPTER SIX:
Sibiloi, Central Island, South Island, Saiwa Swamp and
    Mount Elgon   64

CHAPTER SEVEN:
Marsabit, Losai, Shaba, Samburu, Buffalo Springs and
    Laikipia Region   72

CHAPTER EIGHT:
Lake Nakuru, Lake Bogoria, Mount Longonot and
    Hell's Gate   90

CHAPTER NINE:
Mount Kenya National Park   102

CHAPTER TEN:
Aberdare National Park   106

CHAPTER ELEVEN:
Masai Mara and Ruma   118

CHAPTER TWELVE: 130
National Parks Guide   142
Travel Tips   146
Selected Animal and Bird Gallery   150
Check List   156

INDEX   158

INTRODUCTION

K enya is a land of contrasts; its habitats vary from the snow-covered shoulders of Mount Kenya, montane forests, tropical rainforests, dry semidesert and savannahs, to the mangrove forests along the coast. Examples of all of these habitats are protected by National Parks and Reserves.

This variety of habitats and the wildlife they contain is unsurpassed anywhere else in Africa. In the northeast are the arid lands of Samburu, Buffalo Springs and Shaba reserves, where a visitor can see wildlife that is found nowhere else, such as the endangered Grevy's zebra, the long-necked gerenuk, beisa oryx, reticulated giraffe and some very special birds. In the southwest there is the world-famous Masai Mara National Reserve, well known for its abundance of wildlife (and where it is not at all unusual to be able to see and photograph all of the Big Five – black rhino, buffalo, elephant, leopard and lion – in a single morning) and where, between July and September, the famous wildebeest migration is to be found. In between these two extremes are the mountain national parks of Mount Kenya and the Aberdares, and the Great Rift Valley. Certainly no safari can be complete without a visit to Lake Nakuru National Park and its flamingos. To complete the variety, there are a number of marine national parks and reserves along the coast.

Top Spots to See Animals

Masai Mara National Reserve: big cats and the famous wildebeest migration.
Buffalo Springs/Samburu National Reserves: gerenuk, beisa oryx, reticulated giraffe and leopard.
Lake Nakuru National Park: flamingos, rhinos and leopard.
Amboseli National Park: elephants and views of Kilimanjaro.

Opposite top: A lioness and her cubs in the Masai Mara National Reserve.
Opposite centre: A private vehicle on safari in Amboseli National Park, with Kilimanjaro in the distance.
Opposite bottom: The distinctive Vulturine Guineafowl occur in flocks in dry bush country.

Introduction

Where to Spot the Big Five

Lion: a nocturnal hunter, but the easiest cat to see in the Masai Mara during the day.
Leopard: shy and nocturnal, it can usually be seen in the Masai Mara, Samburu and Lake Nakuru reserves on early morning and late afternoon drives.
Elephant: seen in most wildlife areas (except Nairobi and Saiwa Swamp national parks); the best place is Amboseli, around swamps at midday.
Buffalo: the most dangerous of Africa's animals, it can best be seen in the Masai Mara National Reserve and the Aberdare National Park.
Rhino: both black and white species are mostly confined to protected areas; see them in Nairobi, Nakuru and Aberdare national parks; Solio Ranch and Lewa Conservancy.

Kenya's national parks were founded in 1946. They offer the visitor a chance to experience and observe wildlife in its natural state in stunning scenic backgrounds. The wildlife that a visitor will see in the national parks and reserves has become so accustomed to safari vehicles, and their often noisy occupants, that the animals no longer run and hide, but carry on with their normal life. Prides of lions will often continue sleeping, which can at times be a little annoying for the visitor wanting to photograph a fierce lion! One thing is for sure, anyone visiting Kenya will never forget their amazing experiences and many visitors will return again and again.

It can be said that safaris started in Kenya. The word safari simply means 'a journey' in Kiswahili. In 1909 President Roosevelt set out from Nairobi's famed Norfolk Hotel on his famous year-long safari with two white hunters, JR Cuningham and William Judd, 15 askaris (soldiers) and 265 porters. Porters were paid $US4.50 per day, a licence to shoot an elephant was US$85.00, and for a rhino or a hippo it was US$15.00. On this safari Roosevelt and his son Kermit collected 1100 specimens, which included 17 lion, 11 elephant and 20 black rhino. The oldest operating safari company in Africa, Ker & Downey Safaris, based in Nairobi, celebrated its 60th birthday in 2006.

Safaris are a very important source of income for Kenya, being second only to agriculture in revenue earnings. So by visiting Kenya you are helping the economy and all of Kenya's people.

So *Karibu* (welcome), and enjoy your safari in Kenya.

PART ONE: PLANNING YOUR TRIP

When booking your safari it is very important to book with a reputable company, preferably a member of KATO (Kenya Association of Tour Operators). Ensure that your driver/guide is at least a Bronze level member of the KPSGA (Kenya Professional Safari Guides Association) and your tour leader is at least a Silver level member of the KPSGA. Pick an itinerary that stays at a destination for two or (even better) three nights. There is nothing more exhausting than to keep moving on every night, with long drives between destinations.

Part One: Planning your trip

Types of safari – special safaris
While most visitors take a general wildlife safari, you can book a safari specializing in a particular subject.

Above: A family of cheetahs sitting on a tourist vehicle, a not unusual sight in the Masai Mara National Reserve.

Balloon safaris
Balloon flights are available in the Masai Mara and in the Rift Valley, and can be arranged with your tour operator or from your camp or lodge. They take place at dawn which means an early wake-up as you have to drive to the launch site. In the Masai Mara there are a number of balloon companies.
Governors' Camp Balloons: based at Little Governors' Camp, www.governorscamp.com
Mara Balloons: based at Keekorok Lodge, Mara Safari Club, Mara Serena Lodge.
Trans World Safaris: tours@transworldsafaris.com
There are also balloon flights available over the Rift Valley. Guests are picked up from their lodge or camp at Lake Naivasha or Lake Nakuru. **Go Ballooning Kenya:** www.goballooningkenya.com

Bird shooting safaris
The shooting season for sandgrouse, guineafowl, francolin and spurfowl is 1 July to 31 October. The season for doves and pigeons is 1 June to 31 March. Operators include:
Ker & Downey Safaris: www.kerdowneysafaris.com

Introduction

Top Spots to See Birds

Kakamega Forest,
Buffalo Springs/Samburu
national parks (mountain),
Mida Creek (coast),
Arabuko-Sokoke Forest Reserve
(coast).

Kenya's Ornithological Heritage

Kenya has 1092 bird species. In
Africa only Zaire – four times larger
in area than Kenya – has more
species. Kenya holds the record for
the largest number of birds seen in a
24-hour period: 340, seen by Terry
Stevenson, John Fanshaw and Andy
Roberts (a team from the USA has
recorded a higher total in South
America, but a substantial number
of the birds were only heard and not
seen). Kenya also holds the world
record for the greatest number of
birds seen in a 48-hour period: 496,
seen by Don Turner, David Pearson
and the world-famous wildlife
film-maker, Alan Root.

Robin Hurt Safaris: www.robinhurtphotosafaris.com
Kulalu Camp, Galana Ranch: nick@swiftmalindi.com
Kalacha Camp, Chalbi Desert: www.tropicair-kenya.com
David Mead: www.kerdowneysafaris.com

Bird-watching safaris

With 1092 species recorded, Kenya is a prime birding destination.
On a two-week safari as many as 500 species can be seen, while on
a three-week safari during October through to March, when many
Eurasian migrants visit, seeing 700 species is a distinct possibility.
Bird Ventures (Origins Safaris): www.originsafaris.info
Ben's Ecological Safaris: www.tcfb.com/bestours

Camel safaris

Camel safaris take place in northern Kenya where the camel is
most suited. Safaris last from a few days to a week. Sleeping on a
camp bed (covered with a net) under the stars is an unforgettable
experience. Although visitors can ride a camel if they wish, the
real wonder of this type of safaris is walking. On these safaris
visitors are escorted by colourful Samburu tribesmen.
African Frontiers: www.geocities.com/african_frontiers
Sabuk Camel Safaris: www.eco-resorts.com/SabukCamels.php
Bobong and Ol Maisor Camels: olmaisor@africaonline.co.ke

Climbing safaris

To climb Africa's second highest mountain, Mount Kenya, is the
ambition of climbers worldwide. A climb to the twin peaks, Batian
(5199m/17,058ft) and Nelion (5188m/17,022ft), requires serious
ice-climbing experience, but for lesser skilled climbers and
walkers, Point Lenana (4985m/16,355ft), higher than Mont Blanc,
is a good alternative. There are three climbing routes: the
Naro-Moru Route, Sirimon Track and Chogoria Route. There is
also an interesting Summit Circuit that circles the mountain.
Naro Moru Lodge: www.alliancehotels.com
Mountain Club of Kenya: www.mck.or.ke
Tropical Ice Safaris: www.tropical-ice.com

Cultural safaris

Most safari camps and lodges offer visits to local villages. In the
northern districts its possible to visit isolated tribes in the Lake

Part One: Planning your trip

Turkana area, which is often described as the 'Cradle of Mankind.'
Origins Safaris: www.originsafaris.info/cradle-of-mankind.htm

Elephant safaris
In the Samburu National Reserve it is possible to join elephant researchers while they study the local elephant, and in Nairobi it is possible to visit Daphne Sheldrick's elephant orphanage.
Elephant Watch Safaris: www.elephantwatchsafaris.com
Sheldrick Animal Orphanage:
www.sheldrickwildlifetrust.org

Fishing safaris
Kenya has a lot to offer, from trout fishing in streams and mountain tarns on the Aberdares and Mount Kenya, and Lake Turkana in the hot far north, where you can fish for tiger fish, giant Nile perch, barbel and tilapia, to excellent sport fishing in the Indian Ocean. Guests staying at Mfangano Lodge and Rusinga Lodge, on Lake Victoria, can fish for Nile perch and tilapia. Sea fishing is on offer at most of the coastal hotels.
Brookside Fishing Flies Company:
www.flyfishingkenya.com
Ker & Downey Safaris: www.kerdowneysafaris.com
Hemingways Resort, Watamu: www.big-gamefishing.net
Sea Adventures Ltd., Shimoni: hemphill@biggame.com
Peponi Hotel, Lamu: www.peponi-lamu.com
Kingfisher Boats, Malindi: www.kenyasportsfishing.com
Howard Laurence-Brown, Mtwapa:
www.kenyadeepseafishing.net

Flying safaris
With over 400 airstrips in the country, an excellent domestic schedule, and charter airlines available, flying is becoming more and more popular. Domestic flights with Air Kenya and Safarilink from Nairobi's Wilson Airport fly to all the major safari destinations, while the charter airlines will fly you virtually anywhere.
Schedule Airlines
Air Kenya: www.airkenya.com
Safarilink: www.safarilink.co.ke
Air Charter Services
Boskovic Air Charters: www.boskovicaircharters.com

Scenic Beauty Spot

Great Rift Valley: there are stunning views looking down into the Great Rift Valley from near Nairobi and Maralal.

Best Times to Visit Kenya

It's possible to enjoy a safari all year round – even in the rainy season it rarely rains for more than a few hours each day and then usually only in the evenings. The most popular time for safaris is July to September. This is the time when the famous 'migration' takes place in the Masai Mara and when most schools in Europe and the USA are closed for the summer holidays.

Introduction

East African Air Charters: www.eaaircharters.co.ke
Everett Aviation (helicopter charters):
www.everettaviation.com
Tropic Air (based out of Nanyuki): www.tropicair-kenya.com
Naivasha Aviation Services (based out of Gilgil):
www.simpsonsafaris.com

Getting married

For some time now, it has been popular to get married while on holiday. More and more safari camps and lodges now offer this service too. At Governors' Camp in the Masai Mara, as well as regular marriage ceremonies, they can also arrange for couples to get married in a Masai *manyatta* by a Masai *labon* (holy man). This kind of marriage is not legal back home, of course. Information and photography: www.lynseyphotos.com

Golfing safaris

Below: Governors' Il Moran Camp on the banks of the Mara River in the Masai Mara National Reserve.

Few countries can offer golfing holidays that include wonderful wildlife and beautiful beaches. At some of the golf courses you may even have to wait for a hippo or a group of warthogs to move before you can tee off! There are 40 golf courses in Kenya, ten of which are used for championship events. Many of the

Part One: Planning your trip

courses are at an altitude of more than 1500m (5000ft) and are ideal for golfing all year round.
Kenya Golf Safaris: www.kenya-golf-safaris.com
Leisure Golf Club: www.golfinginkenya.com

Helicopter safaris
Tropic Air, based in Laikipia, offer visitors the unprecedented opportunity to discover and explore northern Kenya's remote and stunning areas with the ultimate in speed and comfort. Their Eurocopter is equipped with fly-fishing rods, so it's possible to fly to remote tarns and streams on Mount Kenya and fish for trout.
Tropic Air: www.tropicair-kenya.com

Horseback safaris
Several companies offer safaris by horseback. Itineraries include the Masai Mara, Amboseli, Chulu Hills and the stunning scenery of the Great Rift Valley. A new circuit takes in Meru and Laikipia and finishes in the Masai Mara. On these safaris your accommodation is in mobile camps that are set up for you each evening. It is also possible to take horse rides while staying at various safari lodges, such as Borana Lodge and Wilderness Trails Lewa Downs.
OffBeat Safaris: www.offbeatsafaris.com
Safaris Unlimited: www.safarisunlimited.com

The Safaricom Marathon
Runners from all over the world come to Lewa Downs to compete in the Safaricom Marathon. This is the only marathon in the world where runners run through a wildlife reserve. Although predominantly a fund-raising event, many professional runners also take part. The funds raised are used for education, health care and wildlife conservation in the area.
Safaricom Marathon: www.lewa.org/lewa_marathon.php

Railway safaris
East African Steam Safaris run two-day rail trips from Nairobi to Mombasa. A refurbished Beyer Garratt is used to pull the train. Stops are made at various vantage points for photography and for a candlelight dinner.
East African Steam Safaris: tannereps@iconnect.co.ke

Essentials for Your Medical Kit

Anti-malarial drugs
Aspirin (or similar)
Antihistamine (for insect bites and allergies)
Oral rehydration powder
Insect repellent
Lip balm
Alcoholic swabs
Scissors
Tweezers
Plasters (Band-Aids)
Anti-diarrhoea pills and laxatives (consult your pharmacist for advice)
Throat lozenges
Antiseptic cream
Insect bite cream
Eye drops
Any other medicines and toiletries you regularly use
Energy bar/drink for walking safari

Introduction

Photographic safaris

It is possible to book a special photographic safari with most safari companies. Origins Safaris are the most experienced company in this field.

Origins Safaris: www.originsafaris.info
For Wildlife Filming, contact: samuels@swiftkenya.com

Scuba diving

Dogs Breath Divers: www.dogsbreathdivers.com/kenya
Ocean Sports: www.oceansports.net

Volunteer holidays

Join researchers as they radio track animals and monitor the behaviour of various species at the Taita Discovery Centre.
Origins Safaris: www.originsafaris.info

Sites of historical or cultural interest
Fort Jesus, Mombasa

This 16th-century stronghold was built by the Portuguese to protect their trade routes to India. The architect was Italian, so the structure has similar features to an Italian fortress of the time. The fort, whose walls are 15m (50ft) high and 2.4m (8ft) thick, stands on an old coral ridge at the entrance to the Old Harbour, Mombasa.

At the end of the 17th century, the Sultan of Oman sent an army to seize the fort; the siege lasted almost three years before it finally fell into their hands. In 1728 the fort was recovered by the Portuguese without a struggle, but relinquished again later to remain under Arab rule until 1895, when Mombasa became a British protectorate. The fort was bombarded by the British Navy in 1878 and 1895, when it became a prison under British protection. On 15 August 1960, Fort Jesus was declared a national monument.

Gedi Ruins

Sixteen kilometres (10 miles) south of Malindi, the ruins of an old Arab town, set in the midst of the coastal forest, provide an atmospheric reminder of the past. Gedi was founded in the 14th century and flourished during the late 14th and 15th centuries. It was abandoned in the early 17th century, probably because of

Part One: Planning your trip

increased pressure from the warlike Galla tribe as they moved southwards. The word 'Gedi', or, more correctly, 'Gede', is a Galla word meaning 'precious'; it is also a personal name. Gedi was originally surrounded by a 2.7m-high (9ft) wall, which has at least three gates. The northwestern part of the town has been excavated and covers an area of about 18ha (44 acres).

Among the excavated ruins are the Great Mosque (originally constructed in the 15th century and rebuilt 100 years later), the Palace, the Dated Tomb – inscribed with its Arabic date AH802 (1399) – and the Pillar Tomb. A number of wells are now the home of barn owls.

Interesting birds can be seen at Gedi, among them the Lizard Buzzard, Palm-nut Vulture, Trumpeter Hornbill, Narina Trogon and Black-breasted Glossy Starling. Blue monkeys and red-tailed squirrels also live among the ruins. Gedi is administered by the National Museums of Kenya and is open to the public daily from 07:00 to 18:00.

Below: The ruins of Gedi, an old Arab town founded in the 14th century. Gedi flourished in the 14th and 15th centuries, but was mysteriously abandoned in the early 17th century.

Vasco da Gama Pillar
At Malindi, Vasco da Gama cross and church, built in 1541, are open to the public. Sheik Hassan's pillar tomb, standing beside a 19th-century pillar tomb, can also be seen on the waterfront next to the mosque.

Jumba la Mwtana
The Slave Master's House north of Mtwapa Creek is a monument that forms part of an ancient city that was abandoned some time between the 14th and 15th centuries. The atmospheric ruins, which have been declared a national monument, are set at the edge of the beach among baobab trees and consist of four mosques (one of which is gently subsiding into the sands), some houses and a cemetery.

Aberdare National Park
This was the hideout of the legendary freedom fighter, 'Field Marshall Kimathi'.

Introduction

Treetops
The site where Princess Elizabeth became Queen in 1952.

Kenyatta House, Maralal
The house where Kenya's first president, Jomo Kenyatta, was detained prior to his final release in 1961.

Accommodation
A wide range of accommodation is available for travellers going on safari in Kenya, ranging from simple bungalows, small camps, mobile safaris and large tented camps to home-stays and luxury Safari lodges with private suites. Almost the only self-catering accommodation available on safari are those establishments run by the Kenya Wildlife Service, e-mail: tourism@kws.org website: www.kws.org

There is a star system of grading accommodation in Kenya, but unfortunately it is based on a system where a large safari lodge of over 100 rooms will have a high number of stars than a smaller one, simply because it has more than one restaurant or because it has a games room. The smaller permanent tented camps, such as Il Moran Camp in the Masai Mara National Reserve, are often far superior to any safari lodge, but with only 10 tents, it has a rating of only a few stars because it does not have a swimming pool and has only one restaurant!

The type of accommodation you choose can make a big difference to your safari experience. In general, guests receive more personal attention at the smaller tented camps, while the large lodges are far less flexible and tend to stick to more strict schedules – although they do tend to have better food and service. The smaller camps, in particular the mobile camping safaris, will amend their schedules to suit their guests.

Almost all of the large safari lodges and camps have swimming pools, TV rooms and massage rooms, and most are surrounded by electric fences so that the guests do not have to fear encountering an elephant or hippo. But to experience the real Africa it is far better for visitors to stay in the smaller tented camps that have no fences, where they have a good chance of

Part One: Planning your trip

hearing the sounds of the wild while lying in their tent. All in all, staying in a camp is a far better safari experience.

It is also possible to stay at ranches that have wildlife on their land, Loisaba being a good example. Private homes are also available, particularly around Lake Naivasha. The Kenya Wildlife Service has self-catering cottages and houses available in some of the national parks. For information, contact the Kenya Wildlife Service on e-mail: tourism@kws.org or visit their website at www.kws.org

What to pack

Space in the safari vehicle and in small aircraft is limited, so your luggage should be restricted to:

• A bag, preferably a soft one, not exceeding 12kg (26lb) in weight and 65x46cm (25x18in) in dimension.
• A small handbag (airline type) or daypack for money, travel documents and camera equipment.
• A waist pouch or money belt.
• A small fold-up bag to be used on itineraries that include optional short excursions.

Clothing and personal effects

Most people make the mistake of taking too much clothing. Bring comfortable wash-and-wear clothes, both casual and semi-casual. Bright colours and white are not suitable for game-viewing. Please avoid clothing resembling an army uniform (i.e. camouflage clothing). The list of clothing in the panel on page 16 is just a guideline and will depend on the duration of the safari as well as the season in which you are travelling – additional warmer clothing may be required during the rainy seasons (the long rains are in March–June, short rains October–November).

If, during your safari, you are visiting Lamu or Zanzibar, as a form of respect to local customs and the Islamic religion, ladies are requested to dress discreetly by covering their knees and shoulders.

Also remember to pack the personal effects recommended in the panel on this page.

What to Pack – Personal Effects

• Insect repellent
• A good pair of lightweight binoculars for each person
• Sunglasses
• Sunscreen
• Torch (flashlight)
• Medical kit (see panel, page 13)
• One-litre water bottle per person (essential)
• One torch and batteries per person (essential)
• Toilet paper
• Bath soap
• Toothbrush and toothpaste
• Shampoo and hair conditioner
• Deodorant
• Comb/hair brush, nail brush
• Razor and blades
• Lip balm
• Hand cream and moisturizing cream
• Tissues or disposable moist tissues
• Plastic bag (to pack wet/dirty clothing)
• Spectacles (if worn) – some people have trouble with contact lenses and dust
• Pen for immigration formalities
• Note book
• Multipurpose knife (e.g. Swiss Army Knife)

Introduction

PART TWO: ECO ISSUES AND CLIMATE

Habitats and Biomes

Kenya's landscape is characterized by its huge diversity. Almost every known type of landform, from snow-covered mountains and glaciers to desert, occurs within its boundaries, also freshwater lakes Baringo, Naivasha and Lake Victoria, and soda (alkaline) lakes such as lakes Bogoria, Elementaita, Magadi and Nakuru. The land has some of Africa's oldest eroded plains and also some of its youngest, created by recent volcanic activity. Biomes include deserts and semi-deserts, grassland, coastal forest, rainforest, montane forest, ground water forest, highlands, moorland, savannah, mangrove, acacia savannah and acacia woodland.

Kenya's safari code

Keep to designated roads or tracks. Encourage your driver/guide to stay on roads or designated tracks when visiting national parks and reserves. Off-road driving can cause extensive damage to grass and woodland habitats.

Minimize disturbance to animals. Wild animals become distressed when they are surrounded by several vehicles or when vehicles come too close to them. Keep noise to a minimum and never try to attract an animal's attention.

Stay inside your vehicle at all times. Do not stand on the roof or hang out of the windows, and only leave your vehicle at designated areas. Remember, wild animals can be dangerous.

Keep to the speed limit. Most wildlife areas have a speed limit of 40kph (25mph), and animals have right of way – always.

Right: An unusual road sign, erected in an effort to stop colobus monkeys from being run over by speeding vehicles.

Part Two: Eco issues and climate

Support eco-friendly accommodation facilities. Try to stay in lodges and camps that look after their environment and support local conservation initiatives.

Never feed any animals. Feeding wild animals can upset their diet and lead to an unnatural dependence upon people.

Take care not to disturb the ecological balance. Do not purchase, collect or remove any animal products, rocks, seeds or bird's nests from the wild or alter the natural environment in any way.

Take your litter with you. Litter and garbage are dangerous to wild animals. Keep all litter with you and be very careful with cigarettes and matches, which can cause major bush fires.

The protection of Kenya's natural environment is a responsibility that is shared by the tourist industry, the local people and also visitors. As a visitor to Kenya you have the power to influence the behaviour of others. If you see an incident that clearly contravenes any of the above guidelines, please record this and request an incident report form from the reception of your hotel or lodge. If you insist that these guidelines are adhered to, you will be playing an important part in helping Kenya to preserve some of the world's greatest wilderness areas.

Climate

Although Kenya straddles the equator, much of the country is not tropical. Because of the huge variation in altitude there are extensive differences in temperatures; a large amount of the land has an altitude of over 1200m (4000ft) and during the rains may be quite cool for extended periods. Above 2400m (8000ft) it can be cold, with snow falling on the higher slopes of Mount Kenya and sleet and hail falling on the highlands, including the Nairobi area at 1650m (5400ft). The coastal strip and Lake Victoria area are warm to hot with high humidity, while the northeastern and eastern lowlands are hot and mostly dry.

Kenya is influenced by two air masses at different times of the year. A northeasterly air mass originating in Arabia and the Horn

---

Mammals Named After People

Thomson's gazelle was named by Joseph Thomson, an English explorer who explored what is now Kenya in the late 1800s. He wrote a book, *Walk Through Masai Land*, about his travels.

Grant's gazelle was named after James Grant, a British explorer.

Burchell's (common) zebra was named after William John Burchell, an English explorer and collector who explored the interior of Southern Africa between 1811 and 1815 and walked more than 7000km (4350 miles). Burchell was the first European to describe a white rhino.

Introduction

of Africa dominates from November to March, usually bringing hot and dry weather. From April to July a warm, humid air mass brings rain in from the Indian Ocean. It is these air masses that have been used for centuries by Arab and Chinese traders to sail to and from East Africa. Another moist, westerly air mass, originating over the Atlantic Ocean and the Zaire Basin, brings rain to western Kenya, mainly in August.

Rainfall varies greatly – in quantity as well as seasonally. Most of the north and northeast receives as little as 255mm (10in) of rainfall annually, while Mount Kenya and western Kenya average 2000mm (80in), and most highland forests (Aberdares) receive over 1000mm (40in) annually. The costal strip receives over 800mm (32in), but this often rises to 1200mm (42in) between April and July, with May being the wettest month. The Masai Mara National Reserve, which is influenced by the weather of the Lake Victoria area, receives over 1000mm (40in) of rain, mostly from December to May, but it can receive rain showers in almost any month. The area east of the Rift Valley experiences two distinct annual rainy seasons – the 'long rains', between March and May, and the 'short rains', from November to December. These rains are not always predictable. Some years the rains are late or fail completely.

The world's greatest wildlife spectacle

The annual migration of wildebeest and other animals in the Serengeti and Masai Mara is well known. During the course of a year the wildebeest make a trek of anything from 800–1600km (500–1000 miles) as they circle the ecosystem. Their actual route varies from year to year and depends on rainfall that produces the grass on which the wildebeest herds feed. You often read about – or see on television wildlife programs – people talking of the start and finish of the migration. There is no start or finish as such; the migration is a continual movement of the herds in search of food and water. If there is a time that you could call the start of the migration, it is birth. All births take place in the short grass plains in the southeastern part of the Serengeti ecosystem. These plains consist of fine volcanic soils that have been blown there from the Crater Highlands (Ngorongoro crater is one) over millions of years. These soils are rich in minerals, calcium and phosphorus, but for most of the year they are desolate,

Part Two: Eco issues and climate

providing little food and no water for the few Grant's gazelle and ostrich that somehow survive here.

By January or February the rains arrive and the area turns green almost overnight, providing the wildebeest with mineral-rich grazing. These open plains have another advantage for the wildebeest: it is very difficult for any predator to approach the herds without being seen. Within days the female wildebeest herd together and start giving birth; 80% of the females will give birth within a few weeks. This glut of births is thought to be an anti-predator behaviour – with so many calves, it decreases the chances of a calf being singled out by a predator. The predators also become glutted by the sheer numbers of calves available, so more calves will survive the first crucial weeks.

By March/April these open plains start to dry out, forcing the wildebeest to move on. Usually they move in a northwesterly direction towards an area known as the Western Corridor and Lake Victoria, which consists of open woodlands. It is in this area during May to June that the rut (mating season) takes place. By the end of June the grazing begins to get sparse and the herds slowly head northwards towards the Masai Mara National Reserve, the first ones usually arriving during early July. There is a popular misconception that the herds have to cross the Mara River to arrive in Kenya and the Masai Mara National Reserve.

Plants of Special Interest

Mountain national parks: alpine heath zone, groundsels (senecios), and giant lobelia.
Shimba Hills National Reserve: some rare cycads and a small primitive palm.

Below: Landscapes of Kenya – the dramatic Rift Valley view from near Nairobi (left), and a lion in the dry grasslands of the Masai Mara (right).

Introduction

Topography

Kenya has a distinctive topographic profile. The interior is much higher than the rest of the country, and the mountains are roughly in a line running north and south. Its highest mountain, Mount Kenya, is located in approximately the centre of the country. The Great Rift Valley runs from north to south through Kenya, separating the Lake Victoria basin to the west from the hills in the east, which slowly descend into the dry grassy lowlands and coastal beaches. Kenya's topography forms complex ecological zones, including one called the highland zone. This is a region of rolling uplands characterized by cool weather, abundant rainfall, rich volcanic soils, and dense human settlement.

The border between Kenya and Tanzania is a line on the map – not the Mara River. Of course, during the herds' time in the Masai Mara they do cross the Mara River several times as they seek good grazing. When the herds arrive at the Mara River they often stand for hours before they decide to cross, and frequently change their minds at the last minute. Very often the herds of zebra that accompany the wildebeest on their migration make the first move and the wildebeest follow them across the river. Because of this behaviour the wildebeest are thought by some to be stupid, but Dr Richard Estes, who has studied wildebeest for over 30 years, has a theory. The zebra herds are made up of family groups – a stallion and three or four mares and their foals. These family units know each other well and inspire the confidence to decide to cross the Mara River. By comparison,

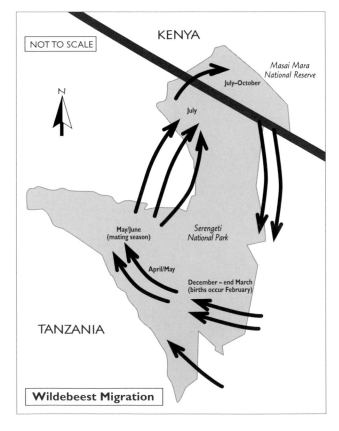

NOT TO SCALE

KENYA

Masai Mara
National Reserve

July–October

N

July

May/June
(mating season)

Serengeti
National Park

April/May

December – end March
(births occur February)

TANZANIA

Wildebeest Migration

Part Two: Eco issues and climate

wildebeest do not have family groups; the only stable association a wildebeest has is between mother and calf. In effect, therefore, a herd of wildebeest deciding to cross the river are almost all strangers to one another.

These crossings can be spectacular to watch and it can be unbelievable at times to see the wildebeest jumping down the river banks, which can be 5–6m (16–20ft) high, without apparently hurting themselves. Once in the river they often have to face some of the largest crocodiles in Africa, but most make it safely across. Problems arise when the river bank they are climbing up gets wet and slippery as more and more wildebeest try to climb out of the river. Many just cannot make it up the steep, slippery banks and fall exhausted down into the river where they drown.

Above: Wildebeest crossing the Mara River in the Masai Mara National Reserve.

During these crossings many calves get separated from their mothers and females can be seen swimming back and forth across the river calling their calves. After a major crossing there are always a few females and calves running back and forth parallel to the herd calling for each other, and it is common to see numbers of sad-looking calves grouped together, not knowing which way to turn. Even though the calves would be eating grass, the chances of them surviving without the protection of their mothers are thought to be slim – no one knows for certain how many do eventually perish without their mothers' protection. The herds usually stay in the Masai Mara until late September, before again heading southwards towards the short grass plains of the Serengeti where the whole drama will begin again. The actual departure date can never be accurately predicted, as again it all depends on the amount of grass available in the Masai Mara and when grazing becomes available in the Serengeti.

NAIROBI, OL-DOINYO SABUK AND AMBOSELI

This chapter covers three very different national parks. Amboseli is perhaps Kenya's best-known wildlife area, while Ol-Doinyo Sabuk is almost certainly one of the least known. Both of these parks are very different to Nairobi National Park, which is the only wildlife refuge in the world situated close to a major city. Amboseli has a Hollywood image: the magnificent backdrop of Africa's highest mountain, with herds of zebra, elephant and wildebeest feeding in the foreground, has been used by film-makers many times. But no matter how many times you have seen Kilimanjaro in films or magazines, nothing can prepare you for your first breathtaking view of this magnificent mountain/volcano. By contrast, the background to Nairobi National Park is the skyline of a major city. At Ol-Doinyo Sabuk, a mountain is the national park and the views, although invigorating, are of farms and plains with the city of Nairobi in the distance. On clear days Kilimanjaro and Mount Kenya can also be seen from here.

Top Ten

Elephants (including some males with big tusks)
Fringe-eared oryx
Lion
Cheetah
Yellow baboon
Saddle-billed Stork
Long-toed Plover (Lapwing)
Double-banded Courser
African Fish Eagle
Pink-backed Pelican

Opposite, top to bottom: A herd of elephants in Amboseli National Park; the bar and dining area at Tortilis Camp, Amboseli; a herd of common (Burchell's) zebra feeding in Amboseli National Park.

Nairobi National Park

Location: 8km (5 miles) from central Nairobi.

Size: 120km² (46 sq miles).

Altitude: 1533–1760m (5030–5775ft).

Of interest: Nairobi is the only city in Africa where one can get into a car outside your hotel and be in wild Africa in 20 minutes (traffic allowing).

Accommodation:

Holiday Inn: www.southernsun.com

Jacaranda Hotel: www.jacarandahotels.com

Hotel La Mada and Oakwood Hotel: www.madahotels.com

Palacina Hotel: www.palacina.com

Fairview Hotel: www.fairviewkenya.com

Norfolk Hotel: www.lonrhohotels.com

Nairobi National Park

Nairobi National Park was Kenya's first national park and it owes its existence to one man, the late Mervyn Cowie. Mervyn had tried for years to get the British government to create the national park and in desperation wrote a letter to the local newspaper calling for all the wildlife in the area to be destroyed as the wildlife was destroying the grazing used by cattle and goats. He signed the letter 'Old Settler'. This created such an uproar that a committee was formed and at the end of World War II (1946) the area was gazetted a national park. Mervyn was its first executive officer.

This unique area is only 8km (5 miles) from the city centre, and at only 120km² (46 sq miles) is entirely within the city's limits. It is the home of an amazing variety of wildlife – 80 mammal species and over 500 bird species have been recorded here. The park, which has an extensive road system, is fenced on only three sides; the fourth boundary is formed by the Athi River, affording access to migrating wildlife. Unfortunately, the area beyond the river – Kitengela, once a traditional Maasai grazing area – is slowly being sold for housing, which is seriously hindering the annual dry-season migration into and out of the park.

Most of the park consists of open grassy plains and scattered acacia bush, intersected by a number of small seasonal rivers and the permanent Athi River, lined by lovely yellow-barked acacia trees, as well as a number of man-made dams holding permanent water. In the west of the park there is an extensive area of highland forest containing olive and Cape chestnut trees.

Nairobi National Park is perhaps the best place in Kenya to see the endangered black rhino, which occur here in good numbers and are quite tame. The black rhino have been so successful here that many have been translocated to other national parks and wildlife areas. The park is also a good

Black rhino

place to see and photograph Africa's largest antelope, the eland, which, unusually, are not at all shy or skittish here. Masai giraffe, buffalo, warthog and both Thomson's and Grant's gazelle are all common. Lion and cheetah both occur and leopards are occasionally seen in the highland forest. Strangely, spotted hyena are seldom encountered, but silver-backed (called black-backed in Southern Africa) jackal do occur. The only major mammal that is not seen here is the elephant, although a few years ago three young males did try to enter the park.

During the dry season (July–October) there is a large influx of wildlife – mainly wildebeest, kongoni (Coke's hartebeest) and zebra – from the Athi-Kapiti Plains into the park. There is a nature trail along the Athi River, which is a wonderful place to walk, especially for birders.

Black rhino (Swahili: *kifaru*)

Rhinos are large, almost prehistoric-looking animals whose numbers have drastically declined during the last 20 years or so. The black rhino is the smaller of the two rhino species, but still weighs an impressive 900–1364kg (2000–3000lb). The average size of its horn varies from 50–90cm (19–35in) for the front horn to just over 50cm (19in) for the rear horn. The average weight of a horn is 2.75–3.5kg (6–8lb).

Black rhino live for 35–40 years and have a gestation period of 15–16 months; only one calf is born. A female produces a calf only about once every four years, which is nursed for one to two years. Because of their low numbers (due to poaching and habitat loss), it is feared that the remaining rhino are so widely dispersed that it is difficult for them to find each other and breed.

Black rhino are browsers with a distinctive pointed prehensile upper lip (while white rhinos are grazers with wide, square lips). They eat a large variety of plants, leaves and plant shoots forming the bulk of their diet.

Rhinos live in home ranges that sometimes overlap those of other individuals, especially at water holes and wallows. These territories are marked by urine spraying and dung heaps; the dung is scattered by the hind feet. Black rhinos are usually solitary, but a female will be accompanied by her latest calf until

Rhino Horn

A rhino's horn, which is not a true horn, is composed of keratin (just like human hair and fingernails) and is not attached to the skull. This horn fetches very high prices. At one time the biggest market for it was North Yemen, where it was mostly used to make the handles of traditional daggers called *Jambiya*. Today the largest market for the horn is China and the Far East, where it is considered an essential ingredient in traditional cures for many illnesses, and as an aphrodisiac. Tests have been carried out to determine if rhino horn does have any fever-reducing effects and it was discovered that if rhino horn was taken in very high dosages it did in fact reduce fever – but aspirin is more effective!

Opposite: *Visitors in Nairobi National Park, in a London taxi, watch zebra feeding, with the skyline of the city in the background.*

Nairobi National Park

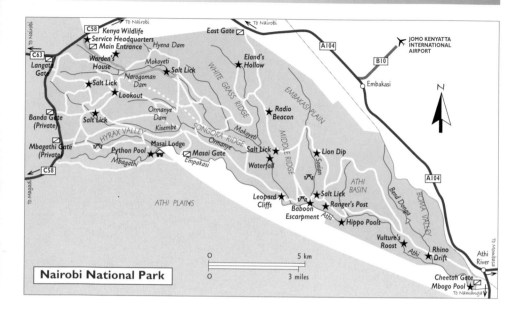

Nairobi National Park

the calf is about three to four years old. When on the move, black rhino calves follow their mothers; this is in contrast to white rhino whose calves always walk in front of their mothers. Their eyesight is very poor, but their hearing and smell are extremely good. This is probably why black rhinos are notoriously ill-tempered and will often charge without apparent reason. For their size black rhinos are very agile and are able to turn quickly, even on the run.

Rhinos are often found with oxpeckers (sometimes called tick birds) on their backs. The birds warn the rhino of danger with a hissing call, and in exchange they feed off the ticks and parasites found on the rhino. In Swahili these birds are called *askari wa kifaru*, which means 'the rhino's guard'.

Oxpeckers (Swahili: *askari wa kifaru*)

Two species of oxpecker occur in Kenya: Red-billed and Yellow-billed. Both accompany large animals and also livestock that have not been treated for ticks. Oxpeckers feed mainly on ticks and blood-sucking flies that they find on their hosts; they comb the hair (in a scissoring action) of their host with a specially shaped (laterally flattened) bill. They also have sharp claws and a very stiff

Oxpeckers

tail that assists them in clinging on to their hosts, especially when the host is moving. As well as feeding on ticks, they also keep wounds clear by eating dead skin and sometimes living flesh. Oxpeckers feed deep in the noses of their hosts and also feed on ear wax. In some parts of southern Africa oxpeckers were eliminated because farmers thought they harmed their livestock. Unfortunately, the livestock then suffered from excessive ear wax and there is now a big movement to reintroduce oxpeckers to those areas again!

Oxpeckers spend most of their time on their hosts; they feed, rest, preen, court, copulate and even occasionally sleep on them (mostly on giraffe, but not buffalo) at night. They pluck their host's fur and use their dung for nests, which are usually in a tree hole or among rocks. Oxpeckers are found in small groups of four to six, but occasionally as many as 20 can be seen feeding on a single, presumably sick, animal. They are co-operative breeders – all of the group will help to feed and rear any young. Red-billed Oxpeckers mostly feed on giraffe, hippo and antelope, such as impala, while Yellow-billed prefer buffalo, rhino, eland, zebra and warthog. Perhaps strangely, they are only very rarely seen on elephants – probably elephants will not tolerate them and can easily sweep them off with their trunk. The few records of oxpeckers seen feeding on elephant have all been associated with sick animals.

Below: A Red-billed Oxpecker clinging to a rhino's head. Oxpeckers feed on ticks, blood-sucking flies and body tissue. In return they act as lookouts for their hosts.

In return for living off a mammal host, oxpeckers act as lookouts. Hunters do not like oxpeckers for this reason; when a hunter (human or animal) is seen, the oxpeckers quickly fly into the sky, scolding loudly as they do so. This can work both ways. Hearing the sound of oxpeckers while walking through long grass can act as an alarm. If they had carried on walking, they might have walked into a solitary old male buffalo, which could have resulted in dire consequences!

Nairobi National Park

Above: A herd of female eland in the Nairobi National Park. These normally shy mammals allow visitors to Nairobi National Park a much closer view than almost anywhere else.

Both species of oxpecker are mainly brown, but Red-billed Oxpeckers, as their name suggests, have a bright red bill and red eyes surrounded by broad yellow eye rings. Yellow-billed Oxpeckers have a yellow bill, tipped in bright red, and bright red eyes. Although their body colour is very similar to that of Red-bills, Yellow-bills have a distinctive paler lower back and rump, which is particularly obvious in flight.

Eland (Swahili: *pouf* or *mbunja*)

The largest of all the antelope, large 1.63m (5.3ft) mature males can weigh almost 700kg (1543lb). Even so, they can still leap almost from a standing position to a height of more than 2m (6.5ft), and youngsters have been known to leap over a 3m (10ft) fence. Eland males weigh on average 500–600kg (1103–1323lb) and females 340–445kg (750–981lb). Both males and females have short spiral horns and a dewlap, but females are smaller and more lightly built. Males slowly become darker, turning blue-grey with age as the skin shows through a thinning coat, and their dewlaps enlarge, often hanging below knee level.

Males regularly thrash the ground or bushes with their horns and often end up with a crown of grass, twigs or weeds. Older males make a loud 'clicking' sound as they walk, which can be heard as

Ol-Doinyo Sabuk National Park

far as 2.5km (1.5 miles) away. This clicking sound was once thought to be coming from the joints or hooves, but it is actually made by the tendons in the front legs. This sound warns other eland who will quickly move out of his path!

Ol-Doinyo Sabuk National Park

Eland are gregarious (herds of up to 1000 have been recorded) but their social organization is different from that of other antelope. Old, dominant males are solitary, while other mature males will form small groups of three to four individuals. Adult females form herds, with the size and make-up of the herd changing daily. Then there are nursery groups consisting of a few adult females and calves, which may not necessarily be their own. One unusual feature of their social system is that adult females will jointly defend calves against predators, including lions.

Eland inhabit open plains and wooded country and they both browse and graze, although they mostly browse. They are also known to dig up large bulbs and tuberous fruits with their horns. They are largely independent of water, although will drink regularly if water is present. Normally very shy, eland have the longest flight distance of any gazelle: 300–500m (328–547yd). However, in the Nairobi National Park and, to a lesser extent, in the Masai Mara National Reserve they are more tame, allowing a much closer approach. Despite this, eland are easily domesticated; they can easily be fattened too. Their meat tastes excellent (and is low in cholesterol) and their milk is creamy. So it is perhaps not surprising that Maasai herders often rear young eland in their herds.

Ol-Doinyo Sabuk National Park

Ol-Doinyo Sabuk, a Maasai phrase meaning 'sleeping buffalo', is a forest-covered hill rising from the surrounding plains. There is only one road (a rough track) that winds its way to the summit through dense highland forest. The view from the summit on a clear day is wonderful: Mount Kenya, Kilimanjaro and Nairobi can all be clearly

Ol-Doinyo Sabuk National Park

Location: 50km (31 miles) from Nairobi.
Size: 18km² (7 sq miles).
Altitude: 1524–2146m (5000–7040ft).
Of interest: Dense highland forest and the graves of early settlers in the area, Sir William Northrop Macmillan and his wife.
Accommodation: There is no accommodation at the park. The nearest accommodation is at the Blue Posts Hotel at Thika, e-mail: bluepostshotel@africaonline.co.ke

Ol-Doinyo Sabuk National Park

seen. Approximately halfway along the road is a panoramic bluff that offers wonderful views over the surrounding countryside. Here are three marble plaques set on slabs of rock; they are the graves of Sir William Northrop Macmillan (a famous hunter and philanthropist), his wife and their servant, Louise Decker. Sir William, who loved this view, was one of the early settlers in this area and owned the nearby 8049ha (19,890-acre) Juja Ranch.

Although the park has a good population of wildlife, including buffalo, bushbuck, leopard and beautiful colobus monkeys, it is difficult to see them as the forest is very thick. Many interesting highland forest birds occur here, such as Hartlaub's Turaco, White-starred Forest Robin and the stunning Narina Trogon.

Amboseli National Park

Amboseli National Park, dominated by snow-capped Kilimanjaro that provides a superb backdrop for photographing the wildlife, is Kenya's most visited wildlife area. Although Kilimanjaro seems close, it is actually located 48km (30 miles) away across the border in Tanzania.

Amboseli was originally designated a reserve in 1948 with an area of 3260km² (1259 sq miles). It was handed back to the Maasai in 1961, but because of conflict between the Maasai herds and wildlife, the reserve was gazetted a national park in 1974 (at a fraction of its original size). Now only 392km² (151 sq miles), the park centres on Ol Tukai, the Maasai word for the local phoenix palm that grows in the area. This area is a magnet for wildlife as it contains many swamps fed by subterranean water draining from Kilimanjaro. To compensate the Maasai, who traditionally watered and grazed their livestock in the area, a number of wells were sunk just outside the national park with funds donated by the New York Zoological Society.

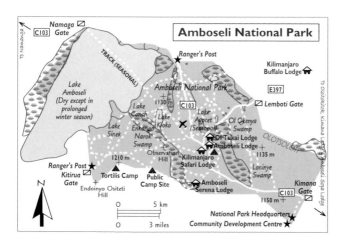

Amboseli National Park

Most of the park consists of a dry, ancient lake bed and fragile grasslands with patches of acacia woodland, while in the southern area there are a number of small rocky volcanic hills. Around the swamps – Ol Okenya, Ol Tukai and Enkongo Narok – the vegetation is lush, with yellow-barked acacia trees and phoenix palms. One of Amboseli's big attractions is its elephants (over 1000); it is possibly the best wildlife area in Africa to experience elephants at close range, and many of the bulls have large tusks. These elephants have never been harassed by poachers and to sit and watch them at close range, feeding and drinking in the swamps with Kilimanjaro in the background, is an experience not to be forgotten. Cynthia Moss and Joyce Pool, with their many assistants, have undertaken extensive studies of these elephants. Cynthia herself has followed their movements for over 30 years, the most extended study of any one species by the same person in Africa.

Apart from elephant, the variety of wildlife includes black rhino, buffalo, Masai giraffe, Grant's and Thomson's gazelle, lion, cheetah and leopard. In the dryer areas of the park, away from the swamps, one can see fringe-eared oryx, gerenuk, lesser kudu and eland. Bird life is prolific too, especially in and around the swamps. Both White and Pink-backed Pelicans, various ducks and cormorants share the waters with the beautiful Pygmy Duck, which is an uncommon bird in Kenya. Kingfishers and bee-eaters use the reeds along the swamp to look out for their prey, and birds of prey are well represented, with African Fish Eagle, Martial Eagle, Eastern Chanting Goshawk and the tiny Pygmy Falcon all occurring.

No visit to Amboseli is complete without a visit to Observation Hill. Walk to the top for a sweeping view over the whole of Amboseli spread out below. You will see the dust trails of animals walking across the expanses of dry plains to water and, towards the south, an almost endless tract covered with acacia trees merging into the base of Kilimanjaro. Some days an opportunistic Maasai warrior in full traditional dress will pose, for a small donation, for a photograph with Kilimanjaro in the background.

Elephants (Swahili: *ndovu*)
The African elephant is the largest living land mammal. An adult bull elephant can weigh as much as 6500kg (14,330lb) and be as tall as 3.3m (11ft) at the shoulder. Elephants spend most of their

Accommodation

Amboseli National Park
Amboseli Serena Safari Lodge:
www.serenahotels.com
Amboseli Sopa Lodge:
www.sopalodges.com
Ol Tukai Lodge:
www.oltukailodge.com
Tortilis Camp: www.chelipeacock.com
Outside Amboseli National Park
Kilimanjaro Buffalo Lodge:
www.africansafariclub.com
Kimana Lodge:
www.africansafariclub.com
Porini Camp: www.porini.com/
amboseli_porini_camp.html
Chyulu Hills National Park
Ol Donyo Wuas:
7 individual cottages,
www.RichardBonhamSafaris.com
Campi ya Kanzi:
www.campiyakanzi.com
Ol Kanjau:
www.bush-and-beyond.com
Umanyi Springs Camp:
tel: 0721 317762.

Amboseli National Park

The Amboseli Elephant Research Project

Amboseli's elephants are the best-known elephants in Africa. In 1972 Cynthia Moss initiated a long-term study that is still continuing to this day. The Amboseli elephants were chosen because they were probably the last relatively undisturbed population in Africa. The local Maasai people never hunted elephants and their presence in the area helped deter any poachers! Over 1200 elephants have been identified individually and each has been assigned a name, number or code. There are currently almost 800 individuals and the birth date of well over half of these is known.

time eating – about 5% of their body weight is consumed each day, and each elephant needs 100–227 litres (30–40 gallons) of water. Unfortunately, they only digest about 40% of the vegetation they eat. Although they prefer grass, they also eat leaves, bark, fruit and seed pods. Elephants can go several days without water, but they prefer to drink and bathe daily if water is available. After bathing elephants use their trunks to blow mud or dust over themselves.

Both male and female African elephants have tusks, whereas only male Asian elephants have them. Elephant tusks are actually very long upper incisors, of which a third of their length is inside the skull. The largest tusk recorded weighed 102.7kg (214lb) and its length was 345cm (11.5ft), but nowadays, because of years of hunting and poaching, it is rare to see one that weighs more than 50kg (110lb). Elephants are 'right- or left-tusked' just as humans are right- or left-handed; they use one tusk more than the other, which makes it shorter and often shaped differently from the other. Their teeth are also very unusual: they break out in sequence from front to rear, with only one tooth and part of another tooth in use at one time. They have 12 teeth, which are slowly worn out one after the other, in both the upper and lower jaws. The last teeth are the largest and usually in use by the time an elephant is in its late 40s; these have to last the animal for the rest of its life. When these teeth are worn out, the elephant cannot chew food very well so it slowly starves to death, usually at about 60–70 years of age. It is not unusual to see old bull elephants spending their last days feeding in or near swamps, where the vegetation may be softer and more easily chewed with their worn-out teeth. This may be why it was thought for a long time that elephants had secret burial grounds.

Another remarkable feature of the elephant is its trunk, which is an asset in so many ways. It is a nose, a hand, a tool for gathering food and siphoning up water, for sucking up dust and then blowing it over the body. It can be used in fighting and for pulling down branches, yet it can also be so gentle as to be able to pick up items as small as a pea.

The elephant's ears are large and are used for cooling on hot days. There are many veins in an elephant's ear and on hot days you can see elephants slowly fanning their ears. This motion helps

Elephants

circulate the blood, which is cooled by about 13°C (9°F) when it returns to the body.

Yet another unusual feature is the female elephant's teats. She has two teats located on her chest between the front legs, which is very different from all other herbivores.

Elephants are gregarious, forming groups that are made up of related females and their young. These groups are led by an old matriarch. At one time it was thought that elephant groups were led by an old bull, but bulls spend most of their time alone or with other bulls, only visiting the groups to check if any of the females are in oestrus. The gestation period is approximately 22 months and usually only one calf is born. Calves nurse for two to four years, using their mouth with the trunk held over the head. It is not unusual to see quite young calves picking up grass and putting it into their mouths. Calves also often reach up and take food out of their mothers' mouths, which may be how young elephants learn what is good to eat. When drinking water, a young calf has to kneel down and drink using its mouth – it is some time before it learns to draw the water up into its trunk and then pour it into its mouth.

Below: Three of Amboseli's tuskers head out of the park at sunset to feed at night. It is a regular occurrence for Amboseli's elephants to feed outside the park at night.

Amboseli National Park

Female calves mature at about 11–12 years of age and stay with their group, while males do not mature until they are 12–15 years of age and are then usually expelled from the herd. This separation is usually a gradual process, with the young bull remaining close to its maternal group. But gradually the females become more and more intolerant of them and they become completely independent, joining up with other males to form bachelor groups. Mature bulls come into musth (a time when their testosterone levels are high – a phase of heightened sexual activity and aggression) when they are about 25–30 years old and wander alone, occasionally joining up with the female groups in case any of the females are in oestrus. During this period, which may last a week or even a month, the male secretes a strong-smelling thick liquid from its temporal glands and dribbles very strong-smelling urine.

Fringe-eared oryx (Swahili: *choroa*)

The fringe-eared oryx is one of two subspecies of oryx that occur in Kenya. The fringe-eared is found south of the Tana River (including at Amboseli) and in northern Tanzania, while the other subspecies, the beisa oryx, is found north of the Tana River and into Somalia and Ethiopia. Fringe-eared oryx differ from beisa in having long, distinctive tassels on the end of their ears and heavier, darker brown coats. Oryx are large antelope with long, spear-like horns and have adapted to living in hot, dry areas. In the arid areas where they live, some of the plants that oryx feed on have adapted to store water or to prevent the excessive loss of it. The marked difference between day and night temperatures causes dew to form which is absorbed by the plant; some plants increase their water content by 25–40%, so the oryx that feed on them get both food and water. This allows an oryx to go without drinking for weeks and, if necessary, months, although where water is available they will drink every few days. Both sexes have horns but those of the females are usually longer and thinner than those of the males. The horns are straight and almost parallel and can be as long as 76cm (30in); the record length is more than a metre (39in). Oryx are remarkably dexterous with their horns – they can easily scratch their backs with them, and can also use them to fend off predators such as lion and leopard. They have even been known to thrust their horns completely through a lion. They are very nomadic, presumably because of their harsh environment, and live in gregarious herds of mixed sexes, numbering 10 to 40 but, occasionally, as large as 200.

Yellow baboon

Yellow baboon (Swahili: *nyani*)

Two types of baboon occur in Kenya: the olive baboon and the yellow baboon. The olive baboon inhabits western and central Kenya, while the yellow baboon can be found in the southern and coastal areas of Kenya. Yellow baboons are smaller, slimmer and lighter in colour and are far less common than olive baboons.

Baboons are extremely social, living in well-organized groups, known as troops, which can number from 40 to 80 members. Each troop (on average 50 individuals) is led by a dominant male who is much larger than the female. Females outnumber males and form the social core of the group, remaining with it all their lives. Young males leave their troop as they become mature and spend time with other troops. When a young male joins a troop he spends most of the time on the edge, interacting with different females until he is accepted into the troop. Within a troop some females are of a higher ranking than others and their young take on this status. Lower-ranking females have to defer to the young of a higher-ranking female, even if it is an infant.

Above: *One of Amboseli's yellow baboons. These baboons have been extensively studied by researchers over a number of years.*

An infant baboon has a pink face and black fur and for the first month of its life it stays very close to its mother, hanging below her stomach as she travels. By 5–6 weeks old the babies can ride on their mothers' backs, hanging on tightly with their hands and feet. After a few months they can ride jockey-style, sitting upright on her back and supported by her tail. From 4–6 months old the young baboon slowly changes colour to dark brown and spends more time with other juveniles; young baboons are suckled for about a year.

Amboseli National Park

Ceremonial Rites

No Maasai ceremony takes place without a bull, an ox or a cow, as the animal's blood plays an important role: while the animal's head is tightly held, the jugular vein is cut using the tip of an arrow or by shooting the arrow directly into the vein (the arrow has a leather thong wrapped around it just behind its tip to prevent it from penetrating too far). Once the blood has been collected in a gourd, the vein is simply pinched and plugged with a wad of dung and mud. The blood is usually mixed with milk, but is also drunk untainted by warriors, by women who have just given birth, or by a person who has undergone circumcision rites.

Baboons live for 20–30 years. Their main predator outside of protected areas is man, but otherwise leopards are their main enemy. Male baboons are fierce, and a group of males will chase off a single leopard or even a lion. Baboons are omnivorous and eat a large selection of food, and although grass forms a large part of their diet, they also eat seeds, berries, pods, blossoms, roots, bark and sap. They eat ants, termites and grasshoppers and have been recorded eating small mammals such as hares, as well as birds, fish and shellfish. Some males have been known to specialize in hunting young gazelle and goats if the opportunity arises.

Right: A Maasai Moran (warrior) wearing an Enkisi-au (lion headdress) signifying that he has killed a lion.

The Maasai people

The Maasai people

The Maasai are pastoralists, herding their cattle, sheep and goats; they also keep donkeys as beasts of burden. The majority of the Maasai still remain firmly attached to their traditional way of life. Second only to their children, the most important aspect of their lives is cattle, which they believe were given to them by their god Enkai; a Maasai of modest wealth will own at least 50. (He will, however, only be considered wealthy if he also has children.) The beasts are rarely slaughtered for meat (special ceremonial occasions aside). Instead they provide the Maasai people with all their needs: milk and blood for nourishment, hides for bedding and for making sandals, and as payment in the case of a dowry or fine.

The Maasai live in an *enk'ang* (often wrongly called a *manyatta*), which is a collection of huts housing Maasai warriors. Low, igloo-shaped huts are constructed by the women out of thin branches and grass, which they cover with a mixture of cow dung and mud. The *enk'ang* is surrounded by a strong thorn-bush fence, and each evening cattle, sheep and goats belonging to all the families are herded into this enclosure until morning. The huts are usually divided into two or three alcoves: one is used as a sleeping area for very young calves, lambs and kids; the others form the Maasai sleeping areas and cooking area.

A cultural feature of Maasai life is the male's passage through four traditional phases, each one marked by an important ceremony. The first one, called the *alamal lengipaata*, is performed just before circumcision. Because the circumcision ceremony only takes place every 12 to 15 years, the age of the boys taking part in the rites varies considerably. At this time, the group picks one of its members as a leader, who then retains the title throughout the lives of people in that particular group. The first phase is followed by *emorata*, or circumcision, initiating the boys into warriorhood. During the ceremony, the boys may show no sign of pain; to do so would be a disgrace. After a period of healing, they become warriors and are known as *morans*. They then become junior elders through the ceremony of *eunoto*, after which they may marry. Finally, with the *olngesherr* ceremony, they become senior elders whose duties are to preside over Maasai affairs. Traditionally the Maasai have no chiefs or headmen; all decisions are made by the senior elders.

Circumcision and Marriage Rites

Maasai girls are circumcised at puberty. Although a ceremony is held, it is limited to family as girls are not separated into age groups; circumcision takes place in the mother's house. Like the boys, the Maasai girls dress in black robes smeared with oil, and around their heads they wear a band with long links of metal beads hanging from it to cover their eyes. After circumcision the girls are allowed to marry, but because men may only enter into marriage once they become elders, the girls' husbands are normally much older than they are.

Passage to Manhood

Once male circumcision has taken place, a period of healing follows during which the boys daub their faces white and wear black robes. They use a small bow to shoot birds, which are fashioned into a special headdress – this is one way in which to prove their manhood and skills. A headdress can have as many as 50 birds. These circumcised young men travel all over Maasailand, and at the end of this period, the warriors grow their hair long, cover their bodies with ochre and dress in their finery.

CHYULU HILLS, TSAVO EAST AND TSAVO WEST

The two Tsavo national parks and the adjoining Chyulu Hills National Park make up one Africa's largest wildlife areas. Tsavo West has spectacular scenery with soaring mountains and the famous Mzima Springs. Kilimanjaro is also visible on a clear day. Tsavo East, by contrast, is a plateau of open thorn bush country with wonderful giant baobab trees, where the Yatta Plateau, the world's longest lava flow, 300km (186 miles) long, dominates the skyline.

The Chyulu Hills are of recent volcanic origin and offer the visitor the chance to walk or take horse rides accompanied with experienced guides. The views from the Chyulus can be quite spectacular with Kilimanjaro seeming to float above the terrain in the distance.

Top Ten

Hirola
Lesser kudu
Klipspringer
Yellow baboon
Striped hyena
Black rhino (Ngulia Sanctuary)
'Red' Elephants
Hippo (view under water at
    Mzima Springs)
Golden-breasted Starling
Rosy-patched Shrike

Opposite, top to bottom: A group of female (and one male) waterbuck in the Chyulu Hills National Park; the beautiful clear water of the Tsavo River near its source at Mzima Springs; in the dry season, herds of animals congregate at a water hole in Tsavo East.

Chyulu Hills National Park

Chyulu Hills National Park

Location: 200km (124 miles) from Nairobi.
Size: 471km² (182 sq miles).
Altitude: 2170m (7120ft).
Of interest: Wonderful walks with great views. Here the popular house plants African violets can be found growing in the wild.
Accommodation: *Chyulu Hills (self-catering three-bedroom guesthouse near the park):* tourism@kws.org
See also panel, page 33.

Chyulu Hills National Park

The Chyulu Hills, lying to the east of Amboseli and running parallel with the Nairobi-to-Mombasa road for 80km (50 miles), became a national park in 1983. The park comprises several hundred small, grass-covered volcanic hills that are only some 400–500 years old, and a number of beautiful forested valleys. It is possible to walk along the crest of these hills, from where the views of Kilimanjaro and the surrounding countryside are phenomenal. There is also a very rough track through the hills, negotiable with a four-wheel-drive vehicle. It is thought that rainfall percolating through the Chyulus feeds the famous Mzima Springs in nearby Tsavo West National Park. A variety of wildlife occurs in the area, including fringed-eared oryx, elephant, Masai giraffe, Coke's hartebeest (kongoni), lion and cheetah. Over 400 species of birds have been recorded here.

Tsavo National Park

This very large wildlife area is larger than Wales and about the same size as the states of New Hampshire and Vermont combined. It has an area of 20,810km² (8035 sq miles) and varies in altitude from 230–2000m (755–6562ft). The Nairobi-to-Mombasa road

Tsavo National Park

splits the park into two halves: Tsavo East and Tsavo West national parks. Since the park was split mainly for administration purposes, the two areas differ markedly. Tsavo East consists of miles of flat, dry thornbush interspersed with magnificent baobab trees and dominated by the 300km long (186-mile) Yatta Plateau, the world's longest lava flow. Although it is dry thornbush country, the vista is of volcanic mountains, hills and outcrops, with magnificent views. Along the Tsavo River there is lush vegetation, comprising doum palms, tamarind and acacia trees. For much of the year Tsavo burns dry and dusty; the red Tsavo dust blankets everything, including the elephants, which are known here for their red colour. Once numbering tens of thousands, drought and serious poaching in the late 70s and early 80s have severely reduced the elephant population, now standing at around 5000–6000. However, their destructive effect on the environment has been lessened as a result, and the vegetation is recovering, in many places thicker than before. After rain Tsavo transforms almost overnight – the grasses push up fresh shoots and many colourful wildflowers, such as the pink and white convolvulus, quickly appear.

Klipspringer (Swahili: *mbuzi mawe*)

This is a small antelope usually found in pairs on kopjes and rocky outcrops. Klipspringers have a very thick coat which is stiff and brittle, unlike any other African antelope. They stand on the tips of their hooves, which are specially adapted for their life on rocks. Klipspringers are very sure-footed and appear to bounce from rock to rock. They are capable of extraordinary jumps and make rapid progress from rock to rock without apparent footholds. In East Africa both males and females have horns but in other parts of Africa only the males have horns.

Klipspringers find all their food, mostly sparse grass and herbs that grow among the rocks, where they live and can manage without water for long periods. The best time to see klipspringers is in the early mornings when they can be seen standing out in the open; they spend the rest of the day lying down in the shade.

Lesser kudu (Swahili: *tandala dogo*)

These shy antelope are smaller and more graceful than greater kudu and have more stripes (11–15) on their flanks. Lesser kudu

Tsavo's Red Elephants

Tsavo's elephants are often referred to as 'red elephants'. Actually the elephants of Tsavo are no different in colour from any other elephants; it's just that the soil in Tsavo is very red in colour and when they bathe or dust themselves they quickly take on the colour of the red soil! Tsavo's red elephants, at one time numbering around 50,000, have dramatically changed the vegetation in the area. During a very severe drought in the late 60s and early 70s, the elephants ate virtually all the available vegetation and badly damaged many of the baobab trees. Together with black rhino, they died of starvation in large numbers. Ironically, before the drought the elephants were the subject of much debate on the issue of culling but, before any decisions were made, nature took its course. Since that time the vegetation has made a remarkable recovery and the elephants are increasing in numbers too.

Opposite: The beautiful Chyulu Hills are some of the youngest mountains in the world. They were formed only a few hundred years ago. On the southwestern side of the Chyulus is the evil-looking black Shaitani (Swahili for devil) lava flow. Surprisingly, black rhino occur in this inhospitable habitat.

Tsavo East National Park

Tsavo East National Park

Location: 200km (124 miles) from Nairobi.
Size: 11,747km² (4534 sq miles).
Altitude: 230–975m (755–3200ft).
Of interest: Lugard's Falls , and the rare and endangered hirola antelope.
Accommodation:
Galdessa Camp: www.galdessa.com
Satao Camp: www.sataocamp.com
Patterson's Camp: pattersons@iconnect.co.ke
Voi Safari Lodge: www.voilodge.kenya-safari.co.ke
Crocodile Camp: www.africasafariclub.com
Taita Hill Lodge and Salt Lick Lodge (situated between Tsavo East and West): www.saltlicklodge.com
Hilton Hotels: www.hilton.com
Taita Discovery Centre: www.originsafaris.info
Ngutuni Lodge (situated in its own sanctuary adjacent to Tsavo East): ngutunilodge@wananchi.com

also have two conspicuous white patches: one on the upper, and the other on the lower part of the neck. Only the males have horns, which are long and spiralled. Lesser kudu live in much dryer country and can survive without water for a long time. They live in small groups of one to three females and their young, while males are mostly solitary. Immature males leave the family groups and for a while join other young males until they are more mature, at about four or five years old. Lesser kudu prefer dense riverine thickets where they are very difficult to see; here they browse on leaves, seed pods and fruits. When disturbed they take flight with large leaps and with their tails curled over their backs.

Red-billed Hornbill (Swahili: *hondohondo*)

This is one of the characteristic birds of the dry bush country and its call, a monotonous 'kok kok kok', is a very common sound of the bush. They are usually found in pairs, often feeding on the ground on seeds and insects such as scorpions and beetles. The male and female are very similar, but the females are smaller and have a shorter beak. Their display is interesting: pairs duet with their wings partially open and their heads bowed; they bob up and down, and at the same time the calling gets faster and faster. Their nesting, like other hornbills (except the Ground Hornbill), is unusual: they nest in a hole in a tree. After mating, the female seals herself in a tree hole with mud, leaving a small slit through which she is fed by the male. The female stays here for the whole of the incubation period. During this time she undergoes a moult,

Tsavo East National Park

growing new feathers, and continues to be fed by the male. When the eldest of the chicks is about 21 days old the female breaks out of the nest and helps the male feed the growing young.

Scarlet-chested Sunbird

Sunbirds occupy a similar niche in Africa to the hummingbirds of the Americas. Most have long bills with which they probe blossoms. Males can be very pugnacious especially during the breeding season. Scarlet-chested Sunbirds can very often be seen feeding on non-indigenous flowers planted in the gardens of safari lodges. Males perch on prominent branches showing off their bright scarlet chests.

Tsavo East National Park

Most of Tsavo East north of the Galana River is closed to the public; only a few professional safari companies are allowed to enter. The park has a very good network of well-signposted roads and tracks and, because the terrain is mostly dry, flat thornbush scrub (the mountain and hills of Tsavo West are missing here) and there are fewer visitors, it has an aura of untamed Africa. The monotonous scrub is occasionally broken by green vegetation along the Galana River and the small seasonal rivers that cross the area.

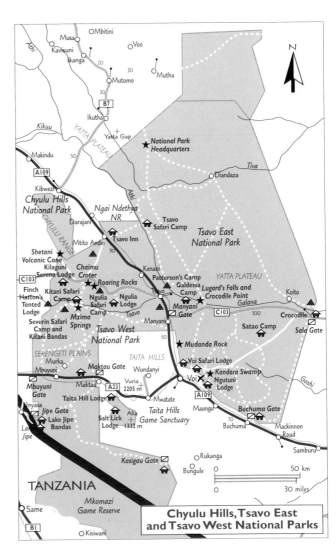

Chyulu Hills, Tsavo East and Tsavo West National Parks

Tsavo East National Park

Hirola or Hunter's Hartebeest (Swahili: *hirola*)

This antelope is similar to a hartebeest, but larger, measuring 99cm (39in) at the shoulder and weighing about 73kg (160lb). Hirola are slimmer-looking and both male and females have long, slender horns, which are very similar to impala horns. Hirola are pale brown in colour with a distinctive white chevron between the eyes and a long hairy tail. They are grazers and can survive without water.

Below: Lugard's Falls are remarkable for the fantastic shapes of their rocks.

The most interesting area to visit is that around Voi, the park's headquarters. Dominated by Voi Safari Lodge set high on a bluff, the Kandara Swamp and Voi River lie to the east. The vegetation is rich along the swamp and river and it is here that most of the wildlife occurs. Also in this area you may be lucky and come across a herd of Daphne Sheldrick's orphaned elephants. To the north of the lodge is Mudanda Rock, a miniature of Australia's Ayres Rock. Two kilometres long (1.2 miles), it stands out prominently from the surrounding plains. Below the rock a natural water hole attracts a great deal of wildlife, particularly during the dry season. There is a parking area to the western side of the rock and a footpath leads to a spot from where one can climb up to the top. From here the views over the plains are wonderful and occasionally one can see elephants and other mammals drinking there.

About 60km (37 miles) north of Voi are Lugard's Falls (named after Captain Lugard, Britain's first proconsul in East Africa) on the Galana River. The falls, actually a series of rapids, are most dramatic and impressive after rain, when the river's flow is constricted in the narrow rocky gorge. Below the falls very large crocodiles can usually be seen at Crocodile Point. Wildlife found here is similar to that found at Tsavo West, but in the area of Satao Camp you have a good chance of seeing the highly endangered hirola antelope (Hunter's hartebeest), relocated here from the border with Somalia in 1996. Tsavo East is good for dryland birds such as the stunning Golden-breasted Starling, Orange-bellied Parrot and the odd-looking Vulturine Guineafowl.

Hirola Conservation

The hirola, also known as Hunter's hartebeest, is one of Africa's most endangered antelope. It is a relative of the hartebeest but has adapted to live in more arid areas. The hirola's range was originally restricted to a small area straddling the Kenya/Somalia border. At some time in the 1970s there was a drastic decline in its population and by 1995 only 300 of the animals were thought to survive in a very small area of southeastern Kenya (the hirola's status in Somalia is unknown). In 1963 a number of hirola (about 20) were moved to Tsavo East National Park and by 1996 they had increased to approximately 80 individuals. In 1995 the

Tsavo West National Park

Hirola Management Committee (HMC) was formed with a mandate to conserve the species. In 1996 a further 29 hirola were translocated to Tsavo East National Park and it is now estimated that there are at least 100 individuals. It must be said that the local people in Ljara are now very protective of 'their' antelope and it took some skilful negotiations by KWS to allow them to move the 29 hirola to Tsavo West National Park.

Tsavo West National Park

Tsavo West National Park is predominantly semi-arid plains broken with granite outcrops and lava fields. The highest and most magnificent, Ngulia Mountain is 1830m (almost 6000ft) high. Tsavo West is the most visited section in Tsavo National Park, offering many attractions apart from its wildlife. The foremost is the famous Mzima Springs where up to 227.3 million litres (50 million gallons) of cool, crystal-clear water flows out of the ground through the porous volcanic rocks. This water is believed to originate from the Chyulu Hills via an underground river. Water from the springs is piped all the way (150km; 95 miles) to the city of Mombasa on the coast. At Mzima there is a car park and visitors are permitted to walk to the springs' source and along a pathway which follows the water. The walk is a wonderful experience. If you are quiet you may be rewarded with the sight of animals and birds coming down to the water's edge to drink, and you are sure to see hippos clearly as they lie in the cool clear water. One can also watch for hippos through the windows of an observation tank sunk into the river, which allows the visitor to enter a cool, new underwater world. Swimming close to the tank's windows are likely to be a number of fish, mostly barbel species. Troops of black-faced vervet monkeys and many interesting birds inhabit the trees around Mzima. This is also one of the few places in Kenya where darters can be seen.

Other interesting places to visit include the Roaring Rocks, which get their name from the sound made by the wind that blows through them. Here, from the top of a 98m (300ft) rock face, there are wonderful views over Tsavo; similar views can be experienced from Poacher's Lookout. The volcanic Chaimu Crater, less than 200 years old and composed of black coke, is well worth visiting and can be climbed if you are interested. This

Tsavo West National Park

Location: 200km (124 miles) from Nairobi.
Size: 9065km² (3500 sq miles).
Altitude: 229–2000m (750–6560ft).
Accommodation:
Finch Hatton's: www.finchhattons.com
Kilaguni Serena Lodge: www.serenahotels.com
Ngulia Lodge: www.kenya-safari.co.ke or www.ngulialodge.kenya-safari.co.ke
Voyager Zawani Luxury Tented Camp: www.heritagehotels.com
Severin Safari Camp: www.severin-kenya.com
Kitani Bandas (self-catering): tel 041 5485 0015 or book through Severin.
Ngulia Self-service Bandas: www.kws.org

Tsavo West National Park

Man-eaters of Tsavo

This is the title of a true account, written by Colonel JH Patterson, who was in charge of building a bridge over the Tsavo River for the Uganda Railway in 1898. For some time, workers were continually being dragged off into the night by two large male lions; the workers believed it was the Devil in the shape of a lion, as the lions were quite fearless. Eventually, in December 1898, after a mounting death toll including 28 Indian workers and a large number of Africans, work on the bridge was brought to a halt until the lions were shot. After many nights of waiting, Colonel Patterson shot the lions. These lions are on display in the Chicago Natural History Museum.

area is a good place to look out for klipspringer (see page 43). It is also a good place for lesser kudu. Other wildlife found in Tsavo include lion, leopard, cheetah, elephant, Masai giraffe, eland, fringe-eared oryx, buffalo, Burchell's zebra, yellow baboon, Coke's hartebeest and Grant's gazelle. Below Ngulia Mountain there is a well-guarded Rhino Sanctuary containing a number of black rhino.

In the southwest corner of Tsavo West is Lake Jipe, 10km (6 miles) long and 3km (1.9 miles) wide, which has the Kenya/Tanzania border bisecting it. Above the lake, the Tanzanian Pare Mountains form a dramatic backdrop, especially at sunset. On clear days, Kilimanjaro can be seen towards the northwest. Although there are a good variety of mammals in the area, it is the bird life that attracts most visitors. The lake shore is the best place in Kenya to see Purple Gallinule, Black Herons, Pygmy Goose and, occasionally, Lesser Jacana.

Hippopotamus (Swahili: kibiko)
After the elephant and white rhino, the hippo is the third largest mammal – a full-grown male can weigh up to 3200kg (7040lb). The name hippopotamus comes from the Greek hippos, meaning 'horse'; in Roman days they were called 'river horses'. Until recently hippos were thought to be closely related to the pig family but recent research using DNA has shown them to be more closely related to whales!

Hippos live in groups of typically 10 to 15, but at times of low water more will crowd together. The resonant honking made by submerged hippos is one of the most familiar and impressive African wildlife sounds. Hippos close both their eyes and nostrils when they submerge, and mature hippos can stay underwater for up to five minutes, but on average they only stay submerged for a minute and a half.

Dominant males control a section of a river or lake shore and tolerate other males as long as they are submissive. At times, though, they drive out other males with great rage, inflicting deep gashes on each other, and they will even attack young males and are known to kill hippo calves. The so called hippo 'yawn' is

Hippopotamus

actually a threat display, usually given by a dominant male, showing off his long, formidable razor-sharp incisors and tusk-like canines. Hippos are very unpredictable; if they are encountered away from the safety of water, anything that gets in the way of them returning to water may be attacked. Many serious accidents have resulted from these encounters.

Hippos feed at night and rest by day in the water. Shortly after nightfall, or earlier if they feel safe, hippos leave the river or lake on well-worn paths, walking for up to 2.8km (1.7 miles), grazing as they go, and return to the river before dawn. During droughts when feed is in short supply they will often delay their return until a few hours after dawn and, in extreme times, will stay out all day seeking shelter from the sun in thick vegetation. Hippos feed on short grass, eating up to 40kg (88lb) a night, using their muscular wide (up to 50cm/20in) lips. Hippos spend most of the day in water shallow enough for them to lie on their bellies with their short legs tucked under, but if there is little human disturbance they will lie out on the bank in the morning sun.

Mating takes place in the water but births usually take place in shallow water with the female partially out of the water. If born in the water the newborn is helped to the surface by the mother. At first a young hippo, which can weigh 25–55kg (55–121lb) at birth, cannot swim, and climbs up onto its mother's neck or back to rest. Young hippos can suckle underwater – they close their nostrils and ears then wrap their tongue tightly around their mother's teat. After about three months young hippos begin to eat grass but continue to suckle until about eight months old. Calves are often left in crèches where they engage in play fights and chase each other around.

Taita Hills Game Sanctuary

Location: 40km (25 miles) west of Voi.
Size: 113km² (44 sq miles).
Altitude: 914m (3000ft).
Of interest: This sanctuary is privately owned and run by the Hilton Hotel chain. This area was once an abandoned sisal plantation which has been transformed into an exciting wildlife reserve containing a large variety of wildlife.

Below: A hippo seen underwater from the windows of the observation tank at Mzima Springs in Tsavo West National Park.

SHIMBA HILLS, MWALANGANJE AND TANA RIVER

The Shimba Hills National Reserve and the adjoining Mwalanganje Elephant Sanctuary are the closest wildlife areas for visitors staying at the beach resorts in the Mombasa area. For these visitors it is just a short drive to experience a part of real wild Africa.

By contrast, the Tana River Primate National Reserve is only for the experienced Africa travellers who are self-sufficient with regard to food, water and fuel. To get there requires a long, hot drive along unmade and mostly unmarked roads.

Top Ten

Sable antelope (Shimba Hills)

Elephants (Shimba Hills)

Cycads (Shimba Hills)

Palm-nut Vulture (Shimba Hills)

Fischer's Turaco (Shimba Hills)

Crested mangabey (only 800 left, Tana River)

Red colobus (Tana River)

Northern Carmine Bee-eater (Shimba Hills and coastal mangroves)

Crested Guineafowl (Tana River)

Pel's Fishing Owl (Tana River)

Opposite, top to bottom:
A dhow off the coast; the rolling forested hills of the Shimba Hills National Reserve; a female elephant feeding with her young at Shimba Hills.

Shimba Hills National Reserve

Shimba Hills National Reserve

Location: 540km (336 miles) from Nairobi, 56km (35 miles) from Mombasa.

Size: 320km² (124 sq miles).

Altitude: 120–450m (394–1476ft).

Of interest: Kenya's last herd of sable antelope, elephants, and ancient cycads. Be sure to spend a night at Shimba's tree lodge.

Accommodation:

Shimba Lodge:

Shimba@aberdaresafarihotels.com

www.aberdaresafarihotels.com

Shimba Hills National Reserve

Shimba Hills National Reserve was established in 1968 to protect one of the last breeding herds of sable antelope in Kenya and to protect a herd of roan antelope that had originally been introduced from an area near Thika, north of Nairobi. Unfortunately, the roan were unable to adapt to their new home and different vegetation and they died out. During the 1990s Masai giraffe were introduced; these have been successful and they are now fully assimilated into this environment.

The reserve consists of rolling hills and forest, with wonderful views of the Indian Ocean. The forest is one of the largest areas of coastal rainforest in East Africa. Mammals to be found here include elephant, buffalo, Burchell's zebra, common waterbuck, lion and leopard. Bird life is good, too; among the more interesting species that can be seen here are the Palm-nut Vulture, Southern Banded Snake Eagle, Grasshopper Buzzard, both Trumpeter and Silvery-cheeked Hornbills, Carmine Bee-eaters, Green-headed Oriole and Fischer's Turaco. Nearby is the Mwalanganje Elephant Sanctuary.

Mwalanganje Elephant Sanctuary

This 24,282ha (60,000-acre) sanctuary is a community-owned wildlife area located adjacent to the Shimba Hills National Reserve. It was established in 1995 by the local Mwalanganje community

Right: A herd of sable antelope in the Shimba Hills National Reserve, the only area where these beautiful mammals occur in Kenya.

Mwalanganje Elephant Sanctuary

with help from the KWS, the US Agency for International Development (through its Conservation of Biodiverse Resource Areas program), the Born Free Foundation and the Eden Wildlife Trust. The sanctuary was set up to create a corridor for the movement of elephants from the Shimba Hills to the Mwalanganje Forest Reserve, and is surrounded by an electric fence.

For many years elephants have traditionally passed through the area, migrating between the Shimba Hills and the surrounding areas. In the late 1980s the elephants started occupying the area more and more, which caused conflict between the elephants and the local people, and as the elephants started destroying crops the farmers retaliated by killing the elephants. To resolve this situation, more than 200 families voluntarily contributed land to the sanctuary, agreeing not to farm it. In return, they became shareholders and managers of the Elephant Sanctuary and received annual dividends from tourism. The local people were also given jobs as rangers and guides.

The Mwalanganje Elephant Sanctuary is the first ever community-owned conservation enterprise dedicated to the protection of the elephant. It has helped to minimize human/wildlife conflicts in the area and has enhanced the socio-cultural and economic well-being of the local community. Apart from elephant, sable antelope, bushbuck, impala, warthog and leopard are also present. Other attraction are the beautiful Kitsanze Waterfall, as well as rare cycads (*cycadaceae*), a primitive group of plants which flourished over 200 million years ago.

Too Many Elephants

Over the years the elephant population has grown causing problems when they raid local farms. Because of this conflict a decision was made to reduce their number by moving some to Tsavo National Park. During 2005 KWS transferred 150 elephants from Shimba Hills National Park to Tsavo East National Park, and more followed in 2006. Elephants are darted in family units and transferred by specially adapted trucks to Tsavo. This is the biggest transfer of elephants ever undertaken in Africa.

Sable Antelope (Swahili: *palahala or mbarapi*)

A male sable, with its distinctive sweeping sickle-shaped long horns, a black satin-like coat and a contrasting white face and belly, has to be one of the most beautiful of all the large antelope. Female sable are a rich chestnut in colour and can easily be confused with roan antelope. Sable antelope were never common in Kenya and the few that are left all live in the Shimba Hills National Reserve. Sables are gregarious, living in small groups in light woodland with clearings. The groups consist of herds of females with their young, bachelor groups of young males and solitary dominant males. The dominant male, which becomes

Tana River Primate National Reserve

Tana River Primate National Reserve

Location: 350km (217 miles) from Nairobi, 160km (100 miles) from Malindi.
Size: 169km² (65 sq miles).
Altitude: 40–70m (130–230ft).
Of interest: This reserve has seven species of primate, plus elephant, hippo, lion, waterbuck and crocodile.
Accommodation: Mchelelo Research Camp run by Institute of Primate Research, National Museums of Kenya: www.museums.or.ke
A self-catering tented camp: tourism@kws.org

Arawale National Reserve

Location: 130km (81 miles) north of Malindi.
Size: 533km² (206 sq miles).
Altitude: 85–100m (280–328ft).
Of interest: This reserve protects Hunter's hartebeest, plus elephant, hippo, buffalo and crocodile.

darker and more obvious with age, stands in a prominent spot in his territory waiting for female herds to pass by. His territory, marked by dung piles, is usually the best grazing in the area, so sooner or later a group of females will arrive. The territorial male will try to keep the female herds in his territory, especially if there is a female in oestrus. Young males are also allowed in his territory as long as they are subordinate and show no interest in the females.

Young bulls generally leave the maternal herd when they are about four years old; by then they have become much darker than the females and are constantly harassed by the territorial males. The young males are very vulnerable to predators at this time, until they can join one of the bachelor herds, while young females stay with the maternal herd for the rest of their lives.

Tana River Primate National Reserve

This reserve was created in 1976 to protect two endangered primates: the crested mangabey and the Tana River red colobus. The reserve on the banks of the Tana River is a relic of the Central African lowland rainforest which at one time stretched across the width of Africa and, because of this, much of the flora and fauna is unusual to East Africa. Although a protected area since 1976, at least 50% of the forest was cut down (between 1994 and 2000) by local people, the Pokomo tribe, who thought that their ancestral land was being taken away from them and given to monkeys.

In all, seven species of primate occur in the reserve, including blue and black-faced vervet monkeys, olive baboons and three different bushbabies (galagos). Also occurring in the reserve are elephants, Kirk's dikdik, leopard, lion, reticulated giraffe, hippo, common and red duikers, Grant's gazelle, buffalo, both Grevy's and Burchell's zebra, lesser kudu, common waterbuck and, seasonally, the rare and endangered hirola antelope.

Arawale National Reserve

Established in 1974, Arewale has no park entrance and there is no visitor fee. This reserve is a sanctuary for Hunter's hartebeest; also occurring there are buffalo, crocodile, elephant, hippo and lesser kudu.

Marine National Parks and Reserves

Arabuko-Sokoke Forest National Park and Reserve

Located south of Watamu, 6km² (2 sq miles) of this forest has been declared a national park. A remnant of the coastal forest, it was once famous for its indigenous rubber trees (*Milicia excelsa*), avifauna and butterfly population. It is the only place in the country where the rare Ader's duiker and the golden-rumped elephant shrew live. Bird species seen here include the Sokoke Pipit and the Sokoke Scops Owl.

Marine National Parks and Reserves
Mombasa Marine National Park

This park, established in 1986, is 10km² (4 sq miles) in area. It was created to protect the corals and coral fishes. The park is surrounded by a 200km² (77 sq mile) Marine National Reserve, where traditional fishing is allowed under licence.

Kinunga Marine National Reserve

This marine reserve lies some 225km (140 miles) north of Malindi. Here visitors can see the rare dugong and green turtle.

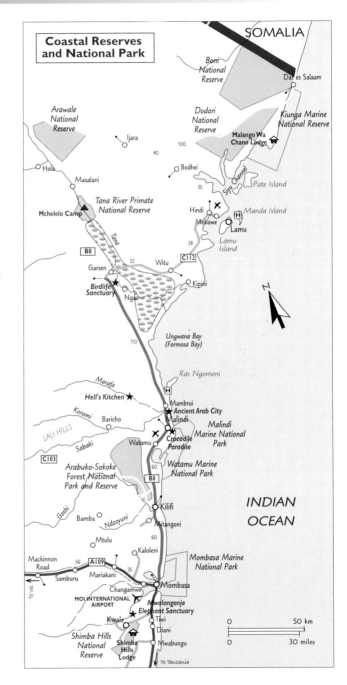

Coastal Reserves and National Park

SOMALIA

Boni National Reserve

Dar es Salaam

Arawale National Reserve

Dodori National Reserve

Kiunga Marine National Reserve

Ijara

Malango Wa Chano Lodge

100

40

Hola

Bodhei

Masalani

35

Pate Island

Tana River Primate National Reserve

Hindi

Manda Island

Mchelelo Camp

Mokowe

Lamu

Tana

Lamu Island

B8

58

52

Witu

C112

Garsen

Kipini

Birdlife Sanctuary

Ngao

N

Ungwana Bay (Formosa Bay)

110

Ras Ngomeni

Marafa

Hell's Kitchen

H

Mambrui

Koromi

Baricho

Ancient Arab City

Malindi

LALI HILLS

Sabaki

Watamu

Crocodile Paradise

Malindi Marine National Park

C103

Arabuko-Sokoke Forest National Park and Reserve

B8

60

Watamu Marine National Park

Goshi

Kilifi

INDIAN OCEAN

Bamba

Ndzoyuni

Mitangoni

Mtulu

60

Kaloleni

Mackinnon Road

56

A109

Mombasa Marine National Park

Samburu

35

Mariakani

TO VOI

Changamwe

Mombasa

MOI INTERNATIONAL AIRPORT

Mwalanganje Elephant Sanctuary

Kwale

Twi

Diani

0   50 km

Shimba Hills National Reserve

Shimba Hills Lodge

Mwabungu

0   30 miles

To Tanzania

ROHOLE, KORA AND MERU

This area is 'Born Free' country made famous by George and Joy Adamson. It is real safari country with open savannahs, baobab trees and dense riverine forest along the banks of the two major rivers which flow through the park and along the Tana River, which forms the southern boundary.

After years of neglect and serious poaching, Meru National Park has been reborn. The park has been restocked with wildlife and, once again, is a wonderful place to visit, especially for birders. Birders should look out for Pel's Fishing Owls and Peters' Finfoot along the Rojeweru River, and also the breeding colonies of Madagascar Bee-eaters along the Tana River. Rohole National Reserve, by contrast, is not open to visitors.

Top Ten

Grevy's zebra
Beisa oryx
Reticulated giraffe
Black rhino
White rhino
Pel's Fishing Owl
Peters' Finfoot
Madagascar Bee-eaters
Visit Elsa's grave
Visit Elsa's Camp

Opposite, top to bottom:
The wonderful view from Elsa's Kopje Lodge; a beautiful male reticulated giraffe crosses a road in Meru National Park; a male elephant feeding under an acacia tree in Meru National Park.

Rohole and Kora National Reserves

Rohole National Reserve

Location: 460km (286 miles) from Nairobi.
Size: 1270km² (490 sq miles).
Altitude: 250–480m (820–1575ft).
Of interest: Dry thorn bush country; wildlife includes elephant, Grevy's zebra and beisa oryx.

Rohole National Reserve

Rohole National Reserve lies to the east of Meru National Park. Although at a lower altitude to Meru, like Meru it consists of dry thorn bush country, with the Tana River forming its southern boundary. Elephant, Grevy's zebra and reticulated giraffe occur but there are no visitor facilities. Rohole is being used as an experiment to see how local tribes can coexist with wildlife.

Kora National Reserve

Kora National Reserve consists of inhospitable, dry acacia thorn bush, interspersed with granite kopjes. During 1983 and 1984 a joint expedition of the National Museums of Kenya and the Royal Geographic Society studied this little-known area, which proved to be a remarkable ecosystem virtually untouched by man. The book *Islands in the Bush*, written by the expedition's leader, Malcolm Coe, records their findings. It was in the Kora Reserve that George Adamson, from 1970 onwards, made his final home. Still rehabilitating lions up to the time of his death, George was gunned down and murdered on 20 August 1989 by Somali poachers. For years access to Kora was very difficult and there are few roads. In 1999 KWS built a bridge over the Tana River linking Meru National Park with Kora, making Kora much more accessible.

Kora National Reserve

Location: 410km (255 miles) from Nairobi.
Size: 1737km² (690 sq miles).
Altitude: 250–440m (820–1444ft).
Of interest: This was George Adamson's last home. During the 1980s the area was studied by a joint expedition of the National Museums of Kenya and the Royal Geographical Society. Out of this came *Islands in the Bush* by the expedition leader, Malcolm Coe. No visitor facilities.

Meru National Park

One of Kenya's lesser-known and less-visited wildlife areas, Meru is perhaps best known for Elsa, the lioness that Joy Adamson rehabilitated to the wilds. This story was made famous by the book, written by Joy, and the film *Born Free*, a story about the lives of Joy, her husband George Adamson and Elsa, the lioness they reared from a cub. Joy also reared a cheetah called Pippa here in Meru, which became the subject of another one of Joy's books, *The Spotted Sphinx*. It is possible to visit Pippa's grave site which is in the riverine forest close to the Rojewero River.

Meru National Park was first gazetted in 1966 by the local county council, the first African council to do so. The park is an area of unspoilt wilderness with views of Mount Kenya and, despite its good network of well-maintained roads, instils the feeling of real wild Africa. The park's attraction lies in the diversity of its scenery and its wide variety of habitats, ranging from forest, dry

Meru National Park

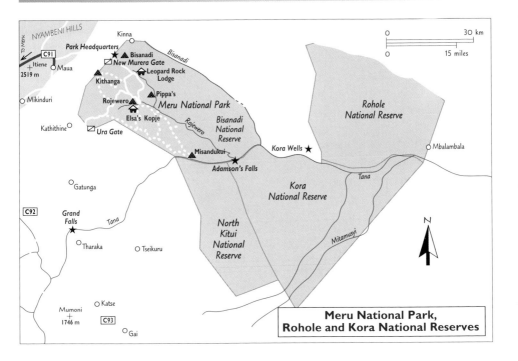

Meru National Park, Rohole and Kora National Reserves

bush and grasslands to swamps and numerous small permanent rivers lined with doum and raffia palms, tamarind trees and various acacias. The Rojewero River, roughly bisecting the park, is the most beautiful of the rivers. Along its banks bird-watchers should look out for the rarely seen Peters' Finfoot and the unusual Palm-nut Vulture.

The eastern part of the park consists of open grassland plains, while the western part is more wooded. There is also a huge contrast in the rainfall; the western area has almost double that of the east. There are a number of prominent inselbergs, including Mughwango (where George Adamson had a camp) and Leopard Rock. There is now a small luxury lodge (nine cottages) on Mughwango with stunning views of the park.

Meru's wildlife, although not as approachable as in other more visited parks, is varied and often numerous. Lion, leopard and cheetah are usually sighted, as well as elephant and buffalo; hippo

Meru National Park

Location: 370km (230 miles) from Nairobi, via Nanyuki.

Size: 870km² (300 sq miles).

Altitude: 366–914m (1200–3000ft).

Of interest: The home of *Born Free*, the book (and film) describing George and Joy Adamson's life rearing a lion cub called Elsa.

Accommodation:

Elsa's Kopje: www.chelipeacock.com

Leopard Rock Lodge: www.leopardmico.com

Meru National Park

Translocated Animals

The total number of animals now translocated to Meru National Park is as follows:

Elephants 66
Grevy's zebra 20
Common zebra 611
Impala 411
White rhino 23
Black rhino 4
Reticulated giraffe 71
Bohor reedbuck 128
Leopard 18

and crocodile are plentiful in the larger rivers. Both Burchell's and the endangered Grevy's zebra occur, as do reticulated giraffe, gerenuk, Grant's gazelle, and both greater and lesser kudu. Over 400 species of birds have been recorded, including Pel's Fishing Owl and African Finfoot.

In the 1980s the park was hit by Somali poachers. Its large elephant herds (more than 3000) were decimated and a herd of white rhino that had been introduced from South Africa were all shot, along with their carers. But Meru is now recovering; during the last few years Meru, with the help of generous donations from Europe, has been rehabilitated. Black rhino and reticulated giraffe have been reintroduced and the road network repaired. Recently IFAW (International Fund for Animal Welfare), in partnership with the KWS and Dr Richard Leakey, committed to a five-year plan costing US$1.25 million. Very soon 66 elephants were translocated from private ranches in Laikipia. These elephants were captured as family groups and moved one at a time to ensure they stayed together. Next, four black rhinos and 20 Grevy's zebra were moved to Meru. In 2002 the Agence Francaise de Developpement (AFD) gave a grant of US$ 7 million; part of this fund is to be used in Meru's rehabilitation.

White rhino (Swahili: *kifaru*)

White rhino are the second largest (in size – hippo weigh more) mammal after the elephant. Males weigh 2040–2260kg (4497–4982lb) and females average 1600kg (3527lb), almost twice the bulk of a black rhino; they have a pronounced hump and a wide, square mouth. White rhino are not white, except at Lake Nakuru National Park, where they take up the colour of the white soda. It is thought they get their name from the Afrikaans word *wyd* (wide), for their wide mouths. White rhino are grazers, using their square mouths to feed efficiently on short grass.

Mature bulls are usually solitary except when they join a female in oestrus. Females have overlapping territories and are generally accompanied by their recent offspring. Juveniles leave their mother at about two to three years old, usually when their mother has calved again. These juveniles often join up together

White rhino

and may temporarily join up with a female without a calf. Larger groups of up to 12 white rhino do occur, mostly during the midday heat, when they lie together in a shady, breezy place.

Baobab tree (Swahili: *mbuyu*)

The baobab is focal to many African legends and superstitions and is revered. With its 'upside-down' look, the baobab looks like a squat prehistoric monster. Legend has it that God, in a fit of anger because the baobab tree could not decide which habitat it required, threw the tree over his shoulder. It landed on its crown and has grown roots upwards ever since. Its grotesquely swollen bottle-shaped trunk and smooth grey bark store water, allowing the baobab to survive in drought conditions. Its thick branches, which look more like roots, are devoid of leaves for much of the year.

Baobabs are among the longest living trees in the world; carbon dating has shown that trees 5m (15ft) in diameter may be 1000 years old. Larger ones may be as old as 3000 years. Portuguese

Below: A white rhino drinking at a water hole; its 'wide' mouth, from which it gets its name, is clearly seen.

Meru National Park

cannonballs from four centuries ago have been found in living trees that line the approach to Mombasa harbour. Many of the older trees are more than 5–7m (15–20ft) in diameter.

This is a very useful tree: its trunk, which is often hollow, holds water for wildlife; its flowers are pollinated by bats and bushbabies, and its fibres are twisted into ropes. Its fruit contains tartaric acid and is high in vitamin C; its pulp, soaked in water, makes a very refreshing drink. During droughts elephants gouge out the trunks with their tusks and eat the moist fibre, causing many trees to collapse. Surprisingly, many survive the elephants' onslaught and continue to grow, even with large holes in them. Baobabs are found in many parts of eastern Kenya below 1300m (4000ft).

Pel's Fishing Owl

This owl is very uncommon in Kenya but it is resident along the Rojewero River in the Meru National Park. They are probably more common than records suggest but unfortunately these owls are very difficult to see as they roost in large shady trees

Doum Palm

overhanging the water. When they are seen, it is usually because they have been disturbed and the only view of them is as they fly away. Pel's Fishing Owls are large (64–76cm/25–30in), rufous-coloured owls which hunt their prey, fish, in shallow water from a low branch or the river bank.

Doum palm (Swahili: *mkoma*)

This distinctive palm, the only one with a divided trunk, is found along river courses throughout eastern Kenya, particularly in hot, dry areas. Its orange fruit, 8–10cm (3–4in) when ripe, is eaten by the local people. Baboons and elephant also eat them. It's not uncommon to see a troop of baboons feeding on the fruit high in the tree with a group of elephant feeding on any that are dropped by the baboons. In fact, it is thought that the fruit has to pass through the gut of an elephant before it can germinate. The nut, called vegetable ivory, is carved and necklaces and buttons are made from it. The leaves are woven into baskets and mats and the Turkana people use the leaves for building their huts. The sap is used to make a strong alcoholic drink.

Below: A herd of endangered Grevy's zebras grazing below a doum palm.

SIBILOI, CENTRAL ISLAND, SOUTH ISLAND, SAIWA SWAMP AND MOUNT ELGON

L ake Turkana and the Sibiloi National Park are often referred to as the 'The Cradle of Mankind.' This is where the Leakey family have researched for many years. The archaeological site at Koobi Fora is well worth a visit, although visitors must either fly there by charter aircraft or tackle some of the worse road/tracks in Africa, including crossing the Chalbi desert. Visitors must be self-sufficient.

Saiwa Swamp National Park is Kenya's smallest national park. This tiny national park is a great place to see the rare sitatunga antelope and spotted-necked otters, which can be viewed from walkways over the swamp and from tree platforms. Mount Elgon National Park, by contrast, is a forest-covered mountain with deep caves into which elephants and other wildlife enter, in search of essential minerals.

Top Ten

Sitatunga (Saiwa Swamp NP)

Spotted-necked otter (Saiwa Swamp NP)

Giant forest squirrel (Saiwa Swamp NP)

Tiang (Sibiloi NP)

Crocodiles (Central Island NP)

Northern Carmine Bee-eaters (Sibiloi NP)

Heuglin's Bustard (Sibiloi NP)

Arabian Bustard (Sibiloi NP)

Colobus monkeys (Mount Elgon NP)

Giant forest hogs (Mount Elgon NP)

Opposite, top to bottom: A doum palm on the shore of the Jade Sea (Lake Turkana); a view of Saiwa Swamp from one of the tree platforms; an El Molo village at Lake Turkana.

Sibiloi National Park

Sibiloi National Park

Location: 720km (450 miles) from Nairobi.
Size: 1570km² (600 sq miles).
Altitude: 200m (650ft).
Of interest: Koobi Fora, where Dr Richard Leakey's team has discovered fossils representing one of man's earliest ancestors.
Accommodation: Visitors may stay overnight at Koobi Fora. The accommodation consists of a number of bandas, but visitors must be self-sufficient. Book through National Museums, www.museums.or.ke

Sibiloi National Park

Sibiloi National Park, situated on the eastern shore of Lake Turkana (also called the Jade Sea because of its unusual blue-green colour which changes as the winds and light change), was gazetted in 1968 to protect the sites of early hominid fossil finds by Richard Leakey's team. Some of their discoveries date back from between 3 million and 1 million years ago. There is a small museum near the park headquarters with exhibits of some of the finds, including part of a 1.5-million-year-old elephant. The national park also includes Central Island, which is formed out of three dormant volcanoes, the highest one reaching to 240m (800ft). The climate is hot; the average temperature throughout the year is 40°C (104°F) and windy. The terrain consists of volcanic rock, desert and dry bush. Vegetation is sparse, with yellow spear grass and doum palms. The almost ceaseless winds in the area have exposed many of the fossil finds.

Sibiloi National Park has a surprising amount and variety of wildlife, despite its being extremely arid and windblown. It includes lion, cheetah, Grevy's zebra, beisa oryx, gerenuk, Grant's gazelle and a unique family member of the topi, called the tiang.

Bird life, too, is varied and at times plentiful, especially during the European winter months, when the lake shore is home to large numbers of wading birds, among them Black-tailed Godwits and Redshanks. For the really keen bird-watcher, the birds found in the arid bush are perhaps the most interesting: Swallow-tailed Kites, Heuglin's and Kori Bustards, Lichtenstein's Sandgrouse, Somali and Carmine Bee-eaters, and both Crested and Short-crested Larks are just a few of the wonderful birds found here.

Koobi Fora

Koobi Fora, on the eastern shore of Lake Turkana, is the headquarters of Sibiloi National Park. The area is virtually uninhabited except for the nomadic Gabbra people. Here is a small museum where some of the Leakey team's archaeological finds are displayed. The area has yielded large numbers of fossils representing both australopithecines and early hominids, including a skull of *Homo habilis* (KNM-ER 1470), one of the earliest recognized species of man, discovered by Dr Richard Leakey.

Sibiloi National Park

It is also here that hominid fossils confirmed that man stood upright more than 4 million years ago.

Even though the area is hot – it can reach 46°C (115°F) – and inhospitable, with almost incessant winds, for anyone interested in archaeology it is a fascinating place to visit. On a walk around the area even individuals with untrained eyes can easily see fossils lying on the surface. It is possible to stay overnight here, but visitors must be fully equipped. A fee of 500 Kenya Shillings per person is charged.

Tiang (Swahili: *nyamera*)

Tiang are close relatives of topi but live in more arid country. The best place to see them is Koobi Fora on the eastern shore of Lake Turkana.

Lichtenstein's Sandgrouse

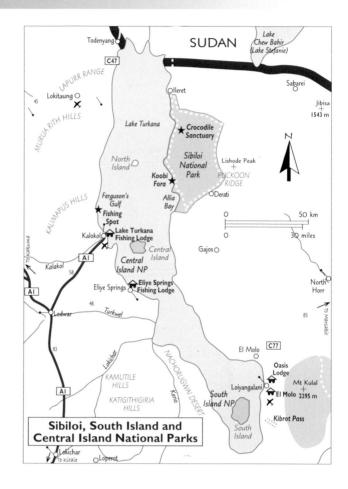

Sandgrouse live in hot, dry, open country where they feed mostly on seeds. These areas are usually far from water. Each morning or evening, depending on the species, large flocks, sometimes thousands strong, fly up to 80km (50 miles) from their feeding or breeding areas to water holes to drink. The sight and sound of thousands of sandgrouse arriving at and leaving a water hole is an amazing experience. On arrival they circle the water hole, land and then quickly run down to the water's edge where they line up, taking several quick sips of water before flying off in a whirl of wings. Male sandgrouse have a special duty to perform while drinking. If the sandgrouse have chicks, the male, who has

Sibiloi National Park

Central Island
National Park

Location: 760km (472 miles)
from Nairobi, via Lodwar, to
Kolokol, then a boat ride.
Size: 5km² (2 sq miles).
Altitude: 460m (1500ft).
Of interest: One of Africa's largest
populations of crocodiles, which breed
in the three lakes on the island.

special belly feathers that can absorb water, crouches down low in the water, thoroughly soaking the belly feathers before setting off on its long flight back to its nest. On arrival at the nest he fluffs out his feathers and the chicks drink from them. Strangely, the female does not have this adaptation. Lichtenstein's Sandgrouse live in the arid, stony areas of northern Kenya and mostly fly to water holes to drink after sunset or before dawn.

Central Island National Park

Central Island lies 15km (9 miles) from the nearest shore of Lake Turkana. The island is formed out of three still steaming volcanoes, the highest 250m (800ft) tall. Each volcano is filled with a lake and each is a different colour; one has a large population of crocodiles, while another is usually fringed with flamingo. There are also a number of boiling geysers on the island.

South Island National Park

South Island is the tip of a volcano lying 6.5km (4 miles) from Lake Turkana's eastern shore and 24km (15 miles) from the southern shore. The island is covered by volcanic ash and at night a ghostly glow from its luminous vents may well be the reason the local people, the El Molo (Kenya's smallest tribe, numbering only a few hundred people), think that the island is a place of ill omen and never visit there. There is no wildlife on the island apart from a small herd of feral goats.

The first known person to visit South Island was the explorer Sir Vivian Fuchs (of Antarctica fame) who landed there in 1934 accompanied by his expedition's surveyor, Snaffles Martin. Fuchs returned to the mainland and sent the team's doctor, Bill Dyson, to join Martin. Fuchs had arranged that Martin and Dyson would send smoke signals every day. After a few days the signals stopped and when Fuchs returned to the island he found no trace of them; neither Martin or Dyson nor their boat was ever seen again. The waters of Lake Turkana are regularly whipped up by 100kph (60mph) winds, which turn the lake into a tempest.

Saiwa Swamp National Park

Saiwa Swamp National Park, Kenya's and Africa's smallest, was created to protect a population of sitatunga antelope. The park

Saiwa Swamp National Park

consists of a long, narrow, swampy valley filled with rushes and sedges, bordered by a narrow band of riverine forest. This is an ideal habitat for the sitatunga, which has evolved specially adapted hooves to live in this swampy environment. A good feature of the park is that there are no roads, so visitors have to do all their viewing of animals and birds on foot. Over the swamp there are wooden walkways leading to several observation towers. The towers have been built along the edge of the swamp to enable visitors to view the sitatunga and other wildlife. From the towers, if one stays quiet and still, it is also possible to see the rare De Brazza monkey as well as Sykes' and colobus monkeys. Other wildlife in this tiny sanctuary are olive baboons, bushbuck, reedbuck, suni, giant forest squirrels and spotted-necked otters.

Sitatunga (Swahili: *nzohe*)

Sitatunga are large aquatic-dwelling antelope, 100–120cm (45–50in) at the shoulder and weighing 45–110kg (100–240lb). Males are larger than females and different in colour, and have spiral horns about 36cm (25in) long. Sitatunga have a shaggy coat which is well adapted to its aquatic environment. The males are greyish-brown in colour while the females are a rich chocolate brown. On the body there are faint white vertical stripes, which are not always readily seen, and there is a prominent white

South Island National Park

Location: 590km (367 miles) from Nairobi, via Maralal, to Loiyangalani, then a boat ride.
Size: 39km² (15 sq miles).
Altitude: 460m (1500ft).
Of interest: This is the scene of a mysterious tragedy involving an expedition led by Vivian Fuchs. Two members of his expedition disappeared from this island.

Saiwa Swamp National Park

Location: 20km (12 miles) from Kitale.
Size: 2km² (0.8 sq miles).
Altitude: 1860–1880m (6135ft).
Of interest: The population of sitatunga which live in this tiny national park.

Left: A male sitatunga feeding in Saiwa Swamp National Park. The sitatunga can be observed from tree platforms which give wonderful views.

Mount Elgon National Park

Mount Elgon National Park

Location: 400km (250 miles) from Nairobi.

Size: 169km² (65 sq miles).

Altitude: 2336–4321m (7664–14,177ft).

Of interest: The lava caves attract elephants, which enter them at night in search of salts.

Accommodation: KWS Bandas: www.kws.org
Nearby Lokitela Farm, bookings through Bush and Beyond: www.bush-and-beyond.com

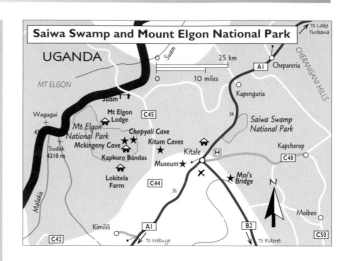

Saiwa Swamp and Mount Elgon National Park

chevron between the eyes. The sitatunga's feet are most remarkable; the hooves are long and splayed, which allows them to walk on soft ground and floating vegetation. Sitatunga are both browsers and grazers, spending their day deep in a swamp, sometimes partially submerged, as they feed on sedges, leaves and grass. At night they often leave the swamp to graze on grasses along the edge of the swamp. They are mostly solitary except at times of mating. The gestation period is about 7½ months and after birth the calf is left 'lying out' (see panel, page 83) for about a month. During 1990 and 1991, with the permission of the Kenya Wildlife Service, 10 sitatunga were released into a swamp at Lewa Downs. This population is now well established and is increasing in numbers.

Mount Elgon National Park

For miles around, Mount Elgon dominates the skyline; it is Kenya's second highest mountain. Part of the mountain, which is actually an extinct caldera, is a national park, one of the most scenic and unspoilt in Kenya. Mount Elgon sits astride the Kenya/Uganda border and is known to the Maasai who once lived in the area as Ol Doinyo Igoon which translates as 'Mountain of the breast'. The highest peak is Wagagai, at 4321m (14,176ft). It is actually in Uganda but climbers are allowed to climb it from the Kenya side of the border. The volcano's caldera is 6–8km (4–5

Mount Elgon National Park

miles) across. The park, founded in 1949, lies on the eastern flank of this volcanic mountain. Elgon's lower slopes are forest-covered, containing some of Kenya's finest *Podocarpus* sp. trees, which slowly give way to beautiful afro-alpine moorlands with giant heaths and giant groundsel. The crater floor, at an altitude of 3500m (11,480ft), comprises a luxuriant groundsel forest and has a number of hot springs which form the source of the Suam River. One of Elgon's special features is that hiking and trout fishing are permitted in the national park.

Mount Elgon also has a number of lava tube caves, some several hundred feet deep. Three are accessible, these being Kitum, Chepyali and Mackingeny. Although the latter cave is the most spectacular, Kitum is the best known as it formed the subject of a wildlife film. The caves and the elephants have been the subject of much research and have been made into a wildlife documentary by the BBC. Mountain vegetation lacks certain minerals which are essential to the health of all wildlife. Because of the lack of certain minerals, local elephants have for hundreds and perhaps thousands of years visited Mount Elgon's caves, particularly Kitum, to gouge into them, sometimes for quite long distances, in their constant search for essential mineral salts. Other mammals, such as buffalo, bushbuck and duiker, also require theses minerals and have followed the elephants' path into the caves. Apparently Mount Elgon's Kitum Cave inspired Rider Haggard's book, *She*.

Left: *Looking down into Uganda from Mount Elgon.*

MARSABIT, LOSAI, SHABA, SAMBURU, BUFFALO SPRINGS AND LAIKIPIA REGION

The Northern Frontier District, Buffalo Springs, Samburu and Shaba Reserves are a must-visit for wildlife enthusiasts. The wildlife here is so different from elsewhere in Africa. Grevy's zebra, reticulated giraffe, beisa oryx, gerenuk and Somali Ostrich are all common here. Cheetah, lion, and leopard are also regularly sighted. Special birds for the birding enthusiasts are Somali Bee-eater, Somali Courser, Vulturine Guineafowl and the stunning Golden-breasted Starlings.

Marsabit National Reserve is a forest-covered mountain which rises out of a desert and was the home of Ahmed, a huge elephant with big tusks, who was protected by presidential decree. Marsabit is still the home of many elephants and some special birds. Losai National Reserve is, by contrast, a lava plateau, with a number of volcanic cones. This area is virtually inaccessible, even by 4WD vehicles, but there is an airstrip which serves a mission station, Ngoronet.

Top Ten

Gerenuk

Beisa oryx

Reticulated giraffe

Grevy's zebra

Greater kudu

Leopard

Vulturine Guineafowl

Somali Bee-eater

Somali Courser

Somali Ostrich

Opposite, top to bottom: A herd of Grevy's zebra in Shaba National Reserve; a family of dwarf mongooses on the alert; a beisa oryx drinking in the Ewaso Ngiro River in the Samburu National Reserve.

Marsabit National Reserve

**Marsabit
National Reserve**

Location: 560km (348 miles)
from Nairobi.
Size: 1500km² (579 sq miles).
Altitude: 420–1675m
(1378–5495ft).
Of interest: Marsabit National
Reserve is the place where American
film-makers Martin and Olsa
Johnson produced some of the
earliest wildlife films in the 1920s.
Accommodation: Marsabit Lodge:
tel: +254 69 2411.

Marsabit National Reserve

Marsabit is a forested mountain, with spectacular volcanic craters, which rises out of the Chalbi Desert. It was first made famous by the American film-makers Martin and Olsa Johnson, who lived there for four years in the 1920s and made some of the first wildlife films. Later Marsabit became known as the home of Ahmed, a huge tusked bull elephant, who was protected by presidential decree. President Jomo Kenyatta declared Ahmed a national monument, granting him presidential protection until his death. Ahmed died as the result of old age in 1974. Ahmed's body has been preserved and is on display at the National Museum, Nairobi.

Greater Kudu (Swahili: *tandala mkubwa*)

The most striking of all the antelopes, the males have long, spectacular spiralled horns which can grow as long as 180cm (7in), forming at least 2½ graceful twists. These beautifully shaped horns have long been prized by hunters and in African culture for use as a musical horn and symbolic ritual object. In some cultures the horns are thought to be the dwelling place of powerful spirits, and in others they are a symbol of male potency. Such long horns should be a hindrance in the wooded habitat where these animals live. But the kudu just tilts back its head and, with its horns lying along its back, walks and even runs easily through dense bush.

Like their relatives, the eland, greater kudu can make spectacular leaps of up to 2.5m (6ft). Greater kudus are tall; males average 135cm (54in) at the shoulder and weigh about 257kg (565lb). Females, as tall but without horns, are noticeably more slender, weighing on average 170kg (374lb).

Greater kudu are browsers living in dry bush areas but in dry seasons they will eat wild melons, other fruits and even Sodom apple and aloes. Females form small herds of 6–10 individuals and are only joined by a male in the mating season. Male kudu are usually solitary, but sometimes form into small bachelor groups. After a gestation period of 7–8 months the females leave the herd to give birth. After birth the female leaves the young calf 'lying out' (see panel, page 83) for four to five weeks, one of the longest periods of all the antelope family; the calf is three or four months old before its mother rejoins its herd.

Losai National Reserve

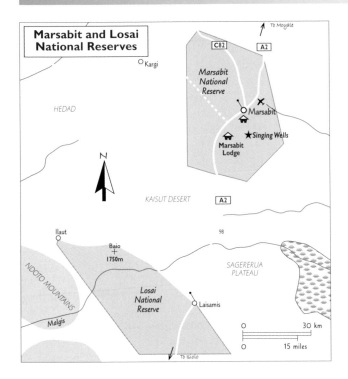

Marsabit and Losai National Reserves

Somali Ostrich (Swahili: *mbuni*)

Somali Ostrich occur in the northeastern dry bush country. Males differ from the Common Ostrich in that their neck and legs are blue. During the breeding season the blue brightens and the bill and the front of the legs become bright pink.

Ostrich have an unusual breeding system, with one major female and five or six minor females laying, on average, 25 eggs in the nest. The eggs are usually incubated by the major female during the day and the male at night. The chicks leave the nest three or four days after hatching and join up with other chicks in the area, forming a crèche which sometimes numbers more than 100. The crèches are looked after by only one adult pair.

Losai National Reserve

This reserve was established in 1976 to protect the habitat and its wildlife. There are no visitor facilities.

Losai National Reserve

Location: 368km (229 miles) north of Nairobi.
Size: 1806km² (697 sq miles).
Altitude: 625–1750m (2050–5740ft).
Of interest: Closed to tourism, Kenya's least-known game sanctuary is located in the Kiasut Desert. The reserve consists of a lava plateau dissected by dry luggas.

Location: 325km (202 miles) from Nairobi.

Size: 239km² (92 sq miles).

Altitude: 700–1500m (2300–4920ft).

Of interest: This is the place where the late Joy Adamson lived while she reared a leopard cub. The reserve is scenically stunning.

Accommodation:

Joy Adamson's Camp (ten tents): www.chelipeacock.com

Sarova Shaba: www.sarovahotels.com

Shaba National Reserve

Although Shaba, lying to the east of the Samburu and Buffalo Springs reserves, is only separated from them by a major highway, it is a very different habitat. It is scenically dramatic; here the Ewaso Ngiro, which forms the reserve's northern boundary for 34km (20 miles), instead of coursing through a plain, runs through deep gorges and waterfalls. Mount Bodech and Shaba Hill dominate the landscape, and the plains are dotted with springs, small swamps and rocky hills. The wildlife is similar to that of the other reserves but generally not as plentiful or as tame.

Shaba is perhaps best known as the one-time home of author Joy Adamson who rehabilitated a leopard called Penny here. The story is told in Joy's book, *Penny, Queen of Shaba*. It was at Shaba that Joy was murdered.

Samburu and Buffalo Springs National Reserves

These two small scenic reserves range in altitude from 800–1230m (2625–4036ft). They sit astride the Ewaso Ngiro River (a Samburu word meaning 'river of brown water') and are dominated by the impressive sheer-walled Ol Lolokwe and the

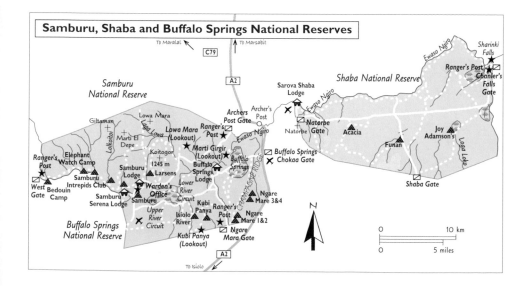

Samburu, Shaba and Buffalo Springs National Reserves

Samburu and Buffalo Springs National Reserves

rocky hills of Koitogor and Lolkoitoi. The river, bordered by a green ribbon of riverine forest made up mostly of tamarind trees, doum palms, Tana River poplars, and the *Acacia elatior*, is the lifeblood of this dry, arid region.

In the Samburu National Reserve north of the river, a narrow plain quickly gives way to rocky hillsides which are home to many leopards, while Buffalo Springs National Reserve is mainly a rolling plain of volcanic soils with dry river beds lined with doum palms.

Buffalo Springs Reserve has two small but important rivers flowing through it: the Isiolo River, which never dries up (the Ewaso Ngiro occasionally does), and the Ngare Mara. There are also the crystal-clear springs which give the reserve its name. Unfortunately, their beauty has been spoilt: one of the springs has had an unsightly wall built around it and its water piped to the nearby small town of Archer's Post, while another has a smaller wall around it and is used as a swimming pool for campers. Fortunately, one small spring has been left in its natural state and its waters flow into the nearby Ewaso Ngiro River, providing a magnet for wildlife.

Near Buffalo Springs is a wonderful area called Champagne Ridge, covered with flat-topped Umbrella Thorn Trees (*Acacia tortilis*), which are characteristic of the area. On either side of the river are extensive areas of Salt Bush (*Salsola dendroides*), which few animals eat because its leaves taste salty, but it does provide cover for lion and cheetah.

It is the unique wildlife that attracts many tourists to this wonderful area and, although there are no large spectacular herds to see, there is a wide variety. Four very special mammals – gerenuk, Grevy's zebra, beisa oryx and reticulated giraffe – are all quite common here and, although there is some seasonal movement out of the reserves, you can usually count on seeing them when you visit here. Other mammals include Burchell's zebra, buffalo, impala, common waterbuck, dikdik (both Kirk's and Gunther's), Grant's gazelle, klipspringer, both greater and lesser kudu and warthog.

Samburu and Buffalo Springs National Reserves

Location: 325km (202 miles) from Nairobi.
Size (Samburu): 104km² (40 sq miles).
Size (Buffalo Springs): 194km² (75 sq miles).
Altitude: 800–1230m (2625–4036ft).
Of interest: Maralal Donkey Safaris in Samburuland, e-mail: info@samburutrails.com www.samburutrails.com
Accommodation: see panel, page 78.

Private Reserves in the Laikipia region

Accommodation in Samburu and Buffalo Springs

Bedouin Camp: reservations@ privatewilderness.com
Samburu Game Lodge: sales@wildernesslodges.co.ke www.discoverwilderness.com
Larsens Camp: sales@wildernesslodges.co.ke www.discoverwilderness.com
Samburu Sopa Lodge: info@sopalodges.com www.sopalodges.com
Samburu Serena Lodge: sales@serena.co.ke www.serenahotels.com
Elephant Watch Camp: www.elephantwatchsafaris.com
Samburu Intrepids: www.heritage-eastafrica.com
Desert Rose Lodge: www.desertrosekenya.com

The highlight of any visit to Samburu and Buffalo Springs is to watch the large numbers of elephant (unperturbed by safari-goers) drinking and bathing in the shallow waters of the Ewaso Ngiro River. Crocodiles and the occasional hippo are present in the river, although it is not an ideal environment for hippos as the dry bush to either side of the river provides them with very little food.

Private Reserves in the Laikipia region

The Laikipia ecosystem covers 809,389ha (2 million acres). Located northwest of Mount Kenya, Laikipia is a sparsely populated area, much of it covered by large, privately owned ranches that include a wide range of landscapes from high plains to forested valleys. On some ranches cattle and sheep share the land with the wildlife. Some are sanctuaries created by the local communities, which have combined small farms and grazing land into large group ranches. (For more information, visit www.laikipia.org)

Lewa Wildlife Conservancy

A member of the Laikipia Wildlife Forum, Lewa Downs, now called the Lewa Wildlife Conservancy, is owned by the Craig family. Originally a cattle ranch where wildlife was encouraged, it now has an amazing variety of wildlife, ranging from elephant and rhino to leopard and dikdik. The wildlife has done so well that, in the case of the reticulated giraffe, it has sometimes done too well. Their numbers increased so much that they were damaging the environment, so several of them were successfully translocated to other wildlife areas including Meru National Park.

It is at Lewa that Anna Mertz, with the help of the Craigs, established the Ngare Sergoi Rhino Sanctuary. Protecting both black and white rhino, it was surrounded by an expensive solar-powered electric fence and patrolled by armed rangers equipped with radios. Later the fence was extended to encircle the entire ranch area, a total distance of 35km (22 miles), and Lewa Downs was renamed. There are now 52 black and 37 white rhino in the conservancy, the figure rising as the population slowly increases. Wildlife that can be seen there include greater kudu, reticulated giraffe, eland, Jackson's hartebeest, both Grevy's and common zebra, gerenuk, impala, Grant's gazelle, bushbuck and buffalo. Among Lewa's attractions are a number of hides (blinds) situated

Borana Ranch

in a swamp, from where it is possible to view the rare sitatunga antelope and many swamp birds. The introduced sitatunga (see page 69) have become more accustomed to visitors and occasionally they can be found feeding in the open on the edge of the swamp. Yet another attraction of a stay at Lewa is being able to walk or ride on horseback among the wildlife. It is also one of the few places in Kenya where guests can take night drives, something that is not allowed in most of Kenya's wildlife areas.

Borana Ranch

Borana is a 14,000ha (35,000-acre) ranch located at an altitude of 2000m (6500ft). Wildlife occurring there includes greater kudu, klipspringer, elephant, buffalo, lion, leopard, cheetah and a variety of antelope. While staying at Borana it is possible to visit the nearby Lewa Wildlife Conservancy to view the rhinos. Other activities are night drives, walks with the local people, and both horse and camel riding. The accommodation is stunning. Borana Lodge has six luxury cottages, each one different, perched on the edge of an escarpment. The view from them is fantastic, with Mount Kenya in the distance and elephants drinking and bathing in a dam below, and also, occasionally, greater kudu drinking. There is also a swimming pool.

Lewa Wildlife Conservancy

Location: 225km (140 miles) from Nairobi.
Size: 9500km² (3667 sq miles).
Altitude: 1615–2896m (5300–9500ft).
Of interest: Both black and white rhino, the rare sitatunga antelope, and greater kudu. Horse riding, hides (blinds) in a swamp.
Accommodation:
Lewa Safari Camp (12 tents):
www.lewa.org
Lewa Wilderness:
www.bush-and-beyond.com

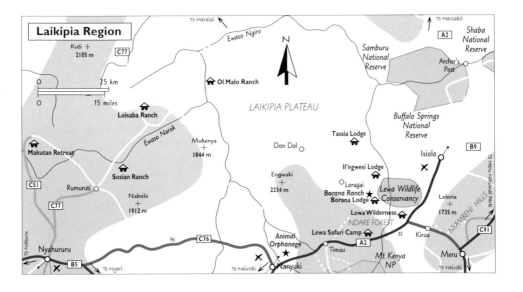

Private Reserves in the Laikipia region

Laikipia Accommodation

Laikipia: www.laikipia.org
Sosian Ranch: www.offbeatsafaris.com
Borana Lodge: www.borana.com
Loisaba Star Beds: www.loisaba.com
Sabuk: www.chelipeacock.com
Sarara: www.bush-and-beyond.com
Ol Malo: www.bush-and-beyond.com
Il'ngwesi Lodge: info@letsgosafari.com
Tassia: www.tassiakenya.com
Mugie Ranch: www.mugieranch.com
Ol Ari Nyiro Ranch: www.laikipia.org

Ol Malo Ranch

Although only 2000ha (5000 acres), Ol Malo is a magic place to visit. It is owned and run by Colin and Rock Francome; an added bonus during your stay here is to talk to the Francomes by an open fire before and during dinner. While the usual drives are available, both day and night, a walk with Colin and one of his staff will remain a highlight of your safari. Also available are camel treks with overnight camping along the Ewaso Ngiro River. Wildlife is varied, with elephants, reticulated giraffe and greater kudu being the main attraction. 'Ol Malo' means 'place of the greater kudu' in the local language. Accommodation is in four beautiful cottages with dramatic views. There is also a swimming pool.

Loisaba Ranch

This 14,000ha (35,000-acre) ranch is located on the edge of the Laikipia plateau. Both day and night drives are available, plus walking, horseback and camel riding. Accommodation comprises seven beautiful cottages, each with a private veranda. There is also a swimming pool and a tennis court at the lodge. Also on the ranch are 'Star Beds' – two rather unusual bush lodges with a difference. One, Kiboko, is set among kopjes and overlooks the Kiboko water hole, while the other, Koija, overlooks the Ewaso Ngiro River. Both are accessible only by camel, horseback or on foot; guests are guided by a team of traditional Samburu and Laikipia Maasai warriors to the sites. At Koija Star Beds, guests cross over the Ewaso Ngiro River on a suspended walkway to the lodge. Both Kiboko and Koija Star Beds comprise two double sleeping platforms and one twin platform. Each double platform is designed for one or two guests. A family platform accommodates four guests sharing bathroom facilities. At Koija two sets of platforms overlook the river and the other has views over a water hole. Each platform is reached by a ladder and has a large double bed, toilet and a camp-style shower with hot and cold water. A thatched roof only partially covers the platform and the beds are on wheels, looking a little like horse-drawn carts, and can be pushed under the thatch if necessary. Normally the beds, which have four-poster insect netting, are left out under the open sky. Each platform is sited to ensure complete privacy. After a wonderful three-course dinner (prepared by specially trained Samburu people) in a thatched dining area, guests retire to their

Sabuk and Ol Ari Nyiro Ranch

star beds. To lie in one of these beds, cosily tucked up against the night chill, listening to the night sounds and looking up at a vista of stars in a clear night sky is a very special experience, and one that you will remember for a long time.

Sabuk

Sabuk is a remote and wonderful wildlife area with a wide variety of animals: greater kudu, elephant, reticulated giraffe, eland and various gazelle can all be seen here. Lion, leopard and cheetah also occur. Sabuk has been conducting camel safaris along the Ewaso Ngiro River for 20 years.

While staying at Sabuk you will be personally hosted by one of the owners, Verity Williams, who has a wealth of experience on safari. Apart from drives, guests can take bush breakfasts and evening sundowners in a wild spot in the area while watching elephants come to drink. Half- or full-day walks or camel treks with local Laikipia Maasai guides can also be arranged. The accommodation comprises five spacious stone cottages, each with a private veranda with stunning views overlooking the Ewaso Ngiro River.

Below: A black rhino browsing on an acacia bush in the Lewa Wildlife Conservancy. This photograph illustrates well the black rhino's pointed lips, in contrast to the wide, square lips of a white rhino.

Ol Ari Nyiro Ranch

This ranch is owned by Kuki Gallmann, the author of *I Dreamed of Africa*. The bush here is rather thick, making wildlife viewing a little more difficult. The real attraction of staying here is the chance of spending some time with Kuki herself; unfortunately though, Kuki cannot guarantee being there during your visit. Guests stay at her home, Makutan Retreat, in three stone-and-thatch cottages, which are built on the edge of the Rift Valley with stunning views of Lakes Bogoria and Baringo.

Grevy's zebra

Il'ngwesi

The Il'ngwesi conservation area is situated next to Lewa Wildlife Conservancy at a lower altitude. The conservation area was created by the local Samburu people with the help of Lewa Wildlife Conservancy. Wildlife in the area includes beisa oryx, reticulated giraffe, Grevy's zebra, gerenuk and dikdik. The Lodge, built by the local people, has six cottages and a swimming pool.

Tassia

Tassia is another conservation area set up by the local people. Visits to the local Samburu people and drives are the main activities here. The Lodge, built by the local people, has six cottages and a swimming pool.

Grevy's zebra (Swahili: *punda milia*)

Grevy's zebra once ranged widely in Ethiopia, Somalia and northern Kenya but now almost all are restricted to parts of northern Kenya. Although they are adapted to semi-arid conditions and require less water than common zebra, they often come into conflict with the nomadic tribes and their livestock (mainly at water points). The Grevy's zebra gets its name from Jules Grevy, president of France in the 1880s, who received one as a gift from Abyssinia. Romans trained them to pull carts in circuses and called them 'hippotigris'.

The Grevy's zebra is taller and larger than the common zebra and its stripes are much narrower and do not reach the belly. Its head is also much bigger and it has very distinctive large rounded ears. Their social behaviour also differs from that of other zebra: Grevy's do not form into large groups and do not migrate in large herds. The adult stallions occupy a territory which they patrol constantly and mark with dung heaps while loudly braying. This distinctive loud braying is a feature that anyone camping near to a stallion's territory will never forget! Loose groups of mares with their young pass through these territories without a problem, but any mare in oestrus can cause fights between males of adjoining territories on their borders. These fights stop the moment the female enters a stallion's territory. Surprisingly, even small bachelor herds are allowed to pass through a stallion's territory if they act submissively.

Gerenuk

Groups of Grevy's zebra appear to have no leaders and, apart from mares with their foals, there are apparently no bonds. Gestation is a little longer than in common zebra – 13 months as against 12 months for a common zebra. Grevy's zebra foals suckle for nine months (common zebra six months) and stay longer with their mothers, so mares usually give birth only once every two years, while the common zebra mares give birth once a year. Grevy's zebra and common zebra occasionally form mixed herds but do not interbreed in the wild. In fact, some researchers consider Grevy's zebra to be more closely related to horses and only called zebras because of their stripes. Grevy's stallions have been bred with horses to produce 'zebroids', but the offspring are sterile.

Gerenuk (Swahili: *swara twiga*)

These elegant, tall, thin, distinctive-looking antelope are common and confiding in the Samburu/Buffalo Springs reserves. Gerenuk is actually the Somali name for these antelopes. They have adapted to feeding at a higher level than other antelopes. They stand erect on their hind legs, with their long necks extended, browsing on leaves out of reach of other similar antelopes. They also use their forelegs to pull down higher branches as high as 1.75–2.5m (6–8ft) off the ground. A gerenuk's head is small, with very large ears; its muzzle is narrow, allowing it to feed carefully between the thorns of acacia trees. It also has flexible upper lips and a long tongue, long eyelashes and sensory hairs on the muzzle and ears to protect the eyes from scratches.

Gerenuk do not require water and get all the moisture they need from the food they eat. Only the males of the species have horns, which are stout, S-shaped and heavily ringed. Both sexes have preorbital glands in front of their eyes which emit a tar-like substance. The males deposit this substance on twigs and bushes to mark their territories. They also have scent glands on their knees and between their split hooves.

Gerenuk live in small groups (2–8) of related females and their young, or bachelor groups or as solitary males. They are found in dry bush country in northern and eastern Kenya below 1220m (4000ft) and apparently were only discovered as a species in 1878.

Antelope 'lying out'

Most female antelope leave the herd to give birth. After birth, the newborn young are left completely alone but well concealed. Depending on the species, they may remain concealed anywhere from a week to a month. The young only emerge when their mother comes to feed them, usually two to four times during a 24-hour period. During this time the calf's scent gland remains inactive and the body wastes are retained until the calf is stimulated to void them by the mother's licking. During 'lying out' the mother remains on guard but stays some distance from the calf's hiding place. When the mother moves her calf to a new hiding place, the calf does not travel beside her but either runs ahead or alternately lags behind her. If the calf belongs to a species that lives in a herd, e.g. impala, when it eventually joins a herd with its mother, it will spend most of its time with other young, only seeking out its mother to feed or when the herd is on the move.

Beisa oryx and reticulated giraffe

Above: A male reticulated giraffe in the Buffalo Springs National Reserve.

Beisa oryx (Swahili: *choroa*)
Similar to the fringe-eared oryx (see page 36), the beisa oryx is greyer and paler and lacks the fringe on the ears. Otherwise their habits and social system are the same. Beisa oryx occur north of the Tana River and are quite common in the Samburu/Buffalo Springs Reserves.

**Reticulated giraffe
(Swahili: *twiga*)**
Ancient peoples revered the giraffe and it is one of the most commonly depicted animals in prehistoric rock and cave paintings. Early written records describe the giraffe as 'magnificent in appearance, bizarre in form, unique in gait, colossal in height and inoffensive in character'. At one time it was even thought to be a cross between a camel and a leopard; this is why even today its scientific name is *Giraffa camelopardalis*. One of the earliest records of giraffe is when one was sent from Malindi to China as a gift in 1415.

Giraffes are the tallest animals in the world, 4.6–5.5m (15–18ft), and full-size bulls can reach up to 5.8m (19ft), outreaching all mammals other than elephants. The reticulated giraffe is the most handsome of all, with its chestnut-coloured body marked with a network of white lines, very different from the jagged blotches of the Masai giraffe.

Giraffe feed by browsing, using their long tongue (18in/45cm) to carefully select foliage, mostly from acacia trees. The narrow muzzle, an extremely flexible upper lip and the long tongue enable it to strip off branches or carefully select individual leaves from between long sharp thorns. Large male giraffe can reach at least 1m (3.3ft) higher than female giraffe and when feeding together the males feed high up while the females feed on vegetation below 2m

Kirk's and Gunther's dikdik

(6.6ft). When drinking, giraffe have either to spread or bend their legs in order to get down to water level. They have very elastic blood vessels and a series of valves that stop the blood rushing in and out of the head when raised or lowered. The giraffe's long neck surprisingly has the same number of vertebrae – seven – as man.

Even though they are often seen together in groups, giraffe form no lasting bonds and only associate with other giraffe on a casual basis. The group is constantly changing in make-up, because giraffe rarely form groups except when feeding on the same tree. Even so, giraffe are rarely out of sight of others due to their high vantage point. Young giraffe form into crèches with at least one adult female nearby.

Giraffes' two main horns differ from those of antelope and deer in that they are unattached to the skull at birth, slowly fusing to the skull at about four years old. During a male's lifetime bone accumulates at the base of the skull, above the eyes and on the nose, forming a massive heavy club which is used to gain dominance over younger bulls. Bulls sparring is called 'necking'; the males stand side by side and in turn swing their heads at each other's head or body. At times these blows can be very heavy but they usually separate before hurting each other too much.

Kirk's and Gunther's dikdik (Swahili: *digidigi* or *suguya*)

Dikdik are very small antelopes, only 35–40cm (14–16in) at the shoulder and weighing 4.5–5kg (10–12lb), hardly bigger than a hare. Gunther's dikdik occur in arid areas in Kenya, north of the Ewaso Ngiro River, while Kirk's prefer a moister savannah habitat. Both Kirk's and Gunther's occur together in the Samburu Reserve.

Male dikdik have small, straight horns which are absent in the females. At times the horns are difficult to see because of a shaggy crest of hair on the crown. Dikdik have large black eyes, which in the Kirk's are surrounded by a white ring, while in the Gunther's the white ring is incomplete. Below the eye is a very conspicuous black preorbital gland. These glands produce a dark, sticky secretion which dikdik deposit on grass stems and low twigs by inserting them into the gland. Dikdik have very large

Kirk's and Gunther's dikdik

Above: A female Kirk's dikdik.
These small antelopes are very
common and quite tame in
the Buffalo Springs and
Samburu national reserves.

noses which are almost like small trunks, being very flexible. The nose, though, is an adaptation for living in hot, dry climates; it has a blood-cooling function: blood is pumped into the nose where it is cooled before being returned to the body.

Dikdik live in pairs and are almost always accompanied by their latest offspring. It is said that they pair for life. They are very territorial; their territories are marked by the secretions from the preorbital gland on the face, foot glands and dung piles. Some of their dung piles (middens) are as large as 1m (3ft), and they have an unusual habit of dropping their dung on top of other animals' droppings, even those of elephants. This habit of trying to cover elephant dung with their own is behind an amusing African story. It is said that one day a dikdik tripped over some elephant dung, so from that day on, all dikdiks have kept piling their dung onto the elephants, in the hope of one day being able to trip up an elephant!

Both male and female help defend the territory, even preventing other females from entering it. The gestation period is just less than six months and a healthy female is able to conceive again in about 10 days' time. Unusually, a female dikdik is able to be pregnant and lactate at the same time. Dikdik are crepuscular (most active at twilight and just before dawn), feeding on the leaves of bushes, flowers, herbs and fruit; they do not need to drink as they get all the liquid they require from their food. When disturbed, they run in a series of zig-zag bounds; their alarm call is a shrill whistle, a 'zik-zik' cry, which is how they got their name.

Dwarf mongoose

The two species are difficult to tell apart: Gunther's dikdik do have a larger nose, and Kirk's have reddish legs while Gunther's are grey. Unfortunately, these two features cannot be completely relied upon, making their accurate identification very difficult.

Dwarf mongoose (Swahili: *nguchiro*)

As their name suggests, dwarf mongoose are the smallest of the six species of mongoose that occur in Kenya. Dwarf mongoose are short-tailed, stockily built and are a speckled reddish-brown in colour. They are highly gregarious, and live in groups of up to 20. They feed on a variety of insects, scorpions, lizards, snakes, birds and small rodents. When they find a snake, it is surrounded and each mongoose pounces at the victim, usually one at a time from different directions. The venom of spitting cobras does not appear to affect them. When hit, they back off, rub the venom off their fur and then go back into the attack.

Their social system is interesting; the group is led by a dominant matriarch who forms a dominant pair with her mate. This pair is the only one in the group that breed but the young are fed, groomed and looked after by any member of the group. The matriarch, being the pack leader, is the first to emerge from the den and is the first to set off foraging each morning. A group's territory averages 2.2km^2 (0.8 sq miles) and is defended vigorously. In the Masai Mara their territories often overlap those of the much larger banded mongoose; interestingly, it is the banded mongoose that give way in any confrontation between the two.

In Kenya's Tsavo National Park an interesting observation has been made. In this arid thornbush area, hornbills regularly forage with dwarf mongoose groups, hopping along the ground with them and eating the same prey. Interesting though, the hornbills give way to the mongoose, even juveniles, if both are competing for the same food item. Although the hornbills catch and eat other rodents which are often the same size as a baby mongoose, they never prey on them. The mongoose benefit from this association as the hornbills give warning calls if they spot any predators, in particular Eastern Pale Chanting Goshawks which are common in this area. When the group is accompanied by the hornbills they feel much more secure so post fewer lookouts.

Lizards

Above: *The more pointed head of this Nile monitor distinguishes it from a savannah monitor, which has a more blunt-shaped head.*

Vulturine Guineafowl

This large, spectacular, tall and long-tailed guineafowl occurs in dry bush country. The sexes are alike. They are very gregarious, usually occurring in large flocks, except when breeding. Their strident, almost metallic call is a feature of the areas where they live.

Somali Bee-eater

Somali Bee-eaters are small pale-looking bee-eaters found in the dry bush and semi-desert areas of Kenya. They are usually found in pairs, except when they have juveniles flying with them.

Agama lizards (Swahili: *mjusi kafiri*)

Lizards are the most abundant and visible reptiles – no one visits Kenya without seeing a few lizards. Red-headed agama are usually seen sunning themselves on rocks. The males have a vivid red-orange head (yellow in northern Kenya) and a bright blue body. Females and juveniles, by contrast, are dull brown with orange patches on their bodies. They live in colonies, with a dominant male who always basks in a prominent spot. When basking, the males bob up and down; this behaviour is sometimes not popular with Muslims, who believe the lizard is mocking their movement during their prayer. They feed mainly on insects.

Savannah monitor lizard (Swahili: *burukenge*)

Savannah monitors are most often seen sunning themselves on the top of a tall termite mound; when alarmed, they quickly disappear down into the mound. In the dry seasons they often aestivate (the summer version of hibernation), mostly hiding in a recess or hole. Occasionally, though, they are found aestivating lying along a tree branch completely in the open. If cornered they can be very aggressive, leaping at an aggressor and lashing out their tails from side to side, which can be quite accurate. They

The Samburu people

can also bite; although their teeth are not sharp, they nevertheless have been known to hang on like a bulldog. These large lizards can be up to 1.6m (5.2ft) in length. They are omnivorous and feed on a variety of food, including small mammals, birds and their eggs, other lizards, insects and carrion. Their enemies are Martial Eagles, and mongoose take their eggs.

The Samburu people

The Samburu are Maa-speaking people who live in the semi-desert of northern Kenya and, like the Maasai, are thought to have migrated southward to their present location several centuries ago. They are herders with cattle, sheep, goats and, more recently, camels. Milk and blood taken from the animals in their herds are their principal foods but they will slaughter a goat or a sheep on special occasions and also during periods of drought. They also collect roots and bark from certain trees to be made into soups. Unlike the Maasai, whose culture and language they share, they are much more tolerant towards other tribal groups.

Below: A young Samburu woman and child milking a goat. The Samburu people rely heavily on goats for their milk but they also utilize camel's milk.

LAKE NAKURU, LAKE BOGORIA, MOUNT LONGONOT AND HELL'S GATE

This part of the Rift Valley is at times the home of millions of Lesser Flamingo and is a must-visit during any safari to Kenya. To view thousands of these birds against a backdrop of steaming hot springs and the sheer sides of the Rift Valley at Lake Bogoria is a sight never to be forgotten. Lake Bogoria is also the best spot in Kenya to see the magnificent greater kudu which, although sometimes difficult to spot, are quite common here. At Bogoria look out for the beautiful desert rose which when in flower is quite spectacular in this dry area.

Mount Longonot is a dormant volcano and it is possible to walk to the crater rim with a ranger escort. Near to Mount Longonot is Hell's Gate National Park which is popular with climbers who love to climb the sheer columnar basaltic cliffs which dominate this special national park. The cliffs are also a breeding place for Rüppell's Griffon Vultures.

Top Ten

Flamingos
Black rhino
Leopard
White rhino
Greater kudu
Great White Pelican
Rothchild's giraffe
Yellow-barked acacia forest
Black-and-white colobus monkeys
Crowned Eagle

Opposite, top to bottom: A breathtaking view of the dormant volcano, Mount Longonot, in the Rift Valley; a spectacular sight of flamingos at Lake Bogoria National Reserve; leopards are common at Lake Nakuru National Park.

Lake Nakuru National Park

Lake Nakuru National Park

Location: 170km (106 miles) from Nairobi.

Size: 188km² (73 sq miles).

Altitude: 1753–2073m (5350–6300ft).

Of interest: Gazetted in 1968, the park is open daily from dawn to dusk (06:00–19:00). Entry by smart card.

Accommodation:

Sarova Lion Hill:
www.sarovahotels.com
Lake Nakuru Lodge:
www.lakenakurulodge.com
Lake Elmenteita Lodge:
www.lakenakurulodge.com
Maili Saba (outside Nakuru Town on the rim of Menengai Crater):
www.mailisabacamp.com
Mbweha Camp (outside park):
www.mbwehacamp.com
Kigio Porini Camp (on the Naivasha – Nakuru Road):
sales@gamewatchers.co.ke

Lake Nakuru National Park

The Rift Valley's most famous lake, Nakuru, is known all over the world for its flamingos and has been recognized as being one of the natural wonders of the world. Roger Tory Peterson, the famous ornithologist, coined the headline phase 'The Greatest Bird Spectacle on Earth' on his first visit to Nakuru.

In 1961, the southern two-thirds of the lake was established by The Kenya Royal Parks as a sanctuary to protect the flamingos, and in 1967 Nakuru was declared a national park, the first one in Africa to be set aside for the preservation of bird life. The park's area was extended in 1969 to encompass the whole lake, and since then has been extended once more; it now covers an area of 188km² (73 sq miles). In 1986 the park was fenced with a solar-powered fence funded by Rhino Rescue Trust (UK) and in 1987 it gained status as an official rhino sanctuary. It is now harbouring a population of over 40 black and over 60 white rhino. In 1990 it was declared a Ramsar site, the first in East Africa, and in 2002 it was declared a World Heritage Site by UNESCO.

But the flamingos, of course, have always been the main attraction. At times there may be almost two million flamingos in residence, forming a stunningly beautiful deep-pink band around the edges of the lake shore. The lake is shallow and strongly alkaline (pH 10.4); this provides the ideal conditions for the growth of blue-green algae on which the flamingo feed.

During 1960 a small fish which is tolerant to alkaline water, *Tilapia grahami*, was initially introduced into the lake to control mosquito larvae; tilapia also feed on the blue-green algae. The tilapia have since multiplied both in number and in size, attracting large numbers of fish-eating birds such a pelicans, cormorants and herons.

Although over 400 species of bird have been recorded at Nakuru, they are not the only attraction the lake has to offer; over 50 species of mammal have been recorded here, and it is perhaps the best place in Kenya to see leopard and both rhino species. Some years ago a number of endangered Rothschild's giraffe were translocated here; they have multiplied and are now a common

Lake Nakuru National Park

sight. In fact their numbers have increased so well that several have been moved to other protected areas including Murchison Fall National Park in Uganda. Another of Nakuru's attractions are the troops of black-and-white colobus monkeys which can be seen in the Yellow-barked Acacia (*Acacia xanthophloea*) forest in the southern part of the sanctuary. This is also a good area to see the magnificent Crowned Eagle, Africa's most powerful, which preys upon the monkeys from time to time. Stretching along the eastern shore of the lake is a magnificent forest of Tree Euphorbias (*Euphorbia candelabrum*), unique in Kenya. It is, in fact, thought to be the largest euphorbia forest in Africa. Depending on local conditions the lake's size can vary between 5km² and 62km² (2–24 sq miles) in area.

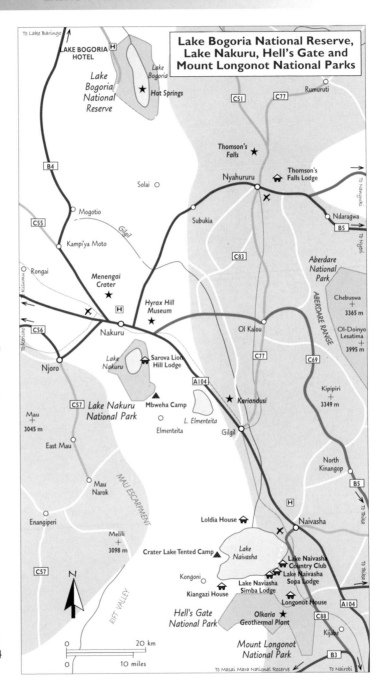

Lake Bogoria National Reserve, Lake Nakuru, Hell's Gate and Mount Longonot National Parks

Lake Nakuru National Park

Lake Baringo

Location: 280km (174 miles) north of Nairobi.
Size: ± 10km (6 miles) long, 6km (3.7 miles) wide.
Altitude: 975m (3200ft).
Of interest: Lake Baringo a well-known birding area (over 450 species recorded), surrounded by dry semi-desert country. Boat trips on the lake are popular – apart from seeing a variety of water birds, hippos and crocodiles are also commonly seen a very close quarters. One of the highlights of a boat trip is buying fish from a Njemp fisherman and then feeding them to the resident Fish Eagles.
Accommodation: see panel, page 95.

Flamingo (Swahili: hero)

The sight of as many as a million or more flamingos fringing a Rift Valley lake, like a river of flame, is one of the most breathtaking sights for many people on safari. The flamingo's name, which in Latin means 'flame', could not be more appropriate for these stunning birds.

Two types of flamingo occur in Kenya: the Greater Flamingo, which stands 1.5m (56in) tall, and the much smaller but much more numerous Lesser Flamingo, which is only 1m (40in) tall. Lesser Flamingo outnumber Greater by 200 to one. Lesser Flamingo eat blue-green algae, spirulina, which grows near the water's surface, while Greater Flamingo sift mud for tiny molluscs and crustaceans, and also spirulina, with their highly specialized bills. In ideal conditions it is thought that Lake Nakuru can produce 8 tons per acre of spirulina in a year. Both species feed with the bill immersed and their heads upside-down. Water is taken into the bill, which acts as a float, by a pumping action of the bird's tongue. The 'water' is filtered through dense filters, called lamellae, which line the inside of the flamingo's bill. Although flamingos find their food in the 'waters' of the alkaline lakes, they need clean fresh water to drink and bathe in. Flamingo congregate in large numbers at points where fresh water enters the lake; at times there can be long lines of flamingo queuing up for their time to drink and bathe. As flamingos spend so long in the caustic water it is very important that they bathe each day so as to keep their feathers in good condition for flight.

Flamingos are highly gregarious and nomadic, and fly in long skeins in a V-formation. Greater Flamingo occur in freshwater lakes and also in lagoons along the East African coast. Apart from being taller, the Greater species differ from the Lesser by being mostly white, with a contrasting bright red panel in the wing. The colours of the bills differ too. The Greater Flamingo has a pink bill with a black tip while the bill of the Lesser Flamingo is bright red with a black tip.

Flamingo are preyed upon by Marabou Storks and Fish Eagles. The storks, which look all the world like undertakers, slowly walk towards the feeding birds. At a certain distance the flamingos

Flamingo

quickly take flight and any ones slow to do so, such as sick birds, are quickly swooped upon by the storks. African Fish Eagles will also prey upon the flamingos, though they use a different technique. The Fish Eagles fly over the feeding flocks of flamingo, causing them to panic and take to the air. Again, if any of the flamingo are slow to take to the air, the Fish Eagle quickly swoops down on it, capturing and then dragging it to the shoreline, where it can be more easily eaten. Interestingly, at Lake Bogoria, Steppe Eagles, which are migrants from Eastern Europe and Russia, have learnt to pirate flamingos from the Fish Eagles. Steppe Eagles patiently wait until a Fish Eagle has caught a flamingo, then several of them will dive down onto the Fish Eagle forcing it to release its prize.

The words of the late Leslie Brown in his book *Mystery of the Flamingos* best describes them: 'In the early morning sunlight the pink of their plumage was exquisite, and their manifest excitement kept a forest of bright red legs and long pink necks always on the move. And they were more beautiful than I have ever imagined they could be.'

Rift Valley Lakes

Almost all of the lakes in the Rift Valley are soda or alkaline as they have no outlet. Their composition of trona or sodium carbonate is as a result of rivers, streams and springs having

Above: A group of Lesser Flamingo displaying along the shore of Lake Nakuru National Park.

Accommodation at Lake Baringo and Lake Bogoria

Lake Baringo Island Camp:
islandcamp@africaonline.co.ke
www.island-camp.com
Lake Baringo Club:
reservations@kenyahotelsltd.com
Budget Accommodation and camping site at Lake Baringo, Roberts Camp:
robertscamp@africaonline.co.ke
Lake Bogoria Hotel:
www.bogoriasparesort.com

flowed into them for thousands of years through mineral-rich volcanic rocks and soils. This, combined with a hot climate, has concentrated the lake waters. However, lakes Baringo and Naivasha are surprisingly fresh, although they too appear to have no outlets. Lake Turkana, too, is only slightly alkaline. Some of the alkaline lakes do contain common salt which is produced in commercial quantities at Lake Magadi.

Rothschild's giraffe (Swahili: *twiga*)

Rothschild's giraffe occur in western Kenya (Ruma National Park) and differ from other giraffe mainly by the colour – rich chestnut patches separated by buffy lines – and having no marking below the knee. Male Rothschild's can have five horns, instead of the more usual two or four. Their social society is the same as that of other giraffes. The Rothschild's giraffe occurring in Lake Nakuru were moved there because of agricultural expansion in their original home, Soy, in western Kenya.

Below: A male mountain reedbuck keeps watch for any rivals and predators that might appear while his females feed.

Leopard (Swahili: *chui*)

An adult leopard weighs 30–80kg (65–180lb), making it much smaller than a lion. Its sandy-coloured coat is patterned with dark rosettes, not spots. Although leopards are mostly nocturnal, in areas where they are not harassed they can often be seen during the day. In fact, if hungry or if an opportunity of hunting arises, they will hunt during the day. Mostly they are found sleeping on a horizontal branch in a shady tree. Leopards mostly hunt by ambush, often leaping from a branch in a tree down onto their prey, usually seizing it by the throat. They usually take their prey high into a tree, well out of the way of spotted hyena or lions, sometimes still eating it days later when it has become rancid. This habit of storing food is very useful when a female has very young cubs as she need not spend time hunting. This means she can spend more time protecting her young from other predators, such as lion and hyena. This is very different from a cheetah mother, which has to leave its young, sometimes for long periods at a time, in order to hunt. Occasionally, though, an agile young female lion will still manage to climb up and take the prey.

Leopards prey on a wide variety of animals – rodents, gazelle, warthog and even fish – and they also readily eat carrion. They are solitary animals, although their home ranges will often overlap. A male's home range will overlap those of several females. When a female comes into oestrus she is accompanied by a male for about a week before they return to their solitary ways. The gestation period is about 90 days, after which two to three cubs are born, usually in a cave, rock crevice or in thick bush. The cubs are born blind and their eyes open after about 10 days. The cubs remain hidden for about eight weeks and, although she will bring them meat at about six weeks, she will suckle them for about three months. Young leopards become independent at about 1½–2 years old but a female cub will often stay with its mother much longer, even when its mother has another litter.

Mountain reedbuck (Swahili: *tohe*)

Mountain reedbuck, smaller than the more common Chandler's reedbuck, inhabit steep rocky open slopes, grassy hills, escarpments and stony ridges. They are delicate and graceful, with a long, soft, greyish-fawn woolly coat which merges well with their surroundings. The horns, only on the male, typical of all reedbucks, are slender and curve upwards and forwards. Mountain reedbucks live in small herds of one dominant male with up to 10 females. They are very shy and alert and have a sharp whistle call when alarmed. Although they are mainly grazers they will browse on leaves and twigs in the dry season. Mountain reedbuck can be best seen in Lake Nakuru National Park and also along the escarpment on the edge of the Masai Mara National Park.

Long-tailed Widow Bird

Widow birds probably get their name from the fact that for part of the year during the breeding season, males grow black feathers over most of their body. Another explanation is that their long black tails are like a widow's train. The Long-tailed Widow Bird is no exception – in the breeding season it grows an extraordinary long floppy tail, while the rest of the body is black except for white-bordered red epaulettes. The male's tail is so long that it is

Hot Springs

Hot springs (*maji moto* in Swahili) and steam jets occur at a number of places in the Rift Valley. The best known ones are on the western shore of Lake Bogoria but there are also hot springs at Lake Magadi, Lake Baringo and at Kapedo, 50km (31 miles) north of Lake Baringo. Interestingly, the water supplying these hot springs at Kapedo is thought to come underground from Lake Baringo and this is the reason that Lake Baringo is a freshwater lake rather than alkaline. Steam jets are often used to supply drinking water. On the slopes of Mount Suswa local people place flat iron sheets over a steam jet and are rewarded by a steady drip of drinkable water. Kenya is now producing electricity from the steam in this area; one-fifth of Kenya's electricity supply is produced this way. Carbon dioxide gas seeping to the earth's surface is compressed into a liquid state and bottled; it is also made into dry ice for refrigeration.

Lake Bogoria National Reserve

Lake Bogoria National Reserve

Acacia No More!

At the 17th International Botanical Congress (IBC) held in Vienna, Austria, during July 2005, all 142 African acacia trees were controversially reclassified under one or the other of two newly constituted genera: *Vachellia*, comprising 73 species, and *Senegalia*, 69 species. The Yellow-barked Fever Tree now becomes *Senegalia xanthophloea*.

difficult for it to fly efficiently, especially in windy conditions. Long-tailed Widow Birds are usually found in marshy areas, where the male bird can be a spectacular sight, flying slowly and erratically, with its tail streaming out behind, looking like a large bustle. Males are polygamous and in the breeding season are very aggressive towards one another during the day but will roost with other males at night.

Yellow-barked acacia forest

Nineteenth-century explorers called this tree the 'fever tree' because it flourished in places of high ground water, which attracted mosquitoes. These beautiful flat-topped trees were believed by the early travellers and explorers to be the cause of malarial fever. The link between mosquitoes and malaria (literally meaning bad air) was not recognized until 1880.

Lake Bogoria National Reserve

Lake Bogoria (formerly known as Lake Hannington) and the surrounding area was established as a national reserve in 1983. Lying close to the base of the Ngendalel Escarpment, which rises 610m (2000ft) above the lake, Bogoria is scenically the most spectacular and dramatic of all the Rift Valley lakes. Long, narrow and deep, it is strongly alkaline and surrounded by dense, impenetrable thorn bush. Around the lake shore are a number of geysers and hot springs, which at dawn can sometimes form a thick mist. When one stands near one of the geysers and peers across the lake through the clouds of hot swirling steam to the towering wall of the escarpment, it is easy to imagine how the earth split apart to form the dramatic, chiselled sweep of the Rift Valley we know today.

There are times when Lake Bogoria is home to thousands of flamingos; to watch skeins of them flying along the lake towards the geysers and hot springs, where they drink and bathe, is a wondrous sight not easy to forget. John Walter Gregory, when he visited the lake during his explorations in 1893, called it 'the most beautiful sight in Africa'. Some years Lesser Flamingos build their cone-shaped mud nests at Bogoria and, though they occasionally lay eggs, strangely enough they have never been known to breed there. Bogoria is also home to a variety of

Rift Valley Volcanoes

mammals: common zebra, Grant's gazelle, impala, klipspringer, dikdik and the magnificent greater kudu, which is both prolific and tame here.

Desert rose (Swahili: *mdiga*)

Desert roses are found in Kenya's hot, arid regions and are thickset shrubs which in the dry season can look like miniature baobab trees. But when in flower they are transformed with striking pink flowers and they become a welcome sight in the drab-looking countryside where they occur. The sap is lethal: it's a potent toxin used to coat arrows.

Rift Valley Volcanoes

The whole length of the Rift Valley is studded with dormant volcanoes varying in size and shape. Some of them have the classic cone shape (Mount Longonot is a good example) while other, much older ones can be difficult to identify as volcanoes, because the original crater has been eroded away with time and only the hard central plug remains. Volcanoes situated in the Rift Valley are: North, Central and South Islands in Lake Turkana,

Lake Bogoria National Reserve

Location: 80km (50 miles) north of Nakuru.
Size: 107km² (41 sq miles).
Altitude: 1000–1600m (3280–5250ft).
Of interest: Flamingos, hot springs, greater kudu.
Accommodation:
Lake Bogoria Hotel: tel: (051) 42733/40748.

Below: *The bubbling hot springs of Lake Bogoria bear witness that this part of the Rift Valley is still very active.*

Mount Longonot National Park

Teleki's Volcano, Kakorinyo, Silali, Londiani, Menengai, Eburru, Longonot, Suswa, Olorgesailie and Shomboli.

Mount Longonot National Park

Mount Longonot is a majestic dormant volcano on the south side of Lake Naivasha. Although dormant, deep below the volcano there is water that is an incredible 304°C (579°F); this water is harnessed in the nearby Hell's Gate National Park at the Olkaria Geothermal Plant which supplies electricity to the national grid. There are a number of natural steam vents in the area which have been used by man for a very long time. The steam is condensed and collected as fresh water – very welcome in this dry area.

There is a well-defined track to the volcano's rim which visitors are allowed to walk, accompanied by an armed ranger. The view from the rim is staggering; the whole breadth of the Rift Valley can be seen, with the Mau Escarpment forming the western boundary and the Aberdare mountain range forming the eastern boundary with Lake Naivasha shimmering below. Joseph Thomson, the famous explorer, made the first recorded ascent in 1884. He wrote, 'The scene was of such an astounding character that I was completely fascinated and felt under an almost irresistible impulse madly to plunge into the fearful chasm'.

There are buffalo and colobus monkeys in the crater and it is sometimes possible to see the rare Lammergeier (Bearded Vulture) soaring by. Accommodation is available at Naivasha town.

Hell's Gate National Park

Hell's Gate, also known as Njorowa Gorge, is a deep gorge with impressive sheer columnar basaltic cliffs. The cliffs are of particular interest to birders and climbers. On the cliffs is a large breeding colony of Rüppell's Griffon Vultures as well as large colonies of Mottled and Nyanza Swifts. Verreaux's Eagles and Lammergeier can also occasionally be seen soaring along the cliff tops.

The gorge is an ancient outlet of Lake Naivasha and has a very prominent lone 25m (82ft) high volcanic plug called Fischer's Tower in its centre. This volcanic plug gets its name from the German naturalist and explorer, Gustav Fischer, who discovered the gorge in

Hell's Gate National Park

1883. There is a Maasai legend which relates how the tower came into being. One day the daughter of a senior member of the Maasai tribe left her home to get married. Tradition had it that she should not look back at her former home, but she turned around and was instantly turned into stone! On the 'tower' are families of rock hyrax and occasionally a pair of klipspringers. Other mammals occurring in the park are mountain reedbuck, eland, Masai giraffe, zebra, impala and both Thomson's and Grant 's gazelle.

Rock hyrax (Swahili: *pimbi*)

Rock hyraxes are small, furry animals weighing 2.5–5kg (5–9lb); they look a little like rabbits without the long ears. It is often said that the hyrax is the elephant's closest relative, but this is not true. The reason they were thought to be related to elephants is that their bone structure in the legs and feet is similar to that of elephants, the fact that males also have internal testes, and also the fact they have a long gestation period – seven to eight months. Rock hyraxes live in family groups of one male along with 20 or so females and their young. Each male defends his territory from other males. Rock hyrax have two or three young which at birth are remarkably developed – they can run about just one hour after birth. The young often form nursery groups. They are diurnal and feed on a grasses, herbage, leaves and fruit. They can survive without water but will drink when it is available. They use regular latrines, which form conspicuous white deposits on the face of rocks. In southern Africa these deposits are scraped off the rocks and sold for medical purposes; it is called 'Dassie Pee'.

Hell's Gate National Park

Location: 95km (59 miles) from Nairobi.
Size: 68km² (26.4 sq miles).
Altitude: 2777m (9111ft).
Of interest: Gazetted in 1984.

Left: A female hyrax, with her young, warming up in the early morning sun.

MOUNT KENYA NATIONAL PARK

Mount Kenya, at 5199m (17,058ft) the country's highest mountain, sits astride the equator; its higher slopes are permanently covered in ice and snow. The national park comprises the mountain above the 3200m (10,500ft) contour plus two salients astride the Naro Moru and Sirimon routes. The mountain is called 'Kirinyaga' by the Kikuyu, to whom it is sacred. The first European to climb Mount Kenya was Sir Halford Mackinder, in 1899. An old extinct volcano, it is made up of three peaks: Batian (the highest), Nelion and Lenana. Of these peaks, the original hard centre core is all that remains; the bulk of the volcano has been eroded away with time.

Top Ten

Scarlet-tufted Malachite Sunbird
Sykes' monkeys
Colobus monkeys
Suni
Crowned Eagle
Red-fronted Parrots
Black-fronted duiker
Giant heaths
Giant lobelias
Giant senecios

Opposite, top to bottom:
Looking over the alpine vegetation on the upper slopes of Mount Kenya down to the Rift Valley; a glacier below the peaks of Mount Kenya; a Sykes' monkey — these monkeys are quite common in the Kenya highlands.

Mount Kenya National Park

Location: 245km (152 miles)
from Nairobi.
Size: 715km² (276 sq miles).
Altitude: 3353m
(11,000ft) and above.
Of interest: The unusual alpine
vegetation: giant heaths, lobelias
and senecios.
Accommodation:
Mount Kenya Safari Club:
Kenya.reservations@fairmont.com
Naro Moru River Lodge:
alliance@africaonline.co.ke
www.alliancehotels.com
Serena Mountain Lodge:
sales@serena.co.ke
www.serenahotels.com
*Warden's Cottage and Sirimon
Bandas (both self-catering):*
KWS Tourism Department
tourism@kws.org

Mount Kenya National Park

Although conceived as a recreation area, the park has a good and varied population of wildlife, and is of geological and botanical interest. Elephant, buffalo and rhino are frequently seen as one slowly climbs upwards, and even when one is in the alpine zone just below the main peaks, there is wildlife in the form of giant rock hyraxes, begging for food from climbers if given the chance.

Scarlet-tufted Malachite Sunbird

Similar to the better known Malachite Sunbird but living at higher altitude, these birds have adapted to live on the special alpine plants that occur there. They feed on insects, flowering lobelias and senecios and nest in tussock grass or in the inflorescences of lobelias and senecios.

Climbing Mount Kenya

Mount Kenya is becoming increasingly popular with mountaineers from all over the world (Reinhold Messner, the first man to climb Mount Everest without oxygen, did much of his high-altitude and ice-climbing training on Mount Kenya). The main central peaks, Batian and Nelion, require ropes, ice axes and a degree of proficiency. Point Lenana by contrast is suitable for climbers with little experience. The four main routes to the peaks are: Naro Moru, the Sirimon and Timau tracks on the mountain's western slopes, and the Chogoria route on the eastern slopes. One can take a circular route or use a different track on the return

Right: Only experienced climbers should attempt to climb Mount Kenya.

Giant rock hyrax

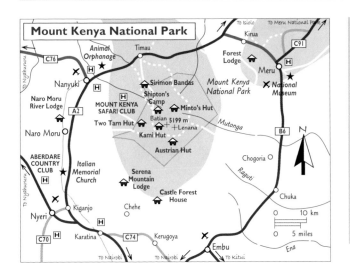

Mount Kenya National Park

Hagenia trees

Hagenia are the dominant tree on the slopes of Mount Kenya, right up to the open moorlands. They are beautiful trees, with feathery leaves and, in season, hanging masses of tiny red flowers. They grow to a height of 20m (66ft) and are often festooned with 'old man's beard'. The wood is hard and dark red in colour, and is used in furniture-making.

journey (only for experienced climbers). Vegetation varies from dense montane forest and bamboo to gnarled hagenia trees draped with 'old man's beard'. Contact Naro Moru Lodge for details.

Giant rock hyrax (Swahili: *pimbi*)

The so-called giant hyrax are rock hyrax, *Procavia johnstoni mackinderi*, endemic to this area, that have adapted to a very cold climate. Their fur is much thicker than that of a normal rock hyrax, making them look much larger. They are quite common on the higher slopes of Mount Kenya where they are fed by climbers.

Sykes' monkey (Swahili: *kima*)

Sykes' monkeys are stoutly built, weighing up to 12kg (26lb), and live in forests. They are closely related to blue monkeys, but are larger and have thick, shaggy coats. They have a distinctive white throat and chest patch, and the bristly tufts of hair on their foreheads give them their alternate name 'diadem monkey'. Their walk is distinctive, moving their back legs in a gentle, trotting gait, and at the same time holding their long tails higher than the body. They live in groups with a dominant male and 10–12 females. Their main diet is forest fruits and insects and occasionally leaves. A good place to see them closely is at Serena Mountain Lodge on the slopes of Mount Kenya.

Afro-alpine vegetation

The height of the alpine heath zone differs from mountain to mountain depending on rainfall and the direction of the prevailing winds. Fascinating are the belts of giant heaths, hung with strands of 'old man's beard'. Giant lobelias, some 3m (10ft) tall, give way to giant groundsels which can grow to 9m (30ft). These high-altitude plants are specially adapted to withstand frost at night; the senecios, for example, close up tightly, only opening when the warm sun strikes them.

ABERDARE NATIONAL PARK

The Aberdare National Park is a wonderful area to visit. A 4WD vehicle is recommended as the roads can be tricky when wet. The scenery is quite spectacular with crystal-clear streams and a number of stunning waterfalls – 'The Guru' has a total fall of 457m (1500ft).

The moorland – with patches of giant heaths, which are so large that they can hide an elephant, and forest patches of hagenia, St John's wort and bamboo – is a wonderful area to explore. In the forest it is difficult to spot any wildlife but if the visitor drives slowly, with luck, leopard, suni and, perhaps, a shy rare bongo can be seen.

Experienced 4WD drivers can get permission from the warden to visit the Salient where Treetops and The Ark are situated. Although the forest is quite thick there is more wildlife here. In the open glades, look for giant forest hog, black rhino, bushbuck and the magnificent Crowned Eagle.

Top Ten

Leopard
Serval (melanistic)
Giant forest hog
Colobus monkey
Sykes' monkey
Suni
Crowned Eagle
Mountain Buzzard
Cinnamon-chested Bee-eater
Stunning waterfalls

Opposite, top to bottom:
A male Malachite Sunbird; the interior of Treetops Lodge, Kenya's most famous tree lodge; a male bushbuck feeding in the open – these normally shy antelope are easily seen by guests staying at Treetops and the Ark.

Aberdare National Park

Aberdare National Park

Now officially called Nyandarua (a Kikuyu name meaning 'a drying hide'), the Aberdares were given their original name by the explorer Joseph Thomson, who first saw the mountains in 1884 and named them after Lord Aberdare, then president of the Royal Geographical Society.

The park consists of the Aberdare mountain range running north to south and a thickly forested Salient which extends down the eastern slopes. On the eastern and western sides montane forest slowly gives way to bamboo and hagenia trees at the higher levels. In the north is Ol-Doinyo Satima, the highest peak at 3995m (13,000ft), and in the south the Kinangop. Between the two is an undulating moorland at an altitude of 3000m (9840ft), with scattered rocky outcrops, forest patches, highland bogs and streams. The moorland is covered in tussock grass, with areas of giant heaths so large they can easily hide an elephant, groundsels (senecios) and forest patches of hagenia, St John's wort and bamboo. A number of ice-cold crystal-clear streams, the Chania, Guru and Karura, cross the moorland, eventually cascading down the slopes in a series of waterfalls. The Guru at one point cascades more than 91m (300ft) down a cliff face and has a total fall of 457m (1500ft). The most accessible and widely photographed are the Chania Falls, sometimes known as Queen's Cave Waterfall after a visit by Queen Elizabeth II, who had lunch in a wooden pavilion overlooking the cascade. These streams hold both brown

Right: *Giant forest hogs eating mud containing essential minerals at a salt lick in the Aberdare National Park.*

Aberdare National Park

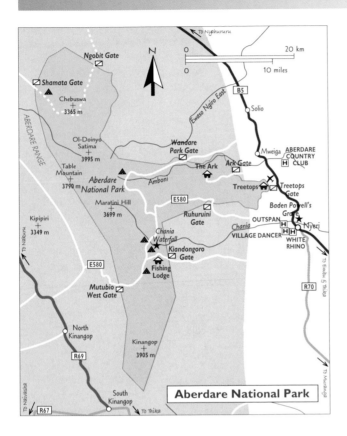

and rainbow trout and there are two fishing camps on the moorland to cater for keen anglers. The heavy rainfall in this catchment area makes the tracks very difficult to navigate and four-wheel-drive vehicles are essential. Animal life is prolific but the thick forest habitat impedes game-viewing. Elephant, rhino, buffalo, giant forest hog, bushbuck and both colobus and Sykes' monkeys are common. Predators are well represented, among them lion, leopard, hyena and serval (many of them melanistic). Bird life, too, is abundant and varied: Cinnamon-chested Bee-eaters nest in holes alongside the park's tracks, the Crowned Eagle – Africa's most powerful – is common in the forest where it preys on suni (a tiny antelope, smaller than a dikdik), while Mountain Buzzards circle over the moorlands and Jackson's Francolins, only found in Kenya, forage for food in the coarse tussock grass.

Aberdare National Park

The most convenient way to visit and experience the Aberdares is to spend a night at The Ark or Treetops, night game-viewing lodges located in the Salient. These two lodges are specifically designed to view the wildlife after dark. Both have flood-lit salt licks and water holes which can easily be seen from the lodges' rooms and balconies. It was at Treetops in November 1932 that Princess Elizabeth, who was on safari with her husband Prince Philip, became Queen Elizabeth II on the sudden death of her father, King George VI.

The whole of this wonderful national park is surrounded by small African *shambas* (farms) and large coffee estates. Because of the conflict between wildlife and farming, the entire perimeter of the national park is in the process of being surrounded by an electric fence, powered by water-driven generators. The enormous cost of this project is mostly being supported by local donations; an organization called Rhino Ark arranges fund-raising events such as motor sport and golf.

Below: The Ark stands looking over a water hole and salt lick, deep in the Aberdare forest.

Accommodation

Accommodation
The Ark
Guests booked into The Ark check in at the Aberdare Country Club where lunch is served. After lunch, they are taken by bus for a 30-minute drive through the Salient and on to The Ark. To enter The Ark guests walk along a raised wooden walkway with great views into the forest. On arrival, guests are briefed on such things as keeping as quiet as possible, times of meals and whether they need waking during the night if any exciting animal arrives at the water hole after they have retired for the night. The rooms are small but self-contained and look out on to the forest. At the end of the building there are two viewing platforms, one glassed in and one open. There is also a ground-level photographic hide where you can be almost at touching distance from the wildlife. After spending a night at The Ark, breakfast is served and guests are then taken back to the Aberdare Country Club.

Treetops
Guests visiting Treetops first of all stop off for lunch at the famous old colonial Outspan Hotel, in the small town of Nyeri. It is here that Lord Baden-Powell on his first visit said the following words: 'the wonderful views over the plains to the snow peaks of Mount Kenya .... The nearer to Nyeri, the nearer to bliss'. In the grounds of the Outspan Hotel there is a small cottage called 'Paxtu'; it is here that Lord Baden-Powell and his wife Lady Olave Baden-Powell spent the rest of their days. They are both buried in the churchyard at St Peter's Anglican Church, facing Mount Kenya. After lunch, guests are taken by bus to Treetops which is just inside the Salient. Treetops sits on stilts and is older and more rustic than The Ark. The majority of the rooms are tiny with no facilities; only the suites have en-suite facilities. There are shower and toilet facilities on the same floor as the rooms. After a night and breakfast at Treetops, guests are taken by bus back to Nyeri and the Outspan Hotel.

Animals
Bongo (Swahili: *bongo*)
The largest of the forest antelope, both males and females have spiralled lyre-shaped horns. They are bright chestnut red in colour, darkening with age, with 12 to 14 narrow white stripes on

Aberdare National Park

their shoulders, flanks and hindquarters. Running along the length of the spine is a black-and-white crest and between the eyes is a very conspicuous white chevron. There are two large white spots on each cheek. Bongos are extremely shy and are more usually found solitary, but occasionally they do form small groups of females and their young. Although mostly nocturnal they are occasionally active during the day. Bongos are browsers and are restricted to the higher elevations, usually occurring between 2100m and 3000m (6890–10,830ft) where suitable vegetation is available year-round. They range widely in the Aberdares, visiting the higher elevations during February and March before descending to the lower elevations during the wet seasons. At certain times of the year their main diet consists of bamboo which unfortunately periodically dies off after flowering. During the bamboo's second year of regrowth the plants become highly toxic; strangely, bongos do not seem to recognize this fact and many of them are poisoned. At one time they could regularly be seen at The Ark but, probably because of a combination of a bamboo die-off and the introduction of lions, they all but disappeared. Unfortunately, in unprotected areas bongos are very easily hunted by groups of hunters using dogs, which force the bongos to bay up, allowing the hunters to kill them easily with spears or guns. Happily bongos are now being seen more often, both at The Ark and on game drives in the area. At one place in the Salient a hide (blind) has been built to give visitors the chance of seeing this beautiful, elusive antelope.

Colobus monkeys (Swahili: *mbega mweupe*)

These beautiful black-and-white monkeys inhabit forests and are usually found feeding high in the trees, at 35–40m (115–131ft), where they can be surprisingly difficult to see. Colobus are very distinctive, with a black body, a contrasting white mantle and a long white bushy tail. Their faces appear to have white whiskers and a beard. The name colobus comes from a Greek word (*colobe*) meaning 'mutilated one' because they have no thumbs. Colobus monkeys spend almost all of their time in trees, rarely descending to the ground. They travel through the trees by jumping, sometimes as far as 15m (50ft), to get from one tree to another. Often they jump spectacularly outwards and downwards with their arms and legs outstretched until they reach another branch.

Colobus monkeys

Colobus live in family groups of 10–20 and they have very well-defined territories. Protection of their territories is mainly by bluff, aided by loud guttural roars. This calling is a distinctive sound heard by people camping in the areas where these monkeys live. Colobus feed almost entirely on young, tender leaves and have large stomachs which can hold the 2–3 kg (4.5–6.5lb) of leaves they eat per day. Most of the feeding takes place in the early mornings and late afternoons; the rest of the day is spent grooming each other, paying particular attention to their long tails, and sleeping while their gut is breaking down the cellulose in the green leaves. Surprisingly, newborn colobus monkeys are pure white and it is not until they are one month old that they slowly change colour. At one time these monkeys were hunted for their beautiful fur which has resulted in their disappearance in some places outside protected areas. Their main natural threat comes from leopards and Crowned Eagles, and on a couple of occasions both leopard and a Crowned Eagle have been found feeding close to each other on parts of the same animal. Which made the kill, the leopard or the bird, is difficult to know. However, the loss of habitat is the most serious threat to their existence.

Above: A black-and-white colobus monkey resting in the forest on the slopes of the Aberdare National Park.

Aberdare National Park

Cape Chestnut

The Cape Chestnut (*Calodendrum capensis*) is one of the most beautiful flowering trees in the highlands of Kenya. It grows up to 20m (66ft) high and during the summer when it flowers, the forests are filled with beautiful rosy pink blossoms. Cape chestnuts are particularly common in the Aberdare National Park and along the Rift Valley escarpment near Nairobi.

Bushbuck (Swahili: *pongo* or *mbawala*)

Bushbuck are beautiful, shy, elusive, forest edge dwelling antelope and when seen are usually solitary, except when a female is with her latest offspring. Only male bushbucks have horns which are 25–55cm (10–22in) in length and grow straight back. The males are bright chestnut but slowly darken with age; some older ones look almost black. The females are similar to young males. Both sexes have distinctive white patches or spots on their ears, chin, tail, legs and neck, and a broad band at the base of the neck. Bushbucks are most active in the early mornings and late afternoons. They feed on a variety of foods, carefully selecting what they eat. They mainly feed on leguminous herbs, shrubs, fruits, pods, tubers, flowers and occasionally grass. If disturbed they often freeze and remain very still – their cryptic colouring is wonderful in helping them blend into their surroundings – or they bound away making a series of barks. Although not territorial, males will fight over any female in oestrus. After a gestation period of six months the female gives birth and then leaves the calf well hidden. The female only visits the calf to feed it during this 'lying out' period (see panel, page 83) which lasts about four months. Their principal predator is the leopard. Occasionally baboons catch and kill the calves, but even so it is quite common to see bushbuck feeding on fallen fruit that the baboons have dropped. Bushbuck are best seen at Treetops and The Ark.

Giant forest hog (Swahili: *nguruwe nyeusi*)

Giant forest hogs are large, ugly members of the pig family, covered in long black hair which becomes sparse with age. The males, which are 50kg (110lb) heavier than the female, weigh 140–275kg (309–606lb), and have large swollen preorbital glands which exude secretions that spread over the face. Both sexes have tusks, the male's tusks being thicker. In Kenya, giant forest hogs occur in highland forest with open areas of grassland. They feed on short green grass, fallen fruits and berries, and they dig out salty earth. Giant forest hogs live in family groups – a female with several generations of her young, 4–12 individuals. The males form small groups and older mature males live alone. While usually nocturnal, they have become diurnal in protected areas. They are best seen on drives in the Aberdare National Park, and at night at The Ark.

Sunbirds

Sunbirds, like the hummingbirds of the Americas, feed mostly on nectar taken from flowers. Of Africa's 70 species, 35 are resident in Kenya. It is possible to see 10 different sunbirds in a day at Naro Moru River Lodge. The birds are characterized by their thin, curved bills and the bright, colourful plumage of the males. When feeding on nectar, pollen from the flower brushes off onto the sunbird's forehead and, as the bird visits other flowers, is transferred from one blossom to another. This method of pollination is an extremely important exchange between bird and flower.

Golden-winged Sunbird

Male Golden-winged Sunbirds are unmistakable, with a long tail, bright yellow wing patches and a large strongly decurved bill. The bill is well adapted to feed on flowering crotalaria (lion's claw), leonotis plants and wild mint, which grow in the highlands where these birds live. Usually solitary, they are mostly seen along forest edges and in gardens. Breeding males have iridescent bronzy gold on head, neck and back, and black wings with yellow patches. The tail is long, with the central tail feathers elongated. The female, by contrast, lacks the long tail and is olive in colour. They are best seen in the Aberdare National Park.

Augur Buzzards

Once the most frequently seen bird of prey, unfortunately their numbers are now much reduced, probably due to modern farming practices. Augur Buzzards prefer open country such as moorlands, mountain forest glades and baobab country. They are usually seen perched on a prominent open branch of a tree or on a telephone pole. Their prey is almost entirely rodents, so they are a very valuable bird to humans. Unfortunately, they are often accused of raiding chicken pens, but all they are doing is looking for rats and mice that are attracted to the chicken food. In the highlands their main prey is giant mole rats.

Below: Augur Buzzards are characteristic birds of the Kenya highlands.

Aberdare National Park

Above: A stunning Hartlaub's Turaco. These turacos, although difficult to see, are common in the Aberdare National Park.

The reason there are fewer Augur Buzzards today is thought to be the practice of spraying agricultural crops with herbicides and pesticides. These chemicals kill any rodents in the area and these are then eaten by the buzzards.

Tree hyrax (Swahili: *perere*)

Tree hyrax are very similar to other hyrax but not as social. They are nocturnal animals and live in highland forest areas. Their loud call, heard after dark, is very unusual. It starts with a squeak, then rises to a squeal and finally ends with a child-like scream. They also have a harsh, rattling cry, like a heavy wooden ratchet being turned slowly, which is heard soon after dark; anyone who does not know them cannot believe that such a sound can come from such a small animal. They are hunted for their fur which is longer, thicker and softer than that of other hyrax. Tree hyrax feed on leaves and fruit, spending most of their time in trees.

Hartlaub's Turaco

Endemic to Africa, turacos are unusual birds. They have strong feet with semi-zygodactyl toes; the fourth is reversible and this allows them to run, climb and bound with amazing agility along branches. The feather colour of most other birds is produced by refraction of light from minute structures in the feathers but turacos have true pigmentation. The red pigment is known as turacin and the green pigment as turacoverdin.

The sexes are alike in colour, mostly green with brilliant crimson-red feathers in the wing, which are usually hidden from sight. However, once a turaco takes flight these crimson-red feathers are revealed, contrasting vividly with the green forest foliage. Turacos feed mostly on fruits, flowers, buds and insects. They are generally shy but their call, a series of loud raucous sounds, betrays their presence. Hartlaub's are resident in the highland forests of Kenya and are quite common in the Nairobi suburbs.

Jackson's chameleon (Swahili: *kinyonga*)

This is a large chameleon, the males being on average 38cm (15in) long. Males have three long horns which they use for fighting other males, while the females may have one or three short horns. The colour of the males is mostly green, while the females are mottled dull green or brown. Jackson's chameleons are found in highland forest, woodland and in cultivated gardens, where their diet consists mostly of insects. Females give birth to live young, usually from seven to 28 in number.

Mackinder's Eagle Owl

These owls are resident in alpine peaks and moorlands on Mount Kenya, the Aberdares and Mount Elgon; there are also small, isolated populations on cliffs, ravines and quarries at Lake Naivasha, Hell's Gate National Park and the area between Mount Kenya and the Aberdares. The best place to see one of these very special owls is along the Nyeri to Nyahururu road. Here local resident Paul Murithi will gladly show you one. Paul has persuaded the local farmers that the owl is beneficial to them because it feeds on rodents. Look out for a hand-painted sign on the roadside, 'Mackinder's Eagle Owl'. For more information, visit Paul's website at: www.owlspot.com

MASAI MARA AND RUMA

Big Cat Country, the Masai Mara National Reserve is lion country; a visitor would have to be very unlucky not to see lions even on a short stay here. Many of the male lions are black-maned and are truly magnificent animals. Cheetah are still quite common, and some of the cheetah are so tame and used to tourists that they often jump up onto the safari vehicle to look for their prey! Leopard, too, are quite common but much more difficult to spot. It is not at all unusual for visitors to see the Big Five (lion, leopard, black rhino, elephant and buffalo) on a morning's drive.

To visit the Masai Mara during the 'migration' is one of the natural wonders of the world. Over one million wildebeest on the move, accompanied by thousands of common zebra and gazelle, is a must to see for all wildlife enthusiasts. Bird-lovers too, will enjoy the Masai Mara which has recorded over 500 species, including 16 species of birds of prey. In the riverine forest bordering the Mara River, huge Black-and-white Casqued Hornbills can be seen and heard, while both Ross's and Schalow's Turaco are more difficult to see as they fly from tree to tree. The very unusual looking Double-toothed Barbet is also found in these forests. Added to all this are the wonderful Mara vistas which just beg to be photographed.

Top Ten

Black-maned lions
Cheetah
Leopard
Black rhino
Topi
Roan antelope (Ruma National Park)
Birds of prey – 16 species
Black-and-white Casqued Hornbill
Ross's Turaco
Stunning scenery

Opposite, top to bottom:
A lioness, feeding on its kill;
a Governors' Camp balloon
floating serenely over the
Masai Mara plains; two
male wildebeest fight in the
Masai Mara.

Masai Mara National Reserve

Masai Mara National Reserve

Location: 275km (171 miles) west of Nairobi.
Size: 1812km² (700 sq miles).
Altitude: 1650m (5414ft).
Of interest: Big Cat country; the famous wildebeest migration; wonderful scenery.
Accommodation: *see panels, pages 130 and 133*

Below: A majestic-looking male black-maned lion, posing for tourists, in the Masai Mara National Reserve.

Masai Mara National Reserve

Kenya's premier wildlife area, the famous Masai Mara National Reserve, is a six-hour drive west of Nairobi. The Masai Mara forms the northern extension of the Serengeti National Park in Tanzania. Wildlife moves freely between the Mara and the Serengeti and it is this freedom of movement which provides the greatest wildlife spectacle in Africa: the annual migration of wildebeest and other accompanying animals. The Mara, as it is generally known (a Maasai word meaning 'spotted' or 'dappled'), is a mosaic of rolling grassland dominated by red oat grass, small bush-covered hills and, along the Mara River and its tributaries flowing towards Lake Victoria, riverine bush and forest.

The reserve is well known for its black-maned lions and their prides, as well as its other abundant resident wildlife, and is one of the few places where it is possible to see the Big Five during a morning's game drive. However, it is perhaps more famous for its annual wildebeest migration – possibly the world's greatest wildlife spectacle (see page 20). The wildebeest population is now thought to number 1.4 million; accompanying them into the Mara may be as many as 550,000 gazelle, 200,000 zebra and 64,000 impala. Added to this are rhino, elephant, buffalo, warthog, giraffe, topi, kongoni (Coke's hartebeest), eland, leopard, cheetah, spotted hyena, and silver-backed and side-striped jackal. Other mammals that can be seen here are red-tailed and blue monkeys, banded mongoose, hippo, Defassa waterbuck, impala and bushbuck – 95 species in all. Many of the cheetah are so tame they seek shelter from the hot sun under the tourists' vehicles and several even climb onto the roofs to get a better view of any prospective prey.

For the bird enthusiast, almost 500 species have been recorded: among these are 16 species of eagle plus many hawks and falcons, six species of vulture, eight of stork, four of bustard (including the Kori Bustard, the world's heaviest flying bird), and nine species of sunbird. In the riverine forest it is possible to see both Ross's and Schalow's Turaco, Double-toothed Barbets and Narina Trogon. With this combination of wildlife and wonderful scenery, all under a great African sky, it is easy to see why the Masai Mara has become so popular among visitors.

Mara cats

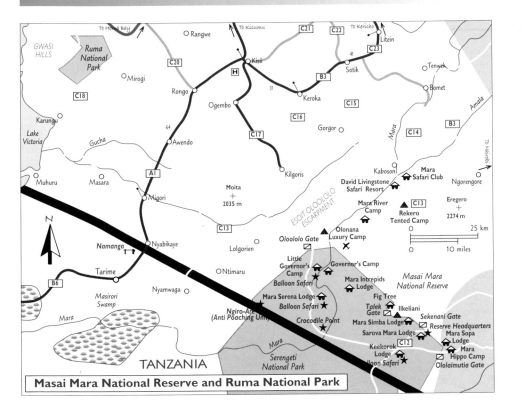

Masai Mara National Reserve and Ruma National Park

While staying in the Masai Mara it is possible to visit Lake Victoria. At dawn, a light aircraft takes tourists to spend a morning fishing or sightseeing on the lake, usually returning after lunch.

Mara cats

Lion (Swahili: *simba*)

Largest of the big cats, males can weigh up to 280kg (620lb), females 30–60 kg (66–132lb) less. Unlike most cats, lions live in a social system – an extended family called a pride. A pride is made up of a group of females, all related to each other (aunts, sisters), and their young, and one or two (occasionally three) males. Pride males are usually males of a similar age and quite often brothers. Generally the females hunt together as a team, but a lioness will occasionally hunt alone. Lions may hunt at any time but prefer night time when they are much more successful; even so, their success rate is only about

Masai Mara National Reserve

Balloon Safaris

The world's first scheduled passenger service by balloon was launched in 1976 from Keekorok Lodge by Alan Root, the famous wildlife film-maker, and the late balloon pilot, Dudley Chignal. Now, at least six lodges offer hot-air balloon flights which, on landing, are followed by a glorious champagne breakfast cooked on site. Kenya is the only country in the world to offer such a high number of passenger balloon flights.

50%. Prey is knocked down and then killed with a bite to the throat or suffocated with the lion's mouth over that of its prey. Males do not often take part in the hunt and have gained a reputation of being lazy. This is not quite true; the male's role is mainly to patrol the territory to protect the pride from other prides and other males who would want to kill any young cubs. It is essential for the females to feel this protection. Of course, if the males are nearby when a kill is made they quickly arrive and take over the kill. When lion prides hunt large animals such as buffalo, very often the males will take part, their weight being very useful in bringing such an animal down. At any kill there is much fighting and squabbling, with the largest and strongest usually getting their fill first.

When prey is scarce the young and cubs often do not get enough to eat and starve. Lions are not always the noble hunters we think they are; it has been discovered that, certainly in the Serengeti, over 50% of the food is scavenged, mostly from hyenas that have originally made the kill. If there is more than one male in the pride, one will be dominant and it is he that will mate with any female in oestrus. Initially, mating takes place about once every 15–30 minutes and lasts for four to five days.

Gestation is on average 105 days and between two and six cubs are born. The cubs' eyes open when they are about a week old and they are helpless for the first few weeks. Newborn cubs weigh about 1.3kg (3lb) and are spotted. Very often one or more females in the pride will give birth approximately at the same time and the cubs are raised together, with any of the lactating females feeding the cubs. At about eight months the cubs are weaned and have lost most of their spots. At 18 months they are mature and it is around this time that young males will leave the pride, although occasionally the pride males will allow them to stay a little longer. These males will usually stay together, often joining up with other young males until they are strong enough to challenge for a pride. Pride males, usually 5–10 years old, are constantly challenged by nomadic males. Once a pride male has been driven out of his pride, he will mostly live off carrion until he dies.

Lions have long been killed in rituals of bravery; the Maasai are a good example of this tradition. At one time a Maasai warrior had

Cheetah

to kill a lion before he was accepted as a man and even now, although against the law, this is still practised. But it is not just in Africa that the lion has been idolized. In England the national football and cricket team have three lions as their emblem and the animal is used in many coats of arms and flags.

Cheetah (Swahili: *duma*)

The smallest of the Big Cats, on average 50kg (110lb), not only is a cheetah the fastest cat, with a top speed of 90–112kph (60–70mph), it is also the fastest animal. Although it is fast, it lacks stamina and cannot run at top speed for long distances; 300m (328yd) is about the limit. A cheetah's body is built for speed; it has a very flexible spine, long, slim, strong legs, a deep chest, a small head and a large heart. Its claws are only partially retractable, giving it extra grip in a chase, and a long slender tail gives it balance when making sharp turns. Although cheetah are similar in colour (tawny-yellow) to leopards, the cheetah has small round black spots on its body, not rosettes as a leopard has. Cheetah also have distinctive 'tear lines' that connect the inside corner of each eye to the mouth. Cheetahs are basically solitary animals, except when females have young or when a

Aloes

Around 60 species of aloe grow in East Africa; some species are eaten by elephants. The sap has been used by local people for many years for burns, insect bites and other injuries. Aloes are now grown commercially in the Rift Valley, for both cosmetic and medicinal use.

Below: A mother cheetah with her cubs in the Masai Mara National Reserve.

Masai Mara National Reserve

Lilies

Flame Lily (*Gloriosa superba*)
Flame lilies appear during the rains;
they have spectacular red flowers
which are often striped yellow or
yellow-green. In Tsavo a variant is
yellow with purple stripes. They are
generally found in dryer areas.

Fireball Lily (*Scadoxus multiflorus*)
The beautiful red flowers appear
before the leaves with the first rains.
Fireball lilies are widespread in rocky
places and open grassland.

male accompanies an oestrus female. Quite often though, young males (usually, but not necessarily, from the same litter) will stay together for a number of years. These coalitions of males are a formidable hunting team and can take on larger prey animals such as wildebeest and zebra. Cheetahs hunt during the day time, usually early mornings and late afternoons, but sometimes also on moonlight nights, and there are even records of them hunting in darkness. Although cheetahs live in the open plains and hunt by speed, they prefer taking cover until they can get sufficiently close to give chase. Then, with a burst of speed, they try to outrun their prey before reaching out with a paw and either knocking it over or hooking their sharp dew claw into it. The cheetah then quickly grabs its victim by the neck, slowly suffocating it. Cheetah often lose their prey to other predators such as hyena, lion, leopard and jackals, and even at times to large numbers of vultures. They eat their prey as quickly as possible, only stopping occasionally to check for danger. A cheetah's main prey is Thomson's and Grant's gazelle and their young, female impala and their young, and also young wildebeest. If a cheetah is disturbed and has to leave its prey it will not return to it; it also does not scavenge. This is a problem in some tourist areas where safari vehicles drive too close to feeding cheetah.

The cheetah's gestation period is 90–95 days after which two to five cubs (sometimes as many as eight) are born, usually but not always in a secluded place. The cubs are quite helpless and very vulnerable at this stage of their life, especially as the cheetah mother has to leave them on their own while she hunts. The cubs open their eyes at about 14–18 days and when they are six weeks old they are able to follow their mother. Before this time, the female cheetah moves her cubs several times to new dens. The cubs are suckled for about two to three months but are able to eat meat at about one month. Cheetah cubs at first have a mantle of long grey hair and their underparts are very dark, very unlike their mothers. At a distance, cheetah cubs at this age look very like the ratel (honey badger), which is reputed to be the fiercest of all African mammals. This is thought by some to be the reason for cheetah cubs looking so much like a ratel. Slowly they become lighter and the spots appear but cubs are sometimes 15 months or older before the grey mantle disappears. Although cheetahs purr, hiss and growl just like cats,

Serval cat and Nile crocodile

they have a chirping bird-like call to keep in contact with each other. Cheetahs are docile by nature and have been trained by man for a very long time, particularly in India. Akbar the Great was reputed to have kept as many as 1000 cheetahs. Their name comes from the Indian word for 'spotted one'.

Serval cat (Swahili: *mondo*)

This is a tall spotted cat, 56cm (22in), with long legs, very large oval-shaped ears and a short tail, weighing from 13.5kg (30–40lb). They are tan-coloured with black spots on the body, a black-and-white ringed tail and very distinctive white marks behind the ears. Occasionally, melanistic individuals occur, particularly in the highlands such as on the moorlands of the Aberdare National Park. Serval cats are shy, solitary and mainly nocturnal. Even if seen during the daytime, usually in the early morning or late afternoon, they can be very difficult to spot.

Their long legs are not adapted for fast running but to enable them to gain elevation when hunting in tall grass. They hunt with head high and ears cocked forward listening for their prey. Once prey is located they creep stealthily towards it, before leaping high through the grass and down onto their victim. Their prey includes young antelope, hares, rodents, snakes, lizards, birds, insects and even frogs. Servals often 'play' with their prey, tossing it high into the air several times before eating it. Where servals occur near man they are serious raiders on poultry, but, in turn, they are often preyed upon by hyena and larger cats, such as lion and leopard. Serval cats have large territories, sometimes as large as 8km² (3 sq miles). Females give birth after a gestation period of about 10 weeks, usually to two to four kittens.

Nile crocodile (Swahili: *mamba*)

Nile crocodiles can often exceed 5m (16ft) in length and weigh up to 1000kg (2204lb). They are fast swimmers and can even run fast on land; they also have excellent sight and hearing. Nile crocodiles are cold-blooded reptiles and depend on the external temperature to maintain their body heat. They can often be seen lying out on an exposed bank warming themselves in the sun. At times they open their jaws which is thought to help them regulate their temperature. When the sun is too hot, they go back into

The Candelabra Tree (*Euphorbia candelabrum*)

This cactus-like euphorbia can grow up to 15m (50ft). It has a short, thick trunk – up to 90cm (35in) in diameter – from which a number of spiny branches spread out, rather like a candelabra. Sometimes also known as a tree euphorbia, it is widespread in grasslands and thorn bush and often grows on termite mounds. It is most common in the Rift Valley, especially at Lake Nakuru, where there is a forest of them growing along the hillside on the eastern side of the lake. This forest of candelabra trees is one of the largest in Africa. Its branches are soft and brittle, and produce thick, sticky latex if broken. This latex is extremely toxic – a single drop in the eye can cause blindness – and it easily blisters the skin. The nomadic tribes of northeastern Kenya have a cure if they get this latex in their eyes: they quickly draw blood from a goat or sheep and pour it into the affected eye or eyes. The pain is quickly reduced and, apparently, the eyesight is not damaged! At times this euphorbia has flowers which are initially greenish-yellow but slowly turn pinkish, in groups of three to six. These flowers attract bees, but unfortunately any honey produced by the bees cannot be eaten, as it irritates and burns the mouth.

Masai Mara National Reserve

Right: *A spotted hyena relaxing in the Masai Mara National Reserve.*

Pyjama Lily

So called because their colour is supposed to be like traditional striped pyjamas, these are a member of the crinum family. These large, bulbous plants, whose heavy green leaves suddenly spring out of the ground during the rains, have long, tubular flowers coloured white with delicate pink stripes. They are widespread in Kenya.

the water to cool. Nile crocodiles are reputed to be able to stay submerged for up to one hour. Nile crocodiles have a varied diet ranging from insects when young to large mammals such as zebra, wildebeest and humans when adult. Prey is ambushed or stalked along the water's edge, with only the crocodile's eyes and nose visible above the water. Occasionally, if prey is a short distance from the river bank, they lunge completely out of the water to seize it and will sometimes use their tail to knock the victim into the water. Once in the water the prey, depending on its size, is thrashed around until a limb or part of the body is wrenched off. Also, when several crocodiles are feeding on a carcass at the same time, they will bite the carcass and then rotate several times until a piece of the victim is torn away. Crocodiles are unable to chew; they simply raise their heads and let the food fall down into the throat. Digestion is very slow and there have been incidents where a large crocodile has been shot and its victim has been recovered almost unmarked from inside the body. The female lays hard-shelled white eggs, usually 30–50, in a hole which she digs in a sand bank, usually near the water's edge. She covers the eggs after laying. Interestingly, the temperature of the buried eggs determines the sex of the young. When the young begin to break out of the eggs, the female crocodile digs into the hole and assists the young out of the eggs, even carrying them in her mouth down to the water where she can release them. Crocs have hardly changed since the days of the dinosaurs; a wonderful example can be seen at Koobi Fora on the shores of Lake Turkana.

Spotted hyena

Spotted hyena (Swahili: *fisi*)

The spotted hyena is both a skilful predator and an efficient scavenger. It weighs 40–86kg (88–189lb) and stands 70–91cm (28–36in) high at the shoulder. Unusually in the mammal world, the female is larger, on average 6kg (13lb), than the male and is dominant to the males. The sexes are very difficult to distinguish, apart from their size. For a long time hyenas were thought to be hermaphrodites, having both male and female sexual organs, and it was thought that they could change their sex at will! This was because the females' genitalia look very similar to those of the males. The reason for this, and the fact that the female is larger than the male, is thought to be so that the female can protect her young. It also gives her unimpeded access to any food. Hyenas live in clans of 30–80 adults. Within a clan of hyena there is a dominant female and it is this female that will often initiate a hunt. Interestingly her offspring usually eat better, grow faster and obtain higher ranking later in life. Spotted hyenas are social and communicate with calls and postures. When excited they hold their tails over their backs and when fighting the tail is held out straight, but when walking the tail is usually hanging down. If afraid, such as when they are chased away from a kill by lions, they slink away with the tail between the legs.

Clans consist of related individuals and they vigorously defend their territories from other clans. These territories are patrolled and marked with their anal glands and droppings. More often heard than seen, their long-distance call, a repetitive 'whoo-up', carries for up to 5km (3 miles); their well-known 'laugh' is a social appeasement call. A den, in which they raise their young, is usually situated in the centre of the territory and often on high ground, with good drainage and a good view of the surrounding area. The den will have several entrances that connect to underground tunnels; some dens have been used from time to time for many years. Two to four young are born (although rarely more than two survive) in a natal den, or a thicket or hollow near the den, after a gestation period of 90–110 days. Spotted hyena cubs are born with their eyes open but are initially partially blind. They are suckled for an unusually long time, 12–18 months, although they will start eating meat from kills made near the den from about five months old. This is thought to be because spotted hyena do

Gardenias

Gardenias are small trees and shrubs often eaten by elephants and giraffe which frequently crop them tightly, making them stunted and almost unrecognizable. Gardenias have heavily scented, creamy yellow flowers. In the Masai Mara they are often used by lions and cheetah to rest under during the hot hours.

Masai Mara National Reserve

Right: In the Masai Mara National Reserve, the icon of a male topi standing on a termite mound is a common sight.

not regurgitate food to their young and often have to hunt long distances from their den. In some areas, or at certain times of the year when their prey is scarce, they may be away from the den for up to a week at a time. Hyena hunt individually or in a group, mostly at night, their prey usually the more vulnerable animals such as young wildebeest rather than swifter, more abundant prey. They hunt by running down their prey and can run for long distances and as fast as 64kph (40mph).

Spotted hyena have massive, strong teeth and powerful jaws which can crack bones easily – the strength of a hyena's jaws has been measured at 800kg/cm^2 (4520lb/sq in). Their digestive system is able to digest and break down bone, chitin and semi-poisonous compounds which are digested in only a few hours. The hyenas' massive teeth are able to cut through bones and skin, including that of elephants and rhino, leaving only the horns, hooves and some hair. It is this ability to utilize the remains of large animals more completely than any other carnivore that makes the hyena such a special animal. Other carnivores waste up to 40% of their kills. Interestingly, in the Ngorongoro Crater researchers found that it is more often the case that lions scavenge hyena kills than the other way round. This is almost certainly true in other wildlife areas too.

Unfortunately, hyena occasionally do kill human babies and small children and attacks on adults have been recorded. This may have arisen because some nomadic societies dispose of their dead and fatally ill by leaving the bodies outside the villages for the hyenas to eat. Although modern man mostly despises the hyena, in ancient Egypt they were domesticated, fattened and eaten.

Topi (Swahili: *nyamera*)

Topi are a familiar sentinel in the Masai Mara where their habit of standing on top of termite mounds is such a part of the scene. Males weigh on average 130kg (287lb) while the females are a little smaller, weighing about 108kg (238lb). They stand about 1–1.3m (3.25–4.25ft) at the shoulder. These antelopes have a short, glossy coat which is conspicuously coloured red-brown to purplish with distinctive blackish patches on the face, upper forelegs and on the hips and thighs. Their legs are yellowish, making them look as if they are wearing long stockings. Topi are almost exclusively grazers, living in open grasslands. They have a long, narrow muzzle and mobile lips which are adapted for selective feeding, eating only the tenderest green blades of grass. They are mostly gregarious, living in herds of 15–20, but at times congregate in much larger numbers. Usually a herd, which consists of one male and several females with their young, will hold a territory, defending it from other topi.

In the Masai Mara females form herds and move through the territories of different males. In these territories the male will have a small area of bare, trampled earth, very often an old termite mound on which he stands. This area is marked by dung piles and grass stems are marked by scent from his preorbital face glands. The male topi stands on these prominent mounds advertising his presence to all other male topi in the area. The males vigorously defend these territories from other males. Male topi fight by facing up to each other then going down on their knees to fight each other with their horns. Mating takes place

Nandi Flame Tree (*Spathodea campanulata*)

Called *kibobakasi* in Swahili, this tree is also known as the African tulip tree. It is native to western Kenya but has been planted throughout the country. When in flower this indigenous tree, standing 5–10m (16–33ft) in height, is spectacular. Its blooms are trumpet-shaped, about 12cm (4.7in) long, coloured orange/red, fringed with gold, and with a yellow-tinged throat. These flowers hold copious amounts of watery liquid.

Masai Mara National Reserve

within the territory and after a gestation period of eight months a single calf is born. Like other antelope the calves spend their first days 'lying out'. Reputed to be the fastest antelope with a bounding gait, they can outrun most predators.

Wildebeest or Western white-bearded gnu (Swahili: *nyumbu*)

The western white-bearded gnu is one of five distinct subspecies of wildebeest or gnu that occur in Africa but is the only one that still occurs in large migrating herds. Male wildebeest stand 125–145cm (50–58in) tall at the shoulder and weigh 120–270kg (265–600lb); the females are a little smaller, weighing about 45kg (100lb) less. Wildebeest are often called 'the clowns of the plains' because of their strange looks and, at times, their apparently strange behaviour. In fact, they are a very successful animal, exploiting the grasslands of the Serengeti/Mara fully to their benefit. They have an ability to locate unerringly areas of good grazing. Wildebeest are a keystone species and certainly not a clown; they have shaped and dominated their ecosystem for more than a million years. Wildebeest are pure grazers, inhabiting the open grassy plains, migrating only to follow the favourable conditions of grass.

Most wildebeest births take place in the early mornings, the actual birth taking about 1½ hours. The female wildebeest can delay delivery at any time if disturbed, at least until the calf's head and trunk emerge. Females lie on their side for delivery and the moment the calf is expelled the mother begins licking it. The newborn calf can stand within a few minutes and immediately seeks its mother's teat to suckle. Newborn calves are light tan in colour and are very active and able to run after about five minutes. As soon as the calf can run its mother quickly joins up with other females with calves to form a maternity herd. It may take from one to two days for the mother and calf to bond together and, should they become separated during this time, the calf easily becomes lost and tries to follow whatever is close by. It may be another wildebeest, another animal or a tourist vehicle or even, occasionally, a predator such as a lion. Any of these contacts can be disastrous to the calf. After two or three days the calves are able to keep up with the herds and their chances of survival are much improved. The main predators on the calves are hyena, but

Accommodation in Masai Mara

Mara Simba Lodge: simbalodges@mitsuminet.com
Mara Siria Tented Camp: www.mara-siria-camp.com
Mara Porini Camp (18km from the reserve; six tents on the banks of the Laetoli river: www.porini.com
Naibor Camp: theartofadventures.com
Ol Seki: info@bush-and-beyond.com
Olonana Luxury Camp: www.sanctuarylodges.com
Rekero Tented Camp: info@bush-and-beyond.com
Richard's Camp: www.chelipeacock.com
Saruni Camp (spa treatments inclusive): www.sarunicamp.com
Sarova Mara: www.sarovahotels.com
Sekenani Camp: www.sekenanicamp.com
KWS Research Station (offers self-catering accommodation): tourism@kws.org

Wildebeest

Left: *Wildebeest crossing the Mara River during their famous migration.*

lions, leopard and cheetah all take their toll. The calves are suckled for about four months but begin to eat grass at about 10 days old.

During the mating season, the large herds split up into smaller herds with five or six male wildebeest establishing territories within the herd. The males mark their territory with the scent glands on their face and between the two halves of their hooves. They also defecate and urinate at certain spots in this territory. The territorial males seem to go crazy, frantically leaping about, scent-marking nearby bushes and trees, and at the same time

Masai Mara National Reserve

grunting and snorting and foaming at the mouth. This may well be another reason why they are called 'clowns of the plains'. During this time territorial bulls have little time to eat or rest. The female wildebeest are only in oestrus for one day, so the males' behaviour is understandable – they have so little time to mate with the females.

Thomson's gazelle (Swahili: *swala tomi*)

Known to everyone as 'tommy' or 'tommies', Thomson's are much more numerous than the similar Grant's gazelle, although not as widely distributed. These small, graceful gazelles measure on average 62cm (24in) at the shoulder and weigh 17–29kg (37–64lb); the females are a little smaller. Males have strongly ridged horns while the females have short, pencil-thin horns, often malformed and broken, or none at all. Some scientists believe the females are slowly evolving and will eventually be hornless. This theory does seem a little odd though, because female Thomson's gazelle do try to protect their young by using their horns to fend off smaller predators such as silver-backed and side-striped jackal. Thomson's gazelle are well adapted to the open plains, where they are often seen with the similar-looking Grant's gazelle and other plains mammals, such as wildebeest and zebra. They migrate alongside wildebeest and zebra exploiting, like them, seasonally available grazing. They prefer short, green grass, so being among larger mammals is an advantage as the larger mammals either eat or trample down the long grass making the shoots of new grass more easily available. In the dry season they will browse on shrubs, legumes, seeds and even the fruits of the Sodom Apple (*solanum* sp.), which are poisonous to most other mammals. In burnt areas that have recently received rain Thomson's gazelle will sometimes congregate in large numbers to feed on the new shoots of grass that quickly appear.

They are dependent on water and sometimes are forced to walk up to 15km (9 miles) to find it. Otherwise they spread out over the plains, mostly in family groups of anything from five to 50. In the early mornings and late afternoons, the herds come much closer together; at this time the young often play, sprinting around the herd, with bouts of stotting or pronking (bouncing on stiff legs). Males take up territories and mark the boundaries with

Thomson's gazelle and Grant's gazelle

dung piles and tiny secretions from scent glands below each eye. These secretions are deposited on the end of growing grass stems by the male turning its head over to one side then carefully inserting the grass stem into his scent gland. These secretions can easily be seen, looking rather like a drop of tar at the end of the grass stem. When marking his territory with dung and urine, the male Thomson's gazelle makes an exaggerated display of defecating and urinating so any other males in sight can clearly see that a territory has been claimed. These territorial marks are made daily, especially if the herds are migrating and new territories must be established. These territories are vigorously defended from other males, with fights being common. The males face up to one another, clashing their horns, but there are frequent stops when both will begin to graze. At the end of a fight both males slowly move apart grazing as they go. Groups of females wander through these territories and the males attempt to keep them there for as long as possible. It is a common sight to see a male attempting to chase a female back into its territory. This is constantly happening so the size and composition of the groups of females are changing throughout the day.

Non-territorial males, usually immature or older males, form small groups of about 10, but occasionally up to 50 can group together. Very often older males keep to themselves which makes them much more vulnerable, so it is not surprising that it is these bachelor males which so often fall victim to cheetahs and leopards. The females breed twice a year after a gestation period of 5–6 months and although births can occur at almost any time of year, the peak time is after the rainy season. After birth, the young are left hidden in a clump of grass but if the grass is short the young are much more vulnerable as they can be more easily seen. The newborn young lie flat on the ground, stretched out absolutely still, and even though they are tawny brown in colour they can be amazingly difficult to see. The females visit their young to suckle them several times a day which is a very dangerous time for both the mother and young. Predation on the young is heavy, with cheetah, lion, leopard, hyena and jackal regularly hunting them. In certain areas baboons, particularly males, actively hunt for newborn 'tommies', and they are also eaten by eagles (such as Martial Eagles), pythons and caracal.

Accommodation in Masai Mara

Campi ya Tembo (book through Cheli and Peacock): tel 020 604054 or 603090/1.
Cottars 1920's: www.chelipeacock.com
David Livingstone Safari Resort: info@mugumo.com
Elephant Pepper Camp: www.chelipeacock.com
Fig Tree Camp: www.madahotels.com
Governors' Il Moran Camp, Governors' Camp, Little Governors' Camp and Governors' Private Camp: www.governorscamp.com
Ilkeliani: www.ilkeliani.com
Keekorok Lodge: www.discoverwilderness.com
Kitchwa Tembo Camp and Bateleur Camp: www.ccafrica.com
Leleshwa Camp: www.leleshwacamps.com
Mara Explorer Camp and Mara Intrepids Camp: www.heritage-eastafrica.com
Mara Safari Club: Kenya.reservations@fairmont.com
Mara Serena Safari Lodge: www.serenahotels.com
Mara Leisure Camp: www.maraleisurecamp.com
Mara Sopa Lodge: www.sopalodges.com

Masai Mara National Reserve

Grant's gazelle (Swahili: *swala granti*)

At first sight these are very similar to Thomson's gazelle, with which they are often found. They are similar in colour but Grant's gazelles are larger, standing 75–91cm (30–36in) high at the shoulder, longer legged and weigh 45–65kg (99–143lb). Females are a little smaller than males and both sexes have horns, although the males' horns are much longer, heavily ringed and thicker than those of the females. Some females have a dark stripe on the body making them look very similar to Thomson's gazelle, but both male and female Grant's gazelle have a white rump patch which extends over the tail, while Thomson's gazelle have a small white rump patch which does not extend over the tail. Grant's gazelle can tolerate very dry conditions, is more of a browser than a grazer and can live in waterless areas.

Grant's gazelle are gregarious, and herds consist of females and their young with a territorial male, or all-male herds. The female herds move through various males' territories while feeding, and each male will try to keep them and mate with any female that may be in oestrus. At the same time the male will often have to defend his territory from other males. Females give birth at almost any time of the year after a gestation period of about four months. Once the fawn can stand and has been cleaned by its mother, it takes its first feed, then moves away, followed by its mother, to a patch of grass

Below: A male Grant's gazelle checking to find out if a female is in oestrus.

Vultures

about 50m (55yd) away from its birthplace, where it will 'lie out' for 2–4 weeks . During this time the mother will stay close by but at times may be as far as 300m (328yd) away. The mother will visit the calf several times a day to suckle and to clean it. She approaches carefully to within about 50m (55yd) of the calf before calling it to her; they briefly touch noses before the calf quickly dives under its mother to suckle. Although the calf will begin to eat grass from about a month old, it is suckled for about six months.

Although Grant's gazelle have preorbital scent glands, they do not use them for marking as Thomson's gazelle do. A male marks its territory with dung piles and urine, doing this in an exaggerated posture so any other male in the area can see him. Grant's gazelle are preyed upon mostly by cheetah and leopard but their young are often killed by jackal. Pairs of jackal hunt for the concealed fawns during their 'lying out' period and although the mother can often chase away one jackal, she has little chance against two.

Ross's Turaco

Turacos are endemic to Africa. All are large, spectacular-looking birds, usually seen when trees are fruiting, or flying from tree to tree when the vivid red patches in their wings are so conspicuously seen. Ross's Turaco are dark, deep blue with an eye-catching bright yellow bill, a bright yellow patch around the eye, and a bright red crest on the top of their head. Turacos feed on fruiting trees and are mostly found in riverine forest. A good place to see them is at Governors' Camp, in the Masai Mara, where they have become used to people and are quite tame. Turacos are unusual in that their feathers have pigments (see page 117).

Vultures

Vultures are a familiar sight on safari, usually seen slowly circling high in the sky looking for any signs of dead mammals. Once a likely source is spotted, such as predators on a kill, or a mammal that has died of natural causes, they quickly spiral down and wait patiently for the predators to finish before they too can begin to feed. This descent is seen by other vultures which immediately descend to the same area. Often the first vultures to arrive are the Lappet-faced (sometimes called Nubian) Vulture, the largest of all the vultures. Lappet-faced Vultures have a large, powerful bill and are able if

The Difference Between Eagles and Vultures

While one is a mainly a predator and the other is a scavenger, the difference between them is mostly in their feet. Eagles and other birds of prey have large, strong feet and sharp talons with which they kill their prey. Vultures, because they do not kill their prey, have small, much weaker feet. The foot of a Martial Eagle is a good example of strong feet and long sharp talons for killing their prey.

Masai Mara National Reserve

Vultures in Trouble

Some time ago it was suddenly realized that the numbers of vultures on the Indian subcontinent had dropped dramatically. This was later found to be caused by the drug diclofenac used on cattle, which destroys the kidneys of any vulture feeding on dead cattle that had been treated by the drug. In Africa, too, vultures are either decreasing or, in some areas, particularly in West Africa, have disappeared completely. In West Africa it is thought that most have been killed by starving farmers during the ongoing Sahel drought. In some areas of Southern and East Africa, vulture parts such as eyes and their flesh and feathers are used by traditional medicine men for various reasons. Vultures are also inadvertently poisoned when they eat animals such as hyena that have been deliberately poisoned as pests in farming areas. It would be a very sad day if there were no more vultures in the African skies. The Red Data Status of East African vultures has recently been revised. The Egyptian Vulture is now regarded as endangered. Rüppell's Griffon Vultures and White-backed Vultures are now near threatened species. White-headed Vultures are now a vulnerable species.

necessary to tear open a carcass that has not been killed by mammal predators. The next to arrive are often the unusual White-headed Vultures which are a little smaller and are reputed to be able to kill small mammals such as hares and newborn gazelles. Like the Lappet-faced, the White-headed has a large, strong bill and is able to tear into any carcass. The next vultures to arrive will be White-backed and Rüppell's Griffon Vultures. Both of these vultures have long, virtually featherless necks, perfect for thrusting deep inside the carcass, and special tongues with backward-facing spines which help them feed inside the body. Rüppell's Griffon Vultures nest on cliffs while other vultures nest on the tops of trees, which means they often have to fly long distances from their nesting sites to areas where food may be available. For instance, there is a large colony of Rüppell's Griffon Vultures nesting on the Gol Mountains in the southern Serengeti National Park in Tanzania. When the famous wildebeest migration is in the Masai Mara National Reserve they may have to fly as far as 160km (100 miles) to find available food.

Two other vultures, one very common while the other has become inexplicably rare, can also be found near a carcass. The Hooded Vulture is quite common and is very often found scavenging in towns. Hooded Vultures have long, narrow beaks, they feed on scraps left by the other vultures and are also able to pick small pieces of meat off the bones and probe into broken bones for the marrow. The last vulture we may find on a carcass is the Egyptian Vulture. These distinctive-looking vultures with a narrow bill feed alongside the Hooded Vultures in a similar way. Egyptian Vultures are perhaps better known for their ability to use a tool. Egyptian Vultures break ostrich eggs by throwing a stone down on to them until they break. Another vulture found in Kenya is the Palm-nut Vulture; they are never found at kills with other vultures as they are solitary and feed on small animals and turtles, which they have almost certainly killed, and on the oil of palm nuts. In the Samburu/Buffalo Springs reserves, Palm-nut Vultures behave a little differently. They can often be seen feeding on bait put out for leopards by the Samburu Lodge and Samburu Serena Lodge, and on occasions they have also been seen feeding on the carcass of a mammal. Yet another vulture which has been recorded from time to time is the European Griffon Vulture. This rarely recorded vulture appears to be slowly becoming more common.

Snake Eagles

Left: A Rüppell's Griffon Vulture about to land among a group of Lappet-faced and White-backed Vultures, feeding on a carcass.

A group of vultures squabbling over a kill is an unbelievable scene. The sound, a variety of screaming, hissing, cackling and grunting, is amazing as they all fight for a piece of the carcass. The Lappet-faced Vultures, being the largest, try to dominate but are usually so outnumbered by White-backed and Rüppell's Griffon Vultures that even they have to back off for a while. But not for long – within a few moments the Lappet-faced will bound towards the kill, then dive onto the other vultures, driving them off for a short time.

Snake Eagles (Swahili: *mwewe*)

This is an interesting family of medium-sized eagles; all have distinctive bright yellow eyes and an owl-like head. They also have long, bare, heavily scaled legs which give them protection from snake bites. Five different species of Snake Eagle occur in Kenya, the commonest being the Black-breasted Snake Eagle and the Brown Snake Eagle which are usually found in open country, while the Western Banded and Southern Banded Snake Eagles are forest-edge birds. The fifth, the Short-toed Snake Eagle, is a rare visitor from Eastern Europe. All are usually solitary and easily seen as they often sit on exposed branches. Black-breasted Snake Eagles and, to a lesser extent, Brown Snake Eagles can often be seen hovering over the open plains. To see such a large bird hovering is quite a sight. When not hovering, they soar quite high in the sky looking out for their prey. When a snake is caught and the eagle needs to take it to its nest to feed its young, it does not carry it in its talons but partially swallows the snake, then flies away with the snake hanging from its bill. Both these species also

Masai Mara National Reserve

occasionally hunt from an exposed branch, dropping down onto their prey. The two Banded Snake Eagle species hunt from a low branch on the edge of the forest, dropping down onto any snake they spot below. When caught, the snake is carried in their talons to a convenient branch, where it is eaten. The Banded Snake Eagle has a distinctive strange mournful *ko-aaagh* call.

Banded mongoose (Swahili: *nguchiro*)

Banded mongoose are a common sight in the Masai Mara National Reserve. They are usually seen in a group, dashing away from a safari car. Occasionally, one or more members of the group will stop running and then stand upright on their hind legs, checking to see if the danger is real. At other times they can be seen in the early morning sunning themselves outside their den which is often in an old termite mound. They are gregarious, living in groups of about 15 to 20 individuals. The group is usually led by a dominant male and female and 3–4 other breeding pairs. The rest of the group is made up of non-breeding lower-ranking adults plus immature and young. Young males are thought to emigrate to other groups. Occasionally, a group can reach up to 40 individuals before splitting up. After a gestation period of two months, up to three or four young are born in the den. Any newborn young in the den are suckled by any lactating female of the group. They forage in a group, keeping contact with chirps and frequent twitters. If any become separated from the main

Warthog

group they become very upset, making a strident, shrilling alarm call. Groups can forage in an area up to 130ha (321 acres) which they defend from other banded mongoose groups. Banded mongoose mainly eat termites, insects and beetles and, only occasionally, snakes.

Warthog (Swahili: *ngiri*)

The warthog is a real character of the African savannah, perhaps nowadays better known as 'Pumba', the warthog character that starred in the film *The Lion King*. Warthogs weigh 90–113kg (200–250lb), the females being smaller, up to 22kg (50lb) lighter than the males. Although they are certainly not beautiful, they are fascinating animals. Warthogs are very distinctive, with a head that is large in comparison to its body, three pairs of warts on each side of its head, very often large sharp tusks, and a thin tail with a tuft of hair at its end. When running, warthogs characteristically hold their tails upright which always causes amusement among visitors. The tuft on the end of the tail is thought to act like a flag so any piglets running behind their mother can easily follow their mother and each other. Male warthogs fight either at a close distance or charge each other head-on; the warts act as pads protecting the eyes and face. Warthogs have four tusks; the ones in the upper jaw curve upwards and outwards, sometimes forming a semicircle around its snout. The tusks in the lower jaw fit against the upper ones and wear to a very sharp cutting edge which can cause serious cuts to

Left: A big male warthog poses for the photographer.

Ruma National Park

Accommodation at Lake Victoria

Lake Victoria Mfangano Camp:
info@governorscamp.com
www.governorscamp.com
Rusinga Island Lodge:
reservations@privatewilderness.com
Guests staying at Rusinga Island
Lodge and Mfangano Lodge
can arrange visits to Ruma
National Park.

Ruma National Park

Location: 30km (19 miles)
from Mbita.
Size: 120km² (46 sq miles).
Altitude: 1200–1600m
(3937–5249ft).
Of interest: This park was
previously called Lambwe Valley.
Some of Kenya's last roan antelope
can be found here, plus Jackson's
hartebeest and Rothschild's giraffe.
Ruma is also an important
wintering area for the endangered
Blue Swallow.

any predator trying to kill them. Warthogs usually trot, but can run surprisingly fast if chased by a predator. They are mainly grazers and are often seen kneeling as they graze short grass. They also dig up tubers and roots with their snout and tusks, a habit which causes much damage in agricultural areas. At times, particularly during droughts, warthogs will scavenge on carcasses left partially uneaten by predators. A large male warthog has been seen chasing a cheetah off its kill, a Thomson's gazelle, then beginning to eat the gazelle itself. Warthogs can survive without water for several months, can tolerate high temperatures and are able to conserve water inside the body. When water is available they will drink regularly and they enjoy mud wallows. Warthogs usually live in family groups of a female and her young; males only join a family group for mating. After a gestation period of about 175 days a litter of two to four young is born. Female warthogs have only four teats and each piglet will suckle exclusively from one teat – even if a piglet dies the remaining piglets will not suckle from the available teat. The young suckle for at least four months but start eating grass when about two months old. At night warthogs live in holes which they have excavated from existing smaller holes made by other animals. Warthogs reverse themselves into these holes so that they can defend themselves with their sharp tusks. Even so, they are often dug out of these holes by lions.

Ruma National Park

Originally established as a game reserve in 1966, mainly to protect a small herd of roan antelope, Ruma became a national park in 1983. It is only 30km (19 miles) from Homa Bay at Lake Victoria. The park is infested by tsetse fly, which has protected the area from encroachment by farmers. Recently though, the nearby research centre (International Centre for Insect Physiology and Ecology, or ICIPE) has devised new ways of controlling the tsetse and there is now pressure on the government to degazette the park. The park lies in the flat floor of Lambwe Valley bordered by the Kanyamaa Escarpment. The terrain is mainly rolling grassland, with tracts of woodland and thickets dominated by acacia and balanites species which tolerate the black cotton soil. Interesting wildlife found here includes Jackson's hartebeest, Rothschild's giraffe, topi, oribi and Bohor reedbuck. Bird life is good, with resident Bare-faced Go-away Birds, Mariqua Sunbirds and Silverbirds, and the area is an important

Roan Antelope and Oribi

wintering ground for the beautiful endangered Blue Swallow which breeds in South Africa. There is however no accommodation at Ruma; the nearest is at Mbita Point, 30km (19 miles) away.

Above: A group of roan antelope feeding in the Ruma National Park.

Roan Antelope (Swahili: *korongo*)
Roan are large and aggressive antelope, the males having horns which can grow to, on average, 70cm (27in) long. They are grazers and live in herds of up to 20; young males are tolerated within the herd until about two years old. Males live alongside the herd and actively exclude other males.

Oribi (Swahili: *taya*)
Oribi are small, graceful antelope with long legs and neck and a silky fawn/reddish-brown coat. Both sexes have a distinctive black spot below the ear and the male has thin horns, 8–19cm (3–7.5in) long. Males are territorial, mostly found with one mate, but occasionally a male will have two or more females resident within his territory. The oribi is a grazer which prefers grass that is shorter than itself but at the same time it needs cover nearby in which it can hide.

NATIONAL PARKS GUIDE

List of National Parks

Tsavo East NP

Tsavo West NP

Aberdares NP

Mt Kenya NP

Lake Nakuru NP

Amboseli NP

Nairobi NP

Meru NP

Kora NP

South Island NP (Lake Turkana)

Hells Gate NP

Mt Longonot NP

Ol Donyo Sabuk NP

Marsabit NP

Sibiloi NP: size 169km², altitude 2336–4321m

Saiwa Swamp NP

Ndere Island NP (Lake Victoria): size 4.2km², gazetted in 1986

Malka Mari NP

Chyulu Hills NP

Central Island NP (Lake Turkana)

Ruma NP

Arabuku Sokoke NP

List of National Reserves

Marsabit NR

South Turkana NR

Nasolot NR: size 92km², altitude 750–1500m

Nyambene NR

Shaba NR

Buffalo Springs NR

Bisanadi NR: size 606km², altitude 320–360m.
This reserve is adjacent to Meru National Park and is a dispersal area for wildlife from Meru. There are currently plans to upgrade this reserve.

Rahole NR

North Kitui NR

Lake Bogoria NR

Opposite, top to bottom:
A normally shy and nocturnal side-striped jackal at dawn in the Masai Mara National Reserve; a male African (Cape) buffalo accompanied by a cattle egret; a herd of beisa oryx in Buffalo Springs National Reserve.

National Parks Guide

Kamnarok NR: size 88km^2
Kerio Valley NR
Kakamega Forest National Reserve: size 45km^2,
altitude 1520–1680m
Kakamega Forest is the easternmost remnant of the equatorial
rainforest that once stretched across Africa. Known as a bird-
watching destination, some 10–20% of reptiles, mammals and
birds found here occur nowhere else in Kenya.
Masai Mara NR
South Kitui NR
Mwea NR
Arawale NR
Boni NR
Dodori NR
Tana River Primate NR
Shimba Hills NR
Chepkitale NR
Losai NR
Mt Kenya NR
Laikipia NR

Below: A male Defassa
waterbuck feeding on the shore
of Lake Nakuru National
Park, with flamingoes in the
background.

Other Kenyan National Parks

National Sanctuaries
Maralal
Lake Simbi
Ondago Swamp
Kisumu Impala Park

Marine National Parks
Mombasa Marine NP
Watamu Marine NP
Kisite NP
Malindi Marine NP

Marine National Reserves
Malindi Marine NR
Watamu Marine NR
Mombasa Marine NR
Mpunguti NR
Kiunguti NR
Kiunga Marine NR

Biosphere Reserves
Kiunga Biosphere Reserve: size 250km^2
Mt Kulal Biosphere Reserve: size 7000km^2
Malindi/Watamu Biosphere Reserve: size 261km^2
Mt Kenya Biosphere Reserve: size 715km^2, includes Mt Kenya National Park at 580km^2

KWS Tourism Department
KWS Headquarters, tel: +254 (020) 501081 or 602345, e-mail: tourism@kws.org website:
www.kws.org

Wildlife Conservation: Who owns What
Kenya has a total of 64 national parks, reserves and marine national parks and reserves; almost 10%
of the country's land area is devoted to wildlife conservation. The national parks are owned by the
government. A portion of the revenue earned by the parks and reserves is allocated to the local
people living in the area; no human settlement is allowed. Local county councils own the national
reserves; wildlife is protected and has precedence, some human habitation is permitted, and livestock may share the area at times. As for game sanctuaries and conservation areas, landowners can
establish such areas to protect a particular animal or certain species of plant life. They are allowed
to use the rest of their land for other purposes; a good example of this practice is Lewa Wildlife
Conservancy.

National Parks Guide

Entry Requirements

Passport, valid from date of entry, is required by all. Nationals of the following countries do not need visas to travel to Kenya: Bahamas, Bangladesh, Barbados, Botswana, Brunei-Darussalam, Cyprus, Dominica, Ethiopia, Fiji Islands, Gambia, The, Ghana, Grenada, Jamaica, Kiribati, Lesotho, Malawi, Maldives, Mauritius, Namibia, Nauru, Papua New Guinea, Samoa, San Marino, Seychelles, Sierra Leone, Singapore, Solomon Islands, St Lucia, St Vincent & The Grenadines, Swaziland, Tanzania, Tonga, Turkey, Tuvalu, Uganda, Uruguay, Vanuatu, Zambia, Zimbabwe.

NB If you are NOT a citizen of any of the above countries and you wish to enter Kenya, you MUST OBTAIN A VISA IN ADVANCE, particularly if you are proceeding to Kenya from a country where there is a Kenyan Embassy, High Commission or Consulate to issue visa.

Applications from nationals of the following countries have to be referred to Nairobi for approval: Afghanistan, Armenia, Azerbaijan, Cameroon, Iran, Iraq, Lebanon, Libya, Mali, Nigeria, North Korea, Pakistan, Senegal, Somalia, Tazikstan, Yemen, Stateless Persons. Persons falling under this category are advised to apply at least three months before the proposed date of travel to Kenya.

Health
Malaria

Malaria is very common in Sub-Saharan Africa. The pre-dominant species is *Plasmodium falciparum*, the most dangerous of the four species of human malaria (the others are *P. Vivax, P. Ovale* and *P. Malariae*). Malaria causes an estimated 2.7 million deaths per year, with most of these deaths occurring in Africa. Ninety percent (90%) of the world's malaria cases occur in Africa. Chloroquine resistance is widespread in Africa. Now, malaria outbreaks are being reported in some locations of Africa that had been previously thought to be at elevations too high for malaria transmission, such as the highlands of Kenya. Some scientists hypothesize this is due to climatic change, while others think it is due to human migration. Also, malaria has resurged in certain locations of Africa that had previously had effective control programs, such as Madagascar, South Africa, and Zanzibar. Malaria occurs in over 100 countries and territories. This use of prophylactic medication for malaria is very controversial, so visitors are recommended to contact their own doctor for advise.

Anthropod-borne Diseases

Anthropod-borne diseases such as malaria, plague, relapsing fever, Rift Valley fever, tick-bite fever, and typhus (mainly tick-borne) have been reported from most of this area. However, except for malaria (chloroquine resistant) in certain areas, they are not likely to be major health problems for the traveller. African sleeping sickness (trypanosomiasis) can occur. Various forms of filariasis, leishmaniasis, and tungiasis (skin penetration by larva of the female sand flea) may be found in some areas of Kenya.

Food- and Waterborne Diseases

Food- and waterborne dis-eases are common in some areas, particularly amebiasis and typhoid fever. Hepatitis A occurs in this area. Schistosomiasis is uncommon but does occur in some of Kenya's lakes.

Travel tips

Health Requirements

Recommended vaccinations for all travellers:
• Hepatitis A
• Typhoid
• Yellow fever (arriving from a yellow-fever-infected area)
• Polio
• Hepatitis B
• Rabies
• All travellers should be up to date on tetanus-diphtheria, measles-mumps-rubella, and varicella immunizations.

Health Precautions

• Drink only bottled water and drink it often to avoid dehydration.
• Avoid overexposure to the sun; most of Kenya's safari destinations are situated at high altitude (e.g. Lake Nakuru is at 6000ft, and Masai Mara at 5400ft), so it is very easy to get sunburnt.

Distances from Nairobi

Amboseli to Nairobi
  220km (137 miles)
Aberdares to Nairobi
  210km (130 miles)
Baringo to Nairobi
  280km (174 miles)
Masai Mara to Nairobi
  360km (224 miles)
Mombasa to Nairobi
  500km (311 miles)
Samburu to Nairobi
  355km (221 miles)

4WD Vehicle Hire

For safari-goers interested in hiring a 4WD vehicle, there are several options in Kenya:

Glen Mathews:
4WD self-drive Land Rovers equipped with winches and roof racks; e-mail: fourwdm@ iconnect.co.ke

Roving Rovers: fully equipped (camping) Range Rovers; website: www. rovingrovers.com

Tough Tracks: for vehicle hire and also hiring camping equipment; website: www.toughtracks.com

Avis Rent-A-Car:
www.avis.co.ke

Hertz: www.hertz.co.ke

Photography

Although Kenya is famous for being a land of photographic opportunities you must not attempt to photograph subjects such as the president, military installations, military personnel in uniform, police, prisons and prisoners. Remember that you should never photograph people without first asking their permission – Muslim women in traditional dress often dislike being photographed, and Maasai and Samburu warriors will expect to be recompensed for posing.

Film, both slide film and colour negative film, is widely available in Nairobi and Mombasa and in almost all safari lodges and camps. It is much cheaper in Nairobi – Expo Camera Centre on Mama Ngina Street is the cheapest. Camera batteries and video cassettes are not readily available from the camps and so it is advisable to stock up in Nairobi or Mombasa.

Still Photography

Two lenses are all that is needed for most wildlife photography, the exception being bird photography. A 28–85mm lens is adequate for photographing scenery and people, and a 100–300mm lens is ideal for taking general wildlife photographs. For bird photography, on the other hand, a lens of 400mm or more is required, especially for close-up photographs. There is often a temptation to make use of x2 extenders to double the magnification of the lens. Be warned that this makes focusing more difficult, and often the results are disappointing. However,

National Parks Guide

certain camera manufacturers such as Canon and Nikon produce a x1.4 extender, which, when used on a fixed 300mm or 400mm lens, can result in excellent photographs.

The really enthusiastic photographer is advised to bring two camera bodies. The second body is useful if you come across problems and it can also be loaded with a higher-speed film for those difficult shots early in the morning or late in the afternoon. For high-quality photography, slow film such as 50ASA, 64ASA or 100ASA should be used. It is also a good idea to fit a filter on the front of any lens to circumvent the dust problem. Use a small tripod that can rest on the vehicle's roof, or a beanbag to help keep the camera steady. To avoid missing any good shots, keep your camera ready to use. It is a good idea to have the camera switched on, resting on your knee and covered with a towel or kikoi (colourful African cloth).

Video Photography

Many visitors nowadays prefer using video cameras to still or movie cameras. The modern video camera is small and compact, making it very easy to use. Rather than moving it freely around, rest it on your vehicle's window-frame or roof, using a beanbag to keep it steady. (Bean bags are only supplied by one or two of the top safari companies so check before arrival). Better results will be obtained by letting the object move into or out of the viewfinder as opposed to following it as it moves. If possible watch a couple of wildlife films before you come on safari and note how the professionals do it.

Another tip is to keep the camera angle as low a possible, particularly if the subject is close, as it makes the subject much more impressive. The temptation is to stand and photograph out of the roof hatch and then have to look down on the subject which is not good photography.

Do not forget to use your video camera at night – it is amazing how well a video camera works in darkness, so if you are lucky and have a roaring lion outside your room or tent, have a go and film it (keep inside your room, of course); even if the picture is unclear, you will at least pick up the wonderful sounds.

Sound can either enhance or spoil the final result. Wind is perhaps the biggest problem, followed by chat from your safari companions. A special directional microphone fitted with a good wind cover is the answer to this problem.

Digital Photography

Many visitors now use digital cameras, ranging from the simple point-and-shoot variety to expensive ones with interchangeable lenses. In a digital camera, film has been replaced by a memory card (CF Compact Flash is the most common) which is available in various sizes from 128 MB to 8MB (in Nairobi 1MB is probably the largest available). Depending on the mode you select to capture your photographs in, RAW or JPEG, you can take as few as 20 images in RAW and nearly 300 images in small JPEG on a 128MB CF card. In large JPEG setting, 50 images are available on a 128MB CF card. Most photographers select Large JPEG but if you want to sell your photographs to a magazine its better to use the RAW setting. Many hotels, lodges and camps do not stock memory cards, so it is a very good idea to bring several spare cards on safari; even if they are available, they will be far more expensive than at home. Some digital photographers bring their laptop computers and download their photographs each day, but the extra weight may be a problem on small charter aircraft. Another solution is to carry a portable CD burner, and download your photographs onto CDs.

A problem for interchangeable lens cameras on safari is dust. When changing lenses some dust will enter the camera and will be attracted to the camera's charged sensors. This dust may be invisible to the eye, but will show on photographs. An air bulb can sometimes remove dust but in extreme cases the camera will have to be returned to the manufacturer for cleaning. DO NOT use an air can aerosol to clean a sensor because this can cause permanent damage. Because of this, many photographers never change a lens during a safari drive.

Binoculars

In order to benefit fully from your safari, it is essential that you have a pair of binoculars. Binoculars of the size 7X35 or 8X40, generally small in size and reasonably light in weight,

are strongly recommended. The first 7 or 8 represent the magnification and the second 35 or 40 refer to the diameter of the front lens in millimetres. Generally the larger diameter of the front lens, in relation to the size of the eye piece lens, the greater the amount of light gathered and, therefore, the brighter and clearer the image. Another easy way to check out the brightness of binoculars is to divide the second number (35) by the magnification (7) and the higher this number is (5) the brighter the binocular. It is a big temptation to buy larger magnification binoculars such as 10X40 or 10X50, but these tend to be heavy and cumbersome and are also difficult to hold steady. Fortunately with modern technology it is possible to purchase binoculars that have large magnification but have an image stabilizer system, unfortunately though, they are heavy and require batteries (dry cells) to run the stabilizing system.

Water

Water is a precious commodity in Africa. Please use water sparingly and do not waste it (e.g. when brushing teeth). Try to avoid unnecessary washing of hair, lengthy showers, etc.

Good Reading

Kingdon, Jonathan: The Kingdon Field Guide to African Mammals (1997). Natural World Academic Press. Estes, Richard: The Behaviour Guide to African Mammals (1992). University of California Press.

Selected Animal and Bird Gallery

Elephant

White Rhino

Hippo

Buffalo

Blue Wildebeest

Burchell's Zebra

Banded Mongoose

Dwarf Mongoose

Reticulated Giraffe

Sykes' Monkey

Vervet Monkey

Lesser Bushbaby

Warthog

Yellow Baboon

Honey Badger (Ratel)

Colobus Monkey

Rock Hyrax (Dassie)

Nile Crocodile

Savannah Monitor Lizard

Agama Lizard

Animals

Lion

Cheetah

Caracal

Serval

Spotted Hyena

Leopard

Bongo

Hirola

Roan Antelope

Sable Antelope

Beisa Oryx

Oribi

Bushbuck

Eland

Reedbuck

Mountain Reedbuck

Impala

Kudu

Grant's Gazelle

Thomson's Gazelle

Sitatunga

Suni

Common Duiker

Klipspringer

Selected Animal and Bird Gallery

Fish Eagle

Crowned Eagle

Martial Eagle

Verreaux's Eagle

Southern Banded
Snake Eagle

Western Banded
Snake Eagle

Black-chested
Snake Eagle

Pygmy Falcon

Eastern Pale
Chanting Goshawk

Swallow-tailed Kite

Crested
Guineafowl

Vulturine
Guineafowl

Mottled Swift

Kori Bustard

Heuglin's Bustard

Jackson's
Francolin

Green-headed
Oriole

Black-tailed Godwit

Birds

Greater Flamingo

Lesser Flamingo

Pink-backed Pelican

White Pelican

Marabou Stork

Saddle-billed Stork

Pygmy Goose

African Finfoot

Lesser Jacana

Long-toed Plover (Lapwing)

Black Heron

Bare-faced Go-away Bird

Double-toothed Barbet

Sokoke Pipit

Narina Trogon

Schalow's Turaco

Ross's Turaco

Fischer's Turaco

Blue Swallow

Hartlaub's Turaco

Selected Animal and Bird Gallery

Long-tailed Widow Bird

Trumpeter Hornbill

Ground Hornbill

Silvery-cheeked Hornbill

Red-billed Hornbill

Northern Carmine Bee-eater

Cinnamon-chested Bee-eater

Madagascar Bee-eater

Black-and-white Casqued Hornbill

Somali Bee-eater

Scarlet-tufted Malachite Sunbird

Scarlet-chested Sunbird

Red-fronted Parrot

Orange-bellied Parrot

White-starred Forest Robin

Purple Gallinule

Black-breasted Glossy Starling

Golden-breasted Starling

Golden-winged Sunbird

Birds

Rüppell's Griffon Vulture

Lappet-faced Vulture

Hooded Vulture

White-backed Vulture

Palm-nut Vulture

Mackinder's Eagle Owl

Lammergeier

Egyptian Vulture

Pel's Fishing Owl

Sokoke Scops Owl

Augur Buzzard

Grasshopper Buzzard

Lizard Buzzard

Klaas's Cuckoo

Lichtenstein's Sandgrouse

Yellow-billed Oxpecker

Two-banded Courser

Somali Courser

Rosy-patched Shrike

Red-billed Oxpecker

Check list

Top Mammals
- [ ] [ ] Ader's duiker
- [ ] [ ] Banded mongoose
- [ ] [ ] Beisa oryx
- [ ] [ ] Black rhino
- [ ] [ ] Black-fronted duiker
- [ ] [ ] Blue monkey
- [ ] [ ] Bohor reedbuck
- [ ] [ ] Bongo
- [ ] [ ] Buffalo
- [ ] [ ] Burchell's zebra
- [ ] [ ] Bushbaby
- [ ] [ ] Bushbuck
- [ ] [ ] Caracal
- [ ] [ ] Chandler's reedbuck
- [ ] [ ] Cheetah
- [ ] [ ] Coke's hartebeest (Kongoni)
- [ ] [ ] Colobus monkey
- [ ] [ ] Common duiker
- [ ] [ ] Common zebra
- [ ] [ ] Crested mangabey
- [ ] [ ] De Brazza monkey
- [ ] [ ] Defassa waterbuck
- [ ] [ ] Dwarf mongoose
- [ ] [ ] Eland
- [ ] [ ] Elephant
- [ ] [ ] Fringe-eared oryx
- [ ] [ ] Gerenuk
- [ ] [ ] Giant forest hog
- [ ] [ ] Giant forest squirrel
- [ ] [ ] Giant rock hyrax
- [ ] [ ] Golden-rumped elephant shrew
- [ ] [ ] Grant's gazelle
- [ ] [ ] Greater kudu
- [ ] [ ] Grevy's zebra
- [ ] [ ] Gunther's dikdik
- [ ] [ ] Hippo
- [ ] [ ] Hirola (Hunter's hartebeest)
- [ ] [ ] Impala
- [ ] [ ] Jackson's hartebeest
- [ ] [ ] Kirk's dikdik
- [ ] [ ] Klipspringer
- [ ] [ ] Leopard
- [ ] [ ] Lesser kudu
- [ ] [ ] Lion
- [ ] [ ] Masai giraffe
- [ ] [ ] Mountain reedbuck
- [ ] [ ] Olive baboon
- [ ] [ ] Oribi
- [ ] [ ] Ratel (honey badger)
- [ ] [ ] Red colobus
- [ ] [ ] Red duiker
- [ ] [ ] Red-tailed monkey
- [ ] [ ] Red-tailed squirrel
- [ ] [ ] Reedbuck
- [ ] [ ] Reticulated giraffe
- [ ] [ ] Roan antelope
- [ ] [ ] Rock hyrax
- [ ] [ ] Rothschild's giraffe
- [ ] [ ] Sable antelope
- [ ] [ ] Serval cat
- [ ] [ ] Side-striped jackal
- [ ] [ ] Silver-backed jackal
- [ ] [ ] Sitatunga
- [ ] [ ] Spotted hyena
- [ ] [ ] Spotted-necked otter
- [ ] [ ] Striped hyena
- [ ] [ ] Suni
- [ ] [ ] Sykes' monkey
- [ ] [ ] Tana River red colobus
- [ ] [ ] Thomson's gazelle
- [ ] [ ] Tiang
- [ ] [ ] Topi
- [ ] [ ] Tree hyrax
- [ ] [ ] Vervet monkey
- [ ] [ ] Warthog
- [ ] [ ] Waterbuck
- [ ] [ ] White rhino
- [ ] [ ] Wildebeest
- [ ] [ ] Yellow baboon

Top Reptiles
- [ ] [ ] Agama lizard
- [ ] [ ] Crocodile
- [ ] [ ] Jackson's chameleon
- [ ] [ ] Nile monitor lizard
- [ ] [ ] Savannah monitor lizard

Top Birds
- [ ] [ ] African Finfoot
- [ ] [ ] African Fish Eagle
- [ ] [ ] Arabian Bustard
- [ ] [ ] Augur Buzzard
- [ ] [ ] Bare-faced Go-away Bird
- [ ] [ ] Black Heron
- [ ] [ ] Black-and-white Casqued Hornbill
- [ ] [ ] Black-breasted Glossy Starling
- [ ] [ ] Black-breasted Snake Eagle
- [ ] [ ] Black-tailed Godwit
- [ ] [ ] Blue Swallow
- [ ] [ ] Brown Snake Eagle
- [ ] [ ] Carmine Bee-eater

Check list

- [ ] [ ] Cattle Egret
- [ ] [ ] Cinnamon-chested Bee-eater
- [ ] [ ] Crested Guineafowl
- [ ] [ ] Crested Lark
- [ ] [ ] Crowned Eagle
- [ ] [ ] Double-banded Courser
- [ ] [ ] Double-toothed Barbet
- [ ] [ ] Eastern Chanting Goshawk
- [ ] [ ] Eastern Pale Chanting Goshawk
- [ ] [ ] Egyptian Vulture
- [ ] [ ] European Griffon Vulture
- [ ] [ ] Fischer's Turaco
- [ ] [ ] Golden-breasted Starling
- [ ] [ ] Golden-winged Sunbird
- [ ] [ ] Grasshopper Buzzard
- [ ] [ ] Great White Pelican
- [ ] [ ] Greater Flamingo
- [ ] [ ] Green-headed Oriole
- [ ] [ ] Ground Hornbill
- [ ] [ ] Hartlaub's Turaco
- [ ] [ ] Heuglin's Bustard
- [ ] [ ] Hooded Vulture
- [ ] [ ] Jackson's Francolin
- [ ] [ ] Klaas's Cuckoo
- [ ] [ ] Kori Bustard
- [ ] [ ] Lammergeier (Bearded Vulture)
- [ ] [ ] Lappet-faced Vulture
- [ ] [ ] Lesser Flamingo
- [ ] [ ] Lesser Jacana
- [ ] [ ] Lichtenstein's Sandgrouse
- [ ] [ ] Lizard Buzzard
- [ ] [ ] Long-tailed Widow Bird
- [ ] [ ] Long-toed Plover (Lapwing)
- [ ] [ ] Mackinder's Eagle Owl
- [ ] [ ] Madagascar Bee-eater
- [ ] [ ] Malachite Sunbird
- [ ] [ ] Marabou Stork
- [ ] [ ] Mariqua Sunbird
- [ ] [ ] Martial Eagle
- [ ] [ ] Mottled Swift
- [ ] [ ] Mountain Buzzard
- [ ] [ ] Narina Trogon
- [ ] [ ] Northern Carmine Bee-eater
- [ ] [ ] Nyanza Swift
- [ ] [ ] Orange-bellied Parrot
- [ ] [ ] Ostrich
- [ ] [ ] Palm-nut Vulture
- [ ] [ ] Pel's Fishing Owl
- [ ] [ ] Peters' Finfoot
- [ ] [ ] Pink-backed Pelican
- [ ] [ ] Purple Gallinule
- [ ] [ ] Pygmy Duck
- [ ] [ ] Pygmy Falcon
- [ ] [ ] Pygmy Goose
- [ ] [ ] Red-billed Hornbill
- [ ] [ ] Red-billed Oxpecker
- [ ] [ ] Red-fronted Parrot
- [ ] [ ] Redshank
- [ ] [ ] Ross's Turaco
- [ ] [ ] Rosy-patched Shrike
- [ ] [ ] Rüppell's Griffon Vulture
- [ ] [ ] Saddle-billed Stork
- [ ] [ ] Scarlet-chested Sunbird
- [ ] [ ] Scarlet-tufted Malachite Sunbird
- [ ] [ ] Schalow's Turaco
- [ ] [ ] Short-crested Lark
- [ ] [ ] Short-toed Snake Eagle
- [ ] [ ] Silverbird
- [ ] [ ] Silvery-cheeked Hornbill
- [ ] [ ] Sokoke Pipit
- [ ] [ ] Sokoke Scops Owl
- [ ] [ ] Somali Bee-eater
- [ ] [ ] Somali Courser
- [ ] [ ] Somali Ostrich
- [ ] [ ] Southern Banded Snake Eagle
- [ ] [ ] Steppe Eagle
- [ ] [ ] Swallow-tailed Kite
- [ ] [ ] Trumpeter Hornbill
- [ ] [ ] Verreaux's Eagle
- [ ] [ ] Vulturine Guineafowl
- [ ] [ ] Wahlberg's Eagle
- [ ] [ ] Western Banded Snake Eagle White Pelican
- [ ] [ ] White-backed Vulture
- [ ] [ ] White-starred Forest Robin
- [ ] [ ] Yellow-billed Oxpecker

Index

Note: page numbers in **bold** indicate photographs.

Aberdare National Park 15, 106–111, **113**
accommodation 16–17
Afro-alpine vegetation 105
agama lizard 88
aloes 123
Amboseli Elephant Research Project 34
Amboseli National Park **6**, **24**, 32–33, **35**
Arabuko-Sokoke Forest National Park and Reserve 55
Arawale National Reserve 54
Ark, The, Aberdare National Park **110**, 111
Augur Buzzard **115**, 116

balloon safaris 9, 122
banded mongoose **138**, 139
baobab 61
beisa oryx **72**, 84, **142**
Big Five 8
binoculars 149
biomes 18
biosphere reserves 145
bird shooting safaris 9
bird-watching safaris 10
black rhino 27–28, **81**
bongo 111–112
Borana Ranch 79
buffalo **142**
Buffalo Springs National Reserve 76, **84**, **142**
Burchell's zebra **24**
bushbuck **106**, 114

camel safaris 10
candelabra tree 125
Cape chestnut 114
Cattle Egret **142**
Central Island National Park 68
cheetah **9**, **123**–125
Chyulu Hills National Park **40**, 42
climate 11, 19–20
climbing safaris 10
colobus monkey 18, 112–**113**
cultural safaris 10

Defassa waterbuck **144**
desert rose 99

dhow **50**
distances 147
doum palm **63**, **64**
dwarf mongoose **72**, 87

El Molo village **64**
eland **30**–31
elephant **24**, 33–36, **35**, **50**, **56**
elephant safaris 11
environmental organizations 20
etiquette see safari code

fishing safaris 11
flamingo **90**, 94–95, **144**
flying safaris 11
Fort Jesus, Mombasa 14
fringe-eared oryx 36

gardenias 127
Gedi Ruins 14, **15**
gerenuk 83
getting married 12
giant forest hog **108**, 114
giant rock hyrax 105
Golden-winged Sunbird 115
golfing safaris 12
Governors' Il Moran Camp, Masai Mara National Reserve **12**
Grant's gazelle **134**–135
Great Rift Valley see Rift Valley
greater kudu 74
Grevy's zebra **63**, **72**, 82–83
Gunther's dikdik 85–87

habitats 18
hagenia trees 105
Hartlaub's Turaco **116**, 117
health 146
helicopter safaris 13
Hell's Gate National Park 100–101
hippopotamus 48–**49**
hirola conservation 46–47
horseback safaris 13
hot springs 98
hot-air ballooning **118**
hyrax **101**

Il'ngwesi 82

Jackson's chameleon 117
Jumba la Mwtana 15

Kenyatta House, Maralal 15
Kinunga Marine National Reserve 55
Kirk's dikdik 85–87, **86**
klipspringer 43
Koobi Fora 66–67
Kora National Reserve 58

Laikipia region 78
Lake Bogoria National Reserve 98
Lake Nakuru National Park **90**, 92–93, **95**, **144**
lakes
  Baringo 18, 81, 95, 96, 98
  Bogoria 81, **90**, 91, 95, 98, **99**
  Jipe 48
  Magadi 96, 98
  Naivasha 9, 17, 18, 96, 100, 117
  Nakuru 7, 8, 9, 60, 90, 91, 92, 94, **95**, 96, 97, 125
  Turkana 11, **64**, 65, 66, 67, 68, 96, 99, 126
  Victoria 11, 18, 19, 20, 21, 22, 120, 121, 140
Lappet-faced Vulture **137**
leopard **90**, 96–97
lesser flamingo **95**
lesser kudu 43–**44**
Lewa Wildlife Conservancy 78, **81**
Lichtenstein's Sandgrouse 67–68
lilies 124
lion **6**, **21**, **118**, **120**, **121**–123
Loisaba Ranch 80
Long-tailed Widow Bird 97–98
Losai National Reserve 75
Lugard's Falls **46**

Maasai people 39
Maasai warrior **38**
Mackinder's Eagle Owl 117
Malachite Sunbird **106**
malaria 146
marine national parks and reserves 145
Marsabit National Reserve 74
Masai Mara National Reserve **6**, **9**, **21**, **23**, **118**–121, **123**, **126**, **128**, **138**, **142**
medical supplies 13

Index

Meru National Park **56**, 58–60
Mombasa Marine National Park 55
Mount Elgon National Park 70–71
Mount Kenya National Park 102–104
Mount Longonot National Park 100
mountain climbing **104**
mountain reedbuck **96**, 97
mountains
Aberdares 7, 11, 20, 100, 108, 117
Bodech 76
Elgon 65, 70, **71**, 117
Gol 136
Kilimanjaro **6**, 25, 48
Longonot **90**, 91, 99, 100
Mount Kenya 7, 10, 11, 13, 19, 20, 22, 25, 31, 58, 78, 79, **102**–105, **104**, 111, 117
Ngulia 47, 48
Pare 48
Suswa 98
Mwalanganje Elephant Sanctuary 52–53
Mzima Springs **49**

Nairobi National Park **26**, 26–31, **30**
Nandi flame tree 129
national parks 143
national reserves 143–144
national sanctuaries 145
Nile crocodile 125–126

Ol Ari Nyiro Ranch 81
Ol Malo Ranch 80
Ol-Doinyo Sabuk National Park 31–32
oribi 141
ornithology 10
oxpeckers 28–30

passports 146
Pel's Fishing Owl **62**
photographic safaris 14
photography 147–149
pyjama lily 126

railway safaris 13
'red' elephants 43

Red-billed Hornbill 44
Red-billed Oxpecker **29**
reticulated giraffe **56**, **84**–85
rhino **29**
rhino horn 27
Rift Valley 11, **21**, **90**, **99**, **102**
Rift Valley lakes 95–96
Rift Valley volcanoes 99
rivers
Athi 26, 27
Ewaso Ngiro **72**, 73, 76, 77, 78, 80, 81, 85
Galana 45, **46**
Isiolo 77
Mara 12, **21**–**23**, 119, 120, **131**
Rojeweru 57, 58, 59, 62
Suam 76
Tana 36, 51, 54, 57, 58, 84
Tsavo **40**, 43, 48
Voi 46
roan antelope **141**
rock hyrax 101
Rohole National Reserve 58
Ross's Turaco 135
Rothschild's giraffe 96
Ruma National Park 140, **141**
Rüppell's Griffon Vulture **137**

sable antelope **52**, 53–54
Sabuk 81
safari code 18
Safaricom Marathon 13
Saiwa Swamp National Park **64**, 68–**69**
Samburu National Reserve **72**, 76
Samburu people **89**
savannah monitor lizard 88–89
Scarlet-chested Sunbird 45
scuba diving 14
Serengeti-Masai Mara migration 20–23
serval cat 125
Shaba National Reserve **72**, 76
Shimba Hills National Reserve **50**, **52**
Sibiloi National Park 66
side-striped jackal **142**
sitatunga **69**
Snake Eagles 137–138

Somali Bee-eater 88
Somali Ostrich 75
South Island National Park 68
spotted hyena **126**, 127–129
sunbirds 115
Sykes' monkey **102**

Taita Hills Game Sanctuary 49
Tana River Primate National Reserve 54
Tassia 82
Thomson's gazelle 132–133
tiang 67
topi **128**, 129–130
topography 22
Tortilis Camp, Amboseli National Park **24**
translocated animals 60
travel tips 146–149
tree hyrax 116
Treetops, Aberdare National Park 16, 111, **106**
Tsavo East National Park **40**, 45–46
Tsavo elephants 53
Tsavo lions 48
Tsavo National Park 42–48
Tsavo West National Park **44**, 47–48, **49**
types of safari 9

Vasco da Gama Pillar 15
visas 146
volunteer holidays 14
vultures 135–137
Vulturine Guineafowl **6**, 88

warthog **139**–140
water 149
waterbuck **40**
western white-bearded gnu see wildebeest
white rhino 60, **61**
White-backed Vulture **137**
wildebeest **23**, **118**, 130–132, **131**
wildlife conservation 145

yellow baboon 37–38
yellow-barked acacia forest 98

zebra **26**

Imprint Page

First edition published in 2007
by New Holland Publishers (UK) Ltd
London • Cape Town • Sydney • Auckland
10 9 8 7 6 5 4 3 2 1
website: www.newhollandpublishers.com

Garfield House, 86 Edgware Road
London W2 2EA
United Kingdom

80 McKenzie Street
Cape Town 8001
South Africa

218 Lake Road
Northcote, Auckland
New Zealand

14 Aquatic Drive
Frenchs Forest NSW 2086
Australia

Distributed in the USA by
The Globe Pequot Press, Connecticut

ISBN 978 1 84537 558 4

Although every effort has been made to ensure that
this guide is up to date and current at time of going to
print, the Publisher accepts no responsibility or liability
for any loss, injury or inconvenience incurred by read-
ers or travellers using this guide.

Keep us Current
Information in travel guides is apt to change, which is
why we regularly update our guides. We'd be grateful
to receive feedback if you've noted something we
should include in our updates. If you have new information, please share it with us by writing to the
Publishing Manager, Globetrotter, at the office nearest
to you (addresses on this page). The most significant
contribution to each new edition will receive a free
copy of the updated guide.

Publishing Manager: Thea Grobbelaar
DTP Cartographic Manager: Genené Hart
Editor: Thea Grobbelaar
Design and DTP: Nicole Bannister
Cartographer: Nicole Bannister
Picture Researcher: Shavonne Govender
Illustrators: Steven Felmore (birds), Michael Thayer
(reptiles), Penny Meakin, Michael Thayer and Steven
Felmore (mammals)

Reproduction by Resolution, Cape Town
Printed and bound by Star Standard Industries (Pte)
Ltd, Singapore

Acknowledgments: The authors wish to thank
Patrick Reynolds for his valuable help. Also Lis Farrell
and Jeremy Watkins-Pitchford without whom we
could not have
completed this project.

Photographic credits:
Africa Imagery: pages 12, 15, 24 (centre), 50 (top),
56 (centre and bottom), 89, 90 (bottom), 96, 102
(bottom), 106 (top and centre), 110, 113, 118 (top),
126; **Darryl & Sharna Balfour/IOA:** front cover,
title page, pages 6 (bottom), 21 (left and right), 24
(bottom), 40 (top and bottom), 50 (centre and
bottom), 52, 63, 86, 90 (centre), 99, 142 (bottom);
Andrew Bannister/IOA: back cover (top and
bottom), contents page, pages 26, 35, 40 (centre), 42,
46, 69, 72 (top), 102 (top), 139, 142 (centre); **Nigel
Dennis/IOA:** pages 61, 62; **Martin Harvey/IOA:**
half title page, pages 24 (top), 29, 30, 118 (centre and
bottom), 128, 134, 137; **Ian Michler/IOA:** pages 18,
56 (top); **Peter Pickford/IOA:** pages 115, 138;
Ariadne van Zandbergen/IOA: pages 71, 88, 106
(bottom), 131; **Chanan Weiss/IOA:** pages 6 (centre),
102 (centre), 104; **Dave Richards:** back cover (centre),
pages 6 (top), 9, 23, 37, 38, 47, 49, 64 (top, centre and
bottom), 72 (centre and bottom), 81, 84, 90 (top), 95,
101, 108, 116, 120, 123, 141, 142 (top), 144.
[IOA = Images of Africa]

Cover: *Elephants in Amboseli, with Kilimanjaro in the
background (front); Mara River, cheetah in Masai Mara,
African Spoonbills (back, top to bottom).*
Half title page: *Vultures in an acacia tree, Masai Mara.*
Title page: *Elephants in Amboseli.*

Conflict
A N D
Invention

Conflict
A N D
Invention

LITERARY, RHETORICAL, AND
SOCIAL STUDIES ON THE
SAYINGS GOSPEL Q

E D I T E D   B Y

John S. Kloppenborg

TRINITY PRESS INTERNATIONAL
Valley Forge, Pennsylvania

Trinity Press International, P.O. Box 851, Valley Forge, PA 19482-0851

Library of Congress Cataloging-in-Publication Data

Conflict and invention : literary, rhetorical, and social studies on
  the sayings gospel Q / edited by John S. Kloppenborg.
      p.   cm.
    Includes bibliographical references and indexes.
    ISBN 1-56338-123-0 (alk. paper)
    1. Q hypothesis (Synoptics criticism)   I. Kloppenborg, John S.,
  1951-   .
  BS2555.2.C59   1995
  226'.066–dc20   95-24855
                                                               CIP

Printed in the United States of America

95 96 97 98 99 00   10 9 8 7 6 5 4 3 2 1

For

Dieter Lührmann
Paul Hoffmann
James M. Robinson

Sapientiae filiis

Contents

Preface   ix

1. Conflict and Invention: *Recent Studies on Q*   1
   JOHN S. KLOPPENBORG

Part I: THE SOCIAL MAP

2. The Social Map of Q   17
   JONATHAN L. REED

3. Social Conflict in the Synoptic Sayings Source Q   37
   RICHARD HORSLEY

4. The Language of Violence and the Aphoristic   53
   Sayings in Q: *A Study of Q 6:27–36*
   R. A. PIPER

Part II: THE INAUGURAL SERMON

5. Composite Texts and Oral Mythology: *The Case of*   75
   the "Sermon" in Q (6:20–49)
   LEIF E. VAAGE

6. Strategies of Authority: *A Rhetorical Study of the*   98
   Character of the Speaker in Q 6:20–49
   SHAWN CARRUTH, O.S.B.

7. "Love Your Enemies": *Rhetoric, Tradents, and Ethos*   116
   R. CONRAD DOUGLAS

Part III: JOHN THE BAPTIST IN Q ————————————————

8. "Yes, I Tell You, and More Than a Prophet": 135
   The Function of John in Q
   WENDY COTTER

9. "Yet Wisdom Is Justified by Her Children" (Q 7:35): 151
   A Rhetorical and Compositional Analysis of
   Divine Sophia in Q
   PATRICK J. HARTIN

10. Redactional Fabrication and Group Legitimation: 165
    The Baptist's Preaching in Q 3:7–9, 16–17
    WILLIAM ARNAL

11. More Than a Prophet, and Demon-Possessed: 181
    Q and the "Historical" John
    LEIF E. VAAGE

Abbreviations 203

Works Cited 207

Index of Modern Authors 233

Index of Ancient Texts 237

Preface

The essays in this volume are by participants in the Society of Biblical Literature's Q Seminar (1985–89) and Q Section (1990–). While a large variety of topics have been pursued by contributors to the seminar over the past ten years, many of the papers have focused on two major sets of problems — compositional and literary-critical issues, on the one hand, and the question of the social-historical location of Q, on the other. What has been impressive is the significant consensus that has been achieved, particularly on the question of the literary composition of Q and that of its social location, by scholars with very different training and with markedly divergent approaches.

It is a particular pleasure for me to be associated with the scholars represented in this volume, those who have contributed to *Early Christianity, Q and Jesus* (Semeia 55; Atlanta: Scholars Press, 1991), and all those who have participated in the seminar during the course of the last ten years. The conversation, while often heated and contentious, has always been characterized by generosity, erudition, and cooperation.

This volume is dedicated to three scholars who "got the ball rolling" — to Dieter Lührmann and to Paul Hoffmann, whose essays and monographs in the late 1960s and early 1970s signaled the rebirth of Q studies in Germany, and to James M. Robinson, whose essay "LOGOI SOPHŌN" (1964) was instrumental in re-defining the agenda for North American gospel scholarship and in putting Q back on the map of primitive Christianity.

J. S. K.

Conflict and Invention

Recent Studies on Q

Twenty-five years ago Dieter Lührmann published his *Die Redaktion der Logienquelle,* and with that the modern study of Q was born. In 1969 Q, of course, was not a recent discovery but the result of nearly 150 years of Synoptic research. And, of course, important works on Q had been published — by Adolf von Harnack (1907, ET 1908), George DeWitt Castor (1912), J. M. C. Crum (1927), T. W. Manson (1949), Heinz E. Tödt (1959, ET 1965), and James M. Robinson (1964, ET 1971). In 1969 redaction criticism, which Lührmann used, was already a decade old, having been pioneered by his mentor, Günther Bornkamm, among others. With Lührmann's application of redaction criticism to Q, however, Q was shown to be a *document* of early Christianity and a document with a *distinctive theology* in a way that hitherto had not been the case.

From one point of view, Lührmann merely applied redaction criticism to Q and was able to describe the main features of its organization, including the centrality of the motif of opposition to "this generation." In doing this, however, Lührmann underscored the conspicuous lack of any reference to the passion narrative and the lack of a theological appeal to the saving significance of Jesus' death. What Tödt a few years before had described as a "second sphere" of Christianity (1965, 268) had become an important new factor to be reckoned with in the "History of Early Christianity" — the title of Lührmann's fourth chapter (ET 1994).

The same year was important for another quite independent development. Paul Hoffmann published two essays (1969a, 1969b)

John S. Kloppenborg is an associate professor of New Testament at the University of St. Michael's College, Toronto School of Theology.

that would initiate a string of essays (1970a, 1970b, 1971) culminating in his 1972 monograph. Although Hoffmann also noted the
polemic against "this generation," he showed a particular concern
to locate Q and its tradents within the social and political situation of first-century Galilee. Focusing on a variety of Q texts —
the imperatives regarding love of enemies and showing mercy, Q's
prohibition of judging, the third temptation (Q 4:5–8), and the
mention of "children of peace" in Q 10:6 — Hoffmann argued that
the Q group situated itself between the collaborators with Roman
rule and the freedom movements which opposed that rule. In this
context, the Q group

> viewed the path of salvation to be rooted only in following Jesus'
> teachings of doing good and love of enemies. In this sense, it sought
> to call Israel to repentance; as envoys of Jesus, they moved through-
> out the land gathering the children of peace and proclaiming to
> them the imminence of the kingdom. (1969a, 152)

These two foci — description of the literary organization of Q
and articulation of its social location in Galilean society — became
the preoccupation of the study of the Sayings Gospel Q in the
two decades that followed. Although the theological orientation
of Q and the early Jesus groups was still perhaps ultimately the
gravitational center of the various essays and monographs that appeared during this period — over three hundred items alone in the
1980s (see Scholer 1989, 1990, continued by Scholer 1991, 1992,
1993) — the analysis of the theology of the early Jesus movement
and of the Q stream of the Synoptic tradition was now subjected
to two important controls. One the one hand, Q's sayings, with
their peculiar complexion of polemics, extravagant expectations
of God's intervention, and inversionary, even countercultural, wisdom, had to be discussed within a framework that took cognizance
of literary, compositional, and rhetorical features of the collection,
rather than, as in previous scholarship, being used as an undifferen-
tiated fund of materials, all equally important for describing "*the
early Palestinian church.*"

On the other hand, especially from the mid-1970s, there was an
increasing premium placed on the need to coordinate the literature
and ideologies of early Christian groups with a sound analysis of
social *realia* — class structure, economic levels, modes of political
and familial organization, and so forth — and to understand how
particular theological stances could be interpreted meaningfully

in relation to those social "facts." Gerd Theissen's essay "Wan-derradikalismus: Literatur-soziologische Aspekte der Überlieferung von Worten Jesu im Urchristentum" (1973) set a benchmark for the study of the social setting of Q. His thesis that "wandering radicals" were responsible for some of the Q material — a the-sis strongly indebted to Hoffmann's analysis — has proven to be remarkably influential, even if his privileging of itinerancy within Q is now open to serious challenge.[1] The basic picture that he painted of the Galilean society as one fraught with economic un-certainty and social conflict has continued to inform much of the social analysis of the Sayings Gospel Q.

The Social Location of the Q People

Much of the gain of the last quarter century has been the in-sight that, far from being merely a collection of traditions about Jesus and John that some otherwise anonymous Galilean commit-ted to writing, Q is an *argument* for a particular way of looking at Jesus, John the Baptist, God, the history of Israel, the elites of the land, and the other inhabitants of Galilee. It is *invention:* not in the commonplace sense of "fabrication" but in the rhetorical sense of the conceptual process of coming to a position on a par-ticular issue or issues and then "finding" (*inventio*) and arranging resources — some of them drawn from lists of established topics, some recalling the particular pronouncements or exploits of distin-guished persons, some constructed *ex nihilo* — into an argument by which an audience is to be persuaded of the truth of a matter or of the expediency of a course of action.

This type of approach, which might best be termed "socio-rhetorical" — the coinage, I believe, of Vernon Robbins — requires attention both to the literary and rhetorical features of a text and to the probable social context in which it functioned and the par-ticular social problematic it addressed. The latter, of course, can be known only inferentially, by careful coordination of the shape of Q's rhetoric with what is known, largely from Josephus, of Galilee before the Jewish War.

Each of the essays in this volume reflects in varying proportions this modern preoccupation with rhetoric and social description, and each advances our appreciation of the Jesus movement in Galilee represented by Q.

Perhaps one of the most basic questions to be asked concerns

the basis for the conclusion that Q was composed in Galilee or,
at least, reflects in a significant way the Galilean Jesus movement. In the past, this conclusion was based on the mention of
a few Galilean place-names — Bethsaïda, Chorazin, and Capernaum. This, by itself, was an extraordinarily weak argument; few
would argue analogously that the Fourth Gospel's mention of specific sites in Jerusalem is proof that it was written there. For this
reason, Jonathan Reed's essay is of considerable importance both
methodologically and materially, for it sets the discussion of Q's
provenance within the framework of the methods of humanistic
geography, and it considers not only the geographical names but,
more importantly, much more subtle indications of the location,
posture, and allegiances of those who framed and used Q.

His conclusion, that Q's world centers on lower Galilee, and
especially on Capernaum, is not new. But for the first time, this
long-held conclusion receives a solid basis. Q's "map" describes
three concentric circles, with Capernaum and the adjacent hamlets
of Chorazin and Bethsaïda at the center. Jerusalem to the south
and Tyre and Sidon to the north constitute points on the circum-
ference of a second circle, while the edges of a third circle fade into
mythic space, where lie the long-destroyed town of Sodom and the
once-grand city of Nineveh. But Reed does much more than demonstrate why Galilee, after all, was a good choice. He shows how
Q's map is an *argument,* displacing Jerusalem from its position at
the center of things, and how Q treats all cities as insecure places,
fraught with danger and instability. But this is not the reflection of
bucolic yokels who mistrust cities: Reed, by a careful analysis of
the spatiality of Q's languages, provides good reason to think that
those who framed Q were not from the countryside and its hamlets
but from a larger population center.

The two following essays, by Richard Horsley and Ronald
Piper, cohere interestingly with Reed's conclusions. Horsley's essay stresses the intra-Israelite conflict that characterizes Q. Thus
he provides an important corrective to the way in which Q —
and indeed much gospel literature — has been read through super-
sessionist eyes. The lines of conflict in Q are not drawn between
"Israel" and a "Christian" Q group poised on the brink of a gentile expansion but between Galileans and the socially and spatially
remote elites of Jerusalem, between the taxed and the taxers. The
attack on the Pharisees in Q 11:39–52 is not in the first instance
a theoretical reflection on the role of the Law in a Christian so-

ciety but an attack on the political-economic-religious role of the Pharisees and scribes in Herodian Galilee (see also Kloppenborg 1990c).

Where Horsley views conflict within Q on a rather large scale — south versus north, ruling elites versus peasants — Piper chooses a finer focus, examining two groups of Q sayings, Q 6:27–36 and 12:58–59, that provide, on Piper's showing, a telling glimpse at the allegiances and social postures of the Q people. These sayings reflect a rather profound lack of confidence in the norms of social and business intercourse and in the institutions of justice. These are, after all, instruments of social control.

Who would exhibit such a lack of confidence in the scales of justice? Indeed, evidence from Egypt suggests that appeal to the courts was a last, not a first, resort and that the courts often functioned as a form of institutionalized violence (Bagnall 1989). Informal dispute settlement was preferable, at least for those déclassé provincials who lacked the social connections needed to ensure a successful outcome in a lawsuit. But Q is obviously not the product of villagers, as Horsley seems to suggest, since the vast majority of these were illiterate. Its framing, especially if Conrad Douglas is correct in seeing deliberate rhetorical techniques at work in Q 6:27–36, is the work of *scribes*. This was already suggested by the present author (1991) and has been refined further by Piper. Village scribes were the immediate point of contact that villagers had with the administrative apparatus; it was they who would be called upon to frame petitions to the local administrators — compare the rich collections of Egyptian petitions assembled by Octave Guéraud (1931), many of them written by local scribes because the principals were illiterate (see Youtie 1975b); it was they who would frame rental, loan, and sale agreements and who would know as a commonplace the proverb cited in Q 6:38, which in Egyptian loan contracts at least is intended concretely and applied to the actual grain scoop or measure used to dispense both the loan and its repayment; and it was they who wrote marriage and dowry agreements and who would know at first hand the divisive nature of divorce (see 16:18). It was also scribes who could draw upon Israel's epic history and invoke the memory of Abel and Zechariah, Lot and Abraham, Jonah and the Queen of the South, against those whom the Q people regarded as their opponents.

The fault lines are not simply between illiterate villagers and the ruling elites, but between the representatives of the "Great Tradition," to borrow a term from Robert Redfield (1965, 40–59), and the "Little Tradition" as it has been reformulated by scribes of much more modest attainment. For the peasant societies that Redfield described, the Great Tradition, synthesized, rationalized, rendered in epic form, is the domain of the privileged few. These are the "winners" of history who, because of their social standing, are in a position to define in literary terms the meaning of key symbols. Yet the Great Tradition exists in a relation of dependence on the Little Tradition, which is local, unsystematic, and largely oral. The two traditions are not, however, dichotomous; on the contrary, there is a bidirectional movement of intellectualization and rationalization of local tradition by scribal elites and parochialization of scribal tradition in village contexts (see Kloppenborg 1993, 24).

Since in Q we have a literary work, it is necessary to modify Redfield's typology. The struggle in Q is not simply the Great Tradition and its scribal retainers versus the peasant, village-centered, and oral Little Tradition. On the contrary, local tradition has received its own scribal synthesis. This synthesis at points tries to propose solutions to the problems of local conflict that circumvent the channels that the elite might have preferred; it lampoons the conduct of the elites and their retainers (especially in Q's woes); and at points it confronts the elite reading of the tradition with an alternate reading — one that, as Reed argues, displaces Jerusalem from its place of privilege, and one that views the elites as opponents rather than as advocates of the designs of Sophia (Q 7:35; 11:49–51). These lesser scribes also draw on the epic tradition and its heroes, including, as Reed points out, the Galilean Jonah, and rearrange its valences in an way inimical to the readings of the Great Tradition.

Q's achievement is not merely in the codification of the Little Tradition but also in a rhetorical *invention* and arrangement that drew on local tradition, synthesizing it into a coherent alternative to its elite counterpart.

Invention and Arrangement

Most of the literary studies of Q, from Lührmann's *Die Redaktion der Logienquelle* and Siegfried Schulz's massive *Q: Die Spruchquelle der Evangelisten* (1972) through the more recent monographs by myself (Kloppenborg 1987a), Migaku Sato (1988), and Arland Jacobson (1992), have conceived the composition of Q to be mainly a matter of the arrangement of units of tradition. Only a few verses — 10:12; 11:49b; 13:35b — could be ascribed to the redactor of Q. In the more recent studies of Q, moreover, the redaction of Q was not treated as a single compositional moment but rather as a series of compositional acts, each for a particular compositional strata (Kloppenborg, Jacobson) or for a subdocument (Sato).

Although the results of stratigraphic analysis are now widely accepted (see Kloppenborg 1995b), there have been in the 1990s some significant shifts in focus. One the one hand, a few studies have appeared that deliberately prescinded from diachronic analysis and have instead examined compositional features of the "final text" (e.g., Horsley 1991a; Kloppenborg 1990a; Sevenich-Bax 1993). One important development has been the analysis of the rhetorical features of Q, both the compositional models in use (Cameron 1990; Douglas, in this volume) and the rhetorical effect of that composition (Carruth, in this volume). On the other hand, whereas earlier studies tended to view composition rather conservatively — as the arrangement of existing traditions — recent authors have suggested that the framers of Q contributed more substantially to the compositional process (März 1985; Arnal, in this volume).

The dominant model for comprehending how Q was composed presupposes a relatively complex process, with complex blocks of sayings being created by quasi-organic forces, by "growth" from individual sayings to small clusters to larger speeches (see Schürmann 1982, 1991; Zeller 1982; Koester 1990, 137; Kloppenborg 1995b). This model owes much to form criticism and its understandings of the processes by which individual units of tradition grew and aggregated. It should be admitted, however, that this model is only just that; whether compositional analogies can be adduced is another matter.

The scope of Leif E. Vaage's first essay in this volume is modest, addressing the issue of whether there is any evidence that the sermon existed as a unit prior to its incorporation into Q, or even whether smaller clusters had any independent oral circulation. His answer is in the negative.

The claim that the sermon existed in a nearly complete form prior to Q is not a widespread view. Robinson raises this as a possibility but does not pursue the matter (1982, 391), and I, despite the fact that my *Formation of Q* is the focus of Vaage's essay, do not subscribe to this speculation. On the contrary, I suggest that the similar organizations of the so-called Q^1 speeches suggest that they were framed together and belong to the "same compositional phase" (Kloppenborg 1987a, 238). Hans Dieter Betz (1985b, 1985c, 1990) is the most prominent advocate of the view that the Matthean Sermon on the Mount and the Lukan Sermon on the Plain existed, apart from Q, as discrete compositions. Yet both Betz's Sermon on the Mount and his Sermon on the Plain already contain more than Q's sermon. More recently Thomas Bergemann has argued that the sermon does not derive from Q at all but represents an independent, originally Aramaic, composition to which both Matthew and Luke had access (1993).

The more important contribution of Vaage's essay has to do with his challenge to the "organic" model of composition, a model in which independent sayings gradually aggregate into small clusters and finally into the topically organized speeches in Q. The various disjunctions still visible in the sermon are not, argues Vaage, the result of a prolonged series of smaller editorial developments but are just as likely to have been the product of a single act of literary composition.

It is difficult to evaluate this proposal since at present there is no real way to decide which is the more probable. In my view, progress might be made by examining other literatures to obtain clues regarding the "mechanics" of composition. Walter Wilson's (1991) analysis of the composition of various gnomic collections (as a context for his study of Rom 12:9–21) may prove a helpful starting point.

Two of Q's extended compositional units — the sermon in 6:20b–49 and the Baptist materials in 3:7–9, 16–17; 7:18–28, 31–35 — afford the opportunity to examine literary and rhetorical techniques. The contributions of the essays in parts 2 and 3 are many, but of special importance in this regard is the adducing of models from rhetoric (Carruth; Douglas) and drama (Cotter) to render aspects of Q's techniques intelligible. The essays by Hartin, Arnal, and Vaage contribute in a different way, each underscoring aspects of Q's invention that hitherto have not been noticed or pursued.

Because it proceeds comparatively, drawing upon established patterns from Greek and Latin rhetoric, Shawn Carruth's essay is of considerable importance. Although Carruth presupposes much recent stratigraphical — and hence, diachronic — analysis of Q, her interest is the rhetorical features of the finished sermon. Her preoccupation, however, is not on the rhetorical genre of the inaugural sermon but on the way in which a key rhetorical proof, ethos, is established. It has long been recognized that Q is far from a "random collection of sayings" but is rather the product of intentional arrangement. Carruth's essay reinforces and extends this conclusion, not by dwelling on the topical coherences within the sermon, but by focusing on the way in which a variety of devices, all discussed by ancient rhetoricians, establish a coherent image of the implied speaker (Jesus) who stands behind the sermon.

Direct speech, especially the mild rebukes in 6:41–42 and 6:46, is a way of establishing the character of the speaker as a truth-teller. This represents an important corrective to the view, espoused by Schürmann (1969, 366–79) and Jacobson (1992, 103–4), that 6:39–42 forms part of a polemic against opponents. This interpretation misreads the force and intent of the rebukes, which are mild and, as Carruth demonstrates, function to cement the bond between speaker and audience.

Carruth's aside regarding the lack of appeal to external authority is of potential significance for establishing the social location of the tradents of Q. As I have already observed (Kloppenborg 1991), at the earliest layer of Q there are, surprisingly perhaps, no appeals to the Torah as the basis of authority, or to Moses or the prophets, or — assuming that Q 6:23c is redactional (Jacobson 1992, 101, 127; Kloppenborg 1987a, 173, 190) — to Israel's epic history. Such appeals surface only at the second level of redaction, where figures from Israelite history appear. The significance of Carruth's comment has yet to be probed fully. Why, in a speech that promotes what is normally characterized as a countercultural ethic, is the authority appeal restricted to the character of the speaker, and why are the Torah and the prophets absent? Is this because such appeals are not perceived to be useful, either because they are the rhetorical "possession" of the custodians of the Great Tradition (see Kloppenborg 1993), or because they are assumed to support a different ethic, or for some other reason? It might be noted that in the hortatory materials in Q that are ascribed to its formative level, the only figure from the epic history that appears is Solomon (Q 12:27), who is invoked not as a temple-builder or sage but as one attired in finery that pales by comparison with that of the field lilies who, like the Q folk, receive their clothing from God.

Douglas's contribution pursues the issue of rhetoric and Q by arguing that Q evinces at several points the rhetorical pattern of the chreia elaboration. This moves beyond Piper's observations in his important contribution to the 1982 Leuven colloquium (R. Piper 1982 = Piper 1994) and in his 1989 monograph. Where Piper observed compositional patterns in Q but was unable to relate them to contemporary compositional parallels, Douglas proposes the methods of ancient rhetorical schools. An analogous case has been made by Ron Cameron (1990) in respect to Q 7:18–23.

However this process is described, it is clear that Q is the product of intentional and careful composition. Douglas is no doubt right that Q is not the work of itinerants nor of dispossessed peasants; it is the work of scribes (see also Kloppenborg 1991). This, interestingly, is the same conclusion that Piper (in this volume) reaches from quite different observations. Douglas concludes that these scribes, whom Piper regards as already disenchanted, are prepared to imagine another reality in which all goods are not limited and in which honor and its defense are not paramount.

Both Carruth and Douglas draw upon rhetorical patterns in order to render Q's structures intelligible. Wendy Cotter, by contrast, invokes dramatic techniques to help account for the position and function of the Baptist oracle that prefaces Q. One of the unresolved questions relating to Q is, Why John? In ancient sayings collections, whether gnomic or prophetic, one typically finds materials ascribed either to a single putative sage or prophet or, especially in gnomic anthologies, to many. Rarely are there just two. Cotter's essay does not try to account for this conundrum but rather attempts to explain both how Q manages the twosome and negotiates the tensions caused by their contrasting portraitures and how the figure of John is made to serve the characterization of Jesus.

The relationship of John and Jesus is also the focus of Patrick Hartin's essay. Hartin draws important parallels between the emergence of the mythic Sophia at the time of the exile, when Sophia provided a vivid image of the purposefulness and nearness of God's designs, and the use of Sophia imagery in Q^2, when in a similar situation of persecution and failure, Sophia language provided consolation and assurance to the Q people. Hartin's analysis points again to Q's *invention* — its formulation of an "argument" responding to a particular problem of conflict with "this generation" by drawing upon the resources available from Israelite wisdom.

The final two essays return to more traditional critical approaches but arrive independently at conclusions that are as mutually compatible as they are revolutionary. William Arnal proposes a new analysis of John's oracle that has considerable significance for the description of the redaction of Q and for the reconstruction of the "historical John." While most of his predecessors have argued — or assumed — that 3:7–9 is in the main an authentic Baptist oracle that Q has borrowed, Arnal argues with considerable force that it is in fact a product of Q^2 redaction. Vaage's second contribution to this collection makes a similar proposal: there are two quite different profiles of John the Baptist. One, Vaage argues, is from Q's redaction, a "secondary fabrication" in which John is made to serve Jesus as his prophetic precursor. The other, earlier, depiction of John painted him rather as a marginal, Cyniclike figure, an ascetic to whom people had to "go out."

I admit to many reservations regarding Vaage's analysis of Q 7:18–35 and his assigning of Q 7:24b–26, 28a, 33–34 to the formative (Q^1). While the other materials assigned to Q^1 display a rather consistent form (imperatives with buttressing maxims, prefaced with programmatic beatitudes or maxims, and punctuated with warnings), Q 7:24b–26, 28a, 33–34 do not conform to this pattern, nor do they fit with the preceding or following Q^1 speeches (6:20–49; 9:57–60 [61–62]; 10:2–11, 16). Hence, while the sayings Vaage discusses might represent Johannine traditions with which the Q^2 redaction begins, there is no good reason to suppose that they already belonged to Q^1.

Nevertheless, the main burden of Vaage's essay is to underscore the contribution of Q^2 redaction to the depiction of John. This, along with Arnal's essay, will have important consequences for the use of Q in the reconstruction of the "historical John." The conclusions of the two essays also raise to greater urgency the historical question of why the framers of Q felt it necessary to evoke John's memory at all, and having done so, what processes obtained to produce the final Q^2 portrait of John.

Conflict and Invention Together

Explicit characterization becomes important in the Q^2 portions of the Sayings Gospel. It is here that, as Hartin points out, John and Jesus are characterized by associating them with Heavenly Sophia; it is also here that the opponents of the Q people, "this generation," come to prominence. Here too appear witnesses from

Israel's epic tradition — Solomon, Jonah, Abraham, Isaac, Jacob, the Queen of Sheba, Abel, Zechariah, and Lot — standing on the side of the Q folk and their cause. And, as Hartin points out, so intent is the Q^2 material on underscoring "this generation's" rejection of the preaching of Jesus, John, and their followers, that it never gives a clear indication of what that message was. One can see quickly how dramatically the rhetorical posture has shifted, from the hortatory stance of the Q^1 material to the fundamentally defensive stance of Q^2. As a means of defining and sharpening the imaginative boundaries between "us" and "them," Q^2 attacks opponents and characterizes Jesus and his associates by invoking Sophia and her prophetic cohort.

This raises the important question of who is the "us" and who is the "them." A generation of mainly literary approaches to Q dwelt on the language of Q's opposition to "this generation," which was identified by Lührmann and others, including Jacobson and myself, as "Israel." The basis for this identification is clear: various configurations of sayings in Q produce the impression that Q's opposition is not simply to the Pharisees, or some other group, but to a larger entity. Many have pointed out, for example, that whereas most of the woes are directed rather locally against the Pharisees, Q 11:49–51 shifts its complaint and threat to a less well defined but clearly larger group, "this generation." Similarly, the complex found in Q 7:1–10, 18–28, 31–35, while it perhaps emerged from rather local conflict, is now framed by a story that contrasts Israel with Gentiles and concludes with a complaint against this broad and diffuse group, "this generation." Given these (among other) features, it is easy to see the justification for Lührmann's conclusion that for Q, the repentance of Israel was no longer envisaged; only judgment awaited it.

It is important, however, not to confuse rhetoric with social description. Horsley, in his essay for this volume and elsewhere (Horsley 1991c), has pleaded for a view of Q as arising from the struggles of the nonelite of northern Israelite society against the elite. He has proposed alternate readings of various features of Q, in particular, the phrase "this generation" and *krinein* in 22:28–30, that are at wide variance with the usual readings (1991b, 191–92, 196). One may, in fact, turn a sympathetic ear to what Horsley says of Q 22:28–30, especially as it circulated — if it circulated — independently prior to its incorporation into Q. "Sitting on thrones" and "judging the twelve tribes" are perhaps not to be taken as references to judgment but to governance. In the *literary* context created by Q, however, it is not so easy to read 22:28–30 in this way. For it is set alongside the Queen of the South and the men of Nineveh who stand up and *condemn* (*katakrinei*) this generation in the *judgment* (*en tē krisei*) (11:31–32) and alongside the terrifying specter of destruction and sundering of bonds that will occur at the Day of the Son of Man (Q 17:23–37). Little noticed, but even more ominous, is the characterization of that judgment that is given in the parables of the returning master (Q 12:42–46) and the entrusted money (Q 19:12–27) (see Kloppenborg 1995a). Finally, if Arnal's argument (in this volume) is sustained, that Q 3:7–9 is the contribution of the framers of Q^2, the motif of judgment and destruction is rendered even more prominent. Thus *to krinein,* for Q, will not be restoration or renewal but a swift judgment by forces and rules that lie beyond human calculation and control.

Does this mean that the earlier, rather naive descriptions of Q's social setting are to be followed? I think not, for it would be illegitimate simply to read Q's ostensible description of its opponents as a description of its actual situation. Q's rhetoric must be read against a plausible rhetorical situation (see Bitzer 1968). A key part of this situation is the relatively disadvantaged position of the Q people vis-à-vis their opponents, the Pharisees (Mack 1988a, 626; Kloppenborg 1991, 97). As Q 11:39–51 grudgingly admits, the Pharisees can command the best seats in the synagogues; they offer opinions on taxation that are serious enough to invite Q's criticism; and they take an active and public role in memorialization of the prophets. The Pharisees are in a position to define what "Israel" is and how Israel should act. Simply put, they have access to institutional and intellectual resources that the Q people evidently lack. Hence, Q's posture in the woes is one of lampoon or burlesque rather than direct argument *inter pares* — only Matthew will begin to act in this way as he depicts Jesus besting the Pharisees with their own style of argument.

Given the social location of the Q people relative to their opponents, and given the signs of disenfranchisement and disillusionment to which both Reed and Piper point, it is not unexpected that Q's rhetorical posture focuses on an attack on "this generation" or "Israel." This is no more an attack on all Israel than is the Fourth Gospel's polemic against "the Jews." Q attacks those persons who are in an institutional and social position to define and command allegiances precisely by attacking the security and certainty of their primary symbol. Hence, "Israel" and kinship to Abraham are undermined; Gentiles, fiery destruction, stones-become-Abraham's-kin, and even pious Roman officers are brought onto the stage in order to destabilize the opponents. Not that the opponents probably ever heard any of Q's rhetoric. It is for internal consumption, but a key part in Q's efforts to command assent for its own ethic and symbols is the displacement of more dominant values.

Hence, without ignoring the careful analysis of Lührman and the *literary* conclusions he, and others after him, drew, it is possible to read Q's rhetoric within the context of local conflict over particular visions of life in Galilee.

NOTE

1. For a summary, see Kloppenborg 1993, 12–21.

Part I

The Social Map of Q

The Social Map of Q

> I don't know whether you have ever seen a map of a person's mind.
> —J. M. Barrie, *Peter and Wendy* (1912)

"Doctors sometimes draw maps of other parts of you," so J. M. Barrie launches into his fantastic adventure, "...but catch them trying to draw a map of a child's mind, which is not only confused, but keeps going round all the time. There are zigzag lines on it, just like your temperature on a card." The map of Q's geographical and topographical references is not only confused and dizzy but, like the child's mind, troublesome to draw. It is a place where east and west, north and south, meet. Its landscape has mountains, fields, and pastures where wolves stalk lambs. A fox's hole and a bird's nest are visible from the many roads that traverse this land, and one must be ever careful of the brood of vipers out in the wilderness. There are both arid places and torrential floods that can sweep away houses. The cities and villages that dot the landscape — Capernaum, Tyre, Chorazin, and Jerusalem, to name a few — contain a temple, markets, royal palaces, courts, and prisons. Inside, centurions, tax collectors, Pharisees, and sinners converge. Yet homely peasant scenes are also etched onto this map: vineyards, millstones, and barns offer a bucolic repose from the hustle of the city.

This map of place-names and spatial references could scarcely serve as a guide to the itinerary of Jesus' public ministry. The nine different place-names in Q hardly provide a sufficiently representative sample for such a description. Rather than focusing on the historical Jesus, the goal of this study is to examine the place-names and spatial references in Q in order to determine the locale

Jonathan L. Reed is assistant professor of religion at the University of La Verne, La Verne, California.

of the Q community. This study will suggest that the community behind Q should be located in Galilee. The place-names in Q point to Capernaum as an important site to the Q community, and Q's combination of agricultural, rural, and urban imagery makes good sense in a Galilean environment not just for the historical Jesus, but for the Q community as well.

The geographical names and topographical descriptions in Q provide the starting point for a study of the Q community's locale.[1] While the place-names and spatial references in Q refer back to Jesus' activities and are placed on the lips of Jesus, the Q community nevertheless selected the sayings, omitted others, ordered the sequence of materials, embellished some sayings to stress a point, updated other sayings to address a need, and even imagined new sayings or events to fill a void.

Among place-names and spatial references in Q, some do not appear indicative of actual places members of the Q community lived in or visited, while others do. Some place-names in Q are only part of the imaginative world of the framers of Q, while others are part of their real world. Together, both the real and imagined places mentioned in Q make up the *social map* of the community behind Q. This social map shared by the Q community is reflected in the text of Q and can be analyzed and sifted for clues to the actual location of the Q community.

A social map is a community's shared symbolic system of spatial and social orientation (Downs and Stea 1973, 9; Lynch 1973, 303). Contemporary theorists of geography have stressed the social activity at work in the perception of places where people live or wish to live.[2] Every "place" is endowed with social meaning and is much more than a point at which two coordinates intersect — places are centers of meaning, and each place has a particular character to members of any given community (Downs and Meyer 1978, 61). The mention of Jerusalem in the lament in Q 13:34–35 provides an example: here Jerusalem is not merely the capital of Judaea, nor the city perched along the Kidron Valley, nor even that point in Palestine where thirty-one degrees north latitude and thirty-five degrees east longitude intersect. Rather Jerusalem is personified as a character in the Q community's reading of Israel's epic.

The medley of meanings attached to any particular place differs, of course, among individuals. Historically Jerusalem can be seen as the city of both David and Jezebel, as the stronghold that both thwarted Sargon and was crushed by Nebuchadnezzar, and as the pulpit both for Jeremiah and for Zedekiah. Each group makes its own selection from this medley — a Hasmonean aristocrat would not share the same mental pastiche of Jerusalem with a recently circumcised Idumean, and neither would share that of a Galilean. Each individual's social map would be different, based on his or her social group and geographical locale, or home. It is, in fact, the home around which all other places are oriented in a community's social map.[3] The surrounding landscape and more remote places are described in relation to the home.[4] The landscape of each person's social map is a social construct, explicitly and implicitly learned by each member of the group (Gould and White 1974, 52; Lynch 1973, 303). Social maps thus transcend personal idiosyncrasies and "become symbols shared by many" (Downs and Meyer 1978, 71). It is possible, therefore, to examine traces of a community's social map in its traditions and texts in order to learn more about that group's worldview and to locate the home from which this group views the world.

Unfortunately, the numerous examinations of place-names or topographical references in early Christian literature have only anecdotally addressed the question of locating a text and have by and large failed to distinguish the real world of a community from the community's social map.[5] Often geographical references in early Christian texts are studied via a cartographic comparison to see if authors give an accurate geographical description.[6] This strict empirical approach neglects, as Y.-F. Tuan has noted, that in literary texts, "settings are intimately woven with human moods and behavior.... When we study the writings of Joyce and Faulkner [and Q could be added here], we should attend to these intimate pacts between persons and setting rather than isolate the setting with the purpose of seeing whether a particular street or river is accurately located."[7]

John S. Kloppenborg, with his seminal essay "City and Wasteland: Narrative World and the Beginning of the Sayings Gospel (Q)," deserves credit as the first to address the subject of Q's portrayal of a spatial setting directly, rather than casually (Kloppenborg 1990a, 145–60). Focusing on how the technical phrase "the region of the Jordan" in Q 3:3 establishes a "story world" in Q, Kloppenborg distinguishes between the "narrative world" in Q and the real world of the Q community. He concludes that Q's ethos is "quite compatible with the perspective of villagers in agrarian societies" (Kloppenborg 1990a, 155). Unfortunately, this nebulous description is applicable to most of Palestine, the Levant, and the rest of the Roman Empire. While Kloppenborg stresses the creation of a narrative world by the forces behind Q and tries to describe the narrative world's importance to their overall theology, there is, in fact, little evidence for a consciously created narrative world in Q. Q lacks a grand literary design with a concomitant narrative world to move the plot along. None of the place-names or spatial references is strategically placed to alter the mood as one reads through Q, nor do they move the plot along, nor do they create an imaginary setting. Therefore Q's configuration of place-names and spatial images should not be seen as a literary narrative world but should be seen as a reflection of the Q community's social map, which is unconsciously reflected in the text and from which a locale for the Q community can be made more precise.

An examination of the spatial references in the narrative sections of Q reveals the lack of any coherent auctorial or editorial design. John appears *ex nihilo*, as it were, surrounded by "all the region of the Jordan" in Q 3:3.[8] After the Baptist material, Q 4:1 opens the next scene with Jesus being led up into "the wilderness."[9] This is the only proper spatial connection between pericopae in Q that indicates movement from one place to another. The wilderness is, in terms of altitude, "up" (*ana*) from the Jordan rift valley. But the verb *anagō* in connection with the wilderness or interior of a country is commonplace in Greek: based on the spatial imagination that the coastal strip of the Mediterranean littoral, along with certain river arteries or lake shores, constituted the civilized world, movement to the interior "wilderness" regions was thought of as requiring ascension.[10] After the opening scene in the desert, there is a double change of scene in the temptation story: Jesus is transported into Jerusalem (Q 4:9)[11] and then to a place from which he can see all the kingdoms of the world.[12] The next and final spatial reference in a narrative section occurs in Q 7:1 to introduce the story of the Capernaum centurion: "He entered Capernaum."[13]

The only other possible spatial reference outside of the sayings is in the occurrence of the oddly spelled Nazareth ("Nazara") found in both Luke 4:16 and Matt 4:13.[14] The uncertainty of the syntax at this point in Q highlights the lack of any coordinated spatial movement by the framers of Q. Had Q been arranged with a coordinated sense of spatial movement in its sequence, then the position and significance of "Nazara" would be clearer. But there is no sense of movement in terms of a narrative plot in Q: John simply appears preaching in the regions of the Jordan; Jesus is tempted in the wilderness, then delivers the sermon, then enters Capernaum; then another series of his speeches appear.

In contrast to Mark's characterization, Q's slim narrative elements show no interest in an itinerant or mobile Jesus; indeed, the narrative sections of Q give the impression of a sedentary Jesus: the few verbs of movement after Jesus enters Capernaum have John sending his disciples to Jesus (Q 7:19), John's disciples departing from Jesus (Q 7:24),[15] and a questioner coming to Jesus (Q 9:57).[16]

Q's meager narrative sections present a relatively sedentary existence for Jesus in a specific region. Since the few narrative sections of Q are obviously the work of the Q community and cannot be placed on the historical Jesus' lips, they present by inference a likely locale for the Q community. Jesus actively ministers only in Galilee, specifically Capernaum. The other places where Jesus appears lie outside of Galilee: the wilderness and Jerusalem, but both are places to which he is brought. The Holy Spirit leads Jesus to the wilderness, and the devil brings him to Jerusalem.

The distribution of Q's place-names in the sayings material of Q confirms the importance of Capernaum to the Q community and also suggests the environs around Capernaum as the locale of the Q community. If plotted out on a map, the nine different place-names in the sayings material form a set of three concentric circles converging on Capernaum (Q 10:15). Within a short radius from Capernaum are Chorazin and Bethsaïda (Q 10:13). Another concentric circle is formed by the twin cities of Tyre and Sidon to the north (Q 10:13–14) and Jerusalem to the south (Q 13:34). The final concentric circle forms the mythical boundaries of the Q community's social map: the epic city of Sodom to the extreme south (Q 10:12) and the epic city of Nineveh to the extreme north (Q 11:32).

Capernaum is at the center of attention in the woes pronounced on the unrepentant cities (Q 10:15). Bethsaïda and Chorazin, a small city and a village within walking distance of Capernaum at the northern end of the Sea of Galilee, are also targets of the Q community's invective (Q 10:13–14). These three places distinguish themselves from the other six places in Q by the vehemence of their condemnation and by their otherwise anonymity in antiquity (Sato 1988, 198). Israel, Sodom, Tyre and Sidon, Nineveh, and Jerusalem can each claim an important role in the Israelite epic imagination, and they can each boast a long literary pedigree in

the Hebrew Bible as well as in other Graeco-Roman and ancient
Near Eastern texts. But Chorazin, Bethsaïda, and Capernaum lack
such repute. They were, however, judging by the acerbic rhetorical tone of their condemnation and by their incorporation into the
form of a woe oracle, still very important to the Q community.[17]
The three villages' continued significance to the Q community is reinforced in the striking past, contrary-to-fact, conditional phrase:
"Because if the miracles done in you had been done in Tyre and
Sidon, they would have repented long ago, sitting in sack cloth
and ashes" (Q 10:13). The "miracles" alleged to have occurred in
Chorazin and Bethsaïda occurred some time in the past, and the
"long ago" (*palai*) indicates that the community has had to put
up with these villages' obstinacy for some time.[18] Capernaum is
singled out for special condemnation and thus ranks as the most
significant of these three villages to the Q community.[19]

The coastal twin cities of Tyre and Sidon to the north and Jerusalem to the south form the next concentric circle.[20] The choice
to juxtapose Tyre and Sidon with Bethsaïda and Chorazin in Q
10:13–14 — designed to humiliate them — is of considerable significance. As gentile cities,[21] Tyre and Sidon were scorned by the
Israelite prophets, but never as frequently as Egypt, Assyria, or
Babylon, nor any more than other city-states or small countries.
Yet from the a Galilean perspective, Tyre and Sidon were not
merely relics of an epic imagination — they were still real cities in
close proximity to lower Galilee. The choice of Tyre and Sidon as
a contrast to Chorazin and Bethsaïda is not an arbitrary selection
from the Hebrew prophets. These twin cities are precisely what
one would expect a lower Galilean group to select: they are the
closest gentile cities that are part of their past epic traditions and
that are still part of their present social and economic situation.[22]
The majority of coins used in Galilee during the first century bore
the Tyrian imprint — these coins were a daily reminder of Tyre's
economic influence in Galilee.

Significantly, Jerusalem occurs in only one verse in the sayings
material of Q. The double vocative of Q 13:34 begins the lament
over Jerusalem.[23] The tone and perspective of the lament reveal
a certain distance from the city of Jerusalem itself: this distance
has been noted in cosmic terms of the "supra-historical entity" of
the speaker (Bultmann 1968, 114) or described in temporal terms
of the rejection of Jesus' message and messengers as a remote fait
accompli (Sato 1988, 159–60). But this distance perceived by com-

mentators can also be explained in terms of the spatial distance between Jerusalem and the Q community. The oracle presents Jerusalem as a distant, spiritually barren city. There is no illusion of Jerusalem holding a central place in the social map of the framers of Q. It is now,[24] and always has been,[25] a pretentious city.[26] This oracle challenges Jerusalem's claim, implicitly mentioned in 35a, that it houses the divine presence and is the focal point of sacred geography. Indeed, the Q community explicitly states that Jerusalem is forsaken, that it is deserted.[27] Despite the rejection of Judaean claims, the relative disinterest in Jerusalem in Q must be stressed. It is explicitly mentioned only twice: in the temptation and here in the lament.[28] Q ironically points out that Jerusalem's rejection renders its claims to religious centrality even more farcical, but Jerusalem is not singled out as the Q community's primary antagonist, which is more broadly described as "this generation" and which can be found in any city.

The final concentric circle, at the farthest radius from Capernaum, consists of Sodom to the far south and Nineveh to the far north. Nineveh is more remote geographically than Sodom, but in antiquity distances were not measured in miles but by the availability of eyewitness information. From this perspective, both cities are on the periphery of Q's social map, a place where reality blurs with fantasy. The city of Sodom, if it existed at all, was long gone by the time of the Q community. The city of Nineveh, though it still existed, no longer had a social, political, or economic connection with the Galilee of the Q community. These two places are invoked because of their mythical character — they are places unseen by the Q community and hence can serve flat, symbolic roles in its social map: Nineveh is the wicked gentile city that repented,[29] and Sodom is the inhospitable city that was destroyed. Both mythical places are used to shame "this generation," identified elsewhere in Q as Israel (Q 7:9 and 22:30).[30] And one would think that "Israel" was more preferable to Galileans than the more southern designation "Judaean" (*Ioudaioi*), which does not occur in Q at all.[31]

The use of distant ethnic groups to shame one's own group is a common topos in literature of the Graeco-Roman period. Many geographical writers envisioned an "inverse ethnocentric" scheme, in which peoples become more virtuous in proportion to their distance from the author's place of writing, which becomes the target of moral shame.[32] In Q their extreme distance from the community's locale gives the Ninevite and Sodomite — not the Ethiopian or Hyperborean as in Strabo — license to mock the people in the interior, in this case Israel. The twofold "something greater... is here" (*kai idou pleion... hōde* [Q 11:31–32]) in this pericope on the sign of Jonah places the focal point of Q's imaginative world not on Jerusalem but on Jesus. Incidentally, Jonah was not only a northern prophet: he was from Gath-Hepher in Galilee, a site only two miles northeast of Nazareth.[33] The juxtaposition of Jesus and Jonah is therefore particularly appropriate for Q, if read in its Galilean context.

An overview of the place-names in Q highlights the centrality of lower Galilee: at the extremities lie the mythical cities of Sodom and Nineveh, the former to the far south, the latter to the far north; closer to the center lie the twin cities of Tyre and Sidon to the north and Jerusalem in the south; finally, centered around the hub of Capernaum lie the villages of Bethsaïda and Chorazin. The relative lateness of each of the sayings in which place-names occur demonstrates the community's involvement in the selection of place-names and in the shaping of the sayings themselves. Because the place-names all belong to a later stage of Q's development, they are indicative of the Q community's social map, and as was the case with Q's narrative material, not simply reminiscences of Jesus' activities.[34]

If, based on the spatial references in the narrative traditions, the place-names in the sayings material, Q, and the Q community are placed in Galilee, then the amalgamation of images and metaphors from agricultural, rural, natural, and urban life makes sense. Agricultural metaphors pervade Q's sayings from beginning to end. At the outset, John the Baptist scorches his audience with the plea to "bear fruit worthy of repentance," "for the axe is at the root" (Q 3:8–9), and the Coming One with his winnowing fork will clear the threshing floor, put the grain in the silo, but burn the chaff (Q 3:17). Q's Jesus also employs agricultural imagery: the standard measure, customary in produce markets of agrarian economies (*metron* [Q 6:38]); healthy trees bearing good fruit (figs and grapes), rotten trees bearing bad fruit (Q 6:43–44); and the plowing of fields (Q 9:62).[35] The mission speech begins by comparing Jesus' followers to workers at harvest time: "The harvest is large, but the workers are few" (Q 10:2). Other allusions to agriculture dot the sayings of Jesus: grain baskets for storing grain (*modios* [Q 11:33]);[36] spices easily grown on small plots of land (Q

11:42);[37] field hay used for cheap fuel (Q 12:28); grain of mustard seeds and small plots or gardens (Q 13:19; 17:6); cultivated fields (Q 14:18); the salting of dunghills (Q 14:35); millstones (Q 17:2); a sycamine tree (Q 17:6);[38] and people milling grain together (Q 17:35).

With this high density of agricultural images, it is no wonder that Q, the Q community, not to mention Jesus himself, has frequently been located in an entirely rural environment in Galilee.[39] But agriculture was the basis of the entire Roman economy and the primary industry of even the largest provincial cities. We should not, as our awareness of Galilee's urbanization rises, equate urbanization with a decrease in agriculture (Reed 1994a, 47–94; see also D. Edwards 1992, 65–66). The opposite is true: as an area is urbanized, it must develop a more extensive and more efficient agriculture. Douglas Edwards is correct when he writes of the importance of agriculture to the ancient economy in general that "agricultural images in the New Testament, therefore, may neither prove nor disprove a rural provenance" (D. Edwards 1988, 170). This is the case, certainly, in Q.

Only a portion of the agricultural images in Q are associated with activities that take place or items that exist in rural areas outside of the city walls: cutting down trees (Q 3:8–9), winnowing and burning of chaff (Q 3:17), field hay (Q 12:28), fields (Q 9:62[?]; 14:18), salting dung hills (Q 14:35), and sycamine trees (Q 17:6). Each of these activities or items, however, can be imagined in close proximity to either of Galilee's two major cities, Sepphoris and Tiberias, or the major villages of Galilee, such as Capernaum. Furthermore, numerous agricultural items cited in Q can be associated with the larger villages and cities themselves. Granaries are mentioned in Q 3:17 and Q 12:24 — sizable granaries have been excavated in Sepphoris, and Tiberias also would have contained storage facilities for grain. The standard measure is mentioned in Q 6:38 and 11:33 — measures were used mainly in a market setting to buy, sell, distribute, or tax seed or grain, and Sepphoris and Tiberias had the major agoras in Galilee, where the *agoranomos* regulated weights and measures for the entire region (Meshorer 1986; Qedar 1986–87, 29–30). Various spices and seeds are mentioned in Q 11:42; 13:18; and 7:6 — seeds were commonly on sale at markets, and spices could easily be grown in small gardens or pots in the city.[40] Milling grain with millstones is mentioned in Q 17:2 and 17:35 — millstones are ubiquitous in Galilee; excavations at sites of all sizes — Capernaum, as well as Sepphoris and Tiberias — have uncovered millstones.

There are even a series of clues in the agricultural images that betray a more urban perspective on agrarian practices. The phrasing of the mission speech, "Beg the lord of the harvest to send out [*ekbalē* (Q 10:2)] workers into his harvest," recalls the practice of the urban poor, who *went out* into the fields as day laborers in exchange for food during the harvest season.[41] While small farmers or peasants in hamlets would envision workers being brought out to the harvest, the phrase in Q betrays the perspective of those within a city or large village, who envision the harvest as a place to which one is "cast out."

An urban perspective can also be seen in the use of the impersonal passive to describe agricultural practices in Q. The impersonal passive is relatively rare in Greek (Moulton, Howard, and Turner 1963–85, 1:58–59; see also Robertson 1914, 820). In Q, there are only two occurrences: for the picking of fruit in Q 6:44, "They do not gather figs from thorns"; and for the salting of soil and dung hills in Q 14:35, "If salt becomes insipid, . . . they throw it away."[42] The use of the impersonal passive in only these two instances, describing agricultural practices of the countryside, is striking. The saying about figs and thorns ("*They* do not gather" [Q 6:44]) is surrounded by passages addressing the audience with the second person: "Why do *you* see the speck that is in your brother's eye . . . ?" (Q 6:41–42) precedes it, and it is followed by "Why do *you* call me 'Lord, Lord'?" (Q 6:46). The saying on savorless salt, using the impersonal passive "*They* throw it out," is preceded by a saying on the conditions of discipleship, "*Who-ever* finds his life . . ." (Q 17:33), and is followed by a parable that is personalized with Matthew's second-person address: "What do *you* think?"[43] Thus while Q tends to personalize its parables or sayings with the second-person form or address, the only time that the impersonal passive is used is for agrarian practices of the countryside, activities that "they" do.

In addition to these agricultural images, there are also specifically urban images or metaphors in Q.[44] The very word "city" (*polis*) occurs at least three times in Q (Q 11:8, 11). Also mentioned are royal palaces (Q 7:25); marketplaces (Q 7:32; 11:43); plazas (Q 10:10; 13:26; 14:21);[45] a collection of rooftops (Q 12:3); judges and prisons (Q 12:57–59); a city gate (*pylē* [Q 13:24]);[46] city banquets (Q 14:16–24);[47] and banks (*trapeza* [Q 19:23]).[48]

The mission speech assumes that the followers of Jesus will go to cities (Q 10:8–11), where the Q community expects to encounter resistance. Elsewhere two specifically urban institutions are portrayed as the forum for the Q community's encounter with opposition: the agora and courts.[49] Q 7:31–35 links the opposition to both Jesus and John to the marketplace or agora. This generation, considered the opponent by the Q community, is compared to children seated in the agora, playing the flute and singing dirges, with which both John the Baptist and Jesus are out of step (Q 7:32). The imagery in this passage points to the scene one would expect at the vibrant agora of Sepphoris or Tiberias: it is a place where children sit and play, hire their musical services for parties or dirges, where ascetics, gluttons, drunks, tax collectors, and sinners pass through.[50]

The agora is also the locale where the Q community caricatures Pharisaic behavior (Q 11:43). The Pharisees are caricatured as eager to climb the social hierarchy at banquets, synagogues, and in the agora as well. They "love ... greetings in the marketplace" (Q 11:43). In Q, the conflict between the Pharisees and the Q community does not have its primary locus in the synagogue, which is only mentioned here. Rather the conflict between the Pharisees and the Q community seems to be located in an urban setting, at banquets and in the marketplace, and focuses on social status. In several of the woes, banquet and market imagery reappears in the criticism of the Pharisees: in the preparation of cups and dishes prior to eating (Q 11:39–41), in the loading up of goods or merchandise (Q 11:46), and in the setting aside of purchased spices (Q 11:42). The agora in Q is a place of tension and opposition, implying that in the everyday life of the Q community, the agora was frequented.

Q also reflects a concern to avoid another urban institution, the judicial system. Although justice could be meted out on a local level in rural areas, the judicial concerns in Q reflect more formal issues to be resolved at a higher level, such as the courts of Sepphoris and Tiberias: suits, litigation, judges, prisons, magistrates, and rulers. Ronald Piper (chap. 4, below) has pointed out the concern to avoid litigation present in Q 6:27–36, and a cluster of sayings in Q 12 reinforces the vulnerability felt by the Q group toward the courts. The question of how to deal with judicial institutions is acute in Q, and Q's answer, couched in the language of legal and contractual procedures, seems to be: "Avoid the courts at all costs" (p. 60, below).

This advice is explicit in Q 12:57–59, which concludes a cluster of sayings showing the judicial vulnerability perceived by the Q community: settle quickly with a plaintiff, or he'll hand you over to the judge, the judge to the bailiff, and the bailiff will throw you in prison. The view of justice is somber: "You will not get out of there until you have paid your last penny" (Q 12:59). Q 12:4–7 encourages followers of Jesus not to fear those able to kill the body but not the soul, a theme carried over in the exhortation to fearless confession (Q 12:8–9) and in the warning against blasphemy of the spirit (Q 12:10). Members of the Q community are furthermore encouraged not to worry when they are brought before rulers and magistrates (Q 12:11–12),[51] which demonstrates that the courts were not viewed from a distance — they were part of the real world of the Q community.

If the scope is broadened beyond these two urban features, the market and the courts, then dissatisfaction with urbanization in general can be seen in the recurring theme in Q of "going out" as the first step to belief.[52] John's message of repentance is first encountered in the wilderness region of the Jordan (Q 3:2), and those coming out to hear him are said to have fled to him (Q 3:7). The same idea is repeated in Q 7:24–26 with the repeated rhetorical question, "What did you go out to see?" John is found outside the cities in the wilderness, and he is explicitly contrasted with the urban elites, luxuriously clothed and living in palaces. If the "shaken reed" refers to Herod Antipas's numismatic emblem, then he is the one luxuriously dressed, and the city under attack is Tiberias, his new capital (Theissen 1991, 26–42 = Theissen 1985). Salvation outside the city is also a theme in the banquet parable in Q 14:16–24. The servant in the banquet parable, after the wealthy urbanites rebuff the invitation, is told to go outside the city to invite guests (Q 14:21, 23).[53]

The particular amalgamation of urban imagery in Q provides considerable information about the Q community's perception of the city. None of the amenities that urban life offered, such as the baths or the theater, appears in Q. Although Q betrays an awareness of the city, the Q community does not seem to have scaled the social hierarchy of the city very high. Rather, the blend of images portrays a familiarity with those features of and places in the city open to the lower classes and those coming from outside the city: gates, plazas, streets, the agora, banks, and, in the worst case, courts and prisons.[54]

The marketplace and courts, indeed the city as a whole, were perceived with considerable tension by the Q community. Q also presents an anxious image of the civilized order as a whole: one can fall from the height of temples (Q 4:9); houses can be swept away by torrential floods if not built properly (Q 6:48); roofs are not worthy to cover Jesus (Q 7:6); divided houses collapse (Q 11:17); houses can be plundered if not guarded (Q 11:21–22); demons call their abodes "houses" (Q 11:24); murderers build tombs (Q 11:48); the inner temple is filled with blood (Q 11:51); and the home is particularly vulnerable to crime at night (Q 11:39–40).

The need to flee the city and apprehension of civilized life are complemented in Q's social map by an appreciation of nature as the arena for divine disclosure.[55] While, in addition to the tension associated with the city and urban features, Q tends to ascribe to the civilized order danger, chaos, and an absence of the divine, floral and faunal symbols are often used to illustrate Q's positive message. Q tends to ascribe to these aspects of the natural order a sense of comfort, serenity, and divine revelation.

Images from nature are frequently embraced to express Q's vision. Nature is preferred as a simple, serene, and orderly arena: God can raise up children to Abraham from rocks (Q 3:8); trees are praised for their honesty — you can tell them by their fruit (Q 6:44); Jesus even surpasses foxes and birds in their need for a dwelling place (Q 9:58); the simplicity and natural beauty of ravens, lilies, and grass are models for self-sufficiency (Q 12:22–32); meteorological phenomena can be plainly read (Q 12:54–56); and the biological growth of plants is compared to the kingdom of God (Q 13:18–19).

Many of Q's passages bear a striking resemblance to the bucolic aspects of many Roman authors, who as Rome grew in the late republic and Augustan era began to praise the virtues of rural life and the countryside.[56] As Rome expanded, and as Augustus erected more facades and constructed more buildings, numerous authors in Rome struck a chorus on the moral superiority of the rural life, with its nearness to nature.[57] Their turn to nature must be understood in terms of their frustrations with life in Rome.

While I am in no way suggesting a genealogical relationship between such Roman texts and Q, the bucolic Roman poets and authors, by analogy, help us understand parts of Q as a reaction to urbanization in Galilee — on an admittedly minuscule scale.[58] Like these bucolic Roman poets and authors, Q perceives the city or even civilized society from a tense and anxious perspective. It is a dangerous place where hostilities are encountered. This perspective fits the cultural developments of Galilee in the first century C.E. It was during this time that Galilee was subject to urbanization, with Sepphoris and Tiberias being built in its midst.[59]

To summarize: an analysis of the place-names in Q strongly suggests the importance of Capernaum to the Q community; and the remaining place-names, especially Chorazin and Bethsaïda, the negative comparison with Tyre, and a suspicious view of Jerusalem confirm more broadly a Galilean perspective. The particular amalgamation of agricultural and urban imagery, especially the positive example of nature, makes good sense in the recently urbanized Galilee. Although I would not go so far as to locate the entire Q community in the cities of Sepphoris and Tiberias themselves based on the spatial imagery, contact with these cities — illustrated primarily in the market and judicial imagery — on the part of the Q community is certain. Although perhaps more likely at home in such larger Galilean villages as Capernaum, or other sites on the north shore of the lake, the Q community perceived the major cities of Galilee with some apprehension — because they were visited by the members of the Q community.

NOTES

1. Previous research on locating the Q community has analyzed Q's message in an effort to determine the locale from which such a message makes sense. See Mack 1988a, 608–35; Kloppenborg 1990a, 145–60. Kloppenborg suggests a geographical location for Q^1 in the urban sector among the petit bourgeois in the cities of Tiberias or Sepphoris or in the larger towns like Capernaum and Bethsaïda. His approach is, however, quite different than mine. Kloppenborg tries to locate Q^1 where a sufficiently dense scribal sector would have existed to create such sapiential instructions — the two key questions are thus literacy levels in Galilee (of Greek!) and the existence of a concomitant administrative infrastructure in Galilee. I do not seek to contradict Kloppenborg's findings but rather provide an alternative approach, beginning with the spatial references in Q themselves (as Horsley suggests, below, p. 42). On the question of literacy levels and Q, see Douglas's essay, below, p. 122.

2. For a convenient summary of the state of the discipline, see Downs and Meyer 1978. See also Trowbridge 1913; Lowenthal and Bowden 1976; Gould and White 1974; Lynch 1960. Jonathan Z. Smith has borrowed heavily from modern geographical theorists to stress the important

category of "place" in religious thought, ritual, and myth (Smith 1978; 1986, 25–26; 1987).

3. Trowbridge (1913) showed how people hold imaginary maps in their minds that revolve around their homes. See also Lynch 1960; Gould and White 1974, 28–44.

4. Though there are a variety of reference systems by which people orient themselves — egocentric, absolute, or solar — each has the primary function of orienting the home: to help people find their way home, to travel to establish a new home, to orient rooms or huts in a new home. Orientation systems help convert a place into a home. See Lynch 1973, esp. 304–7.

5. Many simply study the historical geography of each place mentioned in the New Testament (see Dalman 1924). Others focus on the literary use of place-names (see the early redaction-critical work of Schmidt 1919, 259–69). For recent studies on the Lukan travel narrative, see Moessner 1989, 21–44; for Mark, see Malbon 1986; Rhoads and Michie 1982, 140–42. Mark, as a literary narrative, is more difficult to locate since a single author has forged a narrative world in which the story takes place. Distinguishing those elements of the story's setting that are shaped by the plot from those elements that unconsciously emerge in the narrative from the author's mental map is a precarious venture.

6. C. C. McCown condemns Luke for his "geographical ineptitude" (1941, 15; see also McCown 1938, 51–66).

7. Tuan 1978, 202. Some literary studies follow this line of reasoning to an extreme and sever the literary text from its historical moorings. Structuralists and some new literary critics have opted out of historical concerns in favor of an understanding of the text as a literary phenomenon. The narrative world within a text has thus replaced the concern to place a text in its original location.

8. The *en tē erēmō* in Luke 3:2 and Matt 3:1 comes from Mark 1:4. But the *pasa hē perichōros tou Iordanou* / *pasan tēn perichōron tou Iordanou* likely derives from Q, though the syntax is uncertain, as Kloppenborg (1990a, 149–50) has convincingly argued; see also McCown 1940.

9. Shawn Carruth of the International Q Project correctly reconstructs Q 4:1 with the Matthean verb (*anēchthē*) and preposition (*eis*). The verb has its only occurrence here in Matthew, and Luke is responsible for shaping the introduction to depict Jesus in the wilderness, where he is guided by the Spirit.

10. See, for example, Herodotus's and Xenophon's descriptions of travels from the coast of Asia Minor into the interior (*An.* 2.6.1). *Anagein* also has the basic meaning "to embark on a journey," specifically of seafaring journeys (so Luke 8:22, and frequently in Acts).

11. Luke's *Hierousalēm* is the preferred reading (so the reconstructions by Harnack, Luz, Polag, Schenk, and Zeller), as opposed to Matthew's *tēn hagian polin*. Robert Gundry notes that the only other occurrence of this phrase in the Gospels is in Matt 27:51b–53, that is, the passage about "holy people" appearing to many in "the holy city" (Gundry 1982, 56). Jerusalem as a sort of Delphic navel is present in Luke's work, and had he encountered the designation *tēn hagian polin* here, he would have readily accepted it. But such a pious designation for Jerusalem is unthinkable from Q's perspective (see above, p. 23, and Horsley's essay in this volume).

12. Gundry (1982, 57) demonstrates how the *oros hypsēlon lian* is very likely Matthew's attempt to style Jesus along Mosaic lines — the vocabulary is also distinctly Matthean.

13. Wegner (1985, 126–27) identifies the Matthean genitive absolute as redactional: this form occurs only once in Q (7:24), and Matthew uses it frequently in this immediate setting (in Matt 8:5–10 as well as 8:1 and 8:28). Furthermore, Matthew could be carrying over the Markan genitive absolute from Mark 2:1 after inserting the cleansing of the leper in between the sermon and the reference to the centurion (Matt 8:1–4/Mark 1:40–45).

14. In a reconstruction of Q 4:16 presented to the International Q Project at New Orleans, November 1990 (see Robinson 1991, 495). Robinson suggests that Nazara probably should be included in Q. See also Robinson 1992b, 361–88.

15. Gundry (1982, 207) suggests that the Lukan *apelthontōn* is original and that Matthew changed the verb to *poreuomenōn* to "show exactness of obedience to Jesus' command (cf. v. 4, where *poreuthentes* occurred)."

16. The *en tē hodō* in Luke 9:57 is not in Q: Luke added it to harmonize with Jesus' alleged itinerancy expressed in the following saying; the *poreuomenōn* is part of Luke's redaction as well (see Bultmann 1968, 28).

17. Bultmann (1968, 112) notes that "we have here a community formulation, since the sayings look back on Jesus' activity as something already completed, and presuppose the failure of the Christian preaching in Capernaum." There are both redaction-critical and tradition-historical grounds for considering Q 10:13–15 as late (see Sato 1988, 199–200, 132; Lührmann 1969, 62–63; and Uro 1987, 110–16).

18. The gospel traditions record no miracles in Chorazin. The miracle occurs only here in Q 10:13. Bethsaïda is also said to be the hometown of Philip, Andrew, and Peter (John 1:44; 12:21) and is where Jesus is said to have healed those in need of cures (Luke 9:10–12). He also is said to have traveled there (Mark 6:45) and even to have healed a man outside of the city (Mark 8:22–23).

19. The composition of the mission speech may seem to suggest that the Q tradents were evicted from Chorazin, Bethsaïda, and Capernaum,

since it links an early kernel of the speech "to shake off the dust from your feet as you leave that city" with the condemnation of the three cities. But the early kernel of the mission speech and the woes against the Galilean cities represent two distinct concerns; the mission represents earlier instructions concerning itinerant preachers, while the woes represent a later communal rationalization of rejection. One should not infer that the advice to itinerants would have been literally followed at a later date by the whole community. Uro (1987, 241–44, esp. 242) has cautioned against identifying the early itinerants with the community as a whole, to whom the later redactors of the Sayings Gospel cater: "The author has used an earlier collection including mission orders, but, as his redaction shows, his primary concern is the situation of the rank-and-file members of the community."

20. Tyre (forty miles) is roughly half the distance that Jerusalem (eighty miles) is from Capernaum. Even Sidon (fifty miles) is closer to Capernaum than Jerusalem. Commentators do not mention the cities' proximity to Galilee but cite exclusively the Hebrew Bible as determinative of Q's source (see Lührmann 1969, 62–63; Sato 1988, 199; Uro 1987, 163–64).

21. The distinction of Gentiles as "other" is apparent in several Q texts: the explicit reference to *ta ethnē* in Q 12:30; the contrast of Israel with the centurion in Q 7:1–10; and Q 13:28–30 are prominent examples (see Jacobson 1982, 365–89). At times in Q Gentiles (those outside) are portrayed more favorably than Israel (those on the inside): in Q 11:31 the Queen of the South is favorably depicted since she came from the corners of the earth. In Q 13:29, people are described as coming from the east and west, the north and south to the eschatological banquet, while Q's intended audience will be locked out.

22. Contra Sato (1988, 199 n. 283), who describes the criteria of selection as "the Gentiles of the past (Tyre, Sidon, the Queen of the South, the Ninevites)." Sato's limitation of his investigation to a diachronic study, linking Q with the Hebrew Bible, is apparent.

23. The rut of previous scholarship on the lament runs deep; for a discussion of the relevant issues and bibliography, see Steck 1967, 40–58.

24. Note the present indicative of *aphietai*. Sato (1988, 157) awkwardly suggests that the context implies an eschatological-future sense to the present *aphietai,* despite the fact that this tense is a rare exception to the usual *hnnh* + imperfect/future of the Hebrew Bible's announcements of judgment. But Sato (1988, 158) correctly notes the pessimism in this oracle with regard to the possibility of Jerusalem's repentance: "Whoever wants to hear something hopeful in this sentence doesn't take seriously the painful lament 'Jerusalem, Jerusalem,' and its genre."

25. The present participles in Q 13:34a portray Jerusalem as continually, throughout history, having rejected the advances of YHWH or divine Wisdom. The aorists of *ēthelēsa* and *ēthelēsate* are significant in that these

advances came to an end some time ago, pointing to the late redactional date of this saying.

26. Steck (1967) has outlined the features and development of the Deuteronomistic view of history within texts of the second temple period and has shown that the theme serves either in rationalizing a recent catastrophe (such as 722, 586, or 167 B.C.E.) or in using a past catastrophe to inspire a repentant attitude in the present. But in Q 13:34–35 the theme of the rejected prophets is used simply to condemn Jerusalem.

27. In light of the contrast set up between the wilderness and the city (see Kloppenborg 1990a), the *erēmos* of Matthew may well be Q's reading. The quotation *eulogēmenos ho erchomenos en onomati kyrios* (Ps 117:26 [LXX]), which had been resignified as an acclamation of the priests to the pilgrims at the Feast of Booths (*m. Sukk.* 3.9), was added to mock the Jerusalemite religious activities: until Jesus and his message are recognized, the priests' performances will ring hollow.

28. Implicitly Jerusalem is also in mind in the description of bloodshed in the temple in Q 11:51, but Jerusalem is hardly the "focus of unbelief and non-acceptance" (Kloppenborg 1990a, 154).

29. It should be noted that Nineveh and the allusions to the Jonah stories are distinctly northern Israelite traditions and are hence an appropriate choice for Galileans. In fact, virtually all of the epic figures in Q date to before the divided kingdom (Abel, Jacob, and Isaac [13:28]; Solomon [11:31]; Abraham [12:27]; Noah [17:26–27]; Jonah [11:29–32]; Zechariah [11:51]); there is no David, who founded Jerusalem (Matt 12:23 is Matthean), and no Moses. Nor are they particularly Judaean: Isaiah is for the poor, critical of Judaea, and Solomon is a negative example — richly dressed but not as nice as the flowers; see Horsley's comments on Q as part of a renewal of Israel in Galilee (below, p. 45).

30. "This generation" occurs in minimal Q at 7:31; 11:29, 31, 32, 51. There are no redactional clues to suggest that Q 22:28–30 is late since it coheres well thematically with the previous two sections (Lührmann 1969, 75) and does not seem to be redactionally connected with them. I presume only on tradition-historical grounds that it is late.

31. The *presbyterous tōn Ioudaiōn* in Q 7:3 is certainly Lukan. Surprisingly, Wegner (1985, 166) considers Lukan redaction here only "not impossible," in spite of the fact that *Ioudaiōn* would be a hapax legomenon in Q.

32. Romm 1992, 47. Considered from this perspective, Horsley might be right: the use of Gentiles in Q might be primarily to shame Israel and is not an announcement of a gentile mission (see Horsley, below, p. 38).

33. Gal (1992, 18) notes that the site was continuously inhabited from the Iron Age through the Roman period.

34. Each of the place-names in the sayings has been assigned to Q^2 by Kloppenborg 1991, 101 n. 1.

35. If Luke 9:61–62 is Q. For the arguments, see Kloppenborg 1988, 64.

36. The *modios* was also a common dry unit of measure, and not only a device for storage (see Plutarch, *Demetr.* 33). Ulrich Luz has refuted Joachim Jeremias's claim, based on a cursory reading of Strack-Billerbeck's citations, that the *modios* was a common device used to put out lamps (Jeremias 1966, 102). The *modios* was, rather, a ubiquitous item — in agrarian settings — chosen to highlight the absurdity of the illustration (Luz 1985, 221, esp. n. 12).

37. An examination of the habitats of the herbs in the different lists of Matthew and Luke is of little assistance either in determining the originality of Q's list or in determining the locale of the list: all spices could and were grown throughout the Mediterranean basin, including Palestine and Galilee.

38. *Sykaminos* is preferred to Matthew's *horos*. The usual Greek orthography for sycamine tree is *sykomoros,* which may explain the Matthean *horos*. The tree was common to the coastal plane and lower regions of the Levant and Egypt. There was even a port off Carmel called Sykamina (Josephus, *Ant.* 13.332).

39. Based on the imagery of Jesus' sayings, Geza Vermes concludes that he was "an appreciative child of the Galilean countryside" (1983, 48). On Q, see Harnack 1908, 121, and Crum 1927, 62.

40. Note Luke's *kēpos* in Q 13:19.

41. See Garnsey 1988, 44–45. MacMullen (1974, 42, esp. n. 44) has produced an impressive list of inscriptions and passages — from Italy, Greece, Egypt, and Palestine — that describe the custom of hiring out day laborers from the city to work in the fields and vineyards of a city's surrounding area. It is of note that Matt 20:3 (not a Q passage) tells a parable of a householder going into the market to pick up idlers.

42. The Lukan reading *kopria* is preferred (so also the International Q Project: Robinson 1991, 498), although the point could easily be made with the Matthean reading as well: *ei mē blēthen exō katapateisthai hypo tōn anthrōpōn.* Dung heaps (*kopria*) were commonly located on farms in hamlets and rural villages of Palestine where livestock were kept, and salt was commonly used to check the fermentation of the dung heap (Deatrick 1962).

43. *Ti hymin dokei;* Matt 18:12 or Luke's "Which one of you?" (*tis anthrōpos ex hymōn* [Luke 15:4]).

44. Contra Vermes 1983, 48: "The city and its life occupy scarcely any place at all in his teaching."

45. *Plateia* or *diexodos;* 10:10 and 13:26 are in Luke only, but in 14:21, Matthew has *diexodous,* the place where the streets exit outside the city (see *BAGD* 194 for examples).

46. Matthew only; Luke has *thyra*.

47. It is clear from the parable in both Matthew and Luke that the banquet is given in a city, since the servants are asked later to invite those outside the city.

48. Matthew has *trapezitoi* (bankers); Luke has *trapeza*.

49. On the urban imagery in Q 7:31–35 and the connection between the agora and the court in Graeco-Roman cities, see the insightful article by Cotter (1987, 289–304).

50. On descriptions of children, musicians, and street performers in cities' agoras, see Harris 1989, 226; Booth 1980; A. Scobie 1969, 27–29.

51. Matthew has conflated Q and Mark here, so that since he has already mentioned the "governors and kings" in Matt 10:17, he deletes the "rulers and authorities" here.

52. A theme first articulated for Q by Kloppenborg 1990a, 154: "One must 'go out' to see John and to hear his warnings; and the cities are not where Q expects to find a favorable hearing for the messages of John or Jesus."

53. The identification of the city with Jerusalem in Matthew's version is due to his allegory. In Q there was no such Jew-gentile theme, only a story about a banquet being opened up to outsiders, specifically those outside the city, who, from the parable's social criticism, are seen as inferior by society.

54. The banquets, which are criticized as a place where the social elite collect, do not seem to be part of the Q community's social setting (Q 11:43; 14:16–24).

55. On this see Crum 1927, 49–63, and Kloppenborg 1990a, 154.

56. For a list of the appropriate passages, see Stambaugh 1988, 45–47, 61–66.

57. See especially Varro's *On Agriculture,* Lucretius's *De Rerum Natura,* and Virgil's *Eclogues* and *Georgics.*

58. On the degree and definition of urbanization and its extent in Galilee, see Reed 1994b; on determining population numbers as a means of determining urbanization, see Reed 1992.

59. On the impact of these cities, from an archaeological perspective, see Reed 1994a, 47–94, and Reed 1994b.

Social Conflict in the Synoptic Sayings Source Q

Our understanding of social conflict in Q has been skewed by the persistence of Christian theological assumptions. Scholars have long since ostensibly recognized that the notion that "the Jews" or "Israel" rejected the Messiah and were therefore rejected, indeed punished, by God is a prominent piece of early "Christian" apologetics. Unfortunately the notion of the Jews' rejection and the Gentiles' acceptance of the Messiah worked its way into the standard conceptual apparatus of New Testament studies such that it continues to determine exegesis despite our critical awareness of the reality and dangers of Christian anti-Judaism. That we continue to use the concepts "Judaism" and "Christianity" for first-century literature and history may serve to perpetuate the problem. "Judaism" and "Christianity," of course, are both modern conceptual generalizations based on much later literary and other evidence and are inappropriately and unhistorically projected back onto first-century texts, which display striking diversity of origins and viewpoints. Because there was no discernible unitary, much less monolithic, Judaism or Christianity, it would seem appropriate to avoid both terms as much as possible. Instead, we could seek rather to be as precise as possible in historical social-relational terms as discerned through textual and other evidence and checked through studies of comparable social formations of other times and places.

Richard Horsley is professor of religious studies and classics at the University of Massachusetts at Boston.

Unwarranted Assumptions in Previous Discussion

Much recent discussion of Q claims that Q attacks Judaism generally or "all Israel" (for having rejected Jesus and the gospel/God's envoys). This conclusion is based on standard Christian scholarly readings of a few key prophetic sayings in Q. But both the claim and the readings of key terms behind it are based on some unwarranted assumptions.

First, the understanding of Luke 22:28–30 ‖ Matt 19:28 has been influenced by standard English and German (mis)translations of *krinein* as "judging" or *richten*. Far from being negative in connotation, the term is highly positive, even soteriological, as when God "defends" or "delivers" the poor in the Psalms (see, e.g., Pss 9; 10:18; 72:4; 76:9; 82:1–3; 103:6; 140:12; 146:7). As noted some time ago, the Biblical Hebrew *sapat* and its Greek translation *krinein* have the connotation of grace and deliverance, as God defends the rights of the oppressed against the oppressors (Herntrich 1965, 923–32). In Q 22:28–30, the Twelve are portrayed not as judging but as liberating or establishing justice for the twelve tribes of Israel, just as, in *Pss. Sol.* 17:28–32, the anointed son of David effects justice for or delivers the tribes of the people and, at Qumran (in 1QS 8:1–4), "the twelve men and three priests" (who comprise the council of the community) effect righteousness and justice in the land of Israel. Indeed, insofar as this may well have been the concluding saying in Q, the sense of the saying appears to have been virtually the opposite of the commonly assumed negative "judging" of Israel.[1]

The second key but unwarranted assumption is that "the many coming from east and west [north and south]" in Q 13:28–29/ Matt 8:11–12 refers to a "gentile pilgrimage." Contrary to what Joachim Jeremias and others claimed, the key comparative texts (Ps 106:3; Isa 43:5–6) refer not to a gentile pilgrimage but to a gathering of scattered Israelites.[2] On that basis, and because there was no "Christianity" (at the time Q was compiled, supposedly in Galilee) that stood over against "Israel" or "Judaism," "the sons of the kingdom" or "you yourselves thrust out" must refer, not to Israel generally (versus Gentiles), but to some subgroup within Israel.

The third problematic assumption is that Jerusalem (in Q 13: 34–35) and the Pharisees (in Q 11:39–52) are interchangeable with or symbols of the Jews or Israel generally. The high priestly aristocracy still at the head of the "temple-state" in Jerusalem had been charged by the Romans with maintaining law and order in Judaea. These aristocrats may have thought that they represented Palestinian Judaeans generally, even that they were the proper representatives of Galileans as well. It is abundantly clear from contemporary sources such as the Jewish historian Josephus and the Dead Sea Scrolls, however, that many ordinary people and particularly dissident scribes and popular movements had serious ambivalence about, if not outright hostility to, the incumbents in the ruling "house" of Jerusalem. Galilee itself, which had been under Jerusalem rule for only a century prior to the birth of Jesus, had been placed under the rule of Herod's son Antipas in 4 B.C.E. Indeed, in much of the biblical tradition, Israel stood over against Jerusalem, even though Second Isaiah and others writing from the perspective of the Jerusalem ruling class used "Zion" as a symbol for the whole people. The Pharisees, of course, were just one among the "parties" or "philosophies" of the Judaeans, according to Josephus, and, in the minds of the Judaean and Galilean common people, did not represent "Israel" any more than did the high priestly families who had been installed by Herod only a generation before.

With those readings of key proof texts as based on unwarranted assumptions, the principal bases disappear for claiming that Q directs prophetic judgment against Israel. If anything, based on a more appropriate reading of Q 22:28–30 and 13:28–29 and on the claim that long-standing Israelite expectations are being fulfilled in Jesus' activity in passages such as Q 7:18–23, 10:21–24, 11:14–20, and 12:51–53, Q envisages a renewal or restoration of Israel.

The Christian theological reading of Q as proclaiming the judgment of Israel, however, has received powerful if unintended reinforcement from recent hypotheses of redactional strata in Q.[3] In particular, the hypothesis that a formative "sapiential" stratum of basically community teaching was redactionally reframed by the addition of an "apocalyptic" layer of judgment against the impenitent and the opponents of the Q community sets up a whole redactional layer of five substantial speeches, not simply a handful of prophetic sayings, to be understood as addressed against "all Israel."

Criticisms of such redactional hypotheses have been voiced recently, particularly criticism of the division of Q into separate "sapiential" and "apocalyptic" strata.[4] The latter division is based on "several common features" ostensibly found in the speeches of the respective layers of Q.[5] Three general, common features are claimed for the redactional judgmental speeches: the *form* of "prophetic judgment and apocalyptic words" and chriae; *motifs* related to judgment, such as the parousia and Israel's rejection juxtaposed with Gentiles' positive response; and a *projected audience* of opponents and the impenitent. Only the latter two must be addressed briefly here.

Supposedly the target group in all five judgmental discourses (Q 3:7–9, 16–17; 7:1–10, 18–35; 11:14–26, 29–32, 39–52; 12:39–59; 17:23–37) is "all of Israel." Close examination of those five speeches, however, indicates that only limited sections of the material are ostensibly directed at the "out-group" of opponents and the impenitent. Most of the material in those five clusters of sayings appears to be exhortations and sanctions addressed directly to the "in-group" of the Q community (Q 7:18–23, 24–28; 11:14–26; 12:39–59; 17:23–37). There seems no reason to think that "this generation" in Q 7:31; 11:29–32, 50–51 refers to Israel as opposed to Gentiles. The only occurrence of "Israel" in Q is in 7:1–10. The point of the story about the Gentile who responds to Jesus with faith is to challenge Israel to fuller response, not to exemplify a mission to Gentiles. The "historical" illustrations of the Queen of the South and the Ninevites in Q 11:31–32 are hardly gentile responses to Jesus, providing no basis for the notion of "gentile faith" as an sign of condemnation for Israel. The preaching of John about the coming baptism by Spirit and fire is double-edged, positive-salvific as well as negative-judgmental (cf. the double-edged thrust of the kingdom in Q 11:20 and 10:9, 11). Q 7:31–35 is a vindication of Jesus and John vis-à-vis outside critics but not explicitly judgmental. We are left with only two subdivisions of one of those five speeches as prophetic sayings addressed ostensibly to the impenitent and/or opponents, that is, Q 11:29–32 and 11:39–52, also the sayings in which "this generation" is focused. It seems unwarranted, therefore, to believe that a whole redactional layer of Q was directed against Israel and to proceed with a redactional judgmental stratum as a working hypothesis about Q. Rather, Q will be assumed unitary (with the possible distinction of particular earlier and later components).

Toward an Appropriate Procedure on Q in Historical Context

Standard study of Synoptic gospel materials has purposely isolated Jesus' sayings from their literary context. Yet it is a truism, and should be a fundamental procedural axiom, that meaning depends upon context. Thus, unless we are satisfied to have modern scholars construct the context for meaning without serious attention to the original historical context of meaning, we must attend carefully both to the historical literary context and to the historical cultural and social context.[6]

John Kloppenborg's and others' composition criticism has been an important step in recognizing the character of Q as literature (Kloppenborg 1987a, esp. chaps. 4 and 5; Jacobson 1992, chap. 4). Q is not a collection of sayings so much as a series of sayings-clusters or discourses, each focused on a particular subject and having a particular function for a movement or community.[7] In this respect Q bears greater similarities to the *Didache* than to the *Gospel of Thomas*. This means that Q must be approached discourse by discourse, considering particular sayings as parts of whole discourses rather than in isolation. The character of Q as literature also bears implications for the degree to which it must be considered in historical cultural and social context. The *Gospel of Thomas,* which is truly a collection of Jesus sayings, or a Sayings Gospel, presents Jesus' sayings in isolation or in limited combinations apparently for individual contemplation and spiritual insight. The hermeneutics implied in the collection of sayings itself indicates that social context was not particularly important for the spiritual meaning to be discerned. By contrast, Q appears to be directed toward the concerns of a movement or community. Its implicit hermeneutics indicates that the historical social context is of considerable importance. Because the available text of Q is limited and provides limited historical social information, however, consideration of the likely historical social context on the basis of information from other sources becomes all the more important.

The Historical Context Evident in Q Known from Other Evidence

As with the Gospel of Mark or the Qumran scrolls, the cultural background in Q appears to be Israelite. A number of sayings make reference to and assume familiarity with significant figures and places from the traditions of Israel. As with Mark and the Dead Sea Scrolls, again, the societal context includes Jerusalem as the rejected ruling center and the Pharisees as opponent interpreters of tradition who apparently have some recognized, perhaps official, position. Although Q has precious few place-names, it can apparently be located in Galilee on the basis of the references to Capernaum, Chorazin, and Bethsaïda in Q 10:12–15. In contrast to the scribal and priestly concerns expressed in the Qumran literature, but similar to Mark, the discourses in Q focus on the concerns of ordinary people. This limited information available in the Q discourses enables us to locate Q in Galilee in late second temple times. Given the limited information available in Q itself, a fuller picture of the historical social structure and social relations between Jerusalem, the Pharisees, and Galilee must be sketched on the basis of other sources.

The fundamental social structure of late second temple Palestine involved a primary division and conflict basically between the rulers and the ruled. The rulers, living in Jerusalem, Caesarea, or Tiberias, expropriated tithes and offerings, tribute, and other taxes from the ordinary people, who lived mostly in semi-independent towns and villages.[8] It seems increasingly clear, on the basis of recent sociological analyses, that the scribes and Pharisees mentioned in the Gospels, as in Josephus, were legal-clerical "retainers" responsible for the interpretation and application of the official Judaean laws (see also Saldarini 1988). Galilee, which had not been subject to Jerusalem rule since the ten tribes rebelled against the Davidic monarchy in the tenth century B.C.E., had been taken over by the Hasmonean high priestly regime in Jerusalem apparently in 104 B.C.E., and the inhabitants were expected to live according to the Judaean laws (Josephus, *Ant.* 13.318). It makes sense, both because it was their official role as retainers and because the Hasmonean rulers were preoccupied with wars of conquest and internal political conflicts, that the Pharisees and other retainers were delegated to bring the Judaean laws to bear in Galilee. Since Galilee had only recently been subjugated to Jerusalem rule, however, it is unlikely that local Galilean traditions and customs were brought into close conformity with Jerusalem-based traditions and customs in such a short period of time. Indeed it was likely that there would have been some resentment of Jerusalem rule in Galilee. Insofar as Galileans themselves were probably descendants of former northern Israelites, social life in Galilee would have operated according to Israelite traditions parallel to but somewhat different from those officially recognized in Jerusalem.

Because of the multiple layers of rulers that had been imposed in the middle of the first century B.C.E. when the Romans took control of the temple-state in Jerusalem, the peasant producers had likely come under considerable economic and social pressure, with the attendant indebtedness, hunger, and other symptoms of social disintegration in local communities. The frequent and widespread popular protests, movements, and even extensive insurrections during the last century of second temple times were both symptoms and measures of the extent of the social disintegration.

Levels of Social Conflict in Q

The vast majority of discourses in Q are directed to the movement or community itself. This is true not only of the covenant renewal in Q 6:20–49, the sending out of preachers-healers in 10:2–16, and the exhortation to bold confession in the face of persecution in Q 12:2–12 but also of the sanctioning discourses about the present crisis or the future judgment in Q 12:49–59 and 17:22–37. These discourses directly address or provide windows onto two levels of social conflict, tensions within local communities and latent or overt conflicts between ordinary people and the officials responsible for maintaining the dominant social-economic-religious system.

The tensions within local communities are of two very different sorts, one that Q addresses and attempts to overcome, the other caused or at least exacerbated by the Jesus movement itself. The "sermon" in Q 6:20–49 is much more than a set of sapiential sayings. It is covenantal exhortation, perhaps even an exemplary covenant renewal, beginning with blessings offering the kingdom of God to the poor (functioning as the covenantal "prologue"), providing a "new lease on life" for despairing people subject to poverty and hunger. That forms a basis of hope and motivation for the explicitly covenantal exhortations that follow in 6:27–36, insisting that the people overcome their understandable defensive posture under political-economic pressure, in which they are "at each others' throats," and rather take care of each other in mutual social-economic support.[9] Sanctions on the covenantal exhortation are then given in the double parable, 6:47–49.[10] Depending on how much of a Q discourse can be discerned behind Luke 17:1–4 and whether in function it resembled the fuller parallel in Matthew 18, Q may have included explicit instructions for resolving local conflicts as well. In these ways the teachings of Jesus in Q addressed directly the social disintegration resulting from severe social-economic pressures of heavy demands from multiple levels of rulers.

The Jesus movement, however, generated a certain amount of local conflict itself. This can be seen explicitly in two discourses. Jesus' and/or his followers' preaching and demonstration of the presence of the kingdom and their attempts to renew local community (as in Q 6:20–49) caused divisions in local communities and even in families, as some joined and others did not. This was interpreted in terms of the general eschatological crisis that the movement understood to have been announced by John and Jesus, drawing in particular on the traditional prophetic theme (cf. Mic 7:6) of such familial divisions that would accompany God's decisive deliverance of the people (Q 12:49–59, esp. 51–53). The "mission" discourse anticipates, as it were, the rejection as well as reception that Jesus' envoys (preachers, healers, and organizers) would experience with instructions to enact a curse on the recalcitrant (Q 10:5–11). As indicated in the prophetic woes against the villages of Chorazin, Bethsaïda, and Capernaum (10:13–15), the Jesus movement found itself in sharp conflict with the majority in certain local communities, but the sharpness of their reaction indicates that there had been some engagement and organizing in those villages prior to eruption of such overt hostility.

The second "level" of social conflict indicated in the discourses addressed directly to the Q community is between the people and the officials responsible for the maintenance of the political-economic-religious system. Besides a general popular feeling of oppression and resentment there are particular concerns for repressive action taken against the Q people. At several points in different discourses there are indications that the people generally are experiencing poverty, hunger, and other aspects of social disintegration: for example, the concreteness of the petitions in the Lord's Prayer and a whole discourse devoted to exhortation about overwhelming anxieties about necessities. One of these passages, the blessings (and woes?) in the covenantal discourse, indicates that the response of Q's Jesus to this situation is a proclamation of a reversal of the social order that is imminent or, in effect, already underway in God's offer of the blessings (Q 6:20–21; and delivery of the woes against the rich [6:24–26]?). That there was a certain level of resentment mixed with cynicism is indicated in Jesus' question about the people's response to John: "What did you go out to see? ... A man clothed in luxurious clothing? Behold those who are gorgeously appareled and live in luxury are in royal palaces!" Antipas, of course, had built his royal palace, indeed the whole newly founded city of Tiberias, little more than a decade before Jesus' activity (or roughly a generation before the composition of Q), and the cost of that "development" would have been borne by those taxed to support the regime. Although resentment and cynicism would thus have been exacerbated by Roman political management of Palestine, such attitudes are traditional in virtually any traditional agrarian society. It is clear from the illustration used in Q 12:57–59 that ordinary people such as those involved in the Jesus movement did not trust the "justice" they would receive from the courts operated by officialdom in the ruling towns and cities.

At this level as well as at the local level, of course, the Jesus movement behind Q, in its audacious idea of renewing Israel, had likely caused sufficient social disruption that it had drawn repressive measures down on its head from the authorities.[11] Again, a whole discourse is devoted to reassurance and encouragement about bold confession in the face of trials (Q 12:2–12), and there is that other petition in the Lord's Prayer about not getting into a "test" (11:4). Partly because the text of Q is difficult to reconstruct at this point, but also because of the ambiguity of the term *synagogue*, "assembly," which can refer to an "assembly" and its court at any level from the village through that of a (royal) city to that ostensibly of the whole people, it is difficult to determine whether 12:11 covers local courts or not. It appears from both the Lukan text and the parallel to the Q saying in Mark 13:9, however, that the courts included those of "rulers and authorities," "governors and kings," that is, the official courts of the Romans' client rulers (Antipas and/or the high priests) and their representatives. Of course we cannot determine the degree of persecution or repression being applied; even a few incidents could have evoked the concern expressed in the rhetoric of 12:2–12.

Prophetic Condemnation of Rulers and Their Representatives

Given the amount and degree of social conflict reflected or addressed in the discourses addressed directly to the Q community, it is not surprising to find in Q certain discourses that make a direct attack on the rulers or their representatives. Depending on how we reconstruct the scope and shape of the clusters, there are two or three discourses in Q directed ostensibly against outsiders or opponents. The set of woes against the scribes and Pharisees could not be more explicit; the only question there is whether the previous set of sayings, Q 11:29–32, is to be understood as part of the same discourse with Q 11:39–52 and therefore as also directed against the scribes and Pharisees. The other discourse ostensibly directed at outsiders has been less obvious to scholarly eyes and requires some closer attention. These two discourses suggest the degree to which the Q people were caught up in a structural conflict with the Jerusalem rulers and their representatives, a conflict that on the Q side was articulated in sharp prophetic pronouncements of judgment.

Against the hypothesis of a sapiential discourse beginning with Q 13:24, 26 are the extreme uncertainty as to exactly what the opening sayings would have been and especially the supposedly redactional prophetic sayings and parable that far outweigh and dominate the supposedly original sapiential framing. It makes far more sense to view those prophetic sayings and parable as having formed a prophetic discourse, that is, Q 13:28–29, 34–35a; 14:16–24. Many of Kloppenborg's observations regarding the form and composition of these sayings fit this hypothesis handily, particularly the reconstruction of Luke 13:28–29 || Matt 8:11–12 following Matthew's wording more closely but Luke's order.[12] This discourse then appears to have been directed ostensibly against the Jerusalem rulers.

The prophetic lament in Q 13:34–35a announces explicitly the imminent divine desolation of the ruling house of Jerusalem. Like the traditional Israelite oracular prophets, "Jesus" here speaks for God (or the Wisdom of God). With allusions to the portrayal of God's care for the people in the Song of Moses (Deut 32:11) and to classical prophecies of the desolation of the ruling house (e.g., Jer 22:1–9), this prophetic lament indicts Jerusalem for obstructing God's providential care for "the children," that is, in a standard biblical image, the villages or people entrusted to its government.

The parable of the wicked tenants in Mark 12:1–9 provides a striking substantive parallel of the Jerusalem rulers indicted not only for the injustices of their stewardship of God's people but for violently resisting God's attempts to call them to task. Josephus's account of another "rustic" prophet, Jesus son of Hananiah, provides what looks like a formal as well as substantive parallel of a prophetic lament over the ruling city (*Ant.* 6.300–309). Once we recognize that "many coming from east and west," and so on, in Matt 8:11–12 || Luke 13:28–29 are previously scattered Israelites, and not Gentiles, then the "you" or "the sons of the kingdom" in this saying as well must refer to the rulers, that is, those who (like the aristocracies in most traditional societies) place great stock in their proper lineages, even from Abraham, Isaac, and Jacob. Finally, as recent studies of the parable of the great supper have pointed out, the cast of characters who reject, and are then rejected from, the banquet are very well-off people who can afford to buy another field or multiple yoke of oxen, suggestive of the wealthy elite (see, e.g., Scott 1989, chap. 5).

Thus Q 13:28–29, 34–35, and 14:16–24, that is, what must have been the principal pieces of a whole discourse, can be seen as a prophetic rejection of the Jerusalem rulers over against the people of Israel who are now/imminently being gathered into the banquet of the kingdom. The conflict here is not that of a resentful reform movement against Israel in general, an Israel that has supposedly rejected the movement's message; rather, the conflict is between an Israel renewal movement among the ordinary people of Galilee and the remote rulers in Jerusalem. Not surprisingly, this conflict evident in Q 13–14 follows the same fault lines as the basic structural conflict in Roman Palestine generally.

Nowhere have modern Christian scholarly assumptions played a more decisive role than in standard interpretations of Q 11:39–52, the woes against the Pharisees. On the interrelated assumptions that Jesus' sayings pertain to individual's religion or religious ethics and that "Jesus" is speaking for Christianity against Judaism, interpreters find here a debate about the law and/or more particularly purity laws. Interpretations of Q then range from a radicalization of the law, by taking 11:42 as the key, to a redefinition of purity in ethical terms, taking 11:39–41 and 11:44 as the key. However, only one of the seven woes alludes to the law (tithes, in 11:42), and only two mention purity, and then only as a rhetorical device (11:39–41, 44). A closer look at the woes apart from those assumptions thus indicates that they focus not on the Torah or purity but on the social functions of the scribes and Pharisees.[13] Since it should be obvious on the surface that at least the four woes that do not mention either the Torah or purity concerns (11:43, 46, 47, 52) are focused on the activities of the Pharisees in relation to the people, perhaps it will suffice here to focus on the sayings previously assumed to be about the law.

Q 11:39–41 does indeed begin with reference to the Pharisees' concerns about ritual purity.[14] But both Matthew's and Luke's versions, and therefore almost certainly Q behind them, shift the vessels into metaphors. The point, explicit in Luke's version, is implicit in Matthew's: "Inside you/they [the Pharisees] are full of extortion and rapacity." Nothing too subtle about this woe: the Pharisees' concerns about ritual cleanliness veil (or at least distract attention from) the rapacious effects of their interaction with the people, and the indictment covers both.

Tithes in Q 11:42 were hardly a matter of ceremonial law but of taxes. The reference to "mint, dill, and cumin," items not even certainly tithed, is hyperbole and caricature, probably full of sarcasm or ridicule. The charge that the Pharisees were obsessed with even the minor items, some not even cultivated, serves to indicate how rigorous they were about the principal cultivated products subject to tithes/taxes such as grain, on which the very survival of the subsistence producers themselves depended. And if the Pharisees or scribes, as representatives of Jerusalem, were still insisting on payment of tithes in addition to the taxes that Galileans were paying to Antipas or Agrippa and the tribute they were rendering to Caesar, they were indeed neglecting justice and compassion. (Note the allusion to the prophetic covenantal exhortation demanding *mišpat, ḥeṣed, sedeq, 'emet,* in such texts as Hos 4:1; 12:7; Mic 6:8; Zech 7:9).

The accusation in 11:44 that the scribes and Pharisees are like "unmarked graves" the people walk over unawares may be the most clever woe of all. Like the accusation about cleansing the outside of the cup, this charge mocks the Pharisees' concern with purity. But by charging that they themselves are like unmarked graves from which people are exposed to danger unawares, Q/Jesus shifts the focus to the Pharisees' role or social function in relation to the people. The Pharisees' activities constitute a (hidden) danger to the people.

Throughout these seven woes in Q 11:39–52, the focus is not

on the Torah but on the political-economic-religious role of the Pharisees and scribes. Q's Jesus indicts them for the ways in which they, partly in their role as official interpreters of the official laws and rulings, are contributing to the exploitation of the people, including ways in which their own special concerns for purity codes veil or divert attention from the concrete effects of their administrative-interpretive activities.

When the discourse moves from the indictments of the Pharisees to the declaration of sentence, however, the scope might appear to be broadened, depending on the likely referent of the term "this generation" in Q 11:49–51. "This generation" is also the target of the immediately preceding set of sayings: it is to be condemned at the judgment for not heeding (the preaching of) the presence of the kingdom (Q 11:29–32). Indeed, even though "this generation" occurs only here (Q 11:29–32, 50–51), except for the related usage in Q 7:31, it has been claimed as another key to the secondary redaction of Q as a whole whereby the judgmental sections are directed against Israel generally. Although "this generation" is a vague general term of potential wide reference, there is no indication in Q (or in Mark) that it points to Israel generally. Besides the more general usage, neutrally in Mark 13:30 and pejoratively in Mark 8:38, Mark uses the term specifically in reference to the disciples (!) in Mark 9:19 and the Pharisees in Mark 8:12, the Markan parallel to Q 11:29. If Matt 12:38 represents the order of Q (note Kloppenborg's relocation of Luke 11:16 to match in *Q Parallels* [1988]), then not only Mark but Q as well use "this generation" in reference to the (scribes and) Pharisees in connection with the saying about seeking a sign.[15] Finally, it is pertinent that in the only other Q use of "this generation" (7:31–35), Wendy Cotter found that the imagery of the "children" formally seated as if in court and "addressing" one another implies that these nay-sayers were figures such as scribes and Pharisees (Cotter 1987, 289–304). Thus a number of factors suggest that Q apparently used "this generation" in reference to the Pharisees.

A late rabbinic parallel that Kloppenborg cites as confirmation that "the sign of Jonah" stands in analogy with Jesus' preaching (of the kingdom, which means judgment for the unresponsive) also illustrates that "the Ninevites" stand in analogy to Jerusalem, called the "oppressing city," which thus parallels "the queen of the South," most clearly a ruler (*Lam. Rab.* Proem 31) (Kloppenborg 1987a, 133). That is, with or without a reference to the

Pharisees in the framing of Q 11:29–32, the analogies drawn point to the rulers or their representatives as the ones targeted here, as in 11:39–52 and 13:34–35b. Mark's portrayal of the scribes and Pharisees (esp. 3:22; 7:1–2; and the Jerusalem section), as well as Josephus's depictions of them, indicate that they were based in Jerusalem and functioned as the representatives of the ruling priestly aristocracy.

With regard to both the ruling house in Jerusalem and the scribes and Pharisees, the polemical discourses in Q are not simply criticisms. They are prophetic indictments, a lament over imminent punitive destruction in the one case, a prophetic curse in the other. The prophetic form fits the contents of the indictments, particularly evident in the woes. Just as the classical Israelite prophets pronounced woes against rulers and government officials for their exploitative effects on the people, so these woes in Q indict representatives of the temple government in Jerusalem for their deleterious impact on the people.

The sharpest indictment of all, to which the pronouncement of judgment (the Sophia oracle) is attached, may be the most telling indication in Q of how the Q people understood the most immediate conflict in which they were engaged. Building or tending the graves of revered figures in the tradition would likely have been one of the functions of the scribes and Pharisees as professional guardians of the official traditions. In building/tending the tombs of the prophets, however, the Pharisees, as indicted by Q, are ironically and hypocritically honoring and co-opting the revered memory of figures whom their predecessors among government officials had killed as threatening agitators.

This indictment and judgment, moreover, indicate that the Q people understand John and Jesus as the climactic figures in the long line of prophets murdered by the rulers or officials. Indeed, as indicated in the last Q beatitude in 6:22–23, the Q people apparently understand themselves as continuing the line of persecuted prophets. This may well be rooted in what has been labelled a Deuteronomistic view of history, which had been articulated in Jeremianic preaching (e.g., Jer 7:25–34; 25:4–14) and early second temple covenantal renewal prayers (e.g., Neh 9:5–37) and which had supposedly become widespread in Palestine (e.g., Dan 9:4b–19; *Jub.* 1:7–26). Interpreters of Q proceeding without much attention to the historical social context and searching for an explanation of the redaction of Q by addition of the sharply judgmental sayings have posited a resentment by the Q people for having been rejected by Israel and having "lost" in their bid to "reform" Israel. Such explanations are speculative, with no basis in the text of Q. If our procedure is broadened to consider the historical context of the Q community or movement as located in mid-first-century Galilee, then a very different explanation of passages such as Q 6:22–23; 11:47–51; and 13:34–35b is suggested. As noted at points above, the principal social conflict evident in Q, that between the people and their rulers, parallels the fault lines of the dominant structural social conflict known from other sources. Moreover, as known through Josephus in particular, there were a number of contemporary popular prophets and popular prophetic and messianic movements in Palestinian society with striking similarities to Jesus and his movement(s). Finally, as noted in analysis of the discourse directed ostensibly against outsiders, the charge of having killed the prophets is directed specifically against the Pharisees ("this generation") in Q 11:47–52 and against the ruling house of Jerusalem in Q 13:34–35.

Whatever its eventual "trajectory" or literary fate, absorption into Matthew's Gospel and his community or into Luke's history, Q was the expression of a popular Galilean movement striving for renewal of "Israel" and standing in opposition to and opposed by the ruling institutions and their representatives. This is perhaps portrayed most vividly in their representation of Jesus as the last in a long line of prophets who was, on the one hand, attempting to catalyze a renewal of Israel in Galilee while, on the other hand, attacking the Jerusalem rulers and their representatives.

NOTES

1. For fuller discussion of Luke 22:28–30 ‖ Matt 19:28, see Horsley 1987, 200–206.

2. Jeremias 1958. The Matthean setting has clearly influenced Christian scholarly interpretation of this saying. For example, it is cited from Matt 8:11–12, with the comment "the Gentiles exhibit the faith, … " by Bultmann 1968, 129.

3. Most influential have been Lührmann 1969 and Kloppenborg 1987a.

4. A. Collins 1989, 369–89; Horsley 1989a, 186–203; Kloppenborg 1989, 204–15; Jacobson 1992, 48–51; J. Collins 1993, 165–85.

5. The following focuses on Kloppenborg 1987a, chap. 4.

6. Further ruminations in Horsley 1991b, 175–83.

7. On the following, see further argument in Horsley 1991a, 195–209.

8. For a more extensive sketch of the political-economic structure and situation in Roman Palestine directly pertinent to Q, see Horsley 1989b, chaps. 4–5.

9. This line of exegesis of Luke/Q 6:27–36 is laid out more fully in Horsley 1987, 255–73.

10. See the fuller explanation of Q 6:20–49 as a covenantal discourse by Horsley 1991b, 184–86, and Aitken 1992.

11. For a fuller sketch of the "imperial situation" of Palestine under Roman rule, including Rome's "indirect rule" through client rulers and their officials, and the "spiral of violence" that often resulted, with officials attempting to repress the people's protest or resistance to the hardships they experienced because of the structure of the imposed political-economic arrangements, see Horsley 1987, chaps. 1–2.

12. See Kloppenborg 1987a, 225–32 — that is, once we recognize that the standard scholarly reading of those "coming from east and west" as Gentiles is based on unwarranted Christian theological assumptions.

13. A brief sketch of this point is in Horsley 1991b, 192–93.

14. As documented and explained by Neusner 1976, 486–95.

15. Moreover, if Luke substituted "some" for Pharisees in Luke 11:15 || Matt 12:24, then Q 11:14–20, 23 may also at some point have been an indictment of the Pharisees. That is, all three of these sections, Q 11:14–20, 23, 11:29–32, and 11:39–52, which Kloppenborg's compositional analysis found to be a continuous discourse, would have been ostensibly against the Pharisees, understood in (pre-)Q tradition as "this generation."

The Language of Violence and the Aphoristic Sayings in Q

A Study of Q 6:27-36

The aphoristic — or sapiential — sayings are not usually seen as the obvious place to start if one is attempting to explore the theme of violence and conflict in Q. Attention might more naturally be directed to the prophetic — or perhaps it would be better to say the more openly polemical — sayings, such as to the woes or announcements of judgment (Q 3:7-9; 10:13-14; 11:39-52), or to the sayings referring to the fate of the prophets (Q 6:22-23; 11:49-51; 13:34-35), or to the sayings about not bringing peace but the sword and about introducing divisions on earth (Q 12:51-53). In terms of the stratification of the Q material delineated by John S. Kloppenborg, one would look to Q^2 rather than Q^1 (see in particular Kloppenborg 1987a). Even for those who find such stratifications too stark (such as Richard Horsley[1] and C. M. Tuckett [1991, 213-22]), Q clusters that are *predominantly* "sapiential" would take second place to those that are openly polemical in tone. The object of the polemical attacks, "this generation," at first glance seems to be the Jewish contemporaries of the Q group, but as Kloppenborg has warned, "while ostensibly directed at the 'out-group,' these polemical and threatening materials function in fact to strengthen the identity of the 'in-group' and to interpret for them the experience of persecution, rejection and even the failure of their preaching" (1987a, 168). These materials are part and parcel of the boundary-forming activity that follows

R. A. Piper is reader in New Testament and head of the School of Divinity, University of St. Andrews, Fife, Scotland. This essay is a revised version of a paper presented to the SBL Q Seminar in San Francisco in November 1992.

the experience of rejection. What is more difficult to describe is the *reality* that must underlie these *expressions* of persecution and rejection.

Can anything be said, however, about the more sapiential stratum (or clusters) of Q, in which the rhetoric of reasoned persuasion, rather than polemic, is predominant? Violence was and is part of the fabric of life — and certainly was so in first-century Palestine — so there is no a priori reason why the "sapiential" material should not reflect the subject matter of violence and conflict, even in community-directed sayings. The task will be, first, to identify examples of the language of violence and, second, to go further and make some suggestions about the functions of this language and the social location that can be inferred.

A key text in any such discussion must surely be the instructions about nonretaliation and response to enemies in Q 6:27–36. Violence is to be met with nonviolence. In recent discussion of the social location of Q, these sayings have in fact figured quite prominently.[2] This of course poses the question of whether this teaching about nonretaliation and love of enemies is concerned with "community" and thus the social location of Q at all. Is it, for example, simply presented as an abstract ethical principle or as a radical ethic focused on the individual subject's ability to overcome "self"? If it was aimed at a community or with particular opponents in view, was it primarily anti-Zealot and tacitly pro-establishment in the passivity it espouses? Or was it opposed to the prevailing social-political structures in Palestine?[3]

Although Matthew and Luke agree in their approximate contexts for this teaching in their respective inaugural sermons, they do differ at significant points in their versions of the teaching. The precise Q form of the sayings is in fact of some importance in discussing these issues. In Luke, the exhortation to love one's enemies is followed by the sayings:

> Do good to those who hate you;
> bless those who curse you;
> pray for whose who mistreat you.
> When someone strikes you on the cheek, offer the other also;
> and when someone takes away your cloak, do not withhold even
>   your tunic.
> Give to everyone who begs from you;
> and if someone takes away your belongings, do not ask for them
>   back again.

As is sometimes noted, the phrasing of Luke's version stresses the element of violence in the situations that are depicted — being *struck* on the cheek, followed by when someone *takes away* your cloak, and when someone *takes away* your belongings.[4] His descriptions seem to be of a mugging or robbery.[5] That is apparently why the cloak is mentioned first rather than the tunic; the cloak was more valuable (Luz 1989, 325). Thus although the saying as it stands in Luke is rather anticlimactic (if someone takes something valuable away from you, then give him something inexpensive too!), the imagery is clearly of someone being stripped of clothing. Similarly, someone's *taking away* your belongings seems to be outright theft. The theme of lending is reserved for later in Luke 6 (vv. 34–35). To these examples, Douglas E. Oakman (1991, 163–64) has added others in Luke-Acts that demonstrate Luke's familiarity with the idea that robbery and other forms of violence "were a fact of life, even in village experience" (Luke 10:30; 12:39; 22:36–38, 49–52; 23:19, 32; 39–43; Acts 5:36–37). The parable of the Good Samaritan is an obvious example.[6] But while Luke recognizes such violence as a fact of life, his main concern seems to be to emphasize the *positive* ethic of loving enemies or doing good, being kind and showing mercy to others, that surrounds the non-retaliation teaching in Luke and is also a feature of Luke's Good Samaritan parable. The violence primarily provides an opportunity for commending mercy and kindness.

How far has Luke, however, taken a step beyond Q? Has Luke's motive been to ensure that nonretaliation is not simply viewed as the response of those who were in any case defenseless and had no alternative but to tolerate oppression and try to make friends with the oppressors?[7] The teaching on nonretaliation potentially represents a particularly challenging affront to ancient Mediterranean codes of honor and shame. Luke does not hesitate to confront these codes in other contexts, but the nonretaliation exhortations are distinctive in that they depict the *voluntary* vulnerability of the oppressed to *material and physical exploitation*. This runs counter to Luke's concern for the poor. Furthermore, the exhortations are presented without any supporting argumentation. It cannot be convincingly argued that this voluntary vulnerability to exploitation is in Luke an exhortation just for those who are secure and can morally benefit from a little hardship, perhaps in the cause of social banditry. Indeed, the clause "But I say to you who hear" in Luke 6:27a marks a change from those addressed in the preceding woes (Luke 6:24–26). That change and the extended commands in 6:27 to those who are hated, cursed, and abused make it clear even in Luke that these exhortations about nonretaliation are addressed to an *oppressed* group who are asked to accept further humiliation and loss. As such, these are potentially difficult sayings for Luke.

Luke deals with them in two ways. First, he alters Q's context for the exhortations by placing them amid the positive teaching about loving one's enemies, in imitation of a God who is kind and merciful. Effectively, he switches emphasis from the exploited being encouraged to accept further exploitation to the virtues of love and mercy.[8] Second, he reduces the vulnerability demanded of those who are oppressed by his formulation of this teaching as related to *isolated acts of violence*. One's economic and physical vulnerability — the scale of exploitation — is more limited if the wrong that one suffers is a sporadic and unpredicted violent act (such as being mugged) rather than if it is part of an ongoing exploitative personal or contractual relationship.[9]

The more difficult version of this teaching — and probably the earlier, Q version of this teaching[10] — is better preserved in Matthew, once stripped of Matthew's antithetical formulations.[11] The first saying, about being struck on the cheek, is slightly different in Matthew. While Luke refers to one "who strikes you on the cheek" (*tō typtonti se epi siagona*), Matthew refers to one "who slaps you on your right cheek" (*hostis se rapizei eis tēn dexian siagona*). In view of the relative infrequency of *rapizei* in Matthean vocabulary (only in Matt 26:67 and nowhere else in the New Testament) and in view of Luke's use of *typtein* in three other passages in Luke and five times in Acts, it seems likely that Q should read "slap" (*rapizei*) and that "strike" (*typtonti*) should be seen as a Lukan improvement.[12] If Luke is accordingly to be credited with introducing the word for "hit" or "strike," then this is also consistent with the earlier argument that Luke is responsible for emphasizing a mugging/robbery scenario in these verses.

The specification of the "right" cheek is more difficult to attribute. This refers to a backhanded slap, which represents a more serious insult than being slapped with an open hand (see *m. B. Qam.* 8:6; 1 Esdr 4:30 [LXX]). The reference would thus seem to emphasize an insult rather than a method of mugging or physical brutality (see Weaver 1992, 52). In any case, as Bruce Malina notes, the head or face is one of the most prominent places on the "map" of the physical body as symbolic of honor. A physical af-

front is a challenge to honor, and all the more so if it is directed
to the head (Malina 1981, 35). Walter Wink suggests further that
the backhanded slap was a frequent way of admonishing inferiors,
such as masters their slaves, in which retaliation by the one of inferior status would have been suicidal.[13] If Luke's intention was to
redirect these sayings away from the issue of honor and toward the
issue of armed robbery, as appears to be the case throughout, then
the omission of *dexios* by Luke is understandable.[14] Moreover, the
suggestion that Matthew has redactionally inserted *dexios* simply
for rhetorical reasons seems relatively unpersuasive.[15] The balance
of probability suggests *dexios* was in Q.

After the "slapping on the right cheek," Matthew records:

> If anyone wants to sue you and take your tunic [*himation*],
> let him have your cloak [*chitōna*] as well.

The scene in Matthew is again different from Luke, and thus
the question of the Q version is raised. In the exhortation above,
Matthew presents a legal situation in contrast to the mugging or
robbery depicted in Luke. If someone through legal procedures
(*krithēnai*) lays claim to your relatively inexpensive tunic (*himation*), you should give him your more expensive cloak (*chitōna*)
too. It is frequently suggested that the situation recalls the debtor's
suit in which the garment of a poor person is used as a pledge
against future payments to his creditors (Luz 1989, 325). Even a
court could not compel a debtor permanently to sacrifice his outer
garment, which may explain why the suit is initially for the inner
garment. Exod 22:24–26 (LXX) and Deut 24:10–13, 17 indicate
that when the *himation* was taken in pledge it had to be restored
to a poor debtor before sunset so that he might sleep in it.[16] Moreover, only the poorest would have nothing to give as collateral but
a garment, as Wink notes,[17] and nakedness was strongly against
Jewish sensitivities. Ulrich Luz finds neither Matthew's version of
a lawsuit (with the sequence tunic-cloak) nor Luke's version of a
mugging (with the sequence cloak-tunic) redactional and thus cannot determine which better represents Q here (Luz 1989, 324). In
contrast to Luz, it has been argued above that there is a reason for
Luke changing the version reflected in Matthew.[18]

It also cannot be presumed that Matthew has introduced the
juridical concepts here. First, it is difficult to see Matthew introducing the concept of voluntary surrender by a debtor of even his
minimal rights[19] and relatively easy to see why Luke might wish to

alter it to a situation of theft or compulsion. Second, the surrounding Q material in this cluster of sayings concerning persecutors (Q 6:22–23), "enemies," and "those who hate you" (Q 6:27–35) suggests that *ongoing* relationships are the more consistent emphasis in this part of Q rather than unforeseen acts of violence by assailants (as in Luke).[20] This suggests that Matthew's formulation may be the more original and that Luke is responsible for applying the offenses to acts of violence or compulsion.[21] Third, in contrast to the *lex talionis* of Deuteronomy, which relies upon judicial settlements, Matthew's antithetical teaching of Jesus clearly relies upon *avoiding* legal processes. Thus in Matt 5:39b (insult), 41 (forced labor), and 42 (financial demands), no reference is made to courtroom scenes, and the appearance of a judicial procedure in 5:40 may even be viewed as in some tension with the antithetical construction that Matthew has set up (except insofar as it prevents *further* recourse to law).[22] Finally, legal and judicial concepts are by no means foreign to Q itself, as Q 6:37–38 in the immediate context and Q 12:58–59 show. Matthew's version of Q 6:29b must therefore be taken seriously as representing Q, because Luke's change is easily understood and the evidence for Matthean redaction is far from clear.

This leads then to the third Q exhortation, following that of being slapped and that of being sued for one's garment:

> Matt 5:42: Give to one who begs from you, and do not refuse the one who wishes to borrow from you.
>
> Luke 6:30: Give to everyone who begs from you; and if someone takes away your belongings, do not ask for them back again.

It is necessary again to establish the Q version of this saying. Luke, as throughout 6:29–30, emphasizes the robbery motif: "If someone *takes away* your belongings..." In contrast, Matthew focuses upon a potential debtor: "If someone wants to *borrow* from you..." Again the decisive factor is whether violence was depicted in Q 6:30. In view of the discussion above regarding Q 6:29, we view Matthew's "borrow from you" (*apo sou danisasthai*) as more consistent with the emphasis in Q to focus here not upon isolated acts of violence but rather upon abuse suffered in the context of sustained relationships, emphasizing the reversal of honor-shame codes as well as consequent "judicial" procedures. In support of this one can note the following:

a The "nonviolent" introduction to Q 6:30 in both Matthew and Luke: "Give to the one who begs/asks from you."

b Luke's use of the "borrowing" (*danisasthai*) formulation later in Luke 6:34–35, where he locates the theme of lending without repayment more appropriately in a section on voluntary giving and doing good, away from his section on suffering violence. This suggests that "the corresponding *airein* is LukeR and doubtless used under the influence of the first half of the saying in v. 29b."[23]

c The difficulty of establishing a wording for Q in Luke 6:34, which shows heavy influence of Lukan interests.

d The awkwardness of Matthew's formulation about not refusing one who wants to borrow in the context of his fifth antithesis, which concerns nonretaliation. Even if Matthew has made some redactional alterations to the saying, as will be argued below, he presumably preserves the reference to *borrowing* amid the other nonretaliation sayings in Q 6:29–30 simply because it was here in Q.[24]

Although it is likely that Matthew preserves from Q here the reference to "borrowing" (instead of Luke's "taking away"), it would seem that Matthew has softened the original force of the saying. By restricting the emphasis on "giving" to the "beggar" and by concentrating upon the act of lending rather than on rashly forgoing repayments of a loan (contrast Luke's *mē apaitei:* "Do not ask back again"), the Matthean formulation lacks the radical renunciation of rights that is characteristic of the other sayings in Q 6:29–30. It conforms to more practicable and usual traditions about benevolence.[25] Thus the pattern of the more challenging Q sayings that precede suggests that the Q version here should read:

Give to one who begs/asks from you, and do not ask back from the one who wishes to borrow from you.[26]

In other words, if someone in need wants to enter into a financial arrangement and borrow money, one should give and then not seek recovery of the funds in case of default.[27] Once again the exhortation seems to relate to a situation where some contract or relationship is established and where one's "rights" are being relinquished. The "opponent" is not unknown and unexpected — it is not a hit-and-run type of incident. Surely this is also the implication of the adjacent love-of-enemies teaching about going beyond loving only those who love you and going beyond greeting only those who greet you. Greater demands, in the context of relationships, are depicted. This is the implication too of the preceding Q "persecution beatitude" (Q 6:22–23):[28] "Blessed are you when people hate you; when they exclude you and reproach you and cast out your name as evil.... For thus did they to the prophets before you." These injuries are not presented just as isolated mishaps. This is "persecution" language — the prophets against society. Such sayings all suggest a pattern of community relationships with those who know the addressees well enough to oppose them. It is also in these social and business relationships (not just in situations where persons are victimized by isolated crimes) that the ancient codes of honor and shame are most active. The language of Q may be less overtly "violent" than that of Luke,[29] but the problems addressed are in many respects more acute.

It is possible to pursue these ideas further. The problems for Q are more acute also because they raise the question of the addressees' relationship to society's institutions of justice. Looked at from the angle of the question, What recourse do I have against someone who takes advantage of me in a local relationship? the answer is not simply: Suffer in silence. The answer seems to be: Avoid the courts at all costs. Give away even more, voluntarily, rather than appeal to secular institutions of justice in cases of being physically abused or sued or even in pursuing a debtor or defaulter. In one sense, this might be seen simply as general sapiential teaching. What sage would not be wary of litigation? Yet its extreme nature seems more likely to reflect at least a profound lack of confidence among the Q people regarding the social and judicial institutions active in their sphere. Again, this judicial interest cannot simply be attributed to Matthew. It can hardly be accidental that the next section of the Q sermon (Q 6:37–38) continues the very vocabulary of warning against judicial procedures: "Do not judge, and you will not be judged; for by the measure with which you measure, it will be measured to you."[30]

Before investigating the implications of this for the social location of Q, it may be helpful briefly to broaden the range of the Q material that is considered. A telling parallel to this viewpoint can be found in another saying that is sapiential in form, although appearing later and somewhat awkwardly at the end of a series of sayings about judgment in Q 12. Q 12:58–59 shows the same concern to advise avoidance of judicial proceedings:

Come to terms quickly with a plaintiff against you while you are going with him on the way, lest the plaintiff hand you over to the judge, and the judge to the guard, and you be thrown into prison. I tell you, you will not leave there until you have paid the last quadran.[31]

Here judicially sanctioned "violence" is clearly in view, but it is viewed from the more vulnerable perspective of a debtor rather than a lender. Interestingly, the advice of Q again is not, "Neither a borrower nor a lender be." Perhaps such an option was not a realistically open one, although Q may hint at this elsewhere (see Q 11:9–13). The advice of Q is simply that whether as borrower or lender, make peace with and even give way to your accuser or defaulter. Self-help in settling a dispute appears often to have preceded judicial action. H. J. Wolff's work on papyrus contracts discusses consensual contracts outside the sphere of legislation (Wolff 1970, cited in Llewelyn 1992, 90–91). If attempts on the personal level to reach a satisfactory conclusion failed, then creditors could petition the relevant authority for assistance to enforce their rights under the contract. This assistance may have involved taking the matter to court and obtaining a judgment.[32] The initiative, though, would lie largely with the petitioner rather than with the authorities themselves.[33] Earlier evidence of this procedure is found in the Zenon papyri. Furthermore, J. L. White (1972) has presented a sample of forty-four official petitions from the first and second centuries, which were subsequently analyzed by Llewelyn (1992, 140–45), that show that in the first century persons of the lower social strata did make private petitions to the *strategos,* the chief of police. Such petitions were not the province simply of persons of high social status approaching high-ranking officials.

In such a context, the advice of the Q sayings seems to be to avoid conflict and to avoid any situation at all that might be contested and ultimately go to court.[34] This is not just benefaction; it seems primarily related to situations of vulnerability.

There are of course many other indications in the nonpolemical clusters of Q showing the sociopolitical vulnerability of the Q people. It can be found earlier in Q 12, beginning with the instructions in Q 12:4–7 concerning not fearing those who are able to kill the body but are not powerful enough to kill the soul, and extending to Q 12:11–12, where it is envisaged that one will be brought before "synagogues and magistrates and authorities"

(Luke). As Kloppenborg notes, "12:11–12 describes the forensic scene which the two preceding sayings presuppose, and as we have already suggested, it was this element (along with various catchwords) that occasioned the association of 12:8–9 and 10 with 12:11–12" (1987a, 214). In the sayings that follow in Q 12:22–31 concern is directed to daily economic anxieties about food, clothing, and shelter. Not dissimilar is the encouragement in Q 11:9–13, which follows the Lord's Prayer (Q 11:2–4) with its own petitions about daily bread and "trials." In Q 11:9–13 hearers must ask God for their needs like sons seeking loaves and other food from their human fathers. The "fears" that emerge are as striking as the quite clear attempts to calm them by reason and persuasion.[35]

These "fears" are further testimony to a lack of confidence in normal social and commercial intercourse, as well as being specific fears about the actions of authorities. Thus they are complementary to those Q clusters that express the desire to minimize conflict by not pursuing personal redress. The Q people (like the birds of the air and lilies of the field) are simply thrown back on the providential care of God and on a wisdom that encourages them to keep their heads low regarding any personal distress they suffer. Discipleship may make demands upon them for boldness (Q 12:2–3), but redress for personal injury seems to be viewed as dangerous, counterproductive, or simply wrong.

Does this now allow us to be more precise about the social location of these sections of Q? Kloppenborg's 1991 *Semeia* article suggests that the likely setting for "formative Q" is among the lower administrative sector of the cities and villages in Galilee. The instructional genre would require compilers above the level of peasants, persons with "scribal" abilities, such as those minor officials "ready to assist in the transaction of sales, loans, rental agreements, marriages and divorces" (Kloppenborg 1991, 86). These were neither higher officials nor, presumably, more sophisticated scholars.[36] It is also unlikely that itinerancy was the main mode of their existence. However, they would have been sufficiently in touch with the chronic problems of indebtedness, and perhaps economically affected by these themselves, to attack the prevailing culture and idealize the simple, detached life (Kloppenborg 1991, 87–89). Kloppenborg also speculates that they may have been disgruntled and disillusioned by the administrative adjustments in first-century Palestine.

The interpretation that we have suggested for Q 6:27–36 and

corresponding material in Q would conceivably strengthen such an assessment of the social location of these clusters of Q sayings, placing them close to the sphere of legal and contractual concerns. Such a hypothesis also must address the diverging theories of Wink and Horsley. Horsley has argued for a local, village socioeconomic context for the sayings in Q "rather than the direct face-off between oppressor and oppressed suggested by Wink," who considered the oppressor ultimately to be the Roman occupying power (Horsley 1992, 129). Wink's argument is that "these sayings cannot have been directed against peers but against those in the hierarchical structures of village life who were masters and creditors" and that these would at least encompass the puppets of Rome if not Romans directly (Wink 1992a, 133–34). The suggestion that the location of Q is in the lower administrative sector of the villages and cities of Galilee could conceivably be directed either way — toward local personal situations or toward the administrative structures themselves. Indeed this sector stands at the interface between local, village social concerns about indebtedness and the administrative structures for dealing judicially with such business and social relations, which inevitably would refer back to the cities. The evidence for a lack of confidence in the judicial system, specific fears about "authorities," and a concern to suffer loss rather than seek redress would suggest a clear suspicion about the benefits to be won under higher administrative procedures. This concern may not have been *directly* aimed at Rome, particularly in Galilee, but neither were the structures governing life in Galilee viewed as objects of trust. Even self-help in preference to legal redress was not encouraged in Q 6:29–30. The suspicion about the institutions of power seems to have been sufficiently strong to make voluntary surrender the preferred option.

Is it possible to tell, however, whether economic hardship and social upheaval had already deprived the members of their place in the system or whether they were still active in the scribal and administrative sector?[37] Some progress can also be made here if our preceding observations are correct.

It is sometimes observed that Q 6:30, about making loans without seeking repayment, seems to indicate sufficiently prosperous persons who were in a position to lend money. The scale of lending is, however, not actually prescribed, and so the reference may not indicate much prosperity. Moreover, it is possible that this advice is an extreme example (or "focal instance") set by those who do not have the resources to defend their social position, an example posed as an alternative for those who do have such resources (so Kloppenborg 1991, 88). While ostensibly addressed to lenders, it actually articulates the conflict with lenders and defines what lenders should be like. It may even lay the foundations for the hospitality and help later to be sought by Q workers from their hosts in Q 10. The general vulnerability that has been exposed in the sayings we have examined — and in others at which one could look, such as the mission instructions in Q — seems to make it doubtful that the Q people as a whole were really secure enough to be lenders on anything other than a very minor scale.

But why does Q display such hesitancy about recourse to the courts, whether as borrowers or lenders? It cannot simply be the advice of a good lawyer to a poor client to avoid litigation. As suggested earlier, the action is too consistently one-sided to be legal advice.[38] Furthermore, the fear of such institutions seems to extend in Q 12 to being brought before courts because of the *message* the Q people espoused. Why would the Q people feel vulnerable in this respect? It is unlikely that their views were sufficiently distinct from Judaism or that their message was sufficiently "heretical" to lead to the fear of synagogue expulsions of the kind that might have been faced later by the Johannine Christians.[39] Their vulnerability therefore must be related to their attack on the culture in which they lived, as Kloppenborg and others have rightly shown. If they sought the renewal of the socioeconomic structures of the society in which they lived, as revealed in the Q beatitudes, then surely it would make sense to show wariness toward those very structures in *all their aspects*.

This is effectively what has been found. To give up *entirely* on secular justice, even in personal contractual relationships, seems to rest on an ideological stance. After all, if genuinely injured, sometimes one might expect to win — at least a little, some of the time. Even the peasants did appear to have some right of redress in some situations.[40] But to advocate such a line would be to reaffirm the institutions around them, to affirm that it might be possible at times to have two masters or to affirm two codes of honor — to declare God's renewal of society providing a new honor and dignity for the poor or oppressed, and yet to use the present institutions of society to pursue one's own material claims and affirm conventional codes of honor. Not only does another Q saying, Q 16:13, declare that you cannot serve two such masters, but also the repeated emphasis on trust in God's providence in Q does not encourage this.

The question of honor is also not insignificant here. Malina notes that it was considered highly dishonorable to go to court to seek legal redress from one's equal. Apart from the vulnerability to an uncertain outcome and thus the possibility of public shame, to be forced to go to court to settle a dispute highlights one's inability to deal with one's own problems and equals (Malina 1981, 39). This itself implies dishonor; and this is also why self-help was usually the first line of recourse, as observed above. However, as we have seen, the exhortations in Q 6:29–30 do not even advocate self-help. How then is honor to be preserved in such situations? It is possible to see here a radical reversal of honor codes, but this requires closer examination. It may be more precise to see here a manipulation of the honor codes in favor of the weak and threatened Q people. Whereas, according to those codes, it was highly dishonorable not to respond to a challenge by an equal, there was no dishonor in not responding to a challenge by someone of lesser status (Malina 1981, 36). Indeed, it was dishonorable to respond in such a situation. Thus it is significant that in Q 6:22–23, 27–36 the references to the status of the Q addressees are prominent. Their response is equated with "mercy" (Q 6:36);[41] their call to love enemies is based explicitly upon their status as "sons of your Father/the Most High" (Q 6:35);[42] and the expectation is that their behavior should exceed the expectations that apply to "sinners/Gentiles" (Q 6:32–33). Similarly, in Q 6:22–23 their status is depicted in terms comparable to the "prophets" persecuted in the past. In other words, they are being challenged not by equals but by those of a lesser calling to whom they should show mercy. There is no affront to honor; the honor system has been manipulated to their benefit. As "sons of the Father/Most High," their recourse is to divine help not self-help, which would only bring dishonor upon them. Thus the sayings about encouraging simple trust in their heavenly Father to care for their needs and to meet their fears are completely consonant with this stance. However much their actual powerlessness may give rise to this rationale, the perspective that has been adopted for their "universe" provides a means of coping with their situation of apparent weakness in ways that are not "dishonorable" but that rely upon an assessment of their status that does not derive from society itself.

This makes it more difficult to believe that those responsible for these Q traditions are still local administrators, those with one foot in each camp. They may once have been so. However, whether by hardship (see Kloppenborg 1991, 87–88) or by conviction or by both, they apparently have recognized a fundamental incompatibility between the two worldviews. This has been focused particularly on a rejection of the contractual and legal system. This is not the same as seeking poverty as such (see Robinson 1995) or itinerancy as an ideal in itself[43] but rather seems related to hopes for a renewal of the social structures of their day.[44] Whether they were also attracted to or stimulated by Cynic ideals is yet another debate.[45] They are not even idealistic lawyers working on behalf of the poor. They have lost confidence in the legal system, but they have formulated a new understanding of their own status and have demonstrated an almost naive confidence in the providence of God and the hospitality of those among whom they work. With time, it was probably the judgment of God as well as the providence of God in which they came to hope.

NOTES

1. Horsley (1991b, 180–82) emphasizes the importance of determining the functions and purposes of the individual "clusters" of sayings in Q "regardless of whether one finds a particular hypothesis of stratigraphy convincing" (182).

2. See Kloppenborg 1991, 88; Horsley 1991b, 185–86; see also Horsley 1985, 3–31, and (with regard to Jesus) Horsley 1987, 259–73; Weaver 1992, 34–36.

3. See Schottroff 1978, 9–39. For a general review of some recent work, see Klassen 1992, 1–31, and the bibliography in the same volume (Swartley 1992, 314–22). On the community orientation of these Q sayings, see below (especially n. 43).

4. See Wink 1992b, 104. Wink speculates that because Luke views the whole passage as a response to armed robbery, he has no use for the saying in Matt 5:41 (which Wink attributes "probably" to Q) about the enforced carrying of Roman imperial baggage.

5. See Wink 1992b, 104; Luz 1989, 324: "The Matthean version of 42b is less radical than the Lukan version, which again presupposes the situation of robbery."

6. The imagery of a thief is also found in Q 12:39–40, but here rather differently as a parabolic image in the context of the unknown hour of the coming Son of Man.

7. With respect to the defenselessness of the Q movement, see Robinson 1995.

8. The more developed argument for this is to be found in my re-construction of Q 6:27–36. This was originally formulated in R. Piper 1989, 78–82, corresponding to a large degree with Zeller 1977, 102–3; Schulz 1972, 127–31; Bultmann 1968, 79. A modified version of this reconstruction was subsequently formulated for the International Q Project. In favor of Matthew's order of the sayings on nonretaliation and love of enemies (once stripped of Matthew's antithetical formulations) as better representing the Q order than Luke's sequence are the following arguments:

a. The switch from second-person-plural to second-person-singular ex-hortations in Luke 6:27–36 is an indication that Q 6:29–30 was originally a separate unit, as in Matthew. The content of these sayings is also not directly related to love of enemies in each case. Furthermore, there is nothing to suggest that singular exhortations are more appropriate for the content of Q 6:29–30 than for Q 6:27–28.

b. Q 6:29–30(31) as a separate series of exhortations about non-retaliation, preceding the love-of-enemies teaching as in Matthew, would follow easily on Q 6:22–23, the final Q persecution beatitude.

c. If Q 6:29–31 were a separate group of sayings, then the remaining sayings consisting of Q 6:27–28, 32–33, 35ac appear to be a coherently organized section.

d. Luke's repetition of the love-of-enemies exhortation (in contrast to its appearance only once in Matthew) appears to be caused by the interruption introduced by Q 6:29–30(31).

e. Although it is possible to argue that Matthew is responsible for cre-ating a more "logical" arrangement of two separate sets of exhortations, this convinces only if one can find no good motive for Luke producing the arrangement that he preserves. My argument is that such a motive can be found. The affront to honor and vulnerability to exploitation involved in the nonretaliation teaching were being deliberately subsumed under the positive ethic of mercy and love of enemies.

It is significant that no motivation clauses appear in Q 6:29–30 (in contrast to the extensive argumentation offered for love of enemies). In Q, on my proposal, the sayings about nonretaliation receive in final Q their motivating explanation by the direct proximity to the preceding beatitude (Q 6:22–23), citing the example of the fate of the prophets. In Luke, the necessary motivation was provided by incorporation into the midst of the love-of-enemies teaching. In Matthew, the sayings receive their rationale as an intensification of the law.

I am indebted to James M. Robinson for further clarifying the place of the Golden Rule (Q 6:31) in this argument. If Q 6:29–30 followed in Q directly on Q 6:22–23, then Q 6:31, a universal maxim (known in the plural), would provide a good sequence with 6:30 on the theme of reciprocity. The love-of-enemies sayings would then follow not as a continuation but as a culmination, showing how Jesus' teaching goes beyond reciprocity. The logic of the Q sequence is thus strengthened. For another explanation that attributes the location of the Golden Rule to the Q editor, see Catchpole 1993, 113–15.

Catchpole (1993, 101) objects, however, that such "sandwich structures" (as in Q 6:27–28, 29–31, 32–35) are not a feature of Luke, whose inclination is "to smooth and refine away interruptions, and certainly not to create them." It is clear that Luke has not refined away this one, however, and it is my contention that it is not for reasons of style but for reasons of content that Luke makes the alteration.

9. Acceptance of an ongoing material and physical vulnerability could hardly sit easily with Luke's concern to console the poor. Regarding officials, see the experience of extortion against which John the Baptist warns soldiers in Luke 3:14.

10. See n. 8, above.

11. In contrast to J. Piper (1979, 135), see R. Piper 1989, 78, 226 n. 291; Luz 1989, 273–79, 323–24, 339. The attribution of the antithetical formulations in these cases to Matthew, however, does not require that Matthew also is responsible for separating the nonretaliation teaching from the love-of-enemies teaching (see n. 8, above).

12. The suggestion that Matthew is making a deliberate link with the passion narrative may imply a Matthean change in Matt 26:67 as plausibly as a change here (but cf. *rapisma* in Mark 14:65).

13. Wink 1992b, 105. Wink also interestingly suggests that turning the other cheek was a means of robbing the oppressor of the power to humiliate, presenting a cheek that cannot normally be backhanded!

14. J. Piper (1979, 58) considers the reference to the right cheek to be a "legal technicality" that Luke has removed; see also Catchpole (1993, 24–26), who argues that the version in Matthew is typical of "the recurrent pattern of Jesus' teaching which often takes as its starting-point the most trivial offence by the Christian disciple or the most extreme offence against him." This pattern is not completely consistent, however, as Matthew himself shows.

15. Luz 1989, 325. Catchpole (1993, 24–26) does acknowledge that there are other instances of Matthew introducing *dexios* redactionally (Matt 5:29–30; 18:8–9), but Catchpole notes that the right-left order is conventional and that the insertion in Matt 5:29–30 may be reminiscent of the text in 5:39.

16. See Horsley 1987, 268. But note also the ostracon-text referred to by Fitzmyer 1981, 639.

17. But if Luke's order were original, as Wink suggests, then there is little to explain Matthew's change to a less appropriate image. This is particularly true for Matthew because the movement from the greater to

the lesser is preserved in 5:39, so there would be little reason for Matthew deliberately to reverse that in 5:40.

18. It is possible to agree with Luz, however, regarding his doubts about Matthean redactional activity.

19. This is particularly true in view of his apparent alterations in Matt 5:42 (see below), whereby a radical exhortation to lend even to those who cannot pay back at all is made into a more conventional call to almsgiving and lending.

20. See also Horsley (1987, 262–73), who relates these sayings to local village interaction. He credits Matthew with applying them to enemies who were "outsiders" by putting the instructions into the framework of antitheses, which contrast enemy with neighbor.

21. Whether Luke has also stylistically sought to improve Matthew's Greek in Q 6:29b, however, is more debated; see Hoffmann 1984, 60.

22. Weaver (1992, 53–54): "In distinction from Deut. 19:15–21 the setting of the Matthean text is not that of a court case. Not only is there no mention of an appearance 'before the Lord, the priests, and the judges' (Deut. 19:17); but there is also, significantly, no mention of any 'careful examination' by the judges (Deut. 19:18) to establish the guilt of the antagonist.... While the community is enjoined to take action, as becomes evident from the imperative that follows 'But I say to you,' this action lies beyond established courtroom procedures."

23. Rightly, Catchpole 1993, 112.

24. Catchpole (1993, 112): "*[D]anizein* and *apaitein* together have an association which helps us to understand the presence of Q 6:30 in this setting" (see below). I am also indebted to James M. Robinson for the observation that the use of *thelein,* found in Matthew here, appears to link Q 6:29, 30, 31 and is clearly not due to Matthew since the Golden Rule is located elsewhere in Matthew.

25. So Luz (1989, 329), who also favors the originality of Luke's wording, although for Luz this includes the reference to robbing. Schottroff (1978, 18–20) does cite ancient evidence of it being honorable for a stronger party to show mercy toward a weaker party, but clemency or beneficence toward the poor is hardly the basis for regular financial dealings, as seems to be implied in this Q saying.

26. So also Catchpole 1993, 112, except for our inclusion of *thelein* (see n. 24, above).

27. In many business and contractual relationships in papyrus records provision for "acts of recovery" in case of default is a prominent feature (see Llewelyn 1992, 82–105 with respect to tenancies and lease of boats).

28. Kloppenborg (1991, 90) attributes this saying to Q[1] even though it "signals the beginnings of the formation of social boundaries."

29. The parable of the widow in Luke 18:1–8 also shows that, for his part, Luke has no aversion to recourse to the courts. Indeed, he encour-

ages it! This might also explain his alterations to Q, if Q's wording is closer to that of Matthew in stressing avoidance of legal recourse.

30. Not inappropriately, the cluster of sayings continues with instruction about the hypocrisy of judging one's brother. Thus the cluster of sayings strongly suggests that the problems do not stem entirely from outside the boundaries of normal social (and perhaps commercial) interaction of the Q group.

31. Matthew's location of Q 12:58–59 in his sermon at Matt 5:25–26 is interesting and perhaps significant. In Q, the saying seems to be addressed to "opponents," but (as elsewhere in Q) such "attacks" may in fact serve to strengthen the identity of the "in-group." If so, then the exhortation would be significant for that in-group.

32. The bailiff would serve a writ on the defaulter, who in turn had three options: to pay in full, and the matter would be settled; to do nothing and have his property seized by the state and auctioned until enough was raised to pay the creditor; or to appeal to the authorities, which would require a judicial decision about liability, leaving it to the bailiff then to take any appropriate action regarding enforcement (see Llewelyn 1992, 90).

33. This was apparently true even in cases of theft or assault, where it was up to the wronged party to petition the authorities to investigate the matter. J. D. M. Derrett (1982, 477–564) and Martin Hengel (1968, 1–39) both argue that the administration of law in Palestine was so ineffective in the first century that individuals had to result to self-help (as in the parable of wicked tenants); but Llewelyn more recently has cast doubt on this by appeal to Q 12:58–59 and the third-century B.C.E. Zenon papyri, which refer to authorities taking action upon being petitioned. This may reflect a declining significance of self-help solutions with the extension of Graeco-Roman administration and the state's intervention even in private disputes to prevent more general social unrest, but first-century evidence for this is ambiguous (Llewelyn 1992, 98–99). See below on the issue of self-help as a matter of honor.

34. In general, of course, the legal system appears to have secured the creditor class against the debtor class. The introduction of the *prozbul* by Hillel also secured a loan against annulment in the sabbatical year, in Jewish proceedings.

35. On the argumentation used, see R. Piper 1989, 15–36.

36. Horsley also observes that the instruction may be sapiential, but it is not of the scholarly sort (1991b, 205).

37. Kloppenborg (1991, 88) raises the question without providing any answer.

38. This is different from the more cautious statement: "Often it does not pay to avenge injustice" (Seneca, *De ira* 2.34.1, cited in Schottroff 1978, 17).

39. Horsley (1991b, 195–96) argues that nothing in Q indicates an emergent "Christian" self-consciousness over against Judaism, nor is there any indication of gentile mission. Even Q 22:28–30 is viewed not as a negative judgment on Israel but rather as an expression of a hope for its restoration. Kloppenborg (1991, 94–96) sees the possibility of Gentiles being incorporated into Israel in Q^2 and attributes this perhaps to a change of location to the Decapolis or the coast or the cities and large towns of Galilee. It should be remembered, however, that gentile receptiveness can always be used as a motif to shame Jewish opponents, who are viewed as unresponsive or hostile.

40. Schottroff (1978, 18) cites similar attitudes in Athenagoras and 1 Pet 2:18–25, arguing that the imperative is borne of necessity and testifies to the recipients' dependent state. Their options were not open, but (unlike similar calls to patient endurance in Seneca or the Babylonian *Counsels of Wisdom*) the "Christian texts were quite unaware that it was their powerlessness which played a determinative role in the subject's behavior. An attitude of submission . . . is elevated here with surprising assurance as the ideal." I am not so convinced that the Q addressees' powerlessness was complete and their options entirely closed. Otherwise the exhortation would make little sense. Even if it be argued that the exhortations serve in part to legitimate the low status of the people, other sapiential material in Q goes further to address attitudes of anxiety about physical or material needs (Q 12:22–31) and fears for personal security (Q 12:4–7). These are fundamental fears that remain "options" for all, regardless of status. Moreover, my reconstruction of Q 6:30 depicts a situation of a lender, which again would not be one of complete powerlessness. Undoubtedly a general sense of weakness is to be presumed (and it is unlikely they were unaware of it in sayings such as Q 12:58–59!), but it is doubtful that adopting a simple trust in God's care was the only or even the easiest of the alternatives open to the Q people.

41. Luke's wording ("merciful") here is more likely to represent Q than Matthew's ("perfect"): see Catchpole 1993, 116; Lührmann 1972, 421–22; Schulz 1972, 130; Luz 1989, 346–47; Kloppenborg 1987a, 180–81.

42. For the argument that this refers as much to their present status as to future reward, see R. Piper 1989, 84.

43. That the sapiential material presupposes a concern for communities is argued, for example, by R. Piper 1989, 70–74, 184–86; Horsley 1991b, 197, 205; Kloppenborg 1991, 86–91.

44. See Horsley 1991b, 203–9 and his article in the present volume; Kloppenborg (1991, 88): "[T]hey were prepared to imagine an alternative to the present order." See also Q 12:2–12.

45. Schottroff (1978, 21–22) notes parallels with the portrayals of the Cynics as individuals who suffered abuse in order to highlight "the rottenness of society" but states that if "we compare these legends with Matt.

5:38ff. par. the difference is clear. It is important for the understanding
of the ethical teaching of the synoptics that the subject addressed is not
an isolated individual, but a member of the Christian community." More
recently, Leif Vaage (1995) defends the analogy between Q and Cynicism.
Vaage notes C. M. Tuckett's objection that Diogenes is often depicted
as far from generous to his enemies and therefore that Epictetus simply
describes a Stoic ideal of how a Cynic ought to behave (Tuckett 1989,
366). Vaage, however, replies that inconsistencies among the Cynics with
respect to loving enemies can also be found for Q and Jesus.

Part II

The Inaugural Sermon

Composite Texts and
Oral Mythology

The Case of the "Sermon" in Q (6:20–49)

Increasingly accepted among Q scholars is John S. Kloppenborg's thesis in *The Formation of Q* (1987a) that the early Christian document otherwise known as the Synoptic Sayings Source had at least two (and mostly likely three) identifiable literary strata. These two (or three) distinct intervals of extensive compositional activity in Q are theoretically to be discerned largely on the basis of the following two criteria: (1) continuity of theme, implied audience, and patterns of speech; and (2) the observation of discontinuity or redactional breaks between and within blocks of otherwise cohesive materials.[1] According to Kloppenborg's thesis, the result of such an analysis is a compositional chronology for Q consisting, first, essentially of "wisdom" or "instructional" materials (= Q^1) and, second, of "apocalyptic" or more polemical materials (= Q^2).[2]

At the same time, Kloppenborg, in *The Formation of Q*, is careful to distinguish this literary history of the document from the history of its various "traditions," even though tradition-historical analyses are often part of the set of observations that lead to his literary judgments. In making such a distinction, Kloppenborg reflects the traditional assumption of not a few New Testament scholars that prior to the composition of Q's formative stratum, a number of earlier smaller collections of sayings circulated "orally." Indeed, Kloppenborg's description of the various subsections making up Q's formative stratum as "clusters" belongs to the same "oral" imagination of Christian literary origins.

Leif E. Vaage is an assistant professor of New Testament at Emmanuel College, Toronto School of Theology.

One such "cluster," whose original status as an independent smaller collection of sayings has often been suggested by scholars (though not, in fact, by Kloppenborg), is the so-called "sermon" in 6:20b–49.[3] James M. Robinson writes, for example, in his article "Early Collections of Jesus' Sayings":

> It is particularly the Sermon on the Mount/Plain that has come in question in recent years, as to whether it is to be recognized as a collection in its own right rather than being merely considered a segment of Q. Lc 6, 20–49 does not seem to be just a random segment within a larger whole, for it is a well-rounded unit, beginning impressively with the beatitudes and concluding appropriately with a parable of the house built on rock or sand, to illustrate what doing or not doing Jesus' "words" (Lc 6, 47) ultimately means. Thus one may suspect that it existed as a composition in its own right. (1982, 391)

One may always "suspect" that the "sermon" in Q was originally "a composition in its own right," but what finally constitutes "proof" of this imaginable possibility? In the end, did or did not the "sermon" in Q once exist on its own? How shall we decide? What will make one argument pro or con "more probable" than the others?

The burden of the present essay is to delimit the framework of such a conversation so that its participants will not simply be speaking past each other, owing to the fact that, while we all "see" the "same" things, different categorical frameworks for talking about those things, even if we use the "same" terms, have us drawing quite distinct conclusions. One of the fault lines of disagreement will be the notion of oral composition, that is, whether or not such an activity can be meaningfully discussed and its erstwhile products commonly discerned. It is my opinion that, even if the idea of oral composition per se should prove theoretically defensible, it cannot be instituted methodologically in the study of the Synoptic tradition, that it is thus of no practical use for our present purposes, and that, therefore, such a concept should no longer remain part of the debate.

In what follows, I shall first consider possible evidence from other early Christian literature that Q 6:20b–49 once existed apart from its current presentation in the Synoptic Sayings Source. I shall then review Kloppenborg's composition-analysis of the "sermon" in *The Formation of Q*. In a third section, the relative independent integrity of the "sermon" versus its integration into the rest of Q's

Table 1

Q	Gos. Thom.	Gos. Thom.	Q
6:20b	54	6	6:31
6:21	69b	26	6:41–42
6:22–23	68–69a	34	6:39
6:30	95	43	6:43–44
6:31	6	45	6:45
6:39	34	54	6:20b
6:41–42	26	68–69a	6:22–23
6:43–44	43	69b	6:21
6:45	45	95	6:30

formative stratum shall be considered. And finally the supposition of the "sermon" as an erstwhile oral composition will be entertained. In conclusion, then, beyond summarizing and synthesizing the results of the preceding four discrete investigations, any abiding peculiarities will be noted with additional questions to be pursued.

Documentary Evidence

Other early Christian documents include (variants of) a number of the "same" sayings found in Q 6:20b–49. What do these texts suggest, if anything, about the possibility of an earlier writing that would be the "sermon" circulating apart from its present context in the Synoptic Sayings Source? An obvious case in point is the *Gospel of Thomas*. What does it tell us? The parallels are shown in table 1, from which it becomes immediately apparent that the *Gospel of Thomas* does not share any obvious sequence of sayings with the "sermon" in Q.[4] This is an extremely important observation, if only because one of the fundamental arguments for the erstwhile existence of Q (as a document) has been the shared order of sayings between Matthew and Luke apart from Mark.[5] The absence of any similar correspondence between Q and the *Gospel of Thomas* would suggest, therefore, at least in the case of the "sermon," that no such prior text or earlier independent composition ever existed that was subsequently employed by each evangelist.

The only possible coincidences of order are Q 6:21, 22–23 ‖ *Gos. Thom.* 69, 68 (in both cases, the same two sayings are contiguous to each other, although in reverse order) and Q 6:43–44, 45 ‖ *Gos. Thom.* 43, 45 (the same sequence, though in the case of

Table 2

Luke	Gos. Thom.	Did.	Pol. Phil.	2 Clem.
6:20	54	–	2:3	–
6:21	69b	–	–	–
6:22–23	68–69a	–	–	–
6:27–28	–	1:3	12:3	13:4
6:29–30	–	1:4–5	–	–
6:30	95	–	–	–
6:31	6	–	–	–
6:32–33	–	1:3	–	13:4
6:36	–	6:2	–	–
6:38	–	–	2:3	13:2
6:39	34	–	–	–
6:41–42	26	–	–	–
6:43–44	43	11:8	–	–
6:45	45	–	–	–
6:46	–	–	–	4:1–2

the *Gospel of Thomas* with another saying inserted in between).[6] There are thus only two sets of "matched pairs" of sayings: the repeated association of a pair of utterances with each other — each set, moreover, quite separate from the other. This is hardly a sufficient basis on which to posit the earlier independent existence of the "sermon" in Q.[7]

Of course, one could always argue that the *Gospel of Thomas* has selected sayings from an earlier independent document now imbedded in Q as its inaugural "sermon" and has located these sayings at different places in the *Gospel of Thomas* wherever it seemed best to the "fifth" evangelist. This line of reasoning, however, begs more questions than it answers. There is certainly no way of proving such an "imaginable" occurrence. Moreover, at least half of the "sermon" in Q is otherwise unparalleled in the *Gospel of Thomas*. All of the sayings in Q 6:27–29, 32–36, 38, 40, 46–49 lack counterparts in the *Gospel of Thomas*. Did the latter evangelist simply have no use for these elements of the hypothetical independent sermon that Q 6:20b–49 and the *Gospel of Thomas* would ostensibly attest? How is such an explanation more than an argument from silence?

Further parallels between the "sermon" in Q and other early Christian literature only deepen the conviction that the "sermon"

Table 3

Q	Rom	Jas[8]	1 Pet	Mark	John
6:22–23	–	–	3:14	–	–
			4:13–14		
6:27–30	–	–	3:9	–	–
6:27–28	12:14	–	–	–	–
6:37–38	2:1	4:11–12	–	4:24	–
6:40	–	–	–	–	13:16
					15:20
6:43–44	–	3:12	–	–	–

did not exist as an independent work prior to its composition in the document's formative stratum (see table 2). The parallels to the "sermon" in Q found in the *Didache,* Polycarp's *Letter to the Philippians,* and *2 Clement* are virtually all different from those occurring in the *Gospel of Thomas;* only *Gos. Thom.* 43 and *Did.* 11:8 parallel Q 6:43–44, while *Gos. Thom.* 54 and Pol. *Phil.* 2:3 recall Q 6:20. Moreover, except for Q 6:27–28 (=*Did.* 1:3; Pol. *Phil.* 12:3; *2 Clem.* 13:4), the *Didache,* Polycarp's *Letter to the Philippians,* and *2 Clement* differ completely from each other regarding their respective agreements with the "sermon" in Q (though *Did.* 1:3 and *2 Clem.* 13:4 also recall together Q 6:32–33). Hence it is impossible to claim that there ever existed at any time prior to the composition of the "sermon" in Q an independent work able to account for the charted interconnections between the five documents listed in table 2.

Table 3 lists other parallels to the "sermon" in Q found within the canonical New Testament. Once again, we see the impossibility of positing any shared text as the basis of these sporadic correspondences before the composition of the "sermon" in Q's formative stratum. Most notable is perhaps the fact that beyond the slight agreement of Q 6:37–38 with Mark 4:24, absolutely no relationship otherwise exists between Q 6:20b–49 and the Gospel of Mark. So-called overlaps between Mark and Q are often taken to signal clusters of tradition existing prior to the composition of either of these documents (see, e.g., Laufen 1980; Sellew 1986; Schüling 1991). In this case, the total absence of any such (significant) correspondence would suggest the nonexistence of an earlier composition like the "sermon" in Q prior to the document's formative stratum.

All other parallels to the "sermon" in Q from any as yet unmentioned early Christian document are limited to variants of a single saying.[9] No documentary evidence thus exists that would warrant even the suspicion that the "sermon" in Q once existed apart from its initial composition as part of Q's formative stratum. Are there nonetheless perhaps other grounds for continuing to imagine such a possibility?

Composition Analysis

Kloppenborg sums up his view of the composition history of the "sermon" in Q as follows:

> Composition analysis has shown that a rather complex process contributed to the formation of 6:20b–49. We have already suggested that the association of the beatitudes with the admonition to love one's enemies presupposed that 6:22–23b was already part of the beatitudes, and that 6:35b may have been inserted into 6:35a, c at the time of this addition. Q 6:36 provides a transition between 6:27–35 and 6:37–38. Whereas the first half of the speech concerns violence, generosity and mercy, Q 6:39–45 is unified by the concern with speaking and teaching (or correcting). In typically sapiential style, the speech closes with a mild reproach and a contrast saying designed to express the urgency of attending to the teacher's words. (1987a, 187)

The summary does not say everything. Elsewhere, Kloppenborg notes that the initial beatitudes in Q 6:20–23 "share many of the structural and formal features of the sapiential beatitude, in particular, serialization and placement at the beginning of an instruction." Kloppenborg also states that "Q 6:46, 47–49 provides a good example of the warnings which typically conclude these instructions" (1987a, 188). Though Kloppenborg does not himself draw the conclusion, one might invoke these remarks as support for the suspicion that the "sermon" in Q was once an independent tradition.

But does Kloppenborg's initial summary statement, "Composition analysis has shown that a rather complex process contributed to the formation of 6:20b–49," in fact summarize what Kloppenborg's own measured observations regarding each saying or complex of sayings in this "sermon" would suggest? I think not. What Kloppenborg's composition analysis of the "sermon" in Q successfully demonstrates is simply the fact that this "block" of material in the Synoptic Sayings Source is indeed a composite text. It was not spun out of whole cloth. Exactly what, however, the precise significance is of the various disjunctures that make evident the composite nature of the same "sermon" in Q still remains to be determined.

To say that these disjunctures betray "a rather complex process" behind "the formation of 6:20b–49" presupposes that the "sermon" in Q is the result of a prolonged process of material aggregation (see Kloppenborg 1995b). But, to go straight to the point, why not understand the same set of disjunctures as simply evidence of the less than flawless work of the person(s) who, at a particular time and place, first put Q 6:20b–49 together along with the rest of the document's formative stratum? I assume that there is no reason not to suppose that the formative stratum of Q was in fact composed at a specific time and place.

Let us now look more closely at what Kloppenborg says about each section of the "sermon" in Q. Regarding the opening set of macarisms, Kloppenborg concludes: "The cluster of beatitudes in 6:20b–23 thus contains (at least) three components: 6:20b–21, a *Grundwort,* which was expanded and reinterpreted by vv. 22–23b. Verse 23c is a further expansion of vv. 22–23b" (1987a, 173). Actually, the so-called *Grundwort* in 6:20b–21 is itself made up of three component parts, namely, the three separate beatitudes in Q 6:20b, 6:21a, and 6:21b. All together, therefore, 6:20b–23 has (at least) five notable "breaks" in its conglomeration.[10] In this case, Kloppenborg interestingly reserves judgment about the meaning of such fissures, claiming that "[d]etermination of the stages at which these units were combined must await a discussion of the entire sermon" (1987a, 173).

We move on, then, to the command to "love your enemies" in Q 6:27–35. Kloppenborg writes:

> That 6:27–35 is composite is obvious. The first four imperatives are formulated in the second-person plural and all agree in placing the imperative in first position. Verses 29, 30, on the other hand, are in the second-person singular and follow the form *tō* + participle + imperative (or prohibitive). Most see in vv. 29–30 the combination of two originally independent sayings: an admonition concerning the seizure of goods and a much more general admonition to generous giving (or lending). It goes without saying that the Golden Rule (6:31), formulated in the second-person plural, had a widespread and independent circulation apart from this particu-

> lar context. Verses 32–33 obviously refer back to and presuppose vv. 27–28 while v. 34, which seems to have been formed on analogy to the preceding verses, grounds 6:30 (with *daneizō*). (1987a, 176)

The saying as a whole (6:27–35) is complex, to say the least. Indeed, as Kloppenborg's remarks imply, the verses could be taken to constitute a compositional unit in themselves (see also R. Piper 1989, 78–86). The logical stresses and strains, plus the rhetorical variation from verse to verse, would once again betray the (imperfect) art of early Christian writing, the result of crafting an extended argument from different traditional materials.[11] There is no obvious reason why one must think that the effort to do so in the case of 6:27–35 must necessarily have preceded the composition of the "sermon" itself in Q (6:20b–49).

At this point, however, Kloppenborg adopts the perspective of Heinz Schürmann, who

> suggests that the earliest elaboration of vv. 27–28 was 32–33, 35a, c [hence Kloppenborg's assertion above that "verses 32–33 obviously refer back to and presuppose vv. 27–28"] and that vv. 29–31 and 35b came later. Since vv. 29, 30, 31 appear to be an insertion which interrupts the connection between the imperatives (vv. 27–28) and their elaboration (vv. 32–33), this solution is plausible.[12]

The same argument, however, loses its plausibility if, for example, 6:29–30 does not in fact "interrupt" the "elaboration" of 6:27–28 by 6:32–33 but, instead, itself elaborates 6:27–28 in a specific fashion.[13] Furthermore, the Golden Rule of mutual reciprocity in 6:31, while it may seem to contradict the one-sided reasoning of the sayings in 6:27–35, thus revealing that it was "added later," can also be understood, precisely by virtue of its present position immediately after 6:30 and before 6:32–33, to undergird by further elaborating the preceding instructions in 6:27–30. For if one did not really wish to be hated by every foe and to perpetuate forever the circle of assault and personal violence, by doing unto others what 6:27–28, 29–30 implore, one might eventually hope to receive like treatment in return.[14] Otherwise, as the sayings in 6:32–33 immediately make clear — establishing the argument of 6:27–31 through consideration of the opposite — the Golden Rule serves just as well the interests of tax collectors and Gentiles. Positive reasons are finally suggested in 6:35b for behaving in this admittedly unorthodox manner.

The point is simply that the composite nature of the sayings-complex in 6:27–35 does not require that we imagine "a rather complex process" of antecedent material aggregation, gradually forming what we now know as the discourse in Q on love of enemies, as though the text were a piece of sedimentary rock, laid down in successive waves of application. The development of the discourse in 6:27–35 need reflect nothing more than the progressive elaboration of an argument for which a series of imperatives (6:27–28, 29–30), a well-known proverb (6:31), a couple of comparisons (6:32–33), and a corresponding pair of promises (6:35b) are employed. Again, some textual unevenness is evident. The robe of reasoning in this regard is not seamless. What is not apparent, however, is why such unevenness would necessarily signal a compositional history antecedent to the production of the "sermon" itself in Q (6:20b–49).

Regarding the sayings in Q 6:36, 37–38, Kloppenborg writes:

> Q 6:37a, (b), 38c may have circulated as an independent sapiential admonition, conceivably in a cluster of sayings such as is found now in *1 Clem.* 13:2. In Q, however, it further develops the preceding speech on love of enemies and, more specifically, explicates the programmatic injunction to imitate divine mercy (6:36). (1987a, 180–81)

This is a very telling set of statements. Kloppenborg recognizes that the sequence of sayings here in Q (6:36, 37–38) entails a certain compositional logic. What is said in 6:37–38 "explicates" what has just been said in 6:36, which both in Luke and in Matthew (though to somewhat different effects) is in turn attested to have elaborated the previous sayings-complex in 6:27–35.[15]

> The effect of the juxtaposition of 6:37–38 and 6:36 is twofold: to interpret the ethic of noncondemnation as an act of mercy, and to see this mercy as imitation of divine action. This motif binds 6:36, 37–38 closely with 6:27–35. (1987a, 181)

The coherence observed here between Q 6:27–35, 36, 37–38 is not found in any other early Christian document. It seems logical to conclude, therefore, that before the composition of the "sermon" in Q (6:20b–49), no such combination of sayings had previously been made. The supposition, based on variants of the saying in other documents, that 6:37a, 38c "may have circulated as an independent sapiential admonition, conceivably in a cluster of sayings such as is found now in *1 Clem.* 13:2," whether right or wrong as such, has nothing whatsoever to do with the compositional history of the "sermon" in Q, specifically, the possibility that the same text (6:20b–49) once circulated as an independent work.[16]

Regarding the sequence of statements in Q 6:39–45, Kloppenborg writes: "It is clear that this section of Q is composed of several originally independent sayings: 6:39, 40, 41–42, 43–44, and 45" (1987a, 182). In other words, we face again a composite text. To say, however, that the various sayings in question were "originally independent" connotes more than the text itself can sustain. All we know, in fact, is that variants of (some of) these sayings appear in other documents as well. Nonetheless, Kloppenborg writes:

> Evidently the basis for the association between v. 39 and vv. 41–42 is the common motif of impaired vision and the importance of sighted instruction or correction. Since 6:40 does not share this motif, it is most likely that 6:40 was already attached to 6:39 prior to its association with vv. 41–42. Schürmann rightly observes, "Presumably no one would have encumbered the coherence of vv. 39, 41–42 so severely by a subsequent addition of v. 40." (1987a, 182)

I beg to differ, however, not knowing precisely what Schürmann presumes when he writes, "Presumably." Why should we not rather understand the "encumbrance" represented by the saying in Q 6:40 to the "coherence of vv. 39, 41–42" as the mark of a redactional insertion? Far from being "most likely that 6:40 was already attached to 6:39," it is just as likely, if not more so, that 6:40 was added to 6:39 after 6:39 and 6:41–42 had already been combined, for example, as part of Q's secondary redaction.[17]

"The following cluster of sayings (6:43–45) is also composite," notes Kloppenborg (1987a, 182). Indeed, according to Kloppenborg, the three verses in Q 6:43–45 are made up of four quite different elements: 6:43 is "a proverb"; 6:44a is an interpretation of 6:43; 6:44b represents "further grounding for vv. 43, 44a"; and, finally, 6:45 is "an originally independent saying," now serving as a "commentary word."[18] Only the prior attachment of 6:45 to 6:43–44 is discussed, however, "when this unit was connected with 6:41–42 and 6:39–40" (1987a, 183).

As already observed regarding 6:20b–23, disjunctive features in the sequence of a given set of sayings are not always taken by Kloppenborg to reveal a composition-history antecedent to that of the eventual Q text itself. This is, I think, extremely important to recognize. For it is the rhetorical unevenness of the "sermon" in Q, namely, its obviously composite nature, that otherwise tends rather matter-of-factly to support the presupposition that "a rather complex process contributed to the formation of 6:20b–49." In the particular case of 6:43, 44a, 44b, however, beyond establishing the progressive logic that now links these sayings together, nothing is said about any prior process of their composition as a unit.

At one point when discussing the meaning of 6:39–45, Kloppenborg makes the following remarks:

> Q 6:36 recommends the imitation of divine mercy; 6:39, seen in the context .of vv. 36, 37–38, 40–42, recommends imitation of the *didaskalos* (Jesus) who exemplifies the ethic of nonjudgment as well as nonretaliation, love of enemies and startling beneficence. Q 6:39–45, of course, takes particular aim at teachers (actual or imagined) who do not follow Jesus in his radical lifestyle and ethic. (1987a, 184–85)

These observations are made in debating the question of whether or not the sayings in 6:39–42 were first formulated with outsiders and opponents in view. Once again, however, self-consciously or not, Kloppenborg reveals how the "sermon" in Q (6:36–45) manifests a specific coherence at the level of the text as such, one otherwise quite unparalleled elsewhere. The specific logic, moreover, that conjoins these sayings to one another moves across the "surface" of the text; that is, there is nothing "immanent" in the individual (i.e., "isolated" or "originally independent") sayings themselves that must be imagined to have led to their eventual, albeit protracted, combination.

At least, the thought-pattern suggested by Kloppenborg for the sequence of sayings in 6:36–45 does not demand a process of compilation to have transpired before the "sermon" in Q was itself constructed. The author(s) of the document's formative stratum arranged the various sayings in 6:36–45 in their present order in order to produce the rhetorical effect outlined above by Kloppenborg. In part this took place by making use of a number of so-called traditional materials, but without the use of any prior text that would correspond in any substantial way to the "sermon" itself in Q.

Finally, there is the conclusion to the "sermon" in 6:46, 47–49. According to Kloppenborg:

The parable of the two builders, which has several rabbinic parallels, may well have circulated independently as an admonition to
act upon what one has been taught. Whether 6:46 ever existed as
an independent saying is virtually impossible to determine. Schulz
treats it as a prophetic saying. But the extreme brevity of the saying
as well as the fact that both 6:46 and 6:47–49 speak of "doing my
words" ... suggest that 6:46 may have been formulated specifically
as an introduction for the parable. In the Q context, 6:46, 47–
49 serves as the conclusion to the inaugural sermon (6:20b–49).
(1987a, 185)

Moreover: "Viewed in the context of sapiential and didactic
literature, Q 6:46, 47–49 provides a good example of the warnings which typically conclude these instructions" (1987a, 187). The
properly compositional role played by the sayings in 6:46, 47–49
at the specific level of the "sermon" is thus evident. There is no
basis, however, on which to assume that the same sayings played
any such role prior to the composition of the "sermon" in Q's
formative stratum.

In summary: it was already seen that no documentary evidence
can be produced from early Christian literature for the "sermon"
in Q having existed before or apart from its initial composition as
the opening section of Q's formative stratum. A review of Kloppenborg's composition analysis of Q 6:20b–49 likewise provides
no "internal" grounds for supposing that this text ever circulated
in any fashion whatsoever as an independent work. What about its
relative integrity vis-à-vis the rest of Q's formative stratum?

Independent Integrity or Integral Independence?

One can always opine that the opening "block" of Q's formative
stratum was once a self-sufficient piece of independent "instruction." The literary integrity that characterizes this inaugural section
of the Synoptic Sayings Source would signal the general complete-
ness of a formerly separate composition. Just how independent is
it, however, from the rest of Q? Said otherwise, if the "sermon"
was first created as the opening section of Q's formative stratum,
how does it relate, if at all, to what follows at the same level of
the document?

In a sense, with these questions we come full circle. It will be
recalled that at the beginning of this essay, I quoted a statement by
Robinson regarding why one might suspect that the "sermon" in

Q once existed as a composition in its own right. The heart of that argument was that "Lc 6, 20–49 does not seem to be just a random segment within a larger whole, for it is a well-rounded unit." While this is certainly true as such,[19] is the same "sermon" the only "well-rounded unit" in Q? If not, then Robinson's observations regarding the independent integrity of the "sermon" become essentially inconclusive.

I suggest, for example, that the subsequent set of sayings in Q's formative stratum on "discipleship and mission," consisting of 9:57–60; 10:[2], 3–6, [7], 9–11, [12, 13–15], 16, [21–24], similarly represents "a well-rounded unit."[20] In Kloppenborg's words:

> The basis for the association of 9:57–62 with the mission instructions is presumably the similarity of this homeless and radically obedient mode of existence of the disciples to the itinerant and penniless existence of Q's envoys of the kingdom. The effect of the juxtaposition of the chriae with 10:3–16 is noteworthy: it broadens the original mission instructions by setting them within the more comprehensive framework of a speech on discipleship. For Q preaching the kingdom and following Jesus are one. (1987a, 200–201)

Whatever the composition history of Q assumed here may be, the most notable feature for our present purposes is the overall unity suggested above for the sequence of sayings in Q 9:57–10:16; in view is "a speech on discipleship."

One could add to this the short section on prayer in 11:2–4, 9–13,[21] as well as the longer discussion of anxiety in 12:2–7, [8–9, 10], 11–12, 22–34. Kloppenborg treats the latter sequence as two separate entities, but, in my opinion, this is unnecessary. As Kloppenborg himself writes:

> Although composed of originally independent sayings, 12:2–7 has a unitary thrust. (1987a, 211)

> Although strictly speaking, 12:11–12 goes beyond the sapiential logic of 12:4–7, it coheres with the exhortations in 12:4–7 and 12:22–31 in its hortatory stance and especially in its use of the phrase *mē merimnēsate*. . . . [Q] 12:2–7, 11–12 forms a coherent unit, unified by mode of address (second-person plural imperative), tone (hortatory and comforting), setting (a situation of persecution), and function (to encourage fearless preaching). (1987a, 214)

> Almost immediately following in Lukan sequence is another cluster of Q sayings. Q 12:22b–31 comprises a small collection on the

topic of concern over the necessities of life, and this is followed by
a saying on the acquisition of wealth. (1987a, 216)

[Q 12:4–7, 22–31] counsels the members of the community to
rely completely upon God for provision of their daily needs.
(1987a, 206)

Such comments suggest that the sayings in 12:2–34 together
form as "well-rounded" a unit as the "sermon" in Q (6:20b–
49). The slight "break" to be discerned, perhaps, between 12:2–12
and 12:22–34 is no greater than the similar fissure that occurs in
the "sermon" between 6:20b–38 and 6:39–49.[22] As Kloppenborg
writes: "Whereas the first half of the speech [i.e., the 'sermon' in Q]
concerns violence, generosity and mercy, Q 6:39–45 is unified by
the concern with speaking and teaching (or correcting)" (1987a,
187).

Finally, there is the cluster of sayings in Q 13:24 + 14:26, 27 +
17:33 + 14:34–35.[23] Kloppenborg writes: "The original hortatory
unity forms a rounded discourse on the nature of discipleship, with
a programmatic statement about the nature of discipleship, specific
instructions on following Jesus and a concluding warning" (1987a,
237).

Thus, Q 6:20b–49 is not the only "well-rounded unit" in the
document's formative stratum. At best, therefore, the same fact
can serve as only circumstantial evidence for any judgment to be
made regarding the status of the "sermon" in Q at a previous point
in time.

Does the "sermon" show signs of belonging in an integrated
manner to the rest of Q's formative stratum? Given what we have
just seen, namely, that the formative stratum of Q was composed
of a number of distinct "well-rounded units," it ought not theoretically to surprise us if we were to find that the "sermon" in
Q is relatively self-contained vis-à-vis the rest of Q's formative
stratum. And, in fact, the sequence of larger units in Q's formative stratum, namely, the "sermons" on "discipleship and mission"
(9:57–10:16), "on prayer" (11:2–13), "on anxiety" (12:2–34), and
on discipleship again (13:24–14:35),[24] is neither an inevitable nor
an especially suggestive one.

At the same time, there are numerous places where the various sayings of Q 6:20b–49 are echoed by other statements in the
formative stratum. The kingdom of God, for example, referred
to explicitly in the opening beatitude of the "sermon" (6:20b)

and implied as part of the reasoning of the next two sayings (6:21ab), is, of course, repeatedly invoked throughout the Synoptic Sayings Source.[25] The issue of hunger and getting enough to eat (6:21a) is likewise broached elsewhere in Q (see, e.g., 10:4–6; 12:22–31).

Dealing with enmity and ill-will (6:27–35) is also a concern in other sayings of the document (see, e.g., 10:3–4, 6b, 10–11; 12:4–7, 11–12 [also 12:57–59]), as is the problem of how to manage personal violence against oneself (6:29; see, e.g., 14:27). Imitating God, namely, becoming "sons" of God, promised in 6:35b and enjoined in 6:36, is similarly imagined in the so-called Lord's Prayer (11:2–4), where God is once again called "father" and his treatment of human beings is thought to be paradigmatic for those addressed (11:4a).[26]

The question of leadership or discipleship and the appropriate relationship between leader (teacher) and follower (student) discussed in 6:40 is also apparent in other sayings in Q (see, e.g., 9:57–60; 10:16; 14:26–27; 17:33). Though not stated so baldly, the matter of hypocrisy and behavioral incongruity addressed in Q 6:41–42 is likewise (amply) decried elsewhere (see 11:39–48, 52; further, Vaage 1994, 66–86).

The figure of a tree is used not only in 6:43–44a but also in 13:18–19. Talk of treasure and the heart in 6:45 is, of course, taken up again in 12:33–34. Indeed, it is difficult not to see some sort of dialectical relationship between these two sayings. The question asked in 6:46 ("Why do you call me, 'Lord, Lord,' but not do what I say to you?") is answered not only by the parable that follows in 6:47–49 but even more directly in 9:59–60. The saying in 16:13 about not "serving two masters" or "lords" is also relevant. Finally, the "sermon's" concluding parable (6:47–49) is not the only parable in Q (see, e.g., 13:18–19, 20–21; 15:4–7 [also 14:16–24; 19:12–20]).

Consider in addition the following observations by Kloppenborg:

> This instruction [11:2–4, 9–13] coheres with other parts of Q. Formally, it employs the typical sapiential admonition with a motive clause (cf. 6:27–28, 32–33; 6:37–38; 6:42, 43–44)....Thus, it belongs to the same sphere of interests and applications as the inaugural sermon (6:20b–49) and to the expanded version of the discipleship "speech" (9:57–62 + 10:2–11, 16). (1987a, 206)

In its rhetorical structure it [12:2–12] coincides with several other
Q texts, e.g., 6:27–31, 32–35; 11:9–13; 12:22–31, which also begin with admonitions (6:27–28; 11:9; 12:22b) buttressed either by
rhetorical questions and examples drawn from everyday experience
(6:32–34; 11:11–12; 12:24–26, 27–28) or by proverbial assertions
(11:10; 12:23) or both. (1987a, 208)

In conclusion: Does the "sermon" in Q 6:20–49 show signs of
belonging in an integrated fashion to the rest of the document's
formative stratum? Yes, I would say, as much as any other section
of the same writing as a whole.

Perhaps an "Oral" Composition?

In light of the preceding considerations and the extremely tenu-
ous character of any thesis that the "sermon" in Q might represent
an earlier independent composition subsequently incorporated into
the document's formative stratum, the question now must be addressed that I quickly set aside in the introduction to this essay,
namely, whether the same "sermon" might once have existed as a
separately transmitted oral unit of tradition.[27] If we were to posit
that Q 6:20b–49 once circulated orally as an independent composition before its eventual incorporation into Q's formative stratum,
the insights of Werner Kelber into the nature of orality and the oral
transmission of tradition become immediately pertinent. In *The
Oral and the Written Gospel,* Kelber summarizes well the prevailing assumptions prior to his own work — basically those of Rudolf
Bultmann and his followers — in this way:

> Sayings grew together, multiplied by analogous formation, and un-
> derwent expansion by secondary additions. New sayings joined
> the stream of tradition, developed into groups of sayings, and
> formed catechisms and speech complexes.... Single units showed
> a tendency to grow, to accumulate material, and cluster together.
> Materials in isolated and clustered form joined the stream of tradi-
> tions, were sustained by it, and in turn accelerated the momentum
> toward still larger and more complex formations. One can readily
> form a mental picture of Bultmann's general model of the synoptic
> tradition as a process of aggregate growth. (1983, 4)

This "aggregation" model of "oral tradition" has already been
critiqued above regarding Kloppenborg's composition analysis of
the "sermon" in Q (6:20b–49). Kloppenborg's form- and tradition-
critical observations were earlier seen to be equally intelligible as a

description of how this part of Q's formative stratum was initially written. Kelber's point of view, however, is even more radical in its implications. For it suggests that to the extent that the "sermon" indeed represents oral speech, its previous language and structure were anything but fixed. The composition before us could not reflect an antecedent "oral" work with sufficient stability to be identified as the "sermon," owing to the very nature of orality. Thus Kelber writes:

> In addition to growth and loss, or expansion and compression, a multiplicity of tendencies determines the course of oral transmission. Stock features are combined and reshuffled in endless variations, one theme is substituted for another, the order of sequence is changed, features are adopted from related or unrelated materials, and variant compositions are forever in the making. Taken as a whole, oral transmission shows many faces and inclinations. (1983, 29)

> [The oral history of the "traditional" materials eventually incorporated into Q's formative stratum] would be a pulsating phenomenon, expanding and contracting, waxing and waning, progressing and regressing. Its general behavior is not unlike that of the stock market, rising and subsiding at more or less unpredictable intervals, and curiously interwoven with social and political realities. Or, to use a different metaphor, the oral synoptic traditions represent proliferating tracks going in various directions, some intersecting with one another, others bound for a head-on collision, some running together and apart again, some fading and resurging. But taken as a whole they do not mount up to a preordained march controlled by the law of intrinsic causality. (1983, 31)

In other words, we must assume that in the oral phase of early Christian tradition prior to the composition of Q's formative stratum, nothing like the "sermon" in Q (6:20b–49) could ever have continuously existed. It is as such the creation of the author(s) of the formative stratum of the document. According to Kelber, no antecedent "oral" version of the "sermon" in Q (6:20b–49) would have endured past the moment in which it was first uttered or performed with any guarantee that the next time around, a given saying or sequence of sayings would be maintained as an integral feature of *the* "sermon" and not simply forgotten. According to Kelber:

> [I]f each utterance constitutes an authentic speech act, then the question of transmission can never be kept wholly separate from

composition. In speaking, transmission involves an act of composition, or at least recreation. All too often when we think of
transmission of traditions, we think of it primarily as the passing
on of fixed forms. In other words, we think of it in literary terms.
In orality, tradition is almost always composition in transmission.
From this perspective, too, oral transmission enacts a multiplicity
of discrete instances of speech rather than a continuous process of
solidification of speech into written forms. (1983, 30)

Forgetting is a form of death ever present in oral life. No model
of oral transmission may be said to be valid that does not seriously reflect on and integrate amnesia, broken paths, and rejection
of tradition.... Loss and discontinuity no less than growth and
continuity dictate the realities of oral life. (1983, 29)

The "sermon" would need to have been written down virtually
at the very moment when it was first orally composed in order for
the text that we now read in Q to represent the oral composition
one might presume to posit. But how oral is something committed
immediately and so thoroughly to writing? Are we not back where
we began?

Conclusions: Further Questions and Abiding Peculiarities

The four preceding sections, which probed into the possibility of
the "sermon" in Q having once existed independently as a separate composition, have all rendered negative results. A survey
of the documentary evidence from early Christian literature reveals no reason for supposing that the "sermon" in Q was ever
known apart from its presentation in the formative stratum of this
text. The observations that constitute the basis of Kloppenborg's
form- and tradition-critical composition analysis of the "sermon"
in Q can be applied with equal or greater intelligibility to the
writing of the document itself. The "sermon" per se is no more
"well-rounded" than any other unit or section or "block" of Q's
formative stratum, at the same time that it appears to be as integrated with these other sections of the document as they otherwise
are among themselves. The idea that Q 6:20b–49 might recall a
prior oral composition cannot withstand the recent critique and
description of the nature of orality by Kelber. It would seem that
any thought of the "sermon" as once a separate piece of tradition

before the composition of Q's formative stratum should simply be abandoned.

There are, nonetheless, a number of peculiarities that still persist regarding the "sermon." Robinson has described most of them:

> Matthew respects the integrity of the Sermon on the Mount in a way he does not for any other section in Q. Vincent Taylor has shown that Matthew tends in its way to confirm that the Lukan order of Q is original. For the five main discourses of Matthew, and the Q material in Matthew outside these discourses, when each is considered separately, seem to follow much the same order as that found in Luke. It is as if Matthew thumbed through Q again and again selecting out sayings suitable for the collection he was composing at the time. But in the case of the Sermon on the Mount, and only here, Matthew's collection does not begin toward the beginning of Q and end near the end of Q. Rather Matthew's Sermon retains as its outline the same collection from near the beginning of Q found in Luke's Sermon. Then Matthew gleans from the rest of Q, in much the Q order (Lk 11–13), material to intersperse into Q's Sermon, thereby enlarging it, but leaving it intact. (1982, 391–92)

> If one may discern in Mark 4 traces of a pre-Markan collection, it is possible that what we know in expanded form as the Sermon on the Mount (or Plain) is the outgrowth of another such early cluster of sayings and parables. It uses as its conclusion a double parable exalting Jesus' logoi in much the same way as does Mark 13:31. For the double parable Luke 6:47 ‖ Matt. 7:24 (cf. v. 26) begins: "Every one who comes to me and hears my *logoi* and does them." Hence the term logoi may have functioned as a designation for this early collection [as titles were otherwise regularly placed at the end of ancient documents]. (1971, 94–95)

> The end [of the "sermon"] seems to be the conclusion of a collection, and this not simply because of the occurrence there of the term logoi. Rather the eschatological climax is the same concluding motif that one can sense in the *Didache* (chap. 16), the gospels (Mark 13 parr.), and even in Q (Luke 17:20–37).[28]

> [E]ach of the two small collections from the same period found in *1 Clem.* 13.2 and *Did.* 1.3–6 . . . seem[s] to reflect a similar unity.[29]

The question, however, is whether these (and perhaps other) abiding peculiarities of the "sermon" are sufficiently "weighty" to reverse the otherwise thoroughly negative results of the different investigations conducted above.[30] In my opinion, there is no compelling reason not to assume that Q 6:20b–49 was first composed when the initial stratum of the document was simultaneously written, drawing on "traditional" materials attested elsewhere but otherwise never organized into a "sermon" like the inaugural discourse of Q's formative stratum. The previous "oral" history of these materials cannot be traced or further specified, due to the specific nature of orality. To say more would be the im/purest speculation.

NOTES

1. For a more extensive discussion of these and other related criteria, see Kloppenborg 1995b.

2. According to Kloppenborg, the third compositional level in Q consisted of the temptation narrative in 4:1–13 plus a few additional sayings (11:42c; 16:18) (see Kloppenborg 1987a; further, Kloppenborg 1990c, 35–48). The categories of "wisdom" versus "apocalyptic" as used by Kloppenborg simply reflect traditional form-critical terminology and are not meant to imply mutually exclusive theological or other polarities. Regarding the "wisdom" of Q's formative stratum, Kloppenborg himself (1987a, 318–21) concludes by characterizing it as marked by "two notable departures from the typical form of instruction," as "intensified," as "in effect a transformation of the hermeneutic fundamental to the instruction." As for the "apocalyptic" layer of Q, it turns out to be not that "apocalyptic" after all (see Kloppenborg 1987b, 287–306).

3. See, for example, Wrege 1968; Betz 1985c. As their titles suggest, both scholars have Matthew's "Sermon on the Mount" in mind. More recently, Betz has significantly modified his earlier position (Betz 1990).

4. Notice, furthermore, how the sayings concentrated in a discrete subsection of Q (6:20b–49) occur scattered throughout the *Gospel of Thomas,* virtually from the beginning of the document to its end.

5. See Kloppenborg 1987a, 47–49, 64–80; further, Taylor 1953, 1959 = Taylor 1970, 90–94, 95–118.

6. At a greater level of abstraction, there are two "blocks" of material whose sequence of parallel sayings could be said to be roughly the same: (a) Q 6:20b, 21, 22–23, 30 / *Gos. Thom.* 54, 69b, 68–69a, 95; and (b) Q 6:31, 39, 41–42, 43–45 / *Gos. Thom.* 6, 34, 26, 43, 45. Notice, however, that the sequence of these "blocks" is not the same but inverted, and that in the second case it is not complete. Furthermore, the division between the two "blocks" in Q (6:30, 31) would occur in the midst of what is otherwise a continuous argument (6:27–35).

7. The "basis" of such speculation is eroded even further if Q 6:43–45 par. should actually be seen as a single saying, of which *Gos. Thom.* 43–45 would then be simply a variant.

8. Hartin (1991, 145 n. 1) identifies the following nine "correspondences" between James and the sermon in Q (6:20b–49):

Q	James
6:20	2:5
6:22–23	1:2
6:23	5:10
6:36	2:13
6:37–38	4:11
6:37	5:6
6:43–44	3:12
6:46–47	1:22
6:49	1:23

The cited "correspondences," however, are not all of the same order. Only the two listed in table 3, above (Jas 3:12; 4:11–12), would actually be "parallel" sayings to those of the "sermon" in Q (6:37–38, 43–44). The other seven "correspondences" identified by Hartin are rather more allusions to the Q text itself. In fact, Hartin (1991, 171–72) goes on to conclude that "[w]hile James shows a knowledge of the Q tradition as expressed in the original Q sermon, he also bears witness to how this block of tradition developed within the context of the Matthean community," in other words, the form of Q known to Matthew.

9. The following list does not claim to be exhaustive. It depends heavily on Kloppenborg 1988, ad loc.:

6:20bff. — *Book of Thomas* (NHC II, 7:145.3–8)
6:27–28 — *POxy* 1224 fr. 2 recto col. 1
6:31 — Acts 15:29 (Western text)
6:37–38 — *1 Clem.* 13:1–2
6:40 — *Dial. Sav.* 53
6:41–42 — *POxy* 1:1–4
6:44 — *Apoc. Pet.* (NHC 7, 3:76.4–8)
6:46 — *PEger* 2 fr. 2 recto.

10. The three beatitudes in 6:20b–21ab are indeed more like one another than any one of them is like the fourth beatitude in 6:22–23. At the same time, however, the first beatitude (6:20b) is different from the other two in 6:21ab regarding both the tense of the verb in the second half of the saying (in 6:20b, an implied present; in 6:21ab, the future tense) and the level of abstraction (in 6:20b, the general reference to the "poor/kingdom of God" versus the concrete description of "those who are hungry/weep" becoming "sated/laughing").

11. Indeed, in my opinion, the saying as a whole (6:27–35) represents a rather sophisticated piece of ethical reasoning, whose "logical

stresses and strains" and rhetorical variation serve to enhance its overall persuasiveness. See Vaage 1994, 41–45.

12. Kloppenborg 1987a, 177. The reference is to Schürmann 1982, 137; see also Schürmann 1969, 357.

13. See, for example, Tannehill 1970 = Tannehill 1975, 68–72; or my own alternate reading in Vaage 1994, 42–44, 122–24.

14. Obviously not without a certain cost: see Theissen 1979a, 160–79; further, Vaage 1994, 44–45.

15. See Kloppenborg (1987a, 180): "Since Q already has an adequate conclusion for 6:27–35 in v. 35c, and since Matthew's *oun* in 5:48 is undoubtedly redactional, it seems advisable to regard Luke's formulation — which includes asyndeton in v. 36 and *oun* connectives in v. 37 — as original."

16. At this point in the discussion, to introduce the notion of a possibly "oral" composition without any evidence for doing so besides the customary scholarly desire to discover even earlier separate units of tradition can only obfuscate the contrary state of the textual evidence before us.

17. It is interesting that 6:40 is unparalleled elsewhere, whereas both 6:39 and 6:41–42 have counterparts in the *Gospel of Thomas* (34 and 26, respectively). Cf. the conclusions drawn from this kind of evidence by Crossan 1987.

18. The final suggestion is made following Wanke 1980, 214–15.

19. Though perhaps not so clearly true. According to Kloppenborg (1987a, 187), a notable "break" occurs in the "logic" of the "sermon" between 6:(20b–)38 and 6:39(–49). The same split might also be observed between 6:(20b–)35 and 6:36(–49).

20. The numbers in square brackets identify the verses to be ascribed to Q's redaction. See Vaage 1994, 107–8, 111–14.

21. Kloppenborg (1987a, 203) calls it "a short instruction." See, further, Piper 1982 = 1994.

22. Or between 6:20b–35 and 6:36–49.

23. This is the conclusion of Kloppenborg 1987a, 234–37. The sayings found in 13:25–27, 28–30, 34–35; 14:16–24 are said to have been inserted by the redaction of Q between 13:24 and 14:26–35.

24. The titles in quotation marks are taken from Kloppenborg 1988, xxxi–xxxii.

25. See 10:9; 11:2, 20; 12:31; 13:18, 20; 16:16; further, Vaage 1994, 55–65. The form of the beatitude occurs elsewhere as well, though only at the level of Q's redaction: see 7:23; 10:23; 12:43.

26. Cf. Kloppenborg 1987a, 206: "Like 6:27–35, it [11:2–4, 9–13] portrays God as a generous patron....In both the prayer and 6:27–35 there is an assumed correspondence between the actions of God and those of Jesus' followers: generosity and forgiveness are marks both of God and of the children of God. The invocation of God as *pater* in the prayer

finds a counterpart in 6:27–35 which represents discipleship as imitatio
Dei leading to divine sonship."

27. I leave aside the even more adventuresome speculation that the
"sermon" might have continued to exist independently of the Synoptic
Sayings Source after its simultaneous incorporation into the initial stratum
of the document.

28. Robinson 1971, 94 n. 47. Is the parable, however, in 6:47–49
really an "eschatological climax"? Can it not just as easily be understood
as a "sapiential" analogue of "natural" consequences? It describes the
likely results of two opposing types of response to Jesus' teaching. Kloppenborg (1987a, 185) refers to two rabbinic parallels (m. 'Abot 3:18;
'Abot R. Nat. [A] 24). It is interesting to observe, both at the level of the
"sermon" itself in Q (6:20b–49) and at the level of Q as a whole, that
the parables in the Synoptic Sayings Source are found roughly grouped
together at the end of each composition. Cf. Kloppenborg 1995a.

29. Robinson 1971, 94 n. 47. Though can one really compare 1 Clem.
13:2 (a single verse and variation on the theme of 6:37–38) and Did. 1:3–
6 (a few verses, all related to 6:27ff.) with the "sermon" in Q (consisting
of approximately thirty verses and composed of many different sayings)?
Moreover, as Robinson himself points out, Layton (1968, 343–83) has
suggested that "[i]n the case of the Didache, this may in part be due to
dependence on Matt. and Luke."

30. Given that no substantive evidence exists that the "sermon" in Q
ever existed apart from its appearance in the document's formative stratum, what is the import of the fact that virtually all of the sayings that
make up the "sermon" have a (number of) variant(s) found elsewhere in
early Christian literature?

Strategies of Authority

*A Rhetorical Study of the Character
of the Speaker in Q 6:20-49*

One way of approaching the presentation of Jesus in the Sayings Gospel Q is to be attentive to terminology that designates particular characterizations, such as prophetic Son of God, Son of Man, the Coming One, and Agent of Wisdom. As this is done, one becomes aware that, although the Sayings Gospel presents the speech of Jesus in the foreground, the character of the speaker is closely bound up with the speech (see, e.g., Havener 1987, 67–86).

Beyond whatever designations are applied to him, however, it is also possible to discern a characterization of Jesus in Q on the basis of the formulation of the sayings attributed to him in the collection.[1] Ancient rhetoricians, noting that the speaker's character is a factor in proving a case, have ample discussion on the importance of a speaker's self-presentation and on how that self-presentation might be designed to portray oneself as wise, experienced, forceful, or authoritative.[2] The study that follows will focus on the speaker's self-presentation in one section of the Sayings Gospel, the inaugural sermon in Q 6:20–49. The approach will be to analyze the formulation of the discourse in the unit on the basis of the principles regarding the persuasive effect of the speaker's character articulated in ancient rhetorical theory. Insofar as these principles can be illuminated by observations of modern rhetorical theorists, some of the modern theory will also be drawn upon to reveal more clearly the characterization of the speaker in this unit.

Shawn Carruth, O.S.B. is assistant professor of religion at Concordia College, Moorhead, Minnesota.

Ēthos as a Mode of Persuasion

The importance of the character of the speaker as a means of proof is evident in the work of several ancient rhetoricians. Aristotle insisted that *ēthos* is actually the most effective means of proof (*Rh.* 1.2.4). His older contemporary, Isocrates, claimed "that words carry greater conviction when spoken by men of good repute" and that "the argument which is made by a man's life is of more weight than that which is furnished by words" (*Anti.* 278–80). Quintilian, one of the most insistent proponents of the view that the character of the speaker is essential to good speaking, defines rhetoric as the science of speaking well because this definition includes not only the virtues of oratory but the character of the orator. No one can speak well who is not at the same time a good person (Quint. 2.15.34).

The importance of the good character of the speaker is related to the need for the orator to gain the confidence and the goodwill of the audience. The speaker must be viewed as one who is worthy of confidence, and this impression can be conveyed by displaying one's merit, achievements, and reputable life. The qualities of an upright person are powerful in gaining goodwill, and the lack of these qualities estranges the audience (Cicero, *De Or.* 2.42.182; see also Quint. 4.1.78). Aristotle notes that it is particularly important to win the confidence of the audience when the issue is uncertain and people have differing opinions. In these cases, the confidence people have in a good person is absolute (*Rh.* 1.2.3).

The character of the speaker is especially important to the persuasive effect of deliberative oratory, of which the inaugural sermon in Q is an example. In addition to the qualities of good sense, virtue, and goodwill,[3] it is important that the speaker possess genuine wisdom and particularly authority as well as excellence of character.[4] The orator must unfold an opinion as a person of authority (Cicero, *De Or.* 2.9.35). "All will agree," claims Quintilian, "that the advice given by a speaker should be in keeping with his moral character" (3.8.12). At a later point Quintilian notes that, although examples are of the greatest value in deliberative oratory, "it matters a great deal whose authority is adduced and to whom it is commended" (3.8.36). Cicero's words in the mouth of Antonius summarize the point.

> [T]o give advice for or against a course of action does seem to me to be a task for a person of the greatest weight of character, for to

expound one's advice on matters of high importance calls for both wisdom and ability and eloquence, to enable one to make an intelligent forecast, give an authoritative proof, and employ persuasive eloquence. (*De Or.* 2.81.333)

Aristotle thinks that the proof of the good character of the speaker should be internal to the speech itself and not depend on any preconceived notion or external evidence of good character (*Rh.* 1.2.4). The place to attend most especially to the establishment of the credibility of the speaker is at the beginning of the speech, that is, in the exordium. It is important at the outset to gain the attention and the goodwill of the audience.[5] Aristotle, in fact, thinks that in deliberative speaking the exordium is superfluous unless it is needed for the sake of the speaker.[6] Although the exordium is the place where the authority of the speaker is initially established, the argument from the character of the speaker is not confined to the opening of the speech. Rather, the speaker's credibility and authority must be maintained throughout the speech not only by what the speaker says but by how it is said (Kennedy 1984, 22).

Style, far from being merely decorative, is also a factor in showing the virtue and credibility of the speaker. The words placed in the mouth of Antonius by Cicero express this view:

Moreover so much is done by good taste and style in speaking, that the speech seems to depict the speaker's character. For by means of particular types of thought and diction, and the employment besides of a delivery that is unruffled and eloquent of good nature, the speakers are made to appear upright, well-bred, and virtuous men. (*De Or.* 2.43.184)

The best style is one that indicates the good character of the speaker by showing him or her to be amiable or by indicating his or her good judgment, humanity, and liberality of mind (Cicero, *Part. Or.* 6.22).

The remainder of this study will concentrate on how things are said. It will focus on an investigation of the grammatical formulations of Jesus' inaugural speech in Q in order to show how these forms point to Jesus as one who speaks with authority.[7]

Forms Enhancing the Speaker's Character

Direct Address

Direct address dominates the Q sermon beginning with the beatitudes, which are more likely to have been formulated by Q in the
second person than in the third person,[8] and continuing through to
the final section, which begins with the rhetorical question, "Why
do you call me 'Lord, Lord,' and not do what I say?"[9] This use
of direct address is a device that claims the attention of the hearer
and intensifies the contact between the speaker and the audience
(Lausberg 1973, §758). It is, thus, a device that belongs more
clearly to the proof that depends on the appeal to the emotions of
the audience. Yet since the direct address in the inaugural sermon
is predominantly in the form of imperatives and general wisdom
made specific to the audience in view, it can be effective only if the
audience is convinced of the credibility of the speaker. Here, then,
we shall consider the "I" implied as the one who addresses the
"you."[10] Two aspects of this direct address will be illustrated here,
the example of *licentia* (*parrēsia*)[11] in Q 6:41–42 and the speaker's
self-reference in Q 6:46.[12]

The sayings in Q 6:41–42 exemplify the figure of *licentia*. In
this brief section the speaker chastises the hearers and even directs
a derogatory epithet to anyone who exhibits the behavior being
criticized. The author of the *Rhetorica ad Herennium* notes that
even though frank speech of this kind may seem too sharp, there
are ways of softening it so that the audience will not be angry
but at the same time will be saved from error. One of the ways
mentioned is a direct appeal to the wisdom of the audience (*Rhet.
Her.* 4.37.49). The speaker in the sermon does not make a direct
appeal to the audience's wisdom, but this section is immediately
followed by the proverbial material about good and bad trees and
their fruit. This appeal to general wisdom may perform the function the author of the *Rhetorica ad Herennium* had in mind. He
goes on to take note of the good effect this can have in that the
speaker presents him- or herself as friendly both to the hearers and
to the truth (*Rhet. Her.* 4.37.49).

Outside the rhetorical treatises, others express a similar view
of the manner in which frank speech reveals the character of
the speaker. Dio Chrysostom speaks with admiration of the person who

in plain terms and without guile speaks his mind with frankness, and neither for the sake of reputation nor for gain makes false pretensions, but out of good will and concern for his fellow-men stands ready, if need be, to submit to ridicule and to the disorder and the uproar of the mob. (32.11)

This speaker is characterized as one who is noble and independent (Dio Chrys. 32.11).

In his introductions to selections of moral exhortation in the ancient world, Abraham Malherbe consistently points out the necessity for the moral philosopher to speak frankly to the audience. This is to be done in order to bring the hearers' errors to mind. But it is also to be done with careful attention to the situation and with moderation. Its desired effect must always be the good of the audience.[13]

The use of this figure, then, is capable of portraying the speaker as a person of integrity and as one who has the good of the hearers at heart. Such a speaker is willing to take the risk of alienating the audience because commitment to the truth and to the good of the members of the audience overrides concern for self.

Before moving on to specific formulations, one other aspect of the speech's direct address merits a brief mention. The rhetorical question that opens the concluding section of the sermon at Q 6:46 brings the speaker explicitly into focus: "Why do you call me 'Lord, Lord,' and not do what I say?" Here the attention of the audience is forcefully drawn to the recognition of who it is who speaks.

In this connection it is worth noting that the only "I" implied in the Q sermon is Jesus. Although an editorial introduction must have attributed the sermon to Jesus, an editor never intervenes within the speech itself with a "Jesus said," such as one regularly finds in the *Gospel of Thomas*. The authoritative Jesus is the only one with a voice in the Q sermon, and there is no intermediary between him and those addressed by the words of this sermon. The words referred to in Q 6:47 and Q 6:49 are his own. The authority they carry depends entirely on the wisdom of the one who pronounced them.

Imperatives

The imperatives of the inaugural sermon in Q are one form of the sermon's prevailing direct address. They begin with the double imperative in 6:23, the verse that serves as a transition from the exordium to the *propositio*. The thesis statement opens with the imperative "Love your enemies" in Q 6:27, and the injunctive mood continues through Q 6:42. Imperatives dominate in the section where the issue is stated (6:27–31) and continue into the section where the issue is argued (6:32–45).[14] All together, in these sections there are twelve imperatives addressed by the speaker to the audience.[15]

While deliberative oratory is concerned with persuasion and dissuasion and speeches of exhortation fall into this category, ancient rhetorical theorists give no indication of their understanding of the function of the imperative mood in this type of speech. A perusal of ancient oratory comparable to the inaugural sermon in that it urges people to certain ethical behavior shows that the imperative can be regularly used especially in lists of expected behavior.[16] Yet a sampling of works of ancient literature similar to Q because they contain collections of aphoristic material that is exhortatory in nature does not show that the use of the imperative is consistent. On the one hand, the *Teachings of Silvanus* and the collection included under the "sayings of the wise" in Prov 22:17–24:34 frequently express exhortations in the imperative mood.[17] On the other hand, Epicurus's *Kyriai Doxai,* cited by Hans Dieter Betz as generically related to Matthew's version of the Sermon on the Mount,[18] has no imperatives. In very few places one finds a first-person-plural pronoun (§§2, 11) and a second-person-singular verb (§§23, 24, 25), but, in contrast to the sermon both in Matthew and in Q, the collection is virtually entirely impersonal.[19]

In assessing the rhetorical impact of the use of imperatives in exhortatory material, the observation of the modern rhetorical theorists Chaim Perelman and L. Olbrechts-Tyteca is helpful. They note that the imperative has no persuasive force, and "all its power comes from the hold of the person commanding over the one carrying out his orders" (1969, 158). Thus, when exhortation using aphoristic material is expressed in an impersonal manner, the authority of what is said depends on the reasonableness of the precept. When such precepts are delivered in the imperative mood, however, their force derives from the authority of the one who speaks. The great number of imperatives in a speech unit as short as the inaugural sermon in Q, then, gives a clear impression of the authority of the speaker in the minds of the hearers.[20]

Rhetorical Questions

Another of the figures involving the address of the audience that is amply represented in the inaugural sermon in Q is the rhetorical question. The question is a figure that can add force and vigor to speech[21] and, in some cases, may serve particularly well to emphasize the authority of the speaker. Demetrius notes that when one addresses questions to the audience without disclosing one's own opinion, one forces the hearer into a corner so that the hearer seems to be brought to task and to have no answer (*De eloc.* 5.279). In this case the hearers are rendered speechless, and the speaker remains the only one authorized to speak.

The rhetorical questions of the Q sermon can be shown to add force to the speech and also to be of the kind to which hearers have no answer. In the illustrations that follow particular attention will be given to the effect obtained when the questions have no real answer.[22]

The question "What reward do you have?" occurring in Q 6:31–33, is of the kind that really has no answer. The hearer is brought to task by the question. The inability of the hearer to answer serves to heighten the impression of the speaker's authority. Since the question occurs twice in the unit, it also represents the figure of *adiectio,* a form of doubling that, according to Quintilian, adds, besides charm, force to thought (Quint. 9.2.28).

Each of the rhetorical questions about reward in this unit is followed by another question, "Do not tax collectors/Gentiles [do as much]?"[23] The two sets of questions maintain the force of the speaker's authority.

The pair of questions in Q 6:41–42 represent the category of rhetorical questions called *subiectio* (*hypophora*). With this figure, the speaker asks the addressees what can be said for their position and then states what ought to be so (*Rhet. Her.* 4.23.33; Quint. 9.2.15). Here the speaker asks the addressees "why" and "how" they act as they do. Again, these are questions that really have no answer and thus gain the kind of force Demetrius recognized because they leave the hearers speechless. The speaker's authority is affirmed in the unit by the fact that the statement of what ought to be done comes as an imperative, the form that depends for its force on the personal authority of the speaker.

Quintilian notes that questions can be used to express the attitudes of the speaker and gives a series of examples that can show indignation, wonder, or a sharp command (Quint. 9.2.10–11). The "what" and "how" questions in this unit combined with the epithet *hypokrita* express the offense taken by the speaker at behavior that does not conform to that which is appropriate among those who call one another brother or sister. The questions point to the authority of the speaker to call into question such behavior and to pass judgment on it.

The rhetorical question in 6:44 follows a set of proverbial sayings having to do with the fruit borne by good or bad trees. It represents a conclusion that is to be drawn from the preceding proverbs, but, expressed as a question, it gains in force (see Quint. 8.5.6). By means of the question, the hearers are challenged to draw their own conclusion that, of course, will concur with that of the speaker. In addition to being expressed as a question, the thought demands acquiescence in that it asks the hearers to come to their conclusion on the basis of observation of nature. According to Quintilian, "[T]he mind is always readiest to accept what it recognizes to be true to nature" (8.3.71). No one in the audience will be able to offer a contrary argument or example. The hearers will have to defer to the authority of the speaker.

The question in Q 6:44 illustrates that especially in regard to the use of wisdom sayings by a teacher, the framing of such sayings in the form of questions can function to support the speaker's credibility. The questions in Q 6:39 work in much the same way. While Q 6:44 appeals to commonsense knowledge of the world of nature, Q 6:39 appeals to commonsense knowledge of the nature of human ability. The effect of such rhetorical questions on the hearer is the realization that even a fool would know the answer to the question. This confirms the truth in what is said by the teacher (Perdue 1986, 14).

The last rhetorical question in the sermon introduces the final section of the speech in Q 6:46. It is another of the kind that backs the hearers into a corner and leaves them without an answer. If one hears without acting it is impossible to call this speaker "master." At the conclusion of the speech what matters is not an intellectual assent to the truth of the material but the question of the relationship between speaker and hearers. An appropriate response to this question amounts to an acknowledgment of the speaker's authority as master and action appropriate to that acknowledgment.

Maxims

Since the Q sermon is made up of wisdom sayings attributed to Jesus, a discussion of the use of sayings in ancient rhetoric and the ways their use contributes to or demonstrates the authority of the speaker is appropriate. According to the ancient rhetoricians, the use of maxims gave the impression of the authority of the speaker because their use shows not only the character and wisdom of the speaker but also the ability of the speaker to apply common wisdom appropriately.

Maxims in the rhetorical treatises are defined as concisely expressed statements of what is generally or universally true. While Aristotle says they deal with human actions and what is to be done or avoided (*Rh.* 2.21.2; see *Rh. Al.* 11), Quintilian says they can apply to both things and persons (8.5.3). The maxim is related to the chreia but differs from it in that the chreia is attributed but a maxim is not and in that a chreia can be expressed with actions but the maxim is expressed only in words.[24]

A maxim need not be expressed as a simple statement. Rhetoricians recognize several kinds and several forms of expression. Aristotle points to four kinds. Those without an epilogue either are well known or are clear as soon as they are spoken; those with an epilogue either are part of an enthymeme or are like enthymemes.[25] Maxims can be based on interrogation, comparison, denial, similarity, and admiration. They can express contraries or be given a personal turn (Quint. 8.5.5–7). Authors of the *Progymnasmata* note that maxims can be hortatory, dissuading, declaratory, simple, compound, convincing, real, and exaggerated (Aphthonius, *Prog.* 4; Hermogenes, *Prog.* 4).

Maxims can function as proof in oratory,[26] but they are especially useful for enhancing the character of the speaker. By using good sayings well, the orator also shows his or her character to be good (Aristotle, *Rh.* 2.21.16). Common sayings, since they are general, can seem not to have been formulated for the case at hand but to be simply the "most honorable or honest thing to say or do" (Quint. 5.11.37). The orator using such sayings appears to be a person of honor and honesty. "What sin is there in a good epigram?" asks Quintilian. "Does it not help our case, or move the judge, or commend the speaker to his audience?"[27] Aristotle even notes cases in which a speaker can contradict common sayings and ought to do so when his or her character will thereby appear better (*Rh.* 2.21.13–14).

The connection between the use of maxims and the character of the speaker is also shown by the fact that rhetoricians caution speakers to use them sparingly and comment on who can use them appropriately. Aristotle believes they can be used best by those who are old and experienced. It is unseemly, he claims, for those not advanced in years to use maxims (*Rh.* 2.21.9). Quintilian claims an orator should only infrequently use a maxim in such a way as to give it a personal turn and that care should be taken regarding who does it:

> Such reflections are best suited to those speakers whose authority is such that their character itself will lend weight to their words. For who would tolerate a boy, or a youth, or even a man of low birth who presumed to speak with all the authority of a judge and to thrust his precepts down our throats? (8.5.7–8)

Maxims in themselves carry a certain authority. Common and frequently quoted sayings have the appearance of truth precisely because they are common and all acknowledge them as true (Aristotle, *Rh.* 2.21.11). They can be a kind of testimony all the more impressive because they seem impartial (Quint. 5.11.37). The real force of their use, however, resides in the ability of the orator to use them appropriately.[28]

To illustrate the ways the use of maxims enhances the character and especially the authority of the speaker in the Q sermon, we will examine just two sections, the macarisms in Q 6:20–21 and the group of proverbial sayings in Q 6:43–45, occurring just before the sermon's conclusion. It is particularly appropriate to examine the material at the beginning of the sermon because it is especially important for the speaker's character and authority to be set out at that point. The material in Q 6:43–45 represents an interesting case of amassing proverbial material, a technique frowned upon by Quintilian (8.5.13).

It is generally recognized that the beatitude is a form of aphoristic wisdom.[29] The form is common in Hebrew literature, and there are parallels from Cynic and Stoic circles.[30] As they appear here at the beginning of the sermon, they represent a good example of the maxim with an epilogue of the type that Aristotle considers to be enthymematic in form. Vernon Robbins has shown

how the Q beatitudes would read were they to have their full enthymematic form. The following is adapted from his study of the
Lukan beatitudes (1985, 51):

6:20b	Stated:	Yours is the kingdom of God.
	Unstated:	*You are poor.*
	Conclusion:	Therefore, blessed are the poor.
6:21a	Stated:	You shall be satisfied.
	Unstated:	*You hunger.*
	Conclusion:	Therefore, blessed are those who hunger now.
6:21b	Stated:	You shall laugh.
	Unstated:	*You weep now.*
	Conclusion:	Therefore, blessed are those who weep now.

Robbins points out that it is the particular circumstance of
those addressed as "you" that functions as the demonstrative proof
of the truth of the general statement. These general statements,
"Blessed are the poor," "Blessed are the hungry," and "Blessed are
those who weep," would run contrary to common opinion, and the
circumstances of the auditors as poor, hungry, and weeping do not,
on the face of it, seem especially good reasons for accepting the
truth of the general statements. Because this is contrary to usual
expectations about how reasoning goes, it becomes clear that the
acceptance of the truth of these propositions cannot be primarily
based on their character as statements that everyone would immediately recognize as true. Rather their claim to truth rests solely on
the authority of the one who pronounces them.[31] This appears to
be a case in which one is able to use maxims that run contrary to
commonly held wisdom in such a way as to make one's character
appear authoritative.[32]

The asyndetic series of beatitudes creates what rhetoricians
called the topic of amplification.[33] By this means, many things appear to be said in the same amount of time one thing would be said
if it were formulated using connectives (Aristotle, *Rh.* 3.12.4; see
also *Rhet. Her.* 4.30.41; Cicero, *Part. Or.* 15.53; Quint. 9.3.50).
Thus, Jesus appears to be pronouncing many ways in which the
lives of his hearers are blessed. Enunciating a number of beatitudes does not prove a case, but it does intensify the sense of the
speaker's authority by showing that he or she can illuminate the
situation of the hearers in a comprehensive way.

Here in the exordium of the sermon, where rhetorical principle emphasizes the establishment of the speaker's character, Jesus is shown to be one who overturns common wisdom and lays down a different way of perceiving one's situation. The acceptance of this new wisdom will depend in large measure on the authority attributed to Jesus by the audience.

In the unit Q 6:43–45 four maximlike statements and one question are accumulated. They are: "A good tree does not bear rotten fruit nor does a rotten tree bear good fruit"; "For by its fruit the tree is known"; "Are figs gathered from thorns or grapes from a bramble bush?" "The good person brings good things from the good storeroom, and the evil one brings evil things from the evil"; and "For from the abundance of the heart, the mouth speaks." There are more impersonally formulated sayings gathered here than anywhere else in the sermon. Only the third, expressed as a rhetorical question, implies a speaker and audience. The saying about knowing a tree by its fruit and that about the mouth speaking from its abundance are preceded by *gar,* thus giving these sayings the appearance of functioning as an epilogue or reason for the maxims that precede them. Yet both fail in really providing an explanation and seem rather to be additional maxims that give further insight (see R. Piper 1989, 48–49).

The first way this set of sayings contributes to the characterization of the speaker is in the fact that the first, third, and fourth maxims are based on contraries. Quintilian thinks so highly of this kind of *sententia,* which he calls an enthymeme, that he says it has the kind of supremacy that Homer has among poets and Rome among cities (Quint. 8.5.9). The author of *Ad Herennium* points out that the argument from contraries may resemble a maxim because of its brevity and claims that it is a forcible argument because

> from a statement which is not open to question it draws a thought which is in question, in such a way that the inference cannot be refuted, or can be refuted only with much the greatest difficulty. (*Rhet. Her.* 4.18.26)

Thus, the particular maxims used in this section of the sermon can be seen as particularly forceful in the kind of argument to which they appeal. As the rhetorical questions of the sermon reviewed above allowed no response from the audience, so the maxims collected here allow no refutation on the part of the hearers. Rather their agreement with the point of view of the speaker is required. The authority of the speaker rather than the wisdom of the sayings is shown.

This use of maxims at the conclusion of the main part of the sermon is appropriate in terms of rhetorical sensibility. Quintilian noted that their use as ornament was such that it put the crowning touch on the whole (8.5.10–11), and the author of *Ad Alexandrum* notes that maxims can be added for the sake of style when the case has been proven and no more evidence is needed (*Rh. Al.* 15). Taking into account the fact that when maxims are attributed the authority of the speaker, much more than the truth of the statements, is at stake, the accumulation of so many maxims at the conclusion of the argument section of the sermon has the effect of greatly emphasizing the importance of the authority of the speaker.

Present Tense

Although the treatment of the rhetorical effect of verb tenses is not extensive in the ancient rhetorical treatises, modern rhetoricians have noted that an audience can be influenced by tense (Perelman and Olbrechts-Tyteca 1969, 160). Some attempt to describe at least the function of the present tense is appropriate since it is the tense that clearly predominates in the Q sermon.

One of the effects of the present tense is that it conveys a sense of presence and immediacy (Perelman and Olbrechts-Tyteca 1969, 160). When events are introduced as happening in the present moment, a vivid actuality is achieved (Longinus, *Subl.* 25.1). Although Q 6:41–42 is not the narration of an event, it is a good example of the way the present tense achieves a vivid actuality. By addressing himself directly to the audience and characterizing their behavior, the speaker catches the hearers in the present moment and calls for a response on the spot.

Of course, the present is also the normal tense of maxims and proverbs and functions in these sayings to express something that is generally and universally true, things that are "always timely and never out of date" (Perelman and Olbrechts-Tyteca 1969, 160). The preponderance of gnomic material in the inaugural sermon accounts in great part for the frequency of the present tense. Insofar as gnomic material expressed in the present tense gives the impression of claiming what is to be considered law or normal, the authority of the one who speaks in this way is enhanced. The speaker is authorized to pronounce on what is everywhere and always true.

In the sermon the use of the present tense reflects the speaker's authority to characterize both God and human beings (see Perelman and Olbrechts-Tyteca 1969, 160). God is one who always makes the sun to shine on the wicked and the rain to fall on the lawless (Q 6:35). The general human expectation of reciprocal benefit is the subject of Q 6:31–33, and the general propensity of people to see the faults in others without noticing their own is pointed out in Q 6:41–42. Thus, the authority of this speaker is affirmed on the basis of an ability to state definitively the laws that govern the actions of God and human beings.

Summary

The foregoing has been an attempt to show how the character of the speaker of the inaugural sermon in Q can be discerned by means of an analysis of its formulation with respect to rhetorical principles. The findings will now be summarized.

First of all, the speaker is characterized as one who has a personal relationship with those addressed. This characterization is carried out to a large degree by the direct address that predominates throughout the sermon. Once the speech begins with "Blessed are the poor" (in Q 6:20b) there is no editorial intrusion at all. The direct confrontation of the audience by the speaker creates a sense of immediacy and presence. The use of imperatives, rhetorical questions, and the present tense also contribute to the sense of immediacy and contact between the audience and the speaker.

The predominant notion one gains with regard to the speaker in this text is that he is one in a position of authority with regard to the audience. This portrayal of the speaker is sustained by the frequent use of imperatives and by the types of rhetorical questions that are used as well as by the number of maxims used in the sermon. The authority for their applicability derives from the speaker rather than from the inherent wisdom of the statement. While ancient rhetoricians had a place for citations from other authorities to support an argument,[34] there is no appeal to any authority — divine, scriptural, or otherwise — outside of the speaker's in the Q sermon.

Ancient rhetoricians considered it especially important to establish the speaker's character at the beginning of the speech, that is, in the exordium. The foregoing study has shown that the impression of the speaker's authority is established at the beginning of the sermon but kept foremost in the attention of the audience throughout the speech. The relative weight carried by the ethical proof as compared to the pathetic and logical proofs awaits a careful analysis of these latter two aspects of the sermon. At this point, however, it can be said that the authority of the speaker is of overriding importance as a persuasive aspect in the inaugural sermon in Q.

NOTES

1. Burton L. Mack has noted how rhetorical form presents Jesus as authoritative in Q. See Mack 1990, 33, 51, and 1988a, 617–20.

2. The character of the speaker is one of the three modes of proof set out by Aristotle. He describes them as follows: that which derives from the character of the speaker (*ēthos*), that which derives from the emotional response of the audience (*pathos*), and that which derives from the speech itself (*logos*) (*Rh.* 1.2.3–5).

3. Aristotle specifies these qualities in *Rh.* 2.1.5.

4. Quint. 3.8.12. The author of the treatise *Rhetorica ad Alexandrum* (15), in a discussion of the speaker's opinion as a proof supplementary to those derived from words and actions and persons themselves, notes that a speaker must show that he or she is experienced in the matters at hand and that it is in his or her interest to speak the truth about them.

5. *Rh. Al.* 29. Quintilian thinks that the hearers' belief in the goodness of the speaker will have a good deal of influence in making the audience disposed to listen to the speech (4.1.7).

6. *Rh.* 3.14.12. Aristotle considers the main purpose of the exordium to be to clarify the purpose of the speech. In a deliberative speech the hearers should already be familiar with the subject and no introduction should be necessary.

7. To do a study of this kind, of course, it is necessary to determine as closely as possibly the wording of Q. For the text of Q, reference will be to the reconstruction by the International Q Project working under the auspices of the Society for Biblical Literature and the Institute for Antiquity and Christianity of the Claremont Graduate School in Claremont, California.

8. The International Q Project, hereafter IQP, agreed on the second-person formulation of the beatitudes. See Robinson 1992a, 501–2.

9. This is the formulation agreed upon by the IQP. See Robinson 1991, 495.

10. See Robbins 1985, 54. Robbins uses the work of Emile Benveniste (1971) for his analysis of the second-person form of the Lukan beatitudes. He points out that "you" in discourse takes its meaning from the "I" who speaks.

11. *Licentia* or frank speech includes reprehending the hearers. See Lausberg 1973, §761; *Rhet. Her.* 4.36.48–49; Quint. 9.2.29.

12. Although a self-reference is attested by both Matthew and Luke at Q 6:27, where Matthew has *legō hymin* and Luke has *hymin legō,* the IQP notes that the agreement may be accidental and is undecided about its presence in Q here. See IQP proceedings, 6–9 August 1993, unpublished, pp. 5–6. Because of the uncertainty of the presence of this formulation in the inaugural sermon, it will not be discussed here.

13. See Malherbe 1986, esp. 48, 50, 121. Malherbe cites Dio Chrys. 77/78.37–45; Plutarch, *Quomodo adul* 73C–74E; Epictetus, *Diss.* 3.23. 23–38.

14. The analysis of the structure of the inaugural sermon reflected here is based on a preference for Luke's order in the main section of the sermon as derived from Q. The IQP is undecided on the issue of order. See IQP proceedings, 6–9 August 1993, unpublished, pp. 15–18.

15. The count is based on those included in the reconstructions of the IQP. For Q 6:23, see Moreland and Robinson 1993, 502; for Q 6:27–36, 37–38, see IQP proceedings, 6–9 August 1993, 16–18; for Q 6:41–42, see Robinson 1991, 495.

16. See, for example, the hortatory speeches of Isocrates, *To Nicocles* (esp. 17–40) and *Nicocles or the Cyprians* (esp. 48–62), and Pseudo-Isocrates, *Ad Demonicum.* Imperatives occur also in the exhortatory sections of the *Testaments of the Twelve Patriarchs.*

17. It should be noted that the Near Eastern literary genre designated as instruction, to which Kloppenborg assigns Q, is typified by the imperative (Kloppenborg 1987a, 267). In Kloppenborg's listing of these instructions he describes their contents in terms of the forms they contain (1987a, 329–36). The point being made here is that in the Hellenistic milieu overall, collections of gnomic material were not overwhelmingly imperatival.

18. Betz 1985a, 15. Epicurus's *Kyriai Doxai* are preserved in Diog. Laert. 10.139–54.

19. The precepts of Pythagoras represent another collection of this sort. They are quoted by Diogenes Laertius (8.17–18) and by Plutarch (*De lib. ed.* 12.17). The precepts are prohibitions (formulated with the infinitive).

20. The predominance of imperatives in the sermon is representative of their predominance in the remainder of the material in the first layer of Q. Burton Mack has noted this predominance of imperatives in the early layer of Q and points this out as a trait that "attributes a strong authority to the speaker" (1990, 51; see also p. 33).

21. Lausberg 1973, §766; Quint. 9.2.6, 7; Demetrius, *De eloc.* 5.279. A very helpful description and analysis of the discussion of rhetorical questions in ancient rhetorical treatises can be found in Watson 1989, 311–18.

22. Matthew and Luke do not agree in every instance on the formulation of the sermon material in the form of questions. For these formulations, the reconstruction of the IQP is presumed here. See note 15, above, and for Q 6:39, 40, and Q 6:43–45, see Robinson 1992a, 502.

23. The Q wording is uncertain, but it is clear that the questions in Q were parallel to some extent.

24. Quint. 1.9.3–5; Theon, *Prog.* 202.5; Hermogenes, *Prog.* 7.1; Aphthonius, *Prog.* 3. Scholars are still searching for adequate distinctions between and definitions of short sayings such as proverbs, maxims, and aphorisms. See, for example, James G. Williams (1981, 80), who emphasizes the proverb as stemming from the collective voice of tradition and the aphorism as bringing the voice of the individual more to the fore, and Nigel Barley (1972, 738), who describes the maxim as a saying expressed in general terms that is to be understood literally and the proverb as a saying that is expressed metaphorically and quite particularly. See also John Dominic Crossan (1983, 18–25), who discusses several types of sayings that he includes in the category he calls prose miniature, gnomic discourse, or saying. Crossan concludes his discussion with "talk of a *proverbial* or collective vision and order being countered by an *aphoristic* and personal counter-vision and counter-order" (1983, 25).

25. *Rh.* 2.21.3–6. Quintilian (8.5.4) also distinguishes between a simple *sententia* and one to which a reason has been added. See *Rhet. Her.* 4.17.24.

26. Lausberg 1973, §872; Quint. 5.11.37; 8.5.10. The author of *Rhetorica ad Alexandrum* (7 [1428a]) treats the maxim under the discussion of direct proofs, those that are drawn from words, actions, and persons. These proofs are then contrasted with supplementary proofs: the opinion of the speaker, the evidence of witnesses, evidence given under torture and oaths. As proofs, maxims contribute authority and come close to functioning as legal custom. See Lausberg 1973, §872; *Rhetoric ad Herennium* 2.13.19; Cicero, *De inven.* 2.22.68.

27. Quint. 8.5.32. In this comment Quintilian points out that the maxim contributes to every mode of rhetorical proof.

28. Quint. 5.11.44. This insight is supported by the work of Arland Jacobson, who notes that real wisdom lies not in the content of the proverbs but in their use: "[W]isdom is an attribute not of the sayings but of the speaker" (Jacobson 1990, 83).

29. Beardslee (1970, 36–39) discusses the macarism such as found in Q 6:20b–21 as a special kind of proverb. It is not clear that the ancient rhetoricians would include these macarisms in the category of maxim, but they can be seen as maxims with epilogues. As aphoristic statements they can serve to display the character of the speaker. For the macarism as a sapiential form in Q, see also Bultmann 1968, 72; R. Edwards 1976, 62–65; Kloppenborg 1987a, 188–89.

30. See Beardslee 1970, 36 nn. 13–15; Betz 1985a, 26–33; Downing 1988b, 207; Kloppenborg 1987a, 189; Robbins 1985, 42.

31. See Kennedy 1984, 50. Kennedy is discussing the Matthean form of the beatitudes, which operates on a different logic, but points out the importance of accepting the authority of the speaker for accepting the truth of the propositions.

32. For the beatitudes as contrary to common wisdom see Robbins 1985, 42, and Betz 1985a, 33. Beardslee speaks of "paradoxical present reality" (1970, 37–38). Kloppenborg says the beatitudes, "while not typically sapiential in content, could well be characterized as the 'radical wisdom of the kingdom' " (1987a, 189).

33. For a discussion of amplification as an aspect of oratorical style, see Quint. 8.4.1–29. Aristotle considers the topic of amplification to be one that orators should use in every kind of speech, although he thinks it to be most appropriate to epidictic (*Rh.* 2.18.4–5). Longinus also defines amplification as an accumulation of all aspects and topics in a subject and then strengthening an argument by dwelling upon it. The translator conjectures that Ps-Longinus thinks amplification serves to enhance conviction rather than demonstrating a point (*Subl.* 12.2).

34. *Rh. Al.* 1; *Rhet. Her.* 2.29.46; Aphthonius, *Prog.* 3, 4; Hermogenes, *Prog.* 3, 4; Quint. 5.11.36.

7 _____ R. CONRAD DOUGLAS

"Love Your Enemies"

Rhetoric, Tradents, and Ethos

Rhetoric

Previous research has successfully applied the canons of rhetoric
in late antiquity to early Jewish and Christian writings, including
rabbinic writings, the *Gospel of Thomas,* the Gospel of Mark, and
Paul.[1] There appears, however, to have been little discussion of
rhetorical patterns in the collection of sayings that we call Q. This
essay addresses this deficit and will offer some inferences about the
social background of one such passage. The particular passage chosen as an example, Q 6:27–36, is the "love your enemies" passage,
surely one of the most familiar in the history of biblical exegesis.[2]
Yet rhetorical analysis may further elucidate even this passage. An
appended table shows other examples in Q of the rhetorical pattern
discussed here.

Before discussing the rhetorical pattern applied here, note
should be taken of two significant predecessors. T. Y. Mullins
analyzed the pattern that Q 6:27–36 exemplifies.[3] According to
Mullins, the pattern comprises three to five parts: (1) injunction
of an attitude or behavior; (2) a reason for the injunction; (3) discussion of consequences of behavior; and, optionally, (4) support
by reference to analogous situations; and (5) refutation of a contrary attitude or behavior (1980, 542–43). It is possible to be more
precise than Mullins's general discussion and to relate the structure of these patterns to ancient rhetoric even more closely than
Mullins had.

R. Conrad Douglas holds a Ph.D. in religion from Claremont Graduate School
and currently is a law student.

Ronald A. Piper's analysis of aphoristic wisdom in Q showed a common pattern in "five double-tradition aphoristic collections."[4] This pattern comprises: (1) "a rather general aphoristic saying," either a maxim or an admonition; (2) "a general maxim in statement form that provides ostensible support"; (3) a change of imagery and use of two sayings, often phrased as rhetorical questions and similar to the aphoristic saying in theme but different from it in illustration; and (4) a concluding application that "provides the key for interpreting the meaning."[5] Piper's recognition that "relatively little can be found in the way of parallels to the structure in the Jewish wisdom literature" (1989, 66) should have led him to seek parallels elsewhere. Such a search would have found parallels in the rhetorical practices of antiquity. As Piper repeatedly notes, these collections intend persuasion.[6]

Attending to common rhetorical practice makes it possible to incorporate and to go beyond the acute analyses by Mullins and Piper. Q 6:27–36[7] and other sayings-clusters in Q evince a common pattern reflecting a preliminary training exercise in Greek and Latin rhetorical education. After acquiring basic literacy and before developing full declamations, students would be set to elaborating single sayings. Such an exercise represented "the minimum formal rhetorical equipment of any literate person from the Hellenistic period on" (Cairns 1972, 75, cited by Berger 1984, 1296). The saying elaborated might be a chreia, that is, a succinct anecdote attributed to a significant historical figure, related to some specific situation, and intended to show some notable characteristic of the speaker. Alternatively, the exercise could begin with a maxim (gnome) that encapsulated some bit of proverbial wisdom in a single sentence. A gnome need not be attributed to anyone specific, and some classical writers use the presence or absence of attribution to distinguish between a chreia and a gnome. A gnome might encourage or discourage behavior or simply make an observation about the natural or social order. Whether the saying was a gnome or chreia, elaborations of sayings followed the same pattern.[8]

An elaboration might begin with an encomium praising the speaker; Q 6:27–36 omits an encomium. Then would come the saying (here the one-line exhortation, "Love your enemies" [6:27a]), followed by the paraphrase (6:28b and, probably not part of Q, vv. 27b–28a). Despite different wordings and situations, both the Matthean and Lukan versions of the following verses (6:29–30) further restate the original saying and also belong to the paraphrase.[9] A rationale, often signaled by *gar*, might follow the paraphrase. The summarizing exhortation in 6:31, while lacking this signal, provides the rationale.[10] The next step in the pattern appears in the converses of Q 6:32–34, which point out behavior opposed to the all-inclusive love here enjoined and attribute exclusiveness to stereotyped outsiders (tax collectors and Gentiles; perhaps moneylenders).[11] An elaboration supported a saying's validity through illustrations from nature or society (analogy), from history (exemplum), and from tradition (judgment) (Mack 1988b, 161). The analogy in Q 6:35 sets God's provision of sunshine and rain to the wicked and unjust as a prototype for love of the enemy.[12] As God provides even for the unjust, so God's children ought to love their enemies. An elaboration would finish with an exhortation, either to praise the speaker or to act according to the dictum. Verse 36 provides a concluding exhortation. The conclusion in Q perhaps simply exhorted the audience to "be [or, become] like your Father."[13] The conclusion of Q 6:27–36 becomes the starting point for another elaboration, so that the Q sermon largely comprises a series of elaborations.

The elaboration pattern corresponds to the patterns Mullins and Piper saw. Rules for the elaboration sharpen the analysis and suggest the pattern's rhetorical origins. The elaboration in Q 6:27–36 omits the encomium, the exemplum of a historic figure, and the citation of an authoritative text. The omissions partly reflect the fluidity of the practice. As Burton Mack and Vernon Robbins comment, "We should not think of [the elaboration pattern] as a wooden outline, but as a grammar" (1989, 198). Beyond this, however, the omissions may represent the awkwardness of a nascent movement. Mack and Robbins note that the encomium, exemplum, and judgment are also typically omitted from Markan elaborations. They suggest that people seeking to differentiate themselves from their milieus might have not been able to use the traditional heroic figures from which exempla could be drawn and the authoritative traditions from which judgments could be drawn (1989, 204–5).

The elaboration in Q 6:27–36 follows a common rhetorical pattern. The initial saying (6:27a) exhorts the audience to "Love your enemies." The following lines (v. 28b and, if present in Q, vv. 27b–28a) paraphrase the exhortation, as vv. 29–30 may also. Verse 31 perhaps should be regarded as a rationale. Verses 32–34 provide various converses; v. 35a summarizes the specific behaviors enjoined; v. 35b provides an analogy drawn from nature; and v. 36 concludes with an exhortation.

Tradents

Who might have composed such blocks of sayings? A preliminary caution is justified. Mack comments, "Authorship is therefore essentially ambiguous, for the instruction is clearly addressed to audiences later than the time of Jesus, even though the sayings are attributed to him."[14] Sayings, often free-floating in antiquity and attributable to a variety of figures, do not necessarily provide clear and dependable guides for historians. Any reconstruction would perhaps best be understood as phrased in the subjunctive or with quote marks. *Caveat lector.*

Paul Hoffmann argued that Q 6:27–36 evinces an anti-Zealotic tendency. This view, however, proceeds from questionable assumptions and relies on inadequate evidence. The call for cooperation with forced service in Matt 5:41 and the references to "tax collectors" and "Gentiles" in Matt 5:46–47[15] offer the strongest support for Hoffmann's view. Neither the summons nor the references are indisputably in Q. Hoffmann rightly comments that Matt 5:41 fits exemplarily the contemporary political situation of Palestine (1984, 61). But this remark could apply either to Q or to the Gospel of Matthew. Matthew 5:46–47 mentions not Romans but "Gentiles" — a group much broader than "Romans" — and "toll collectors" as counterexamples.

If Hoffmann's suggestions prove less than helpful, Gerd Theissen and Burton L. Mack provide apparently conflicting yet ultimately complementary reconstructions. Theissen argued in 1979 that the Q sayings reflect the situation of wandering radicals. Theissen correctly interprets Luke 6:29 (someone takes first the victim's coat, then the shirt) as referring to a robbery. His conclusion, that since muggings happen on public streets, Luke 6:29 therefore has the situation of wanderers and travelers in view,[16] is a non sequitur. Theissen also adduces Matt 5:41 but finally admits that the admonition makes sense even for settled Christians.[17] Theissen rightly points out that both Q 6:35 and Q 12:22–32 describe God's care for creation as independent of human virtues and deeds.[18] But human activity contrasts most effectively with the nonactivity of birds and flowers if the listeners themselves work. Moreover, if Q 6:27–36 and other Q passages follow the model offered by the elaboration patterns, then the sayings-complexes are not entirely due to wanderers. The elaborations require settled, literate reflection. Would staff and cloak have been left behind but writing instrument and parchment or ostraka brought along? Yet the wanderers posited by Theissen, if not the authors or tradents of the complexes in their entirety, may still have been partly responsible for them.

In *Jesus and the Spiral of Violence* (1987) and more recently in *Sociology and the Jesus Movement* (1989b), Richard A. Horsley treats Q 6:27–36 and 12:22–31 as examples of "the renewal of local community" and, more specifically, "local cooperation."[19] He suggests that subject peoples tend to sublimate against each other their resentment of domination (1987, 255). Following Tannehill (1970), Horsley views Q 6:27–36 as a "focal instance," that is, a specific and extreme example of a more general outlook to be manifested in attitude or behavior. Horsley argues that, rather than reflecting the experiences of wanderers, the sayings encourage solidarity, including economic cooperation, among peasants: "The messages and the new orientation were: take responsibility for willingly helping one another, even your enemies, in the local village community" (1987, 273). He probably misreads the economic situation by generalizing from conditions that pertained to Judaea but not Galilee.[20] Again, Horsley sometimes distinguishes between Q and later redactional activity, but he seems to assume tacitly that these sayings originated with Jesus. The various sayings may be "authentic," but this should not be merely assumed and cannot be easily determined. Nor does he appear to recognize redaction within the Q tradition. Despite these criticisms, Horsley's basic argument that these sayings address local conditions will be accepted and developed.

In his 1988 SBL seminar paper, Mack rightly mentions a series of sayings applicable to "persons engaged in a variety of life circumstances that may have been experienced in the Jesus movement. One need not assume that the only valid kingdom behavior was a radical homelessness and itinerancy" (1988a, 622). "That Q[1] includes advice on asking as well as on giving to those who beg...means that persons other than impoverished itinerants are clearly in the picture."[21] As Mack also points out, the mission speech addresses a "group which should pray for laborers to be sent out" and "those who are being sent out."[22] Mack opposes an emphasis on "wandering charismatics," yet these statements cohere with Theissen's reconstruction of "early Palestinian Christianity." Mack regards the earliest stage in the Q trajectory as preceding Q^1 and represented by "the set of aphorisms and aphoristic imperatives that were selected for reworking by Q^1 tradents" (1988a, 633). A critical, Cyniclike stance characterized such aphorisms.[23] Q sayings-complexes recurrently expand on such aphorisms, as Q 6:28–36 does on "Love your enemies." Perhaps itinerants were responsible for the earliest stage of Q, thus accounting for the rapid diffusion of sayings attributed to Jesus. Mack's first alternative to the itineracy thesis is to point to itinerant traders.[24] In discussing the commissionings, Mack makes an open-ended comment: "[T]he 'missionary' activity reflected in these instructions could well have been undertaken in the normal course of travel within expanding networks of friends, acquaintances, and trading partners as the Jesus movement spread" (1988a, 623). But would Q tradents have had "trading partners"? Would traders or traveling merchants have preserved, let alone originated, sayings blessing poverty and demanding loans without security? Such a group seems unlikely to have espoused the countercultural attitudes Mack attributes to the early stages of Q. Mack later suggests "a network of small groups meeting in houses" and "personal traffic among houses of hospitality in such a network" (1988a, 634). Who started such a network? Perhaps itinerants did. The aphorisms that were elaborated along the lines discussed above may have represented their outlook.

Much discussion of Theissen's arguments has understandably focused on his *Wanderradikalismus* thesis; after all, his early articles on the Synoptic traditions concentrated on that thesis (Theissen 1973 = 1979c; 1977 = 1979d; 1979a). Yet such a focus takes only incomplete account of Theissen's model. As set forth in *Sociology of Early Palestinian Christianity* (1978), that model can be viewed as a triangle, with itinerants occupying only one corner. Theissen explicitly states, "It is impossible to understand the Jesus movement and the synoptic tradition exclusively in terms of the wandering charismatics. In addition to them there were 'local communities,' settled groups of sympathizers."[25] The combination of these two groups, together with the Son of Man as a legitimating figure, constitutes Theissen's model. Mack's recognition of two sets of "mission" instructions militates in favor of a model incorporating both itinerants and local supporters. Adopting such a model encourages a view of the two groups as sequential yet overlapping and, taken together, as comprising the earliest tradents of Q. In agreement with Theissen, we can say that itinerants may have provided the initial impetus. In agreement with Horsley, it would seem the elaborations do concern conditions in settled communities. Although Mack critiques Theissen, the former's analysis supports viewing both itinerants and local supporters as influencing the development of these sayings-complexes. This agrees with Theissen's statement of the model in his *Sociology*. A diachronic emphasis may be preferable to Theissen's synchronic presentation. But an abrupt and immediately completed change from itinerants to settled communities is unlikely. The activities of the two groups would have overlapped, as the *Didache* shows.[26]

Rhetorical expansion on sayings cannot be attributed to either itinerants (Theissen) or impoverished villagers (Horsley). As we pointed out earlier, itinerants are unlikely to have carried with them the writing instruments such scribal activity presumes. As William V. Harris's comprehensive *Ancient Literacy* shows, literacy was a highly restricted skill in antiquity.[27] In antiquity as often now, the poor, whether urban or rural, lacked basic literacy skills, let alone the rhetorical instruction that the elaboration patterns suggest. Especially in the context of rural villages, scribes would have been those most likely to have had the skills necessary for the elaborations described above.[28] Recurrently papyri from Judaea and Egypt show scribes acting on behalf of their illiterate fellows. Such scribes would certainly not have worked in a social vacuum, and Quintilian does presuppose that unlearned audiences will be able to appreciate rhetoric to some extent (Quint. 3.8, cited by Downing 1985, 99 and 117 n. 9).

Ethos

Anthropological research elucidates the basic orientation that the rhetoric of Q 6:27–36 elucidates. Members of traditional societies characteristically assume that all goods, both material (e.g., land) and social (e.g., honor), are limited. A zero-sum game ensues: gain for one means loss for others.[29] The "limited-good" orientation assumes the natural and social environment to be a closed system with limited basic economic and social resources (Foster, in Potter, Dias, and Foster 1967, 304–7). The result is that available resources cannot be created but only variously apportioned. Concomitantly, the limited-good orientation emphasizes reciprocity within the exchange system.[30] One gives with the expectation of future return: *do ut des.*

Besides material resources, the limited-good orientation also applies to standing within the community, that is, honor.[31] According to Jean Peristiany, honor is the constant preoccupation of individuals in small-scale, exclusive societies where face-to-face personal, as opposed to anonymous, relations are of paramount importance and where the social personality of the actor is as significant as his or her office (1965c, 11).

Jane Schneider has suggested that honor becomes problematic when (1) groups face "competition from equivalent groups"; (2) "contested resources are subject to redivision along changing lines"; or (3) "social boundaries are difficult to maintain, and internal loyalties are questionable" (1971, 2). These situations characterized the Hellenistic and early Roman periods. The primary locus of honor and shame is the group, especially the family.[32] Various cultures links honor with patrilineality. Generations of males transmit honor as a social inheritance, vested in and protected by the fathers.[33] Loss of honor spreads through a family both horizontally between siblings and vertically between parents and children (Pitt-Rivers 1965, 36). The rules of honor also define familial and especially gender roles.[34] Group members who leave a small group where roles and status are clear face challenges to their honor.[35] So long as social authority is "legitimate," that is, recognized and respected as binding, honor is not problematic. "Honour felt becomes honour claimed and honour claimed becomes honour paid" (Pitt-Rivers 1965, 22). When the legitimacy of authority is disputed, honor is insecure and discrepancies in according honor(s) will occur. As a result, a group's member "is forcibly cast in the role of his group's protagonist" (Peristiany 1965c, 11). In addition, the honor-shame polarity is a "zero-sum game."[36] The phenomenon of hubris reflects this zero-sum characteristic. Despite its current inflated meaning, hubris originally meant "behavior intended to produce dishonour or shame to others, on the part of those who derive pleasure from such behavior."[37] The charge of hubris reflects the conviction that there are some people whose status puts their honor beyond or beneath challenge. The claim to such a status, like all claims in honor-shame contests, must be socially ratified or result in derision and greater shame.

Traditional societies, however, are not fully closed systems,[38] for they may offer hopes for transcending the basic assumption of limited good. An idyllic view of the land as granting immortality through inheritance is one example of such a hope. According to DuBoulay and Williams, inhabitants of the Greek village Ambéli see this idyll as realized through harvest and describe the idyll in explicit references to Eden.[39] Another example is hospitality, which expresses this same desire to escape the basic and seemingly ineluctable orientation to limited good. Hospitality is also an exceptional occurrence, extended either to other villagers at times of celebration or, more commonly, to strangers, who by definition are not part of the normal order. DuBoulay and Williams show the ambivalence of this effort to escape the limited-good orientation: "[W]hile within the village consciousness of limited resources, hospitality is felt as a constraint, hospitality to the stranger has to be understood as, amongst other things, an attempt to act as if resources were, as they are in the divine world, unlimited" (1987, 17).

I suggest that the Sayings Gospel offers another instance of the criticism of limited good. Sayings-clusters in Q^1 criticize the assumption that all goods, both material (e.g., land) and social (e.g., honor), are limited. Such sayings as "Love your enemies," "Ask and it will be given to you," and "Don't worry" oppose the limited-good orientation. The elaborations of the sayings further emphasize the belief that, contrary to ordinary experience, neither material nor social resources are limited. Q 6:27–36 addresses the preoccupation with honor endemic to traditional cultures. Intercession can be offered for persecutors. Blows on the cheek[40] are to be treated as meaningless; indeed, the social good of honor is so unlimited that more blows can be invited with impunity. Contrary to normal practice, honor need not be restricted to those likely to return it.[41] The reference to God as Father justifies the challenge to the limited-good orientation and the resulting anxiety and insistence on reciprocity. The Q^1 sayings-clusters assure listeners that they, who are children of God the ideal(ized) parent, will receive what they need. If basic resources, both physical (food, clothing) and social (honor), are not limited, then God's children do not need to worry about either deprivation or opposition. The exemplary nature of God's generosity supports the critique of the limited-good orientation. Freed from anxiety over their continued existence, God's children can imitate God. If God provides even the wicked and unjust, who are God's enemies, with rain and sun, basic necessities for agriculture, God's children can and should treat their enemies similarly. Despite the critique of the limited-good assumption, Q 6:27–36 may have served to strengthen group boundaries that were presupposed.[42] Despite differences in wording between the Matthean and Lukan versions, Q 6:27–36 uses vaguely defined groups of opponents who do not exhibit the desired behavior or attitude to provide converses (6:32–34; cf. 11:11–12; 12:30). The purpose of the pericope was not to strengthen group boundaries, but its converses point toward the use of the reference to God as Father for purposes of demarcation.

Some Progymnasmata in Q Pericopae

STEPS	PERICOPAE		
	3:7–9	6:21–23	6:27–36[43]
1. Encomium/ Introduction	3:7	6:21–22	6:27a
2. a. Saying	3:8a	6:23a	6:27b
b. Paraphrase		6:23b	6:28b–31, 35a
3. Rationale	3:8c		6:31
4. Converse	3:8b		6:32–34
5. Analogy	3:9		6:35b
6. Example		6:23c	6:36
7. Judgment			
8. Exhortation			

STEPS	6:36–45	6:46–49	7:4–9
1. Encomium/ Introduction			7:4–5
2. a. Saying	6:36	6:46	7:6a
b. Paraphrase	6:37a		7:6b
3. Rationale	6:37b–38		
4. Converse	6:41–42	6:49	7:6c–7a
5. Analogy	6:39–40, 43–44	6:47–48	
6. Example	6:45		7:8
7. Judgment			
8. Exhortation			7:9

STEPS	PERICOPAE		
	9:57–(62)*	11:9–13	11:29–35*
1. Encomium/ Introduction	9:57a		
2. a. Saying	9:57b, 59	11:9a	11:29a
b. Paraphrase	9:58	11:9bc	11:29b
3. Rationale	9:58b, 60	11:10	11:30
4. Converse	(9:62)	11:11–12	11:33
5. Analogy		11:13	
6. Example			11:31, 32
7. Judgment			
8. Exhortation			11:35

	12:4–9	12:22–31	12:39–46
1. Encomium/ Introduction		12:22a	
2. a. Saying	12:5a	12:22b	12:40a
b. Paraphrase	12:5b	12:22c	
3. Rationale		12:23	12:40b
4. Converse	12:4	12:30	12:39
5. Analogy	12:6–7a	12:24–25, 27–28	12:42–44
6. Example		12:27b	
7. Judgment	12:8–9		12:45–46
8. Exhortation	12:7b	12:26, 29, 31	

	13:24–30	17:20–30, 37
1. Encomium/ Introduction		
2. a. Saying	13:24a	17:20b
b. Paraphrase		17:21, 23
3. Rationale	13:24b	17:24
4. Converse	13:26–27	
5. Analogy		17:37b
6. Example	13:28	17:26, [28–29]
7. Judgment	13:29–30	
8. Exhortation		17:30

NOTES

1. Among others, see Fischel 1968; Kennedy 1984; Butts 1987; Mack 1987, esp. 15–28; 1988b, 161–65, 179–92; 1990; Robbins 1988; Bjorndahl 1988; Mack and Robbins 1989; Betz 1979; Übelacker 1989; Attridge 1989; Watson 1991.

2. References to Q passages use Lukan chapter and verse numbers.

3. Mullins 1980; for his reference to Matt 5:43–47, see p. 544.

4. See the title of part of chapter 2 in R. Piper 1989. The five collections discussed are Q 11:9–13; 12:22–31; 6:37–42; 6:43–45; 12:2–9. Piper also discusses Q 6:27–36 and Luke 16:9–13.

5. See Piper's summary (1989, 61–77 passim, and esp. 61–65).

6. See, for example, his emphatic statement: "These are not haphazard collections of aphoristic sayings; they display a design and argument unique in the synoptic tradition" (1989, 64; further, 72–74). In view of the use of this pattern elsewhere in the Synoptics, Piper's emphasis on uniqueness may be misplaced at best.

7. The following discussion is based in part on my reconstruction of Q 6:27–36 for the Q Project of the Institute for Antiquity and Christianity. This reconstruction and its database are available to the interested public through the Institute for Antiquity and Christianity, Claremont Graduate School, Claremont, California.

Probably the most contentious issue in reconstructing the Q version of this passage is the order of the sayings. I think that the Lukan order more accurately reflects Q here, as usually elsewhere.

8. For the definition of a gnome and its use to persuade or dissuade from action, see Hermogenes 4, in Walz 1832–36, 1:24–27; Aphthonius 4 in Walz 1832–36, 1:67–72. The outline here follows Hermogenes, as excerpted in Hock and O'Neil 1986, 174–77. For other ancient discussions of elaboration, see *Rhet. Her.* 4.43.56–44.58, where it is called a *tractatio;* Aphthonius, *Prog.* 3.18–75 (Hock and O'Neil 1986, 225–29); Nicolaus of Myra 162–84 (Hock and O'Neil 1986, 261–63). For discussion of Hermogenes, see the introduction by Mack and O'Neil 1986, 155–63; see further, Mack 1987, 15–28; 1988b, 161–65, 179–92; 1990, 43–47; see also Berger 1984, 1092–1110 (chreia), 1093–94 n. 28 (outline of progymnasmata according to Priscian's translation of Hermogenes), 1296–98 (progymnasmata).

9. Schürmann (1969, 345–46, 350–53, 357–58) suggested that the change from the plural of vv. 27–28 to the singular of vv. 29–30 and the resumption of the plural in v. 31 mean these verses were inserted, at the latest in the written redaction of Q. Against this view, see Longinus, *Subl.* 26.3, which advises orators to shift sometimes to the singular for more direct address to their audiences. I am indebted to Shawn Carruth (Concordia College, Moorhead, Minn.) for this reference.

10. Its very general nature and the significant divergence between the Matthean and Lukan placements suggest that the saying in Q 6:31 was previously free-floating.

11. Accepting for "Gentiles" and "tax collectors" the priority of the Matthean version and assuming that Q, as well as Luke, referred to making loans and followed the same format as the other converses.

12. Following the Matthean version here in wording and the Lukan version in limiting the reference to inimical groups. Since the use of *char*-stem words belongs to Lukan redaction here, Q may originally have had *adikous*. However, use of *dik*-stem words is generally characteristic of Matthean redaction.

13. Both the Matthean and the Lukan redactors may have felt such an exhortation was too open-ended and supplied adjectives appropriate to their respective contexts (*teleios* and *oiktirmōn/oiktirmones*). In any case, the saying occupies a hinge position; the Matthean *teleios* refers to the preceding complete, all-embracing nature of the love exhorted, while the Lukan *oiktirmōn* refers to the sayings on judgment that follow.

14. Mack 1988a, 618. For a later statement of Mack's views, see Mack 1993.

15. Hoffmann (1984, 61): "The illustration coheres very well with the contemporary political situation in Palestine."

16. Theissen (1979a, 184): "But a robbery of this kind generally occurs on the open highway, which means that Luke was thinking of the situation of wayfarers and travelers."

17. Theissen (1979a, 184): "All the same, the admonition has a point even for sedentary Christians."

18. Theissen (1979a, 185): "There is no talk here about people working, and certainly not about looking for work." See also ibid., n. 57.

19. Horsley 1987, 255–73, largely repeating Horsley 1986. Horsley's discussion in Horsley 1989b, 124–25, merely summarizes briefly his earlier argument.

20. See Goodman 1983, 417–18, discussed at length by Freyne 1980, 101–207. Freyne finds in Galilee during the Hellenistic and Roman periods a peasant situation, characterized by a wealthy ruling class and a much poorer peasantry, but not a situation of increasing indebtedness and deprivation. For discussion of the sayings here considered against the background of the peasant ethos of limited good, see below.

21. Mack 1988a, 623; surely this is misstated: it is the presence of the sayings about asking that may suggest the role of itinerants.

22. Mack 1988a, 623. This distinction had been previously observed by Zeller 1982, 404–5, 409–10; and Kloppenborg 1987a, 193. For a more recent restatement of his position, see Mack 1993.

23. This is amply illustrated by the material cited by Downing 1988a, 23–29 (6:27–36), 57–58 (11:9–13), and 68–71 (12:22–31), respectively.

24. In Mack 1993 (esp. 114–20), Mack emphasizes how similar the earliest stratum of Q is to the Cynics.

25. Theissen 1978, 17. Similarly, Mack's later discussion describes a "social formation at the earliest stage of the tradition" (Mack 1993, 121).

26. Might the fourth-century relationships of "holy persons" and communities, which Peter Brown explored, have had origins at least as early as the first century? This would neither deny nor underestimate the particular fourth-century factors that Brown sees as operative. See Brown 1971 = 1982, 103–52, and Brown 1976 = 1982, 153–65. See also Draper 1995.

27. Harris 1989. For the prevalence of semiliteracy and illiteracy, understood as difficulty or inability to read and write Greek, in Egypt during the Ptolemaic and Roman periods, see Youtie 1971a = 1973–75, 2:611–27; Youtie 1971b = 1973–75, 2:629–51; Youtie 1975a = 1981–82, 179–99; Youtie 1975b = 1981–82, 255–62. Semiliteracy or illiteracy in Greek did not preclude literacy in indigenous languages, Demotic in the instances discussed by Youtie. Nor did occupancy of an official position entail fluency in Greek; see especially Youtie 1971b. A leading sociologist of the Roman Empire has reportedly estimated a literacy rate in Egypt of 20 percent (Hopkins, cited in Goody 1986, 121).

28. In this regard, see Kloppenborg 1991. If Reed's argument for an urban setting (see above, pp. 25–30) were correct, this would mean a higher rate of literacy but would not change the class constraints. Since Q does not reflect the views of even a nostalgic or romanticizing upper stratum—a point rightly made by Theissen—scribes continue to be the most likely group to have possessed the skills necessary for the elaborations that form Q.

29. Foster 1965, reprinted in Potter, Dias, and Foster 1967, 300–323 (citations are from the reprint). See the critiques by Gregory 1975 and DuBoulay and Williams 1987 and their respective bibliographies.

30. See Gregory's critique (1975, 73–84) and Foster's response (1975, 86–87).

31. The following discussion draws on essays in Peristiany 1965b; Schneider 1971; Denich 1974, 243–62; Malina 1981, 25–50; and Gilmore 1987.

32. Campbell (1965, 145): "Honour invariably has some reference to the corporate family, for in this community the individual can only be taken account of, and evaluated, in relation to his family membership." Peristiany (1965a, 173): "The three social categories with which a Greek identifies himself readily are the family, the community of origin and the nation."

33. Pitt-Rivers (1965, 36): "In both the family and the monarchy a single person symbolizes the group whose collective honour is vested in his person." For the association of honor and patrilineality, see Baroja

1965, 89–93 (medieval Spain); Peristiany 1965a, 179; Bourdieu 1965, 219; Zeid 1965, 252–54.

34. Pitt-Rivers 1965, 69–70; Peristiany 1965a, 181; Bourdieu 1965, 221–22, 239; Denich 1974, 249–50. See also in this regard the discussion below of papyri marriage contracts. Especially but not only in agnatic kinship systems, that is, systems linked through horizontal ties among males, the prescribed roles of women are stringently, sometimes violently, enforced (Denich 1974, 253–55). When nuclear families predominate, people feel less pressure to support the extended kinship system and conform to its norms (Denich 1974, 256–58), resulting in greater possibilities and enhanced status for women. Concern for the honor of female members of a group may avert conflict among males. "A woman's status defines the status of all the men who are related to her, and share therefore the commitment to protect her virtue. She is part of their patrimony" (Schneider 1971, 18). This is especially so when partible inheritance prevails. Male anxiety about female honor thus serves the functions of social control and, among males especially, integration. The unmarried woman no longer subject to her family of origin is an exception to this gender-based differentiation (Pitt-Rivers 1965, 69).

35. Peristiany (1965c, 11): "What is significant in this wider context is the insecurity and instability of the honour-shame ranking. Even when honour is inherited with the family name, it has to be asserted and vindicated."

36. Campbell (1965, 150) says of the Sarakatsani, a Greek nomadic shepherding group: "Since everything depends on the conservation of honour, it is believed that the misfortune of a family which falls from grace through poverty or dishonour in some way validates the status and integrity of others. . . . The values of honour and prestige are exclusive and particularistic."

37. Fisher 1976, 177; see the classical literature cited in this essay and in Fisher 1979; see also MacDowell 1976; Gagarin 1979; Cohen 1991.

38. Foster (1965, 317–21) mentions the idealized and actual roles of wealthy patrons and the hope for good luck.

39. On the basis of field research during 1966–68 and 1971–73 in a Greek, subsistence-oriented village, DuBoulay and Williams (1987, 17) comment: "[I]t is a story which opposes two alternative situations rather than simply presenting one, and in fact to the older generation in particular, the Garden of Eden is as much located in their own experience as the world of the Fall. To the Fall belongs their struggle with the land; to the image of Paradise or the garden belongs their freedom to set food on the table at any time once each crop is harvested and stored."

40. The specification of the right cheek is probably Matthean and emphasizes the dishonoring intent already expressed by the blow.

41. As W. C. van Unnik (1954; 1966) emphasized, use of *agathopoiein*

in the Lukan version reflects an adaptation to and critique of a Hellenistic ethic of reciprocity. However, a critique of reciprocity is evident both in the probable Q version and in later redactions.

42. Lührmann 1972, 426. The tension may, however, already have been implicit in the original saying (6:27a); if all are to be loved, what can it mean to talk about enemies?

43. For Q 9:57–62 and 11:29–35, see Mack and Robbins 1989, 69–84 and 185–91, respectively.

Part III

John the Baptist in Q

"Yes, I Tell You, and More Than a Prophet"

The Function of John in Q

The discussion of John's function in Q presupposes the stratigraphy reconstructed by John S. Kloppenborg. According to his analysis, the material relating to John (Q 3:7–9, 16–17; 7:18–35) belongs to the secondary stage in Q's documentary development. These two blocks of sayings form two of the five Q^2 speeches that now surround the six speeches of the formative stratum of Q (Q^1). Convincing signs of the secondary character of Q^2 are observed by Kloppenborg in the positioning of Q^2 speeches. They assume the introductory and concluding places in the document, and individual sayings interrupt otherwise unitary Q^1 speeches, appending forensic threats to blocks of material that is best characterized as "sapiential."[1]

Kloppenborg states that the Q^2 material is characterized by "the call to repentance, the threat of apocalyptic judgment and the censure of 'this generation' for its recalcitrance" (1987a, 102). These themes do not display an unfocused hostility but rather reiterate the prophetic denunciations of Deuteronomistic tradition. It was O. H. Steck (1967) who demonstrated the ancient four-part pattern: (1) the people sin; (2) God sends the people a prophet; (3) the people reject the prophet; (4) God threatens the people with devastating punishment. This obvious appropriation of Deuteronomistic denunciation in Q^2 material is all the more striking since Q^1 sayings do not display much if any explicit reference to specifically Jewish religious traditions. Scripture is never quoted, and, with

Wendy Cotter is an assistant professor of New Testament at Loyola University, Chicago.

the exception of Solomon "in all his glory" (Q 12:27), no Jewish heroes are mentioned at all. Here, we would want to note that the lack of specific Jewish references does not allow us to conclude that the community represented by Q^1 was necessarily gentile. We can say only that the community does not show interest in appealing to Jewish traditions.

But in Q^2 it is clear that a new strategy has taken over. Besides the Deuteronomistic perspective that characterizes Q^2, three other features show a deliberate and direct appeal to Jewish tradition.[2] First, Scripture is quoted for the first time, and only twice, precisely in the Q^2 cluster given over to John and Jesus (Q 7:22, 27).[3] Jesus appeals to Scripture to ratify his own identity (Q 7:22/Isa 29:18, 19; 35:5–6) and then that of John as his precursor (Q 7:27/Exod 23:20; Mal 3:1). Second, we find for the first time the issue of faithful Torah observance raised (Q 11:39a, 41, 42, 46). Third, heroes and prophets from Old Testament tradition are now called upon to support the teachings of Q^2.[4] Jewish heroes slain for their truthful message and Gentiles who exceed Jews in their faith are meant to provide a paradigm for the Q^2 community.

The turn to prophets is expressed in the way John's opening speech has been fashioned to imitate Old Testament tradition (Q 3:8).

Q 3:7–9, 16–17

Although each of the two logia shows a composite structure,[5] they have been joined to achieve the semblance of a unitary address.[6] Q 3:7–9 imitates a five-step "prophetic announcement of judgment against Israel":[7]

1. *Introductory Address to the Accused:*
   You brood of vipers!

2. *Accusatory Question:*
   Who warned you to flee from the wrath to come? (v. 7bc)
   Bear fruit therefore that befits repentance, and do not begin to say to yourselves, "We have Abraham as our father"; (v. 8a)

3. *Identification Formula:*
   for I tell you (v. 8b)

4. *Pronouncement of Judgment*
   that God is able from these stones to raise up children to Abraham. Even now the axe is laid to the root of the trees. (vv. 8bc, 9a)

5. *Conclusion:*
    Every tree therefore that does not bear good fruit is cut down and
    thrown into the fire. (v. 9b)[8]

The deliberate intention to follow prophetic-speech conventions
can be seen in the way the fruit metaphor in v. 8a and v. 9 is in-
terrupted by v. 8bc — beginning with the identification formula,
"for I tell you" — so that a link is provided between the accusatory
question and the pronouncement of judgment. Another example
is seen in the second logia, Q 3:16–17. Three independent sayings
(vv. 16ac, 16b, 17) have been joined by a catchword. But to achieve
the linkage the contrast of John and the Mightier One (v. 16b)
has been inserted between the contrasts of the baptisms (v. 16ac).
Maintaining *pur* as the catchword is necessary because it joins not
only v. 16 and v. 17 but also the first and second logia (vv. 9, 16).
Two logia must be joined so that the announcement of the Coming One in vv. 16–17, this apocalyptic figure of the end-time, can
share the prophetic credibility established in vv. 7–9 with the more
conventional denunciation. Thus the "Coming One," although this
phrase is not easily recognized as a biblical title, will be assigned
the status of a reliable prophet and will be given holy accreditation
as such.

This carefully constructed speech introduces for Jesus a futurity
that is completely absent from Q[1]. Jesus promises neither a return
meeting with his disciples nor any role of apocalyptic judgment.
John as prophet is the first one, then, who will promise an end-time
judgment and an end-time agent, the Coming One.

Besides the introduction of the apocalyptic end-time and the figure of the Coming One, John's prophetic speech presents the major
themes that will characterize the subsequent preaching of the Q[2]
Jesus:

1. Q 3:7bc: *The perversity of Israel:* Q 7:31–34; 11:19, 39, 44, 47–48.

2. Q 3:8a: *The sterility of Israel:* Q 7:31–34; 11:42, 43, 46; 19:12–27.

3. Q 3:8bc: *The presumption of Israel:* Q 11:29–32, 40–41, 49–51;
   13:28, 34–35.

4. Q 3:7c, 16, 17: *The coming judgment:* Q 11:31–32; 17:31–37.

5. Q 3:16, 17: *The coming agent of judgment:* Q 17:22–27.

6. Q 3:8: *The displacement of Israel:* Q 22:28–30.

This means that Jesus' denouncement of Israel and his promise of a displacement by the Gentiles can in no way be attributed to him as personal and private notions. John has already called out:

> Bear fruit therefore that befits repentance, and do not begin to say to yourselves, "We have Abraham as our father"; for I tell you that God is able from these stones to raise up children to Abraham. . . . Even now the axe is laid to the root of the tree. (Q 3:8–9)

Therefore, Jesus' mourning Israel as forsaken is clearly an echo of God's prophecy:

> O Jerusalem, Jerusalem, killing the prophets and stoning those who are sent to you! How often would I have gathered your children together as a hen gathers her brood under her wings, and you would not! Behold your house is forsaken. I tell you, you will not see me until you say, "Blessed is he who comes in the name of the Lord." (Q 13:34–35)

At the conclusion of the Q^2 document, Jesus will pronounce the displacement of Israel:

> You who have followed me . . . in the kingdom will sit on the twelve thrones judging the twelve tribes of Israel. (Q 22:28–30)

Therefore, Ernst Bammel's statement that "Q turns out to be a justification of John's ministry" (1971–72, 101) is precisely contrary to the case. John's speech provides credibility for the perspectives and Christology of Q^2.

Clearly, John's speech is crucial for Q^2. A closer inspection of its careful construction and its function leads one to see that it is more accurate to understand it as a dramatic *monologue*. In fact, introductory monologues are features of Greek tragedy beginning with Euripides and were therefore familiar devices to the people of the Mediterranean. Tragedies began with a character stepping onto the empty stage to address the audience, preparing it for the dark events of the play to come (Lucas 1923, 11; see also Kindermann 1979, 31–45). F. C. Lucas explains:

> The purpose of these monologues is to give a summary, often extremely prosy, of previous events, and if a god or a ghost is the speaker, of the future course of the plot as well.[9]

In Euripides' *Medea,* it is Medea's nurse who first enters the stage. The audience is given the context of the play by her opening lament:

I wish the Argo had never rowed between the dark Synplegades on the way to Colchis; I wish the pines had never been felled in the glens of Pelion to furnish oars for the heroes who went in quest of the gold fleece for Pelias. For then Medea, my mistress, would not have been stunned by love for Jason and sailed to the city in the land of Iolcus, nor have prevailed upon the daughter of Pelias to kill their father, nor made her home here in Corinth with her husband and her children. (1.1.1–11)

The second part of her speech describes the afflicted state of Medea as Jason prepares to marry the daughter of Creon. Finally she alerts the audience to the violence that will occur in the play:

She hates her children and takes no pleasure in the sight of them, and I fear she intends some mischief. She has a dangerous spirit and will not stand ill treatment; I know her and I fear her, lest she may enter secretly into the palace where the bridal bed is made, and thrust a sharp sword through her heart, or kill the king and the bridegroom as well, and then suffer a worse end herself. She is a terrible woman; not easily will the man who quarrels with her come to sing a song of triumph. (1.1.36–46)

In fact, this is precisely what *does* happen.

It is credible to have Medea's nurse reveal the dark character of Medea because she is the very one who may say, "I know her." John's credibility rests on his prophetic status.

While the technique of the introductory monologue was unknown in Sophocles' day, the use of a prophetic messenger to enter the scene with a prediction of coming disaster was certainly well known. In Sophocles' *Oedipus Rex,* blind Teiresias fulfills this role. Teiresias's speech does not have a prophetic "form"; instead it consists of dark and puzzling asides. For that reason he must be identified in some other manner. Sophocles has the chorus greet him in this way:

But there is one man who may detect the criminal. This is Teiresias, this is the holy prophet in whom, alone of all men, truth was born. (1.1.82–84)

If we were to change the name Teiresias to John, we would have a perfect description of the end-time prophet that Q^2 wants to prepare *its* audience. For that audience, the structure of John's speech and the reputation of John among Christians are all that are necessary to establish him as a prophet "in whom truth was born."

The use of an introductory figure to address the audience was common to all ancient plays. Comedy too had an actor step forward to "warm up" the audience for the fun to follow. The *prologus,* draped in a pallium, took the stage and delivered a monologue designed to charm his audience into keeping their seats for the coming performance.[10] Thus the Mediterranean populace would have been accustomed to these opening monologues that prepared them for what they were to hear and gave an inner insight into the play's significance.

I do not propose that Q is a play or that it was intended for dramatic performance. It is clear, as Kloppenborg has already shown, that Q stands in the tradition of the wisdom-sayings collections. However, as I have shown, John's initial speech in Q does function in the same way as the introductory monologues of plays. The Mediterranean populace was quite accustomed to this preparation, whether it be prior to a comedy or a tragedy. Moreover, not all written plays were performed in the theater. It was quite common for them to be read to an assembled group of the playwright's friends. I suggest that the influence of such introductory monologues may well be responsible for the idea of presenting a preparatory speech of John in Q 3:7–9, 16–17.

Q 7:18–35

The function of Q 7:18–35 requires an independent examination of each of the constituent pericopae (Q 7:18–23, 24–28 [Q 16:16],[11] 31–35) and then an analysis of the effect of the entire composite unit on the rest of Q.

Q 7:18–23

The question of John (Q 7:19) accomplishes two important tasks. First, it tells the reader that John had identified Jesus as the Coming One. This means that Jesus as the Coming One receives a prophetic endorsement. With this title John gives to Jesus his role as an apocalyptic agent of God who will bring judgment to the earth in the end-time.

Second, John's question allows the Q^2 community to focus on the very clear contradiction between the Q^2 expectations of Jesus' apocalyptic-judgment role as Coming One in Q 3:7–9, 16–17 and the Q^1 benign-wisdom role created for Jesus in his first address: Q 6:20b–23b, 27–35, 36–45, 46–49. This contrast is emphasized by the healing miracle (Q 7:1–10) that follows Jesus' initial speech. Even though Jesus will exclaim that the centurion's faith exceeds anything he saw in Israel (Q 7:9), the story does not carry the dramatic apocalyptic-judgment theme that John prepares us to see in Jesus. Instead, it seems to attest the tradition of the merciful, miracle-working Jesus.

By placing the wisdom speech of Jesus as his first and by situating a miracle story immediately after, Q^2 creates the discrepancy in roles that needs to be addressed if the community is to present the wisdom sayings of Q^1 as well as their own forensic, apocalyptic-oriented material.

Jesus' response to John's query shows no eagerness to grasp the title. But neither is the title denied. The argument is constructed so that John himself must come to his own conclusion. Q 7:22 presents actions that further conflict with the promises of John about the Coming One. At the same time these actions do fulfill the prophecy of another prophet, the great Isaiah (Isa 29:18, 19; 35:5–6). It is clear that the one sent from God must demonstrate these signs of salvation. Thus Jesus points to the fulfillment he offers to the Isaian prophecy. The addition of v. 23, "And blessed is the one who takes no offense at me," is an acknowledgment that Jesus' eirenic perspectives may scandalize John and those like him who have not been able to justify the pacific role of the earthly Jesus with the apocalyptic expectations of God's end-time agent.

Here, the Q^2 community affirms the traditions of wisdom and mercy that belong to the earthly Jesus. Jesus' answer to John leaves it to him to accept or reject him as the Coming One. But since Jesus' behavior is justified by the prophecy of Isaiah, that behavior acts as a corrective to John. Clearly, his expectations of the Coming One must accommodate the benign valence of the historical Jesus. So Q 7:18–23 shows that the community must deal with the problem of Jesus' double valence. Q 7:22–23 makes it clear that the identity of Jesus as benign wisdom teacher and salvific miracle worker will not be compromised. At the same time, the fact that John's preaching is given first place in the Q^2 document shows that the community has accepted Jesus as the Coming One. The question remains how Jesus will carry the two valences of wisdom teacher and salvific healer as well as apocalyptic end-time agent of God.

The seeming contradiction will be resolved later. In Q 13:34–35 it becomes clear that Jesus is to come *again*, and here the title *ho erchomenos* is used:

> Jerusalem, Jerusalem, you kill the prophets and stone those who are sent to you! How often would I have gathered your children together, as a hen gathers her brood under her wings, and you refused! Behold your temple is forsaken. *But I tell you, you will not see me until you say, "Blessed is the one who comes [ho erchomenos] in the name of the Lord."*

The idea that Jesus is to come again is not found in the Q^1 stratum. It is only in Q^2 that Jesus is given the role of the future Coming One. His role is further amplified in the last section of Q^2: 17:23, 24, 26–27, 28–30, 34–35, 37; 22:28–30. Here the destruction of the wicked and the displacement of the unfaithful children of Abraham by Jesus' faithful followers are indeed the fulfillment of John's prophecy in Q 3:7–9, 16–17.

Thus, Jesus is able to claim the role of the Coming One even though his earthly life was not characterized by an apocalyptic destruction. He successfully holds two valences because he comes to the earth twice, once as the benign wisdom teacher and healer and again as the one who is the agent of God's end-time judgment. For this reason Q^1 speeches will be retained and transmitted, but with the contextualization of the Q^2 material.

But the resolution of the apocalyptic expectations, represented by John, and of the wisdom teachings/benevolent salvation, represented by Jesus, is not the strategy of Q 7:18–35. Instead, each valence is allowed to stand independently. As we will see, this separateness and double valence will serve to defend Jesus' humiliation and execution by "this generation."

Q 7:24–28

Just as Q 7:18–23 identifies Jesus as the Coming One, so Q 7:24–28 identifies John as the precursor of the Coming One. The status of John must be given credibility by Jesus immediately since Jesus' tough answer to him in Q 7:22 suggests that John might be wrong in his expectations, might be unreliable as a witness to Jesus. Q^2 cannot allow any shadow on John's prophecy or on John himself since he is to give prophetic weight to the revelation of Jesus as apocalyptic Coming One — the valence that Q^2 introduces and allows to control the document as a whole. Jesus must place his own endorsement on John so that he will be accorded the proper respect and his message be accepted as divinely empowered, however puzzling it might be at this point of the document.

The technique of having the main hero endorse the prophet is used in drama as well. In Sophocles' *Oedipus Rex,* for example, Oedipus provides the audience with a legitimation of Teiresias's authority with a speech acknowledging his rightful claim to prophecy:

> Teiresias; seer; student of mysteries,
> Of all that's taught and all that no man tells,
> Secrets of heaven and secrets of earth:
> Blind though you are, you know the city lies
> Sick with plague; and from this plague, my lord,
> We find that you alone can guard us or save us.
> (*Oedipus Rex* 1.1.85–91)

Having been endorsed by the king, Teiresias will win the confidence of the audience regarding his dark predictions of the monarch's end.

Even though the Q document is not drama, one cannot help but notice that the juxtaposition of Q 7:18–23 and Q 7:24–28 will provide a scene of heavenly ratification. It is easy to imagine John's disciples leaving the stage with their enigmatic answer and Jesus now turning to the audience with a monologue directed to them about John's greatness. Jesus will reveal that John is much more than a prophet. He is the prophesied precursor.

Jesus' repeated question to the people about why they have gone out into the wilderness (Q 7:24–26) is a clever argument in which the people are asked to judge their own actions toward John. Why would anyone go into the wilderness? Jesus' first two suggestions, that they have gone to the desert looking for a reed shaken by the wind or for a person in fine clothes, represent contrasting but equally foolish reasons. No one would be looking in the desert for something so commonplace as a shaking reed or for an oddity like a person all dressed up. Jesus' final proposal, that the people are looking for a prophet, is the only reasonable one. This kind of argument absolves the Christian community from having invented a prophetic identity for John. In Q 7:24–26a Jesus establishes that John is already publicly recognized as a prophet. Jesus' revelation builds on the commonly known prophetic identity of John. Jesus claims:

> Yes, I tell you, and more than a prophet. This is he of whom it is written, "Behold, I send my messenger before your face who shall prepare your way before you." (Q 7:26b–27)

This conflation of Mal 3:1 and Exod 23:20 gives John the unique role of precursor.[12]

There are only two direct references to Scripture in Q, and both are located here in Q 7:18–27. The appeal to Isaiah legitimates the Q^1 Jesus as the Coming One. The appeal to Mal 3:1/Exod 23:20 legitimates the Q^2 John as the precursor of the Coming One.

John is lifted up only to lift Jesus higher. Once John is granted the identity of the divinely sent precursor, his prophecies about Jesus are reaffirmed and validated. And Jesus has already validated his own wisdom/salvific role to John. Thus, Q 7:24–26 creates a solid endorsement of John so that Jesus may be doubly endorsed: by God's word in Isaiah and by God's word to John. Both of Jesus' valences are secured.

The role of John as servant to him is reinforced by Q 7:28, where the followers of Jesus are situated in relation to John. Again, John is lifted up: "I tell you, among those born of women there has arisen no one greater than John" (Q 7:28a); but this is only to lift the Christian community even higher: "Yet whoever is least in the kingdom of God is greater than he" (Q 7:28b). Q^2 needs John to bring a divine endorsement to Jesus, to his role as the Coming One, and to Jesus' followers as "insiders." John is still an "outsider." In fact, it is his position as a prophet "outside" the Christian group that gives his prophecy more weight.

Q 16:16

The exact placement of Q 16:16 is unsure. In its Matthean location it acts as a bridge between Q 7:28 and Q 7:31–35.[13] "From the days of John until now the reign of heaven is seized at, and the violent grab it."[14] No matter where it is placed, there is no surprise that John's sufferings would be appropriated by the Q^2 community. The construction of the saying creates a prophetic time period that frames Jesus and his community. By association, then, their sufferings receive the same aura of "martyrdom" as those of John. Far from suspecting any culpability, the audience is ready to grant innocence and even holiness to the community's humiliations. All attacks on the group are seen as the persecution regularly afforded the prophet. Here we see the Deuteronomistic view that characterizes the Q^2 perspective.

Q 7:31–35

This last sayings-cluster could be seen as an expansion of Q 16:16 because it also addresses the rejection of Jesus and John. But a closer examination shows that another facet of Jesus' historical life seems to need defense. To see this, one need only ask why John's *eating habits* would come to mind in a cluster of statements bent on condemning "this generation" for their attack on Wisdom! This question is answered as soon as we notice the particular eating habits described for Jesus. Jesus' sociability is unconventional for a holy man. John's fasting is perfectly conventional. The artificiality of the argument set up in Q 7:33–34 reinforces the idea that Jesus' behavior has been the source of embarrassment.[15]

> For John came neither eating nor drinking, and you say, "He has a demon." The Son of Humanity came eating and drinking, and you say, "Behold, a glutton and a drunkard, a friend of tax collectors and sinners."

Now, there is no tradition from Josephus or from Christian sources that anyone ever accused John of demon possession and much less that they did so because he fasted. As we know, fasting is expected of an ascetic person. Thus Jesus' practice of not fasting seems to create a stir among Christians. The conventionality of John and the unconventionality of Jesus in this matter is clear from Mark 2:18 ("Why do John's disciples fast and the disciples of the Pharisees fast, but your disciples do not fast?") and Mark 2:16 ("Why does he eat with tax collectors and sinners?"). Mark's sources show a concern to address the question of Jesus' lack of ascetic behavior in the matter of food. But John is grouped with the ascetic, with the conventionally pious.

Q 7:31–35 needs to claim that those who criticized Jesus and falsely accused him likewise found fault with John. In this way, John and Jesus can stand together as representatives of wisdom, two sides of the same coin. These two sides — the apocalyptic and ascetic, and the sociable and kindly wisdom — complement each other. And of course Q really wants to claim both of these for Jesus. But for now, John can stand as the ascetic side.

The difficulty is that the historical Jesus displays a lack of conventionality that flies in the face of an end-time expectation. His readiness to eat and drink, to socialize and meet with all sorts of people, invites an insult and doubt about his true holiness. On the other hand, no such problem surrounds John, whether one reads Mark or Josephus.

The problem is solved by inventing an outrageous and unwarranted judgment about John's reasons for fasting. Then, taking the doubts about Jesus to their most extreme and insulting conclusion, namely, that Jesus is a glutton and a drunk, can be similarly labeled outrageous and totally unwarranted. Jesus' face is saved by John.

The sayings-cluster opens with an insulting image that casts the accusers in the role of petulant children who are sitting on the seat of the agora or court, making grandiose pronouncements against their peers.[16] Despite the place in which they sit and the imitation of dignity they adopt, their judgments show them to be no more than willful, immature children:

> We piped to you, and you did not dance;
> we wailed, and you did not mourn. (Q 7:32)

This image is then explained by noting that both John and Jesus were rejected for their way of life, although they followed contrasting paths:

> For John came neither eating nor drinking, and you say, "He has a demon." The Son of Man came eating and drinking, and you say, "Behold, a glutton and a drunkard, a friend of tax collectors and sinners."

As we have observed, the ridiculous interpretation of John's asceticism is sufficient to demonstrate the prejudicial character of the judgment on Jesus. This saying warns anyone else who would question Jesus' lack of asceticism. The criticisms have been located in this counterattack on the community's attackers. Once again, John's reputation serves to protect the holiness of Jesus.

The cluster concludes with the proverb, "Yet Wisdom is justified by her children" (Q 7:35). It serves three separate functions. First, the child image identifies John and Jesus, as well as all those who share their perspective, as the children of Wisdom. Second, the saying indicates that the Q community is willing to accept a broad range of Christian practice. Third, in the conflictual context of Q 7:31–34, the proverb now takes on the character of a threat against those who have opposed and condemned John and Jesus. If Wisdom is to be justified, it can only be because she has been wronged. This is a condemnation of the opponents who pretend to employ Wisdom in their judgments. Q 7:35 promises that it is Wisdom's true children who will vindicate her. Since John's asceticism is really more conventional, the warning about refraining from the defamation of Wisdom might be directed against any disedification over the traditions about Jesus' rather unascetic practices.

To sum up: this cluster defends the historical Jesus' rather free behavior as one legitimate expression of Wisdom. The criticism or even community embarrassment over a hero who is not remembered for fasting or abstinence is attacked by assigning it to the enemies of the community. It is condemned as a superficial view of Jesus' truly wise conduct. And this is accomplished by using John as a partner of Jesus. His completely innocent reputation and his honorable memory shine on Jesus by association. Jesus is the one who is less known and whose behavior is less conventional for a holy person and therefore more subject to criticism. Once John is brought alongside Jesus, their differences in eating and drinking habits can be presented as simply two equal but different modes of Wisdom. This teaching is protected from doubt among community members by having John and Jesus denigrated by the same superficial and pompous opponents. The cluster ends with Jesus promising redress to those who have maligned Wisdom. The reference to Wisdom's children justifying her is clever in that it is broad enough to refer both to the duo of John and Jesus and also to Jesus' followers, the Q^2 community.

Q 7:18–35: The Function of the Unit

In Q 7:18–35 the Q^2 community ratifies the relationship between John and Jesus and the two apparently opposing valences represented by their "historical" lives. This is necessary because Q^2 has material that presents a worldview to be represented by John. It is conventionally prophetic, forensic, ascetic, and apocalyptic in expectation. John's credibility as this prophetic figure must be granted by Jesus somehow since his message will certainly conflict with the benign, nonapocalyptic, wisdom orientation of the Q^1 Jesus sayings that were treasured by an earlier community. John's approval by Jesus means not only that Q^2 views of the kingdom may stand uncontested but that the community's claims about Jesus will stand uncontested. For it is from John that the futurity of Jesus as the Coming One enters Q.

Although Jesus will accept this role later (Q 13:34–35), Q 7:18–35 deals with the necessity of accepting both wisdom traditions and prophetic-apocalyptic traditions as two honorable expressions of wisdom.

The unit accomplishes this by giving honor to each of the pair and then by grouping them together. That is, Jesus first corrects John's singular notion of the Coming One with a scriptural defense of his "historical" benign wisdom as expressed in his miracles (Q 7:18–23). Then in Q 7:24–28 John's credibility as a prophet and as precursor is defended by Jesus. Q 7:28 lifts John up as the most exalted "outsider" only to claim that the least of the "insiders" is above him. Q 16:16 claims John for the community to situate their own sufferings as prophetic and as part of the same persecution operative in this generation. Q 7:31–33 protects Jesus from criticism for his lack of asceticism by claiming that John was equally rejected by vicious superficial minds for his rigor.

Once Jesus has delivered this monologue, the rest of the Q document may flow with material that reflects the benign wisdom sayings of Q^1 controlled and contextualized by the Q^2 material. In those speeches Jesus pronounces denunciations against Israel and refers to his own return. These pronouncements will be quickly seen as reiteration of John's opening speech.

Conclusion

Although Q is not a play, the two sections in which John appears appeal to dramatic conventions well known to audiences accustomed to the theater. Both the speech of John and that of Jesus are better understood as monologues in which the audience is called on to prepare themselves for what is to come.

John acts as the introductory player who calls out the sacred prophecy, who alerts us to the condemnation to come and to the one who will be God's end-time agent. Jesus' monologue is like that of the major player who speaks to his audience, identifying the holy prophet and accepting the mysterious identity that heaven has given to him. He shows us the relationship between the God-sent precursor and himself and leads us to see their mutual innocence. Once Jesus' speech is concluded, the audience is prepared for the uplifting calls to wisdom and the warning of the Coming One of the end-time soon at hand for us all.

NOTES

1. Q^1 is composed of six sets: (a) Q 6:20b–23b, 27–35, 36–49; (b) 9:57–62; 10:2–11, 16; (c) 11:2–4, 9–13; (d) 12:2–7, 11–12; (e) 12: 22b–31, 33–34; 13:24; 14:26–27; 17:33; and (f) perhaps 15:4–7 (8–10?); 16:13; 17:1–2, 3b–4, 5–6. The five blocks of Q^2 are: (a) Q 3:7–9, 16–17; (b) 7:1–10, 18–28, 31–35; 16:16; (c) 11:14–26 (27–28?), 29–32, 33–36, 39b–42b, 43–44, 46–52; (d) 12:39–40, 42–46, 49, 51–59; and (e) 17:23–24, 26–30, 34–35, 37; 19:12–27; 22:28–30. There are also nine interpolations into Q^1 material: (a) 6:23c; (b) 10:12; (c) 10:13–15; (d) 12:8–9; (e) 12:10; (f) 13:25–27; (g) 13:28–30; (h) 13:34–35; and (i) 14:16–24. See Kloppenborg 1987a, 167. See also Havener 1987, 100–101; Mack 1988b, 85–86.

2. A more detailed analysis of these differences is presented in Cotter 1995.

3. For Q 7:22, see Isa 61:1–2; 42:6–7; 35:5–6a; 29:18; for Q 7:27, see Exod 23:20; Mal 3:1. Other scriptural allusions may be present in Q 10:15 (Isa 14:13a, 15); Q 12:52–53 (Mic 7:6); Q 13:35 (Jer 22:5; Ps 117:26 [LXX]). See Havener 1987, 165.

4. Abraham (Q 3:8; 13:28); Isaac and Jacob (Q 13:28); Jonah (Q 11:30, 32); Queen of the South (Q 11:31); Abel (Q 11:51); Zechariah (Q 11:51); Noah (Q 17:26–27); and Lot (Q 17:28).

5. Q 3:7–9 is composed of an introduction (v. 7a) and three independent sayings: (a) a forensic salutation followed by a rhetorical question in the form of an apocalyptic threat (vv. 7b–8a); (b) a rebuke against presumption on one's Jewishness (vv. 8b–c); and (c) a second apocalyptic threat concerning the end-time. The second part of the speech is likewise composed of three independent sayings: (a) a contrast of John's water baptism with the Coming One's baptism of fire and wind (spirit?) (v. 16a); (b) a situating of the baptizers in relation to each other (v. 16b); and (c) an apocalyptic threat about the inevitability of the coming destruction (v. 17).

6. Westermann 1967, 169–94. The full chart of the examples includes Amos 4:1–2; Hos 2:5–7; Isa 8:6–8; 30:12–14; Mic 3:1–2, 4 (pp. 174–75). See also Schulz 1972, 372. For examples of the use of this form in various genres of Christian literature, see Cameron 1984, 30–42.

7. These five steps are outlined by Cameron 1984, 32–36.

8. All Q translations are taken from Havener 1987.

9. Lucas 1923, 9–11. See Bain 1977, 135–47, esp. 138. Also Kindermann 1979, 30. For a treatment of all varieties of monologues and their several purposes as evinced in Roman drama, see Duckworth 1952, 102–9, esp. 107.

10. A terra-cotta statuette of a tragic messenger from Pergamom in the Hellenistic period is located in the Berlin Museum. The figure wears a

mask and the *ogkos,* a convention first initiated by Aeschylus, an arrangement of the hair high on the head and fanned out (see Bieber 1961, 81, 313). The *prologus* of comedy is shown in a miniature drawing from a manuscript of Terrence located in the Vatican Museum. Plautus and Terrence made frequent use of the *prologus* (see Bieber 1961, 153, 318).

11. Kloppenborg (1987a, 112–14) demonstrates that there is no conclusive evidence that Q 16:16 belonged to the cluster of sayings in Q 7:18–35, but he acknowledges that a discussion of John's function in Q should include the saying. We will treat the saying as it occurs in Matthean order although its placement in Luke receives more support as representative of Q order.

12. Although it has been suggested that John's role here is that of an Elijah *redivivus,* such an identity is more in tune with John's portrayal in Mark's Gospel (Mark 1:2). John does not mirror Elijah in Q. As Cameron observes, "[T]here is no evidence that Elijah was imagined as the precursor of the *Messiah* in pre-Christian Judaism" (1990, 40).

13. Lührmann has observed that the position of the saying in Luke is convenient for the evangelist. In Matthew this is less the case since Matthew is focusing on the identity of John in Matt 11:11 and 11:14. Matt 11:12–13 would seem to be something of a digression (Lührmann 1969, 28). Furthermore, most scholars claim that Matthew's version is closer than that of Luke. See Harnack 1908, 16; Hoffmann 1975, 51; Schenk 1981, 44; Zeller 1984, 43, 69; Percy 1953; Jacobson 1978, 79.

14. Translation from Kloppenborg 1990d, 69.

15. A more detailed discussion of the function of the cluster is found in Cotter 1989, 63–82.

16. For a detailed presentation of the forensic image of Q 7:32, see Cotter 1987, 289–304.

"Yet Wisdom Is Justified by Her Children" (Q 7:35)

A Rhetorical and Compositional Analysis of Divine Sophia in Q

The Sayings Gospel Q contains clusters of aphorisms that betray various sapiential emphases.[1] In addition to the aphoristic wisdom advice, Q also bears witness to a tradition where Jesus is presented as Divine Sophia's rejected spokesperson. This twofold sapiential expression reflects two tendencies evident as well within Hebrew wisdom literature. Wisdom instruction and advice, which arose from experience, dominated; but, at the same time a certain reflection on the nature of wisdom developed.

Five passages reflect the Old Testament tradition of Divine Sophia (Q 7:31–35; 10:21–22; 11:31; 11:49–51; 13:34–35).[2] While only two passages in the Sayings Gospel refer explicitly to the figure of Divine Sophia (Q 7:31–35 and Wisdom's oracle in Q 11:49–51), three other passages (Q 10:21–22; 11:31; and 13:34–35) also presume this tradition of Divine Sophia for their argument.[3]

The figure of Divine Sophia developed within the Hebrew writings as reflection upon Wisdom and her relationship to God developed.[4] Proverbs 1–9 seem to have initiated this reflection.[5] There Sophia exists with God before the creation as the first of God's acts: "The Lord created me at the beginning of his work, the first of his acts of long ago" (Prov 8:22). Speaking, as it were, from heaven, Sophia calls upon the people to pay attention to

Patrick J. Hartin is associate professor in New Testament studies at Gonzaga University, Spokane, Washington.

her teaching. As the first of God's creation, Sophia participated in God's wisdom, and she brought all creation into existence. She invites those who are simple and lack understanding to partake of the banquet she has prepared for them (Prov 9:4). Noteworthy in Proverbs 1–9 is the connection between wisdom aphorisms that relate to practical experience and a reflection upon this divine figure, Sophia. An analysis of the origin of these chapters shows that the sayings on practical experience preceded those on the personification of Sophia. A similar progression or development took place in the Sayings Gospel Q (see Whybray 1965, 45).

Ben Sirach continues this reflection on the role of Divine Sophia in chapters 1 and 24. The personification of Sophia becomes more intense and her divine qualities more pronounced. "There is but one who is wise, greatly to be feared, seated upon his throne — the Lord. It is he who created her; he saw her and took her measure; he poured her out upon all his works" (Sir 1:8–9).[6] God communicates this wisdom to creation and to those whom God calls God's friends (Sir 1:10). Chapter 24, where her personification becomes more pronounced, sings the praises of Divine Sophia. She issues an invitation to all to come to her and partake of what she can offer: "Come to me, you who desire me, and eat your fill of my fruits. For the memory of me is sweeter than honey, and the possession of me sweeter than the honeycomb" (Sir 24:19–20).

The book of the Wisdom of Solomon reflects upon the role that Sophia has exercised in the whole course of Israel's history. Chapter 10 illustrates how Sophia has guided and protected the Israelites from their enemies: "But their enemies she drowned and cast them up from the depth of the sea" (Wis 10:19). An important aspect of the role of Sophia is to protect God's faithful in time of persecution and trial. Ultimately God's faithful triumph over opposition because God's power is with them.

Particularly in the centuries following the exilic experience and the prior destruction of the southern kingdom, a destruction that brought about the end of the monarchy, the wisdom tradition endeavored to make sense of what had happened. Resort was made to language and myths found in Egypt (such as those regarding Ma'at and Isis) to express the Israelites' belief in God's purposes. The origin of the personification of Sophia is to be found in this context. A new direction was given to the wisdom of observation — the path to salvation now lies in listening to Sophia, who communicates the ways of God (see Mack 1970, 24, 57).

I shall confine my examination to the two passages in the Sayings Gospel Q that refer directly to the figure of Divine Sophia. Two considerations help this reflection.[7]

1. An emphasis on the composition of these passages will demonstrate how they relate to the rest of the Sayings Gospel Q as well as their position within Q. This examination will show that they belong to that stage of the Sayings Gospel Q at which the focus of attention is on judgments and warnings made against those who oppose the Q community. The composition of this stage should be seen against a background of conflict and persecution. As such these sayings conform to the Deuteronomistic conception of history (Jacobson 1992, 72–76) and belong to the second stratum of Q.[8]

2. I shall pay attention to the rhetorical or persuasive force of these passages within Q. By rhetorical analysis I mean simply an analysis of the persuasive and argumentative power of the passage both taken by itself and in the context of the Sayings Gospel Q.[9] The two passages in question reflect a community that is experiencing opposition, conflict, and persecution from those outside (yet still within Israel) who have refused to accept its message. The emphasis on rejection and persecution betrays this situation. These words must be read on two levels: while they ostensibly refer to the words of Jesus, they in fact reflect the opposition, the conflict, and the persecution that the community of Q is experiencing.

Q 7:31–35: Divine Sophia's Children and Divine Sophia in the Marketplace

Most commentators[10] assign this pericope to a later insertion into the Sayings Gospel Q.[11] Its position in Q is highly significant. Following Arland Jacobson's line of argument, I see its position here as part of the redactor's purposeful design, belonging to what Jacobson terms "the compositional phase" (see Jacobson 1992, 79). The first part of the Sayings Gospel Q commenced with the person of John, gave a brief account of his teaching, introduced Jesus and expressed John's relationship with Jesus (Q 3:2–4, 7–9, 16–17). The essence of the teaching of Jesus, recorded in the Sermon on the Mount, followed (Q 6:20–49). Finally, the section returned to the connection between John and Jesus with Q 7:35 relating that they are both children of Sophia. They remain in the line of Sophia's spokespersons.

The composite nature of Q 7:31–35 has been observed by a wide range of scholars.[12] This corresponds to the developing nature of the aphoristic parable, as indicated by John Dominic Crossan (1983). This section (Q 7:31–35) undoubtedly has seen growth and development over time. In a masterful essay Ron Cameron (1990, 35–69) has argued that Q 7:31–35 has been closely woven into the wider context of Q 7:18–35, in which all the features of a developed chreia operated.[13]

Divine Sophia's communication to humanity is well expressed in Wis 7:27: "Although she is but one, she can do all things, and while remaining in herself, she renews all things; in every generation she passes into holy souls and makes them friends of God, and prophets." Against this background of Hebrew wisdom thought, John and Jesus are the ones in this generation to whom Divine Sophia has communicated herself. As the children of Sophia they stand in the same line as all her spokespersons throughout time. Characteristic of the prophetic line are the opposition and rejection that the prophets experienced. Not to be outdone, John and Jesus also experience rejection by "the children of this generation."

This passage demonstrates the opposition, in effect the situation of conflict, that exists between "this generation" and the children of Sophia, of whom John and Jesus are preeminent.[14] Two contradictory lifestyles are juxtaposed and rejected by those outside the Q community.[15] The judgment against John is that he is possessed because he fasts. The judgment against Jesus is that he is a glutton, a drunk, and someone who associates with those members whom society considers most base. Because the accusations against John are so unwarranted, the same conclusion is drawn with regard to Jesus. These statements demonstrate the unreasonable rejection of Jesus and John.

Q 7:35 is a proverb[16] acting as a culminating conclusion to the entire pericope: *kai edikaiōthē hē sophia apo pantōn tōn teknōn autēs*.[17] Reference is made to the children (*tekna*) of Sophia, recalling the children of Sophia in Sir 4:11.[18] While Sophia exalts her children in Sirach, in Q 7:35 the roles are reversed. Sophia is the one who is maligned, and it is the task of her children, in this instance John and Jesus, to defend her.

Sophia is personified in this Q passage. She sends out messengers who ultimately are rejected. Among them are John and Jesus, and through their actions the righteousness of Sophia shines forth. The Lukan formulation is judged to lie closest to Q (see Hoffmann 1972, 197–98; and Hartin 1991, 125–26) and reads: *kai edikaiōthē hē sophia apo pantōn tōn teknōn autēs* ("Wisdom is justified by all her children" [Luke 7:35]).[19] In Matthew (11:19) the formulation has been changed to read: *kai edikaiōthē ē sophia apo tōn ergōn autēs* ("Wisdom is justified by her deeds"). In Matthew there is a conscious effort to identify Jesus with Sophia. Matthew, then, presents Jesus as Sophia incarnate. A development has occurred between Q and Matthew with regard to Jesus' relationship with Q.

Reading this proverb in the context of the entire parable (together with its application), one notices how the movement has changed. The parable opened with a reference to children (*paidia*). These children exercise the function of pronouncing judgment, particularly on John and Jesus. As such they are the spokespersons for this generation in its opposition to John and Jesus. In the concluding proverb reference is once more made to children (*tekna*). The choice of a different noun for "children" suggests that the referent is different too. The "children" now are the children of Sophia (*tekna sophias*), not the children of this generation (*paidiois tēs geneas tautēs*). The children of Sophia are, in the very first instance, John and Jesus. The logic of this argumentation can be expressed in this way:

Premise 1: The children of this generation opposed John and Jesus.

Premise 2: John and Jesus are the children of Sophia.

Conclusion: The children of this generation oppose Sophia's children.

The children of Sophia are more than just John and Jesus — they are all who accept the will of God in their lives. In this way the people of the Q community are drawn into this confrontation.[20] They are those who follow John and Jesus, and, as such, they too are spokespersons for Sophia. In the opposition that they encounter they are reexperiencing the opposition of the children of this generation to John and Jesus. It is important to stress this wider conception of the children of Sophia because there is the tendency to see the notion in a very individualistic way as relating only to John and Jesus.

The reader is led to view the superficiality within this generation. Opposition exists between the children of this generation and the children of Sophia, John and Jesus. The very accusations leveled against John and Jesus are without any legal justification.[21]

This section must function at a stage within Q when the emphasis on the conflict between the followers of Jesus and this generation becomes more pronounced.

This passage betrays a background or setting whereby the Q community is experiencing opposition and conflict. The framing of the Sermon on the Mount (Q 6:20–49) has now taken place within the context of the introduction of John the Baptist and the relationship of Jesus to John. In contrast to the wisdom and prophetical-eschatological direction of Jesus' teaching in the sermon, John's teaching bears a decided apocalyptic stance. John proclaims destruction on this generation for its way of life and for its refusal to pay attention to his message. Both John's and Jesus' message present a challenge to this generation — they offer two different approaches of wisdom. But this generation refuses to give heed to their message. They are both rejected. Without doubt a strong tension has developed between the message of Jesus and this generation. The original sapiential speech of Q was addressed to the Q community to encourage it to embrace a particular lifestyle. This new framework implies that this generation — a wider context than the Q community — has refused to give attention to the message of Jesus.

Q 11:49–51: Divine Sophia's Role of Doom

The two witnesses to the Q text (Luke 11:49–51; Matt 23:34–36) are extremely close. One noteworthy difference in the two accounts is the actual speaker of these words. While Divine Sophia speaks these words in Luke, Jesus himself is the speaker in Matthew. I have argued elsewhere (Hartin 1991, 117–18) that the speaker in Q accords best with the way in which Luke has presented the matter, that is, with Divine Sophia addressing these words. Matthew has once again changed this saying according to his tendency to equate Jesus with Sophia incarnate.

This is the strongest condemnation that is issued against "this generation." This time Divine Sophia addresses her proclamation directly to this generation. The book of the Wisdom of Solomon provides the background to this passage. In Wis 10:1–4 Divine Sophia is seen to be operative throughout Israel's history of salvation:

> [Wisdom] protected the first-formed father of the world, when he alone had been created; and she delivered him from his trans-

gression, and gave him strength to rule all things. But when the
unrighteous man departed from her in his anger, he perished because in rage he killed his brother. When the earth was flooded
because of him, Wisdom again saved it, steering the righteous man
by a paltry piece of wood.

In Wis 7:27, Wisdom is also judged to be in operation in the world
at every age and in every generation:

Although she is but one, she can do all things; and while remaining
in herself, she renews all things; in every generation she passes into
holy souls and makes them friends of God, and prophets.

In these two passages Divine Sophia involves herself in salvation
history. She communicates herself to people and makes them both
friends of God and her spokespersons. In Q 11:49–51 the same
theme occurs. Divine Sophia sends prophets to act as her envoys.
In doing so her envoys encounter opposition, persecution, even
death. This rejection is total, as is evident from the reference to
the blood of the prophets that had been shed from the time of Abel
to the time of the prophet Zechariah. But this persecution did not
end with Zechariah; it continues to this present generation: "Yes,
I tell you, it will be charged against this generation" (Q 11:51).
Clearly, the Q community must be experiencing some form of violent opposition. This passage, then, puts their persecution into
perspective.

Examining the position of Q 11:49–51 in the Q document, one
notes that it is placed in the midst of a series of woes against the
Pharisees (see Kloppenborg 1987a, 144). Q 11:47–48 addresses
woes against the Pharisees because of their hypocrisy: they erect
graves to the prophets whom their fathers had killed. Q 11:52 follows this Sophia passage with a further woe, this time directed at
those lawyers who prevent others from entering the kingdom. The
main purpose of this passage is to give expression to the rejection
of Divine Sophia's messengers by the religious leaders of Israel.[22]
This rejection has occurred consistently throughout Israel's history.
Now, however, with the rejection of Jesus and his followers, the
situation has become more critical.

Noticeable here is the theme of the rejection of God's messengers, whereby the Deuteronomistic understanding of history has
been joined together with the Sophia motif. The incorporation
of a theme of judgment exercised by Sophia is something new
in the context of the Sophia personification of the Hebrew writ-

ings. There her role was that of coming among humanity to offer salvation. Now, Sophia stands in the position of a judge to exercise judgment: *nai legō hymin, ekzētēthēsetai apo tēs geneas tautēs* ("Yes, I tell you, it will be charged against this generation" [Q 11:51b]). Sophia is the agent who sends the emissaries who are ultimately and inevitably rejected. The Q tradition addresses itself to the "final" generation in which Sophia's prophetic word of doom is to be fulfilled.

The Function of the Divine Sophia Pericopae within the Sayings Gospel Q

Besides the two passages referred to above, three other passages indirectly presume the tradition of Divine Sophia (Q 10:21–22; 11:31; and 13:34–35). All these passages were probably woven together into Q at the same time, namely, that period when the sapiential substratum of Q was undergoing an apocalyptic-Deuteronomistic revision (referred to as Q²). A number of important emphases emerge from this study of the Sophia passages.

1. The Q community reflected upon this experience of failure in their proclamation to the rest of Israel. They had recourse to the myth of Divine Sophia in order to provide a solution to their problems. A new dimension occurs within the development of this myth of Divine Sophia. In the Hebrew writings the emphasis was upon Divine Sophia coming among humanity to offer salvation. In the Sayings Gospel Q the emphasis has now turned to the theme of judgment that is exercised through Sophia's representatives. Something similar had already occurred in the context of the Hebrew wisdom traditions. The experience of failure and opposition to their religion, as occurred from the time of the exile onward, led the Israelites to acknowledge the function of Divine Sophia, who fulfills God's purposes. Despite oppositions and setbacks, God has a decided plan for his people. In like manner, the opposition, rejection, and persecution that the Q community experiences are given meaning through recourse to the figure of Divine Sophia.

2. A characteristic feature of these Sophia passages is the stress placed upon the rejection of God's messengers by "this generation."[23] This is clearly viewed from the perspective of the Q community as it experienced conflict and rejection from the wider community of the people of Israel.[24] These spokespersons of the Q community stand in the same line as all the prophets

of the past. This experience of opposition and violence that the Q community is presently enduring is the motivating force behind the development of the Q^2 redaction, of which the Sophia passages form an important part.

3. I have drawn attention to the characterization given to Jesus by these pericopae. His rejection is a paradigm for the rejection of the Q community, who are his messengers. Jesus is in fact the eschatological emissary of Divine Sophia. In Q 7:35 Jesus is presented as the culminating emissary of Divine Sophia, and the other Q passages related to Divine Sophia tend to support this understanding. For example, in Q 11:49–51 there is no direct reference to Jesus, but the very fact that "this generation" is condemned and found guilty of the persecution and death of all those prophets who had preceded implies that the fate of Jesus forms part of this long history (R. Piper 1989, 169). In Q 11:31 Jesus is referred to as proclaiming a message that is greater than *the* representative of Wisdom in the Old Testament, namely, Solomon. In this Jesus is once again *the* representative of Wisdom.

Dieter Lührmann (1969, 24–48) was the first to emphasize the importance of the opposition to "this generation" as a key to the redaction of Q. As such Jesus in these Sophia passages is the representative of Sophia in the judgment of this generation. This is the perspective through which these Sophia pericopae in the Sayings Gospel Q approach Jesus. Only in the Gospel of Matthew does a further development take place. There Jesus is viewed as Sophia herself or as Sophia incarnate (see Hartin 1991, 132–34).

4. Sophia opposes those who hold authority in Israel. They are concerned with the protection and the preservation of the Torah. Even the blessing of the unlearned in Q 10:21–22 is an indirect criticism of the *sophoi kai synetoi* (the wise and the intelligent). Jacobson emphasized the full irony of this statement by arguing that it is "a sarcastic inversion of a current Jewish claim" (1978, 155). Once again in line with the other Sophia sayings, criticism is being directed against "this generation" and especially at its leadership for its failure to understand and appreciate the significance of the proclamation of Jesus and that of the Q community. In Q 11:49–51 Jerusalem, which represents the religious leadership of Israel, is held responsible for the rejection of Sophia's emissary. In contrast to this is Sophia's message, which is proclaimed as *sophia* or *kērygma* (proclamation) and not as Torah. Sophia's message is embraced by her children (Q 7:35) or by the unlearned (Q 10:21).

5. A critical situation of opposition and conflict is envisaged as the setting for these Sophia passages. Ronald A. Piper (1989, 177) has distinguished between the purpose of the aphoristic wisdom sayings and that of these Sophia sayings. While the aphoristic sayings aim at exhorting and encouraging the hearers to a particular style of action and way of life, these Sophia passages aim at helping the community of Q come to an understanding of what happened to Jesus.[25] While I do agree that this is a possible way of viewing the purpose of the different wisdom material in the Sayings Gospel Q, the intention of the redactor of Q^2 in incorporating the Sophia passages into the instructional was not, to my mind, to provide an understanding of what happened to Jesus per se. The concern of the Q "preachers" was with their present situation: this is the consuming focus of their attention. In order to give it meaning they refer to Jesus as the founding figure, showing that what they presently experience by way of opposition and persecution is what had already been experienced by him. The opposition that Jesus experienced is used to give meaning to the opposition that they are experiencing.

Like the prophetical oracles of Israel's past, both the oracle of doom (Q 11:49–51) and the lament against Jerusalem (Q 13:34–35) drew attention to the fate that is to befall "this generation" because of their rejection of Jesus and his followers. In no way do the oracles intend to bring about the conversion of this generation — in fact this generation's persistent opposition is presupposed. Exactly the same was true with the prophets of the Old Testament. The oracles against Tyre, Phoenicia, Babylon, and so on, were directed more to the people of Israel in an attempt to assure them of God's protection and the punishment of those who desert God's ways.

The followers of Jesus are hence being *persuaded* to understand their own rejection through the rejection of Jesus. They are to view it against the background of the Deuteronomistic conception of history whereby the constant rejection of prophets occurs. In speaking about the fate of Jesus the emphasis is not on his death-resurrection, for this is not a feature of Q; instead, the fate of Jesus includes the total rejection of Jesus' proclamation by his own people, a rejection that is demonstrated most forcefully in the lives of Jesus' followers. The rejection of the Q community and its preachers is a rejection of Jesus, just as a rejection of the spokespersons of Divine Sophia is a clear rejection of Sophia herself.

6. These passages betray a concern far more for the acceptance of the messengers than for an acceptance of a detailed content. The type of response that is called for involves an openness that resembles that of "infants" (Q 10:21–22). In Q 11:31–32, for example, mention is made of both this *sophia* of Solomon and the *kērygma* of Jonah. However, nothing in effect is said of its content — it is rather the response of "this generation" that is the focus of attention. This contrasts with the aphoristic tradition where the emphasis does fall upon the content of the message that is being proclaimed.

7. These Sophia passages also bear an eschatological stamp. The handing over of all knowledge by the Father to the Son (Q 10:21–22) is clearly an eschatological event — the communication of revelation from the Father. The theme of eschatological judgment also permeates these Sophia passages: reference to the Queen of the South and the people of Nineveh appearing at the end to issue judgment over the people of this generation is also very evident (Q 11:31–32). In the oracle of doom (Q 11:49–51) Sophia takes an overview of the whole history of salvation, and she shows how the death of the prophets occurs throughout this period.

8. The rhetorical force of these Sophia passages, which issues forth in a condemnation of those outside the Q community, is aimed primarily at promoting adherence within the community. The traditions related to Divine Sophia in the Sayings Gospel Q are understood predominantly in a collective sense (and not an individualistic sense). Hence, it is the community of Q that is judged to follow the work of the prophets and in this experiences persecution and opposition. This has importance when considering the absence of any real references to the death of Jesus. The persecution of which the Sayings Gospel Q speaks is characterized by the Deuteronomistic understanding of prophecy and what happens to the prophets who are Sophia's envoys (Q 6:23; 11:49–51; 13:34–35). An examination of the Sophia passages has clearly shown that in places where one would have expected to find references to or reflections of a passion theology, nothing occurs.[26] Q has a totally different conception of suffering and vindication. It is far more a communitarian, rather than individualistic, experience. For this reason the Sayings Gospel Q aims at providing support for those of the Q community who are experiencing persecution and suffering. The aim is not to trace some event in the past. The Q redactor is interested in the present. The Sophia passages illuminate the expe-

riences of the present and give meaning to the lives of the members of the Q community to adhere to the proclamation that they have received. The importance of the words of Jesus in Q does not stem from his death and resurrection but from the very course of his ministry, where his words are presented as words of Sophia.

NOTES

1. This has been ably demonstrated by R. Piper (1989).

2. I refer to the Q sayings by their Lukan location because Luke is generally understood to have preserved the order of Q better. In this I follow the system employed by the International Q Project of the Society of Biblical Literature (IQP). This does not mean that one is endorsing the Lukan reading — this can be established only through painstaking research.

3. R. Piper (1989, 162–73) discusses the arguments for and against designating passages as dealing with the figure of Divine Sophia. He also considers Q 9:58 as containing a " 'Sophia' allusion." However, the allusion is I feel too remote to deserve any substantial consideration.

4. The exact origin of this myth of Divine Sophia has been the subject of much discussion and research over the past decades. One thing that does emerge from these examinations is that the presentation of Wisdom varied and received different emphases as the context and time of its use changed.

5. Mack (1970, 46–47) noted the possibility that Job 28 could be responsible for introducing this figure into the Old Testament.

6. All quotations are from the New Revised Standard Version of the Bible with Apocrypha (1990) unless otherwise noted.

7. R. Piper (1989, 163) draws specific attention to the fact "that most of the synoptic sayings which seem to allude to Sophia are double-tradition material, but also distinctive emphases have been suggested for these sayings."

8. Here I endorse and make use of the direction that John Kloppenborg (1987a) has opened up in dealing with the stratification of Q.

9. Quoting an economist (McCloskey 1982), Stanley Fish (1990, 210) argues that " 'assertions are made for purposes of persuading some audience' and that given the availability of a God's-eye view, 'this is not a shameful fact' but the bottom-line fact in a rhetorical world."

10. It is not my intention here to argue for a particular reading of Q. My purpose is to see how it fits into the composition of the Sayings Gospel Q and how it functions within the Sayings Gospel Q.

11. Jacobson (1978, 24–98) argues that this pericope should be seen as bringing to a conclusion the first section of Q. Kloppenborg (1987a, 107–

21) views this pericope as part of Q^2, belonging to a section (Q 7:1–10, 18–23, 24–26 [16:16], 31–35) that is united around the theme of "this generation's" failure to respond to the proclamation of the kingdom.

12. See in particular Cotter 1987, 293 n. 19; Lührmann 1969, 29–30; Schulz 1972, 225–28; Steinhauser 1981, 73; Kloppenborg 1987a, 110–12.

13. Cameron (1990, 51) demonstrates how the rhetorical composition operates in Q 7:31–35. Among the elements he notes are the following:

- *Statement of analogy:* 7:31–32. Here a parable is used to demonstrate what "this generation" is like.

- *Statement from example:* 7:33–34. The purpose of this statement is to substantiate the truth of the previous parable by citing an example from the realm of the behavior of John and Jesus that proves the point of the parable.

- *Concluding periodization:* 7:35. This saying serves the purpose of vindicating Wisdom by means of her spokesmen, John and Jesus.

14. Although John and Jesus are mentioned together, they are not treated as complete equals. This is particularly observable from the reference that is made to Jesus as the Son of Man. This title occurs in Q only within the document's second layer (Q^2) (Lührmann 1969, 97). The apocalyptic figure of the Son of Man has been read back onto the earthly life of Jesus. See Vaage 1991b, 103–29, for a detailed examination of the Son of Man sayings in Q.

15.   (*a*) *John fasts.* He rejects eating bread and drinking wine.
    (*b*) *The conclusion* they draw is: "He has a demon."
    (*a1*) *Jesus eats and drinks.*
    (*b1*) *The conclusion* they draw is: "He is a glutton, a drunk,
     a friend of tax collectors and sinners."

16. Lührmann (1969, 29) suggests that this may have originally been a Jewish parable.

17. The language of the law courts is evident throughout this pericope. The parable commenced with the scene of the children sitting in the agora. This is an image that Cotter (1987, 302) has demonstrated "does not draw us into the world of children, but into the world of adults, and in particular the centres of civic justice, the courts." Then, the concluding proverb takes up this legal language once again when it speaks of the children of Wisdom justifying her (*dikaiōthē*). Through the actions of Sophia's children, her truth will be legally reinstated.

18. *Hē sophia huious autēs anypsōsen kai epilambanetai tōn zētoutōn autēn* (Sir 4:11); "Wisdom teaches her children and gives help to those who seek her."

19. The NRSV translates it as, "Nevertheless, wisdom is vindicated by her children." I prefer to translate *dikaioō* as "to justify," in place of "to vindicate," as this is closer to the traditional way in which *dikaioō* has been translated into English and understood.

20. Hoffmann (1972, 229–30) supports this interpretation in saying that those who stand behind Q are also in opposition to this generation and are reflected in this saying.

21. As Cotter (1987, 302) says: "No matter how these 'children' adopt dignified behavior, it is plain from the content of their objections, that they are, after all, only shallow children."

22. This is the point that Richard Horsley emphasizes in his contribution in this volume (p. 49), where he argues that the conflict is between those trying to reform Israel and the religious elite of Jerusalem.

23. Steck (1967, 269) notes in particular how Q 11:49ff. and 13:34–35 continued the Deuteronomistic tradition of the fate of prophets. Tuckett (1983, 164–66) demonstrated that a very characteristic motif of Q is the bringing together of the Deuteronomistic tradition and Sophia reflection, as can be seen especially in Q 7:35; 11:49–51; and 13:34–35.

24. Note the perspective of Horsley (above, p. 44), which sees the opposition as not between the whole of Israel and the members of the Q community but rather as coming from those retainers who tried to apply the laws of Jerusalem to Galilee.

25. R. Piper (1989, 174) says: "Thus the 'Sophia logia' are used mainly with respect to understanding Jesus' fate; the aphoristic collections for encouraging anxious followers in their present crises."

26. It is true, as Kloppenborg (1990b, 80) argues, that "it seems likely that if Q sees any theological significance in the death of Jesus, it does so through the optic of deuteronomistic theology. On this view, persecution and death are the 'occupational hazards' of the envoys of God or Sophia."

Redactional Fabrication and Group Legitimation

The Baptist's Preaching in Q 3:7-9, 16-17

The Q picture of John the Baptist is fraught with interpretive difficulties.[1] Some texts present Jesus and John as nearly equal colleagues: Q 7:35, for instance, refers to both as children of Wisdom. Elsewhere in the document, however, this inexplicably high assessment of John is flatly contradicted: for example, in Q 7:28, which apparently goes so far as to exclude John from the kingdom. Not content to contradict itself over John's status, Q also invokes nearly every imaginable role for John, seemingly without consideration of a coherent presentation: he is variously the Elijianic precursor, the greatest of the old age, a prophet of doom, a baptizer, an opponent of Israel, the harbinger of the kingdom, a colleague of Jesus, and a wise man.

Overview of the Scholarship

With few exceptions, scholars have assumed that some sense can be made of this incoherent data. It is argued that, despite the inconsistency of Q's presentation of John, a coherent view of John's status and role *can* be teased out of the material. Thus according to T. W. Manson (1949, 41) or, more recently, Ivan Havener (1987, 53, 63–65), Q promotes a negative view of John as a prophet of doom whose limited and judgmental words are compared unfavorably with the positive message of Jesus. A. D. Jacobson and John

William Arnal is a doctoral candidate at the Centre for the Study of Religion, University of Toronto.

Kloppenborg, conversely, see Q as having high esteem for the Baptist, whose harsh message makes him a prophetic ally in the Q condemnation of Israel.[2] They attribute discrepancies in this picture to modifications undertaken before or after the Q redaction. The approaches of James Robinson (1975, 4–6) and Walter Wink (1968, 18, 24–26) see an initial high assessment of John as necessarily mitigated by increasing concern with the christological status of Jesus.

In my view, no such reconstruction of a coherent Q redactional presentation of John's role convincingly explains the discrepancies in the Q presentation of him. It seems that the logical mind of the modern scholar attempts to find a coherent message among irreconcilable statements; or the scholar assumes that the Q redactor had little control over the traditions used in the document. Thus this redaction is held to have modified a perspective on John it disagreed with by introducing blatant contradictions into the text rather than by simply omitting the offending material. But what coherent role can possibly be expressed by the statement that John is both within (16:16) and outside (7:28) the kingdom? Perhaps Q's redaction allows these contradictions to stand because it does not in fact care about John's role or status at all. The assumption that Q regards John in a speculative fashion should be reevaluated.

The perspective I have just described, however, is in part related to the view that John's preaching in Q 3:7–9, 16–17 is basically historically authentic. The majority of scholars appear to regard this preaching as genuine historical reminiscence.[3] Harnack's exuberant assessment of Q's historical reliability (1908, 246–52) seems to remain the norm for John's words, if no longer for those of Jesus. Even those scholars who divide the preaching into originally separate elements on form-critical grounds seem to believe that the majority of its material nevertheless goes back to the Baptist.[4] Bultmann's observation that 3:7–9, at least, may easily be read as an early Christian composition put on John's lips[5] has not met with general approval. On the contrary, the allegedly non-Christian character of the material continues to be invoked to defend its historicity.

Such an understanding of the historical value of the material has influenced the scholarly understanding of Q's perspective on John's role. When Q 3:7–9, 16–17 is viewed as genuine historical reminiscence, it comes to be held as the starting point for Q's reflection on John. Beginning with his historical message, the Q redactor, it is imagined, speculates on the relationship of this message to Jesus, wisdom, and salvation history. The belief that Q's John has a coherent status and role is not, of course, *entirely* due to the view that his words in Q are authentic. But in all such reconstructions the function of the preaching is to provide a sample of the Baptist's words, upon which the document's evaluation of his status and role is based. When John is seen as a negative figure, his "historical" preaching functions as a sort of "bad example" and serves to emphasize his inferiority. When he is a positive figure, he is positive because the Q community approves of his words. The "preservation" of his preaching, contrasted with Mark's "abbreviation" of it, is further evidence for his high status and prophetic role. The general consensus that Q provides a reliable indication of John's message virtually necessitates that this preservation be due to Q's speculative concern with John's role and status.[6]

Reconstructing the Text

The foundational text, then, for assessing Q's regard for the Baptist is Q 3:7–9, 16–17. Fortunately, problems of reconstruction are rather limited. The divergences between Matthew and Luke are largely cosmetic and have little effect on our reading of the text's original significance. A few other problems of reconstruction are more consequential. These include the opening to John's speech and difficulties with the wording of 3:16, which overlaps with Mark and hence makes reconstruction that much more difficult.

Several scholars have noted the likelihood that both Matthean and Lukan versions of the brief introduction to John's speech in Q 3:7a are redactional, or at least that the original wording has been changed, since not much verbal agreement is found between the evangelists here.[7] What agreement does exist here between Matthew and Luke can conceivably be explained as determined by the Markan context (Mark 1:5–6), where the crowds are likewise described as *having come, to be baptized, by him*. That is, the agreement shared by Matthew and Luke in this description can be explained on the basis of their knowledge of Mark alone, without recourse to Q. If Q did indeed have a description of the *coming* of John (as is generally supposed, although the exact character of such a description seems beyond recovery),[8] it is only necessary for Q to read here "he said" (*elegen/eipen*). Matthew's and Luke's failure to depart significantly from their Markan source here renders it highly improbable that the Q opening to this chreia provided any more informative a description than this bare indication of speech. It is not impossible, of course, that Q contained a more specific description of John's audience, but that such a description was present is incapable of proof and generally unlikely. Q 3:7–9, 16–17 probably contained no indication of any precise group singled out for polemic. The words are offered acontextually, or at least with very little context.

Conversely, the Lukan reading of "the one who is stronger than I is coming" (*erchetai de ho ischyroteros mou estin*) in Q 3:16 seems to be following Mark here (1:7 — identical, except Luke adds *de*), while Matthew witnesses to an independent version: "*the Coming One* is stronger than I" (*ho de... erchomenos ischyroteros mou estin*). This version clearly does not depend on the Markan wording and uses terminology ("the Coming One," as a title) that is prominent elsewhere in Q (7:19; 13:35); it thus seems best to regard this participial form, that is, Matthew's version, as the original Q.[9]

In light of these comments, the original Q text of John's preaching, reconstructed from Matthew and Luke, would appear as follows:

3:7 He said..., "You brood of vipers! Who warned you to flee from the approaching wrath?

3:8 Make, therefore, fruits worthy of repentance, and do not presume to say to yourselves, 'We have Abraham as a Father.' For I tell you [*legō gar hymin*] that God is able to raise up children [*tekna*] to Abraham from these stones.

3:9 Even now [*ēdē de kai*] the axe is laid [*keitai*] to the root of the trees. Therefore every tree not making good fruit is cut down [*ekkoptetai*] and is cast [*balletai*] into fire.

3:16 I, on the one hand, am baptizing you with water. But the Coming One [*ho erchomenos*] is stronger than I, whose sandals I am not worthy to carry. He will baptize you with holy wind/spirit [*pneumati hagiō*] and fire. [cf. Mark 1:7–8]

3:17 His winnowing-fan is in his hand to clear his threshing floor, and he will gather the wheat into his barn, but the chaff he will burn with unquenchable fire."

The first step in a reevaluation of John's role in Q involves calling into question the prevailing wisdom that the preaching reconstructed above is largely authentic. There are in fact several good reasons to doubt the historicity of the material. First, with the exception of 3:16, the actual material in Q is absolutely without parallel in any other contemporary presentation of John. Thus we have absolutely no external support for or confirmation of these traditions by which to support the scholarly trust in them. Q 3:7–9 and 3:17 categorically fail the criterion of multiple attestation. Moreover, the substance of John's message in this extra Q material is incompatible with any of the other extant descriptions of the Baptist. There is little reason to trust Q when all the other sources for John contradict the Q picture. John's preaching in Q is vituperative, polemical, and threatens a "coming wrath" that is to be effected by an apocalyptic thresher-figure. Not one of these ideas is even alluded to in the other gospel materials or in Josephus. Indeed, Josephus (who is our only source not concerned to place John within the context of Jesus' special status) not only fails to present John's message as one of eschatological doom but actually offers a picture of John rather incompatible with such a view:

> John was a pious man, and he was bidding the Jews who practiced virtue and exercised righteousness toward each other and piety toward God, to come together for baptism. For thus, it seemed to him, would baptismal ablution be acceptable, if it were used not to beg off from sins committed, but for the purification of the body when the soul had previously been cleansed by righteous conduct. And when everybody turned to John — for they were profoundly stirred by what he said — Herod feared that John's so extensive influence over the people might lead to an uprising (for the people seemed likely to do everything he might counsel). (*Ant.* 18.5.2 [LCL])

As John Kloppenborg argues, "[T]he portrait of John in Q differs markedly from the impression left by Josephus' treatment of John" (1990a, 150). We might expect that Josephus has "deapocalypticized" this portrait. As something of an apologist for Judaism in light of the Jewish Wars, Josephus clearly does not wish to present the people and the figures who exercise influence among them as fiery-eyed apocalyptic fanatics. There is little reason, a priori, to consider Josephus any more reliable a source than Q. But Mark, who would have little apparent reason for so doing, agrees more with Josephus than with Q in characterizing John's message as more hortatory than polemical, more occupied with ritual (baptism) than with apocalypse. Q's John, then, differs markedly from any other independent treatment of the Baptist known to us. The idiosyncratic picture of the Baptist implied by his preaching in Q renders that preaching unconfirmed and suspect.

In addition, the character of the traditions that make up this speech hardly inspires confidence in its historicity. Many critics regard the preaching as composite. Q 3:7–9 is generally separated from 3:16–17, and vv. 8 and 16b are viewed as interpolations into these blocks (see esp. Kloppenborg 1987a, 102–4). Each block, then, is held to have circulated independently under the rubric of "prophetic and apocalyptic sayings."[10] But if Q 3:7–9 is conceived as originally independent, it requires a narrative opening that both identifies the speaker as John and explains against whom the passage's vituperation is leveled. Without an indication of audience, the criticism contained in this material is unfocused and hence nonsensical. This is to say that vv. 7–9 cannot have been an originally independent *saying* but must, if ever independent, have taken the form of an apothegm. Its narrative setting, presupposed by the Synoptic evangelists, is inseparable from its content. But the material does not correspond well to this form either. The erstwhile narrative framework[11] does not simply provide the occasion for the saying but here provides the entire *rationale* and *motive* for it. The saying, moreover, is hardly a witty concluding utterance, as is typical and expected for apothegms (see Bultmann 1962, 40; Stein 1987, 170); rather, it serves to reflect on whatever situation the narrative has created. However, in the context of Q, regardless of how the document originally introduced this saying, its juxtaposition with 3:16 serves to identify the speaker, and the presence of similar polemical material on the lips of Jesus makes it clear, *within the document as a completed and integral whole,* that John's words are directed against impenitent Israel. The point, then, is that Q 3:7–9 does not correspond well to the form we would expect orally circulating material to take. It is difficult to imagine that it ever circulated outside of a larger written document (upon which it depends for its necessarily contingent meaning). And it is simplest to assume that the first such *document* in which it appeared was Q itself.

Conversely, both the original independence of 3:16, the saying about the Coming One, and its ascription to John are practically proven by its independent appearance in Mark (1:7–8). It does not follow that Q's version, which adds the words "and fire" and the apocalyptic description in v. 17, is superior to that of Mark. Many scholars, however, seem to regard this additional material as secondarily omitted by Mark, rather than secondarily added by Q.[12] Such an assertion flies in the face of the recognized tendency of the tradition to explicate sayings and add circumstantial details (Bultmann 1962b, 32; Stein 1987, 181), which is precisely the way the additional Q material operates. This being the case, it is a priori more likely that Mark, not Q, contains the more ancient form of John's messianic predictions. Whether the Markan version is in fact reliable is a question that goes beyond the limits of our discussion. The point is that the Markan version of this traditional (i.e., pre-Q) saying seems more likely to represent the older form of the saying, historically accurate or not.

Thus the form of John's preaching in Q may be viewed as a secondary development of the tradition. The first block in it, Q 3:7–9, resists form-critical classification, and the second block, 3:16–17, in the absence of any indications to the contrary, receives a secondary formulation in Q. It would thus seem that, while some of the material in v. 16 may or may not derive from the "historical John," there is good reason to doubt the Baptist provenance of the remainder of that preaching. We might justifiably ask, then, whence the remainder of this secondary material derives.

There are several reasons for ascribing this material to Q's redaction.[13] The assessment that the Baptist's speech is not specifically "Christian" and does not fit well with the description of Jesus — the main reasons for the acceptance of its authenticity — is correct only if we are comparing it to, say, Mark or Paul. But if one compares the Baptist material to the theology of Q as a whole (and especially to the themes typical of Q's later Deuteronomistic redaction), quite a striking correspondence emerges. John castigates those who refuse repentance and pronounces their future doom, ideas typical of the polemical redaction of the document. Israel's sinfulness and rejection, a major theme of this layer of the document, are stressed by John in 3:8. This rejection of claims to national privilege is repeated in Q 7:9; 10:10–15; and 11:29–32. The prediction of an eschatological figure, here designated by the title *ho erchomenos,* not only coheres in substance with the Son of Man figure used to designate Jesus in Q but is deliberately identified with Jesus in 7:18–23 and also appears on Jesus' lips in 13:34–35. John's *erchomenos* is described with the same ideas and words used in Jesus' own *self*-description in Q 12:49: "I have come to cast [*balein*] fire [*pyr*] upon the earth, and how I wish that it were already [*ēdē*] kindled!"[14] The harsh tone of John's preaching is hardly unique in Q: elsewhere Jesus uses equally harsh words to denounce "this generation" (see Q 11:39b–44, 46–52; 12:57–59; 17:2), a generation in need, precisely, of "repentance" (see Q 10:13; 11:32). Nor does John's message entirely ignore the positive elements in Q's presentation of the kingdom (a feature actually more characteristic of Q^1 than Q^2). The function of John's *ho erchomenos* is partly "to gather the wheat into his barn," an allusion to the promise to those who will repent (so also Fitzmyer 1981, 475). The imminence of these events, a theme apparent throughout Q (e.g., in Q 11:29–33, 51; 12:39–40, 49), is stressed in 3:9 with its use of *ēdē de kai* and the present tenses *keitai, ekkoptetai,* and *balletai.* Thus, as John Kloppenborg states, "[T]he motifs which characterized John's preaching soon emerge in Q, figuring prominently in Jesus' own preaching" (1987a, 95). This of course suggests that John's words *do* have a content with special significance in the early Jesus movement and, more precisely, for the people responsible for Q. In light of the likely secondary character of the Baptist's preaching and its hermeneutical dependence on the document as a whole, there seems little reason not to associate the composition of this preaching with the person(s) responsible for the compilation of the entire text. John's words do not differ from those of Jesus; instead they are practically a *summary* of the Q^2 message.[15]

John's preaching also echoes the typical *style* and *vocabulary* of the Deuteronomistic Q redaction. The polemic directed against the crowds or against an unspecified "you" occurs elsewhere in Q, in 11:29–32, 44; and 12:56. The use of *tekna* (in preference to *pais/paidion*) as a positive metaphor specifically referring to the repentant upon whom God bestows beneficence is repeated in Q 11:13; 7:35; and 13:34, the latter two texts very likely added to the clusters in which they appear at the later redactional stage of the document.[16] The use of harvest imagery for the judgment occurs in Q 10:2 and 19:21. And the use of *ballein* in the sense of "to cast away" appears in Q 12:28, 49; and 14:35. Jesus' use of aphoristic wisdom throughout Q^1 is paralleled by John's use of an aphorism in 3:9b: "Every tree not making good fruit is cut down and cast into fire." Arland D. Jacobson (1982, 375) has also noted that Q as a whole is distinctive in its use of rhetorical questions and invidious comparisons, two forms of rhetoric that appear most strikingly in John's inquiry, in v. 7, as to who warned the "brood of vipers" to flee from the approaching wrath. And Kloppenborg

(1990a, 144, 149–50) has noted that John's preaching alludes to the story of Lot and Sodom and that a similar fascination appears not only in Q 17:28–30 but in the redactional phrase at 10:12. John also uses the standard prophetic/sapiential phrase of Q, *legō hymin*. Finally, the form of the whole speech, as an apothegm enclosing prophetic judgment sayings, is typical of the form of most of Q's Deuteronomistic material.

It may also be argued that the title used by John, *ho erchomenos,* is in its application to Jesus a redactional creation. Culled in part from the messianic proof text in Ps 117:26, "Blessed is the One Who Comes (*ho erchomenos*) in the name of the Lord," which is quoted explicitly in Q 13:35, it may also be resonant with Mal 3:1–2:

> Behold, I send my messenger to prepare the way before me, and the Lord whom you seek will suddenly come to his temple; the messenger of the covenant in whom you delight, behold, he is coming, says the LORD of hosts. But who can endure the day of his coming, and who can stand when he appears? For he is like a refiner's fire and like fuller's soap.

The first part of this text, notably, is applied to John elsewhere in Q (7:27) and in Mark 1:2. The traditional association of this segment of the passage with John renders plausible the notion that the remainder of the text may have partially inspired Q's rendering of John's words about fire in 3:16 and his characterization of Jesus as the *erchomenos*. Theodotion's version of Daniel witnesses to a literal rendering of the Aramaic of the Son of Man text in 7:13 as *hōs huios anthrōpon erchomenos ēn,* a rendering that could also have been available to the much earlier Q redactor. In any case, the title seems to function as a redactional "correction" or replacement of the more traditional Son of Man vocabulary.[17] It is unique to Q and shows no indication of having had a prior history.[18] Its first occurrence in Q is in the Baptist's preaching. The second is at Q 7:19, where John is made to ask if Jesus is indeed the *erchomenos*. Notably, in this instance, the understanding and significance of the title are literarily dependent upon the initial reference in 3:16 and are therefore to be attributed to the redaction of Q as a whole. The final reference occurs in 13:34–35, a text that may be regarded as redactional in its themes and vocabulary.[19] A logical progression develops among and between these three references (so also Kloppenborg 1987a, 94), beginning with the expectation of the *erchomenos,* moving on to identify him with Jesus, and finally predicting his future return. Such a progression, spanning the work as a whole, is undoubtedly to be attributed to redaction.

Thus in light of the apparent secondary character of Q's presentation of the Baptist's words, its egregious coherence with not one but nearly *all* of the themes, motifs, and stylistic features of Q's Deuteronomistic redaction, its use of redactional terminology, and its function within a progression that operates across Q as a whole, it is difficult to conclude that John's preaching is anything *but* a redactional composition. How, otherwise, are we to account for so many of the typical features of Q and its redaction being present in a single pericope? It is almost as if the redactor is offering an abstract of his work.[20]

The material was probably put together in the following fashion: 3:16, apparently an independent saying traditionally attributed to John, was modified by the addition of the words "and fire" and by the reference to the *erchomenos.* The order of its clauses, particularly the placement of John's reference to his unworthiness, was changed in order for the saying better to accommodate additional material fore and aft. This traditional saying was then framed by references to fire (coherent with the reference to fire interpolated within it). The image of the thresher in v. 17 is a clear allegorical development of the description of the baptism of holy *wind (pneuma)* and fire in the preceding verse: the wind will separate the chaff, and fire will burn it. The Q redactor has then taken the Jesus aphorism from the sapiential layer of Q, in 6:43–44 ("[N]o healthy tree bears bad fruit;...a tree is known by its fruit"), has recast it in an apocalyptic fashion, and has surrounded this modified saying, *which is literarily dependent upon the earlier recension of Q* (Q^1), with material of his own composition in Q 3:7, 8b, and 9a. Thus despite being drawn haphazardly from different sources, John's preaching as a whole exhibits a good deal of coherence. The theme of judgment pervades the whole, and John not only proclaims Jesus but proclaims with Jesus' voice and indeed his very *words* in v. 9b. It is therefore possible to argue that the redactor of Q^2, or at least the group out of which this redaction grew, has used a traditional saying in which John predicts the coming of the Messiah (?) as the starting point around which was composed the remainder of the Baptist material, patterned after the message and image of Jesus throughout Q^2.

Conclusion

In light of these remarks, then, we should be open to the possibility that the Baptist's preaching in Q has been composed in order to express those very ideas and motifs that are special concerns to the people responsible for the document. These observations would suggest that Q did not *inherit* its image of John; it *created* that image. If so, it is no longer necessary to presume that Q's idea of John is the result of reflection upon the significance of his preaching. That preaching is in fact created after Q's own image. John introduces and supports the ideas attributed, throughout Q, to Jesus. The three dominant characteristics of the Q program — the proclamation of Jesus as the Coming One, the threat of judgment, and the polemic against Israel — are here undertaken by John as well. Indeed, John is even made to replicate the *form* of Jesus' message, using aphoristic wisdom and the *legō hymin* address. And Jesus' very words are found on John's lips in 3:9b, a feature that provokes a conscious comparison of these two nearly identical preachers.

Notably, the confusion over John's role and status appears in this block as much as anywhere else, suggesting that Q redaction, or the Q "community," does *not* in fact have a consistent idea of John's role. The redactor refuses to speculate as to the place of John in the history of salvation. John comes across in this preaching as, variously, a prophet, a baptizer, a wise man, and an Elijianic precursor-figure. Moreover, his high status is affirmed by the independence accorded his message and simultaneously denied by his proclamation of Jesus as the stronger Coming One. These various images and evaluations of John cannot be made consistent because the redactor was not concerned with consistency. What all these contradictory presentations have in common is their *deployment* in the service of casting John's message as identical to that of the people responsible for Q. The unequivocally positive presentation of John as a prophet, baptizer, and sage is an incidental by-product of the *function* of his preaching to reiterate Q's polemical and eschatological teachings. The more ambivalent view of John as a precursor-figure operates in the service of Q's desire to have him affirm the special status of Jesus. The same phenomenon occurs throughout the rest of Q's John material. The various roles he is given throughout Q are bound together by all serving the same *function*: they stress John's congruence with the Q people themselves — as, practically, a paradigmatic Q disciple — by presenting him as either opposed by Israel, proclaiming the eschaton, or attesting to Jesus. Thus while John's status and roles in Q, and in the redactional preaching material, are not consistent, their manipulation to present John's message and situation as identical to that of Q *is* consistent. Diverse material is collected or created to serve this end.

The question subsequently arises as to why Q would want to use the Baptist in this fashion. The answer should be clear: John, a figure who stands outside the community, is, in reiterating the precise message of Q and of Q's Jesus, made to legitimate the beliefs of the embattled Q people.[21] As an independent and generally respected witness to the various aspects of the Q faith, John is invoked as "proof" of their legitimacy.[22] As such, he is not elevated above Jesus or even the Q prophets; it is rather his independence from them that enables him to fulfill this function. The Q message is shown to be valid by its appearance in the mouth of John. His attestation to the unique status of Jesus shows that Q's faith is not idiosyncratic. The opposition of John to Israel discredits Q's opponents and illustrates their unreasonableness; thus criticisms of the Q community are defused and its defensive negative appraisal of "this generation" confirmed.[23] Q's John, therefore, is the product neither of theological speculation nor of historical reminiscence, but of the very real needs of a marginal community to find outside support. The resultant image of the Baptist has little to do with rarefied theological reflection (aloof from the realities of social intercourse) and even less to do with historical reality.

NOTES

1. An earlier version of this essay was read at the annual meeting of the Canadian Society of Biblical Studies, Queen's University, Kingston, Ontario, May 29, 1991. Work on this essay was supported by the Social Sciences and Humanities Research Council of Canada in the form of a doctoral fellowship.

2. Jacobson 1982, 380–81, 386–87; 1978, 28–30, 97; Kloppenborg 1987a, 107, 115, 117, 168.

3. See Kraeling 1951, 35–94; C. Scobie 1964, 60–71, 75, 77, 83; Farmer 1962, 956; Wink 1976, 487.

4. See Dibelius 1935, 230–31; Bultmann 1968, 11, 165; Hoffmann 1972, 28–31 (in part); Neirynck 1982, 54; Kloppenborg 1987a, 102–3 n. 2, 104–5.

5. Bultmann 1968, 117. Lührmann (1969, 31) also notes the amenability of 3:7–9 to Christian concerns.

6. Even März (1985), who argues that the entirety of the saying in Q 12:49 was a construction of the Q redaction and who makes this argument in part on the basis of the text's striking coherence with and structural symbiosis with John's preaching in 3:16–17, does not appear to grasp some of the implications of his argument. If John's description of the Coming One in Q 3:16 is of such interest to Q redaction that a saying later in the document would be constructed out of whole cloth just to establish a connection with this preaching; and if, moreover, part of the argument in favor of viewing Q 12:49 as a redactional composition is its structural function with respect to Q 3:16 (and the surrounding material); then the inverse surely follows: John's preaching will presumably be as subject to redactional modification as 12:49 in light of this overriding interest in identifying Jesus as the Coming One; and the structural role of the material, necessarily reciprocating that of 12:49, will surely open it up to as much a priori suspicion as it does in the case of 12:49. Yet März does not follow up these implications, instead appearing to assume, in broad agreement with other scholars, that 3:16 constitutes bedrock historical material from which characterizations of Jesus are then compared; and the surrounding amplifications of 3:16 in vv. 7–9 and 17 are ignored.

7. Beare 1962, 38; Davies and Allison 1988, 301; Manson 1949, 39.

8. There is some speculation that such a description may underlie the minor agreements between Matthew and Luke in Luke (Q?) 3:2–4 par. (see Crossan 1983, 342; Jacobson 1978, 28–30; Polag 1979, 28; Streeter 1924, 291). Others would suggest that these agreements are quite easily explained as independent modifications of the Markan text (see Fitzmyer 1981, 452; Kloppenborg 1988, 6). Kloppenborg, it appears, has since changed his mind (see Kloppenborg 1990a, 147–49). It seems necessary to posit *some* kind of introduction to John's words in Q, especially as they stand at the beginning of the text, but its precise character is highly debatable.

9. So Kloppenborg 1987a, 102 n. 1; Harnack 1908, 3; see also C. Scobie 1964, 65–66. Polag (1979, 28) takes the opposite view, regarding the Lukan wording as original.

10. See Bultmann 1968, 11, 117, 165. In this collection Wendy Cotter also makes this point forcefully: two main logia (Q 3:7–9 and vv. 16–17) comprise this speech. She writes: "Although *each* of the two logia shows a composite structure, they have been joined to achieve the semblance of a unitary address" (p. 136, emphasis added).

11. Without prejudice to the extent and character of such a narrative introduction. See above, n. 8.

12. See, for example, Jacobson 1978, 31–32, 34–35; Kloppenborg 1987a, 102–5. See also Davies and Allison 1988, 307.

13. It should be noted that what is meant here is *not* merely that this material was incorporated into Q as a document only at the time of the major (Deuteronomistic/polemical) redaction, a conclusion that would of course have no logical bearing on the material's historicity (or vice versa). Rather, the material appears to have been formulated and composed by the same hand responsible for drawing together the major, Deuteronomistic redaction of Q. Note that the increasingly standard stratification of Q into two major layers — a formative collection of sapiential material and a secondary redaction emphasizing polemical themes — is assumed in what follows. "Q[1]" is used to designate the initial layer, while "Q[2]" signifies both the Deuteronomistic/polemical material added at the redactional phase and the concerns of that phase as a whole.

14. On this correspondence, see März 1985. As already noted, März uses this correspondence to argue that it is 12:49 that is a redactional creation on the part of the compiler of Q. It is worth reiterating, however, that the correspondence extends beyond affinity with merely 3:16 to the surrounding material (see n. 6, above). In light of this broader correspondence and the interest shown by the redactor (especially visible precisely in his or her creation of 12:49) in the characterization of Jesus in John's preaching, we might plausibly expect a redactional intervention in the text of John's preaching of the same sort as occurs in 12:49. There is no good reason that any of März's observations regarding 12:49 should not apply equally well to 3:7–9, 16–17.

15. Wendy Cotter (in this volume) likewise recognizes the programmatic character of the speech (Q 3:7–9, 16–17) for the rest of Q.

16. Note that both Q 7:35 and 13:34–35 serve as summarizing "commentary words," providing the interpretive key to the clusters they conclude; additionally, these texts make little sense as independent sayings. Thus at the very least we can conclude that these statements were composed and situated where they now appear at the latest stage in the development of the larger clusters that they conclude. This in itself does not prove them to be compositions/additions made at the level of Q[2] redaction but at least makes such a contention plausible, particularly given the fact that themes reinforced by such summary statements are easily coordinated with the main themes of Q[2] redaction. On this latter point, regarding 13:34–35, see n. 20, below. Note also that 11:13 likewise serves as a concluding summary to the speech in Q 11:9–13. This observation, however, raises the difficult issue of the relation of Q[1] composition/redaction to that of Q[2] and the social continuity (or lack thereof) between the two recensions, an issue far beyond the scope of this essay.

17. That the Q redactor may here be nuancing or "correcting" an earlier, traditional title is important. It may be assumed that Q represents a combination of traditional materials, sayings that have been modified

in line with redactional interests and sayings that have been constructed wholesale either by the redactor or within his or her circles. It consequently makes little sense to object that John's speech does not employ Q's favorite title for Jesus ("Son of Man"), when in fact it is clear that this title predates the redaction of Q^2. It is precisely the fact that the *erchomenos* title does *not* permeate all of Q's sayings (many of which are to be deemed traditional), but only appears at a limited number of critical junctures, that makes it so clear that the title is a redactional one. This methodological principle may be extended to other material as well. Thus, it is not sufficient to state that a given theme in John's preaching does not cohere perfectly in its nuances with that theme as articulated in the mass of other sayings to demonstrate that the speech is not redactional. Instead, some attention must to paid to whether the different minutiae that are being noted stem from the document's redaction or from the traditions on which the redactor drew.

18. Actually, the term does occur in the Baptist's preaching in John 1:27. The fourth evangelist here follows Matthew's wording almost exactly, reading *ho opisō mou erchomenos* (Matthew: *ho de opisō mou erchomenos*). This Johannine text is sometimes cited as an independent witness to the Matthean reading of the Q text (e.g., by Kloppenborg 1987a, 102 n. 1). Such an understanding would of course make it less likely that the title, and its ascription to the Baptist, originated with Q redaction. But the Johannine reading can be explained without such a hypothesis. The phrase *ho erchomenos* does not here function as a title. The gospel writer is very interested in playing on the irony of John's temporal precedence to Jesus, the Preexistent One (cf. also 1:15), and it is this Johannine idea that lies behind the evangelist's wording. The idea that Jesus is *stronger* than John is not a concern to the evangelist — it goes without saying! Hence the traditional (=Markan) wording of this saying was probably modified by the evangelist himself in order better to express his unique concerns. That the result is similar to the Q wording need not indicate dependence on prior oral tradition. The correspondence is easily understood in terms of independent, coincidental, and actually quite theologically different reworkings of that traditional text.

19. Particularly in light of its mythification of the conflict between Jesus/Wisdom and Israel. See Vaage 1988b, 599–601. See also n. 17, above.

20. Indeed, this speech is most appropriate to fulfill a programmatic role (as noted by Cotter; see n. 16, above) because of its placement at the opening of the text. The location of this preaching, then, and its consequent function to lay out and introduce the central tenets of Q's ideology should make the *extent* of the material here attributed to redactional composition far less surprising than it might be otherwise. Notably, the same phenomenon recurs in Mark (introductory proof texts regard-

ing the Baptist), Matthew and Luke (infancy narratives), John (prologue), and Thomas (sayings about interpretation). It is precisely at the opening of a document, in other words, that prominent redactional intervention is most to be expected.

21. Kloppenborg (1987a, 168) acknowledges the legitimizing effect of the presentation of John in the polemic against Israel. Horsley (1989b, 109) goes further, seeing in Q 7:18–28 (and elsewhere) a series of exhortations and rationalizations for the community. It should be noted that the remaining Baptist material in Q (i.e., 7:18–35 and 16:16) presents John — and makes use of him — in the same fashion as does 3:7–9, 16–17, although the degree of redactional intervention in this material is (unsurprisingly) rather more limited than in the preaching.

22. Again, see Cotter (above, p. 138): "Ernst Bammel's statement that 'Q turns out to be a justification of John's ministry' is precisely contrary to the case. John's speech provides credibility for the perspectives and Christology of Q²."

23. Cotter 1987, 289–304, and 1989, 63–82, offers a similar assessment of Q 7:31–35. See also Mack 1988a, 616.

More Than a Prophet, and Demon-Possessed

Q and the "Historical" John

═══

John is never mentioned in the canonical New Testament beyond the four Gospels and Acts, not even in connection with the early Christian practice of baptism. Apparently for Paul and his imitators, for the writers of the Petrine and Johannine epistles, for the authors of Hebrews and James, and for the author of Revelation, it was simply not important or possible to remember anything significant about "the Baptist." Neither for their respective theological programs nor for their different social situations was it deemed necessary or convenient to invoke or elaborate the memory of this man.[1]

In extracanonical Christian literature, there is likewise a striking absence of references to John until the advent of explicit commentary on the New Testament writings, and even then, commentary concerning John is remarkably spare until the fourth century c.e.[2] For example, John is mentioned only once in the *Gospel of Thomas* and, then, only in a saying (46) parallel to Q 7:28;[3] or again, John is mentioned once in the *Apocryphon of James* (4:2) in a passage recalling Mark 6:27–28.[4] Not without justification, therefore, does Helmut Koester begin his introductory discussion of John the Baptist with the assertion: "Our primary sources for the life and ministry of John the Baptist are the canonical gospels."[5]

The established "database" for reconstructing the "historical" John is thus already small from the beginning. It shrinks even fur-

---

Leif E. Vaage is an assistant professor of New Testament at Emmanuel College, Toronto School of Theology.

ther once we recognize that neither Matthew nor Luke-Acts can be invoked as independent witnesses in this regard, given that their respective literary elaborations of Mark and Q, both of whom had developed their own portraits of John, make everything that Matthew and/or Luke-Acts might wish to say about John liable to the suspicion of being a redactional construction.[6] One would have to be able to demonstrate beyond all reasonable doubt that one or the other evangelist simply could not have invented the tradition that he or she is otherwise alone responsible for "preserving."[7]

Beyond Q, therefore, we are left essentially with Mark and John (plus a controverted passage in Josephus) as the primary touchstones for developing whatever "historical" portrait of the desert drifter we might wish to paint.[8] Although it is clear that whatever is said in any of these sources must ultimately be compared with the witness of the other (two or three) texts for the purposes of "historical" inquiry, the particular vision of each writing must also be rigorously respected at the outset, if only to permit the original and limited variety of distinct perspectives regarding John to be recognized and appreciated. In what follows, therefore, I will concentrate almost exclusively on the testimony of Q.[9]

Both Mark and John make clear in the prologue to their respective Gospels what they understand the significance of John's memory to be. For Mark, John is first and foremost "the Baptist,"[10] that is, "the one baptizing in the wilderness and preaching a baptism of repentance for forgiveness of sins" (1:4), by whom "the entire region of Judaea and all the inhabitants of Jerusalem" were "baptized in the Jordan River confessing their sins" (1:5), including Jesus (1:9). It is precisely in this capacity that John also serves in Mark as Jesus' designated forerunner or foreshadow, "my messenger before you, who will prepare your way" (1:2), after whom "comes one stronger than I" (1:7) who "will baptize you" not with water but "in holy spirit" (1:8). Like a number of other promises in Mark, the latter event never actually occurs within the narrative time frame of the Gospel, although Jesus immediately becomes in Mark (1:10, 12) the one suffused by the Spirit, whose personal holiness (1:24; cf. 3:30; 6:20) is then opposed to the "unclean spirits" otherwise routinely cast out by Jesus in Mark (1:23–28; 3:11; 5:1–18; 6:7; 7:24–30; 9:14–27).

It is Mark who highlights both the ritual practice of baptism by John as well as the parallel between John's start and finish and the life and death of Jesus (Mark 6:14–16, 17–29, 30–32). At the same time, the biblical citation in Mark 1:2 leaves no doubt at the very beginning of the Gospel that John is hardly to be confused with "Jesus Christ son of God" — in contrast to Q (7:27), which uses the same scriptural passage to characterize John, but only as an intervening last-ditch "containment strategy" between the absolute high praise of John in Q 7:24b–26 and Q 7:28a, and otherwise recalls the two men in Q 7:33–34, 35 as being "different, but equal." The strict distinction in Mark 1:2–3 between John and Jesus is then reiterated through the contrast between the fasting of John's disciples and the Pharisees and the eating habits of Jesus' own followers in Mark 2:18–20.

The description in Mark 1:6 of John "dressed in camel hair and wearing a leather belt around his waist" obviously recalls the description in 2 Kgs 1:8 of Elijah the Tishbite. Together with the mistaken comment of certain people in Mark 6:15 that Jesus, initially confused with John, was rather Elijah, it prepares for the discussion after Jesus' transfiguration in Mark 9:11–13 about Elijah coming first, that is, already having come, presumably in the person of John, and the correlative impending destiny of Jesus as the Son of Man.

It is significant that John's baptism is said in Mark (1:4) to be "a baptism of repentance." This contrasts with Q (3:7b–9), which also speaks of repentance with regard to John, but only in reference to the charge by John to do something "worthy of repentance" and not to imagine anything else, for example, submission to baptism as a sufficient defense in the face of the wrath to come.[11] In this regard, Q agrees with Josephus, who likewise comments that John

> had exhorted the Jews to lead righteous lives, to practice justice toward their fellows and piety toward God, and so doing to join in baptism. In his view this was a necessary preliminary if baptism was to be acceptable to God. They must not employ it to gain pardon for whatever sins they committed, but as a consecration of the body implying that the soul was already thoroughly cleansed by right behavior. (*Ant.* 18.117)

No new "historical" information regarding John is provided by the Gospel of John that is not already found in Mark.[12] As Josef Ernst writes:

> The Baptist [in John] is, indeed, precisely not the false Messiah, the Antichrist, or one who comes in his own name (5:43) but, rather, the ideal witness to Christ. John appears as the model Christian

preacher, as the prototype of the true evangelist, as the person sent by God (1:6; 3:28) to lead others to faith in Christ (1:7, 8, 19, 20, 29–34; 3:26, 28; 5:33f.). (1989, 215)

Regarding the Gospel of John, Walter Wink concludes:

> The Evangelist has thus projected upon John his own all-consuming purpose: "that you may believe that Jesus is the Christ, the Son of God" (20:31; cf. 1:7, 29, 34, 36)....The Evangelist's portrait of John is thus intended more for the church than for Baptist circles. Far from being an enemy, John is Jesus' "best man" (3:29). In the same absolute sense as in Mark, John is still the "beginning of the Gospel" (John 1:6–8, 19ff.). He stands with Jesus as a witness against "the Jews" (1:19ff.; 5:32ff.), his witness is equivalent in value to that of the Old Testament (5:33ff.), and he assumes the role of the first confessing Christian (1:29ff.). John's "Christianization" is now, in this Gospel, made complete. The "baptizer" has become "the friend," the forerunner has become "the voice," the prophet has become a saint. (1968, 106)

In terms of the Gospel of John, John is the first and final "sign," the shadow at dawn, manifesting the emergent meaning of "the word made flesh," the ultimate truth of Jesus. Thus in 10:41, the last we hear of John in the Gospel of John, it is said just before Jesus' final and culminating "sign" of raising Lazarus from the dead both that John himself "did no sign" (i.e., nothing comparable to what is recorded of Jesus in the preceding chapters; hence John is hardly to be mistaken for Jesus) and that "everything John said about this one [namely, Jesus] was true" (see Bammel 1965, 181–202).

The Redaction of Q

Especially since John S. Kloppenborg's work *The Formation of Q: Trajectories in Ancient Wisdom Collections* (1987a), it has become important when interpreting the Synoptic Sayings Source to consider the literary-compositional "level" at which any utterance or group of utterances is found in the document. Regarding John, two sets of sayings come into question, namely, the opening pericope in Q (3:7b–9, 16–17) and the more extended text in 7:18–35 (including 16:16). According to Arland D. Jacobson (1992, 77–129), these two units (3:7b–17; 7:18–35) together constitute the enclosing frame of Q's first major section (3:7–7:35).

According to Kloppenborg, both units (3:7–17; 7:18–35, along with 7:1–10) are to be ascribed to Q's secondary redaction. Although Kloppenborg does not himself understand the determination of literary stratigraphy to indicate a particular judgment about the antiquity or authenticity of the traditional material contained in a given stratum of Q, in my opinion, the attribution of a group of sayings to Q's redaction must diminish the likelihood of their reliability as "historical" testimony, for the same reason that Matthew and Luke were earlier said to be essentially untrustworthy as witnesses to the "historical" John because of the redactional nature of their compositions (see, further, Vaage 1988a; also Vaage 1991a).

How is John depicted by Q's redaction? What, in other words, is the dominant image given of the man by the final version of the Synoptic Sayings Source? At this level of description, I have no quarrel with the perspective of Kloppenborg and other scholars on the general shape of the memory of John in Q. In Kloppenborg's words:

> Although John's baptizing activity is presupposed by 3:7a and 3:16a, Q's interest in John resides elsewhere. John is primarily a prophet of the coming end. Formally as well as materially the composition [3:7–9, 16–17] is dominated by prophetic features. Q 3:7b–9 is a prophetic reproach of impenitence and the announcement of judgment, and 3:16–17 describes that judgment in detail. Materially, the two pericopae [3:7–9, 16–17] reflect the deuteronomistic pattern in which the prophets are interpreted as preachers of repentance and as heralds of judgment. (1987a, 105)

Both in 3:16 and in 7:18–23, 27, 28b, John is made to occupy a subordinate position to Jesus. In 7:18–23, answering John's inquiry as to whether or not Jesus is the one to come, Jesus emerges as the long-awaited figure, the designated successor to the end-time prophet. John is thus a precursor, aware that he is not the real thing and visibly anxious to find out who is.[13]

Likewise in 7:27 — plainly an addition to the preceding "negative" characterization of John in 7:24–26 — the figure of John is raised up to the level of God's appointed *aggelos* and effectively made equivalent to the person of Elijah, the final messenger expected to appear before the end, even as John is simultaneously demoted once again below the rank of Jesus. That John was sent "before your face" means paradoxically coming first, but decidedly in second place: "to prepare your way before you."

By the time of Q's redaction, it is clear that the "least" person "in the kingdom of God" is now considered greater than John (7:28b). The fearsome dieter (7:33) who otherwise was thought by some(one) to be the highest of all mortals (7:28a) is now put in his place. Indisputably awesome and correct, John ceases with Q's redaction (7:28b) to be the decisive player in the field. Indeed, he may no longer even be part of the game, given that Jesus and, by extension, all those identified with him "in the kingdom of God" presently supersede the former "superman" — precisely as John himself already foresaw in 3:16.

In 16:16, John embodies the end of "the law and the prophets." They endured "until" him. John is either the culmination of whatever "the law and the prophets" stand for or the premonition of something new. In either case, he remains a transitional figure, pivotal and significant, but clearly not the desired "thing itself."

In Q 7:35, the last saying of the section, John seems suddenly to be placed on a par with Jesus, insofar as both John and Jesus are together here called "children of Wisdom." Each would participate — in the specific way that 7:33–34 has differently described — in the Deuteronomistic scheme of divine envoys sent to Israel to proclaim repentance to the nation, only to be ultimately rejected by the "children of Abraham" (see Q 3:8; 7:32).

The proper characterization of John and Jesus has ceased, however, at this point in the proceedings to be of primary interest to the Q redactor. The focus of attention has rather shifted to "this generation" (see Q 3:7b; 7:31). It was these persons' similar disregard for both John and Jesus — who otherwise for Q's redaction, as seen above, had clearly distinct portfolios — that alone permits the unified judgment to be made that we now find in 7:35. The example of the two contrary figures thus serves, in the end, to sustain what John alone proclaimed at the beginning of Q, namely, the threat of wrath to come against a brood of unrepentant siblings.

Q 3:7b–9, 16–17

The opening pericope of Q (3:7b–9, 16–17) is still read by many scholars (e.g., Ernst 1989, 55) as a set of sayings either by or about the "historical" John. One reason for this assumption is the fact that the statement in 3:16 is a repeat offender with "multiple attestation" in the discourse of the canonical Gospels and Acts.[14] Of all the sayings in Q associated with John, this was clearly the most popular.

Despite Kloppenborg's claim that the group of sayings in 3:7b–9, 16–17 "is not an original unity but the result of the juxtaposition and editing of smaller units of tradition" (1987a, 102), the image of John created by these verses is plainly uniform.[15] Throughout the passage, John is consistently identified with the threat of impending wrath, root metaphors of cutting and harvest, the need for repentance, the impotence of traditional connections, and the speaker's own ancillary role in this drama. Although the water John used to baptize might have served to arrest the promised fire into which all deadwood would be thrown, the same practice is immediately declared unequal to the impending baptism of a stronger one "by holy spirit and fire," said to be simply "unquenchable" for all unheeding chaff.[16] Ostensible cracks and fissures in the final literary formulation of this unit hardly detract from the singular thrust of its general portrait of John.[17]

Only in 3:16 is any reference unambiguously made to baptism in Q.[18] As already noted, the speaker's water rinse is here contrasted with the coming stronger one's baptism by holy spirit and fire. The point of the saying, especially in conjunction with 3:17, is to predict an imminent harvest purge in which whatever or whoever corresponds to "chaff" will be destroyed by "unquenchable fire."

There is no suggestion that the speaker's baptism by water in 3:16 anticipates in any way the second more blistering bath. It simply underscores in terms of a particular action — the shared verb *baptizein* — the fundamental difference otherwise to be observed between the speaker "I" and "the one stronger than I." All we are told about the speaker's baptism by water is that it hardly equals what comes next.

Only through a possible structural symmetry between 3:16–17 and 3:7b–9 might the water baptism referred to in 3:16 be understood as equivalent to the act of "producing fruit worthy of repentance." The expression "producing fruit worthy of repentance" (3:8a), however, first contrasts with the attempt to "flee from the coming wrath" in 3:7b. It is then made in 3:8a to conflict with the search for refuge in one's family lineage or the fact that "we have Abraham as our father." In 3:9, we are not told exactly what "fruit worthy of repentance" might be, only that "every tree not producing good fruit will be cut down and thrown into the fire."

By inference alone we might conclude that the statement in 3:16, "I baptize you with water," finally makes clear what the "fruit worthy of repentance" mentioned in 3:8a concretely entails. But, again, there is no suggestion that the "wheat" to be gathered into the granary in 3:17 — the undiscussed "good fruit" of 3:9 — became so by having first been water-soaked.

In 3:7b–9, it is clear that whatever the "fruit worthy of repentance" might be in 3:8, it is only by actually producing such fruit that one could hope to avoid the crackling fate of every tree "not producing good fruit." It is not clear, however, that in 3:16a being baptized with water has much to do with the scenario to follow, insofar as there is another baptism heralded in 3:16b–17, "by holy spirit and fire," with which "the one stronger than I . . . will himself baptize you." Unless, of course, we are to imagine at this point a sequence of events like the different stages of a Roman bath: first the cold plunge, then the hot shower.

Once the winnowing fork gets going in 3:17, what saves you from the flames is being wheat — an identity, perhaps, roughly equivalent to the status of being a good fruit-bearing tree.[19] But is it finally the speaker's baptism by water that makes one "wheat" or a "tree producing good fruit"? Are we to assume that the act of putting forth "fruit worthy of repentance" is mistakenly identified at this point in Q with the necessary, though otherwise indeterminate, labor of irrigation? If, as Kloppenborg writes, "John's baptizing activity is clearly presupposed in . . . 3:16a," it is hardly clear, even at the level of Q's redaction, how this same activity was conceived to render any particular benefit.

This is as close as John gets in Q to being a "baptist." Such water-work was thus hardly the man's distinguishing trademark for the Synoptic Sayings Source. Even in 3:7b–9, 16–17, the activity of baptism figures basically as an aside in a combined polemic against complacent "children of Abraham" and the prediction of warmer days ahead. Otherwise, as we shall now see in 7:18–35, among the various characterizations of John made in this section, "baptizing" is never mentioned again. For Q, it seems, at every stage of its compositional development, the "historical" John was never especially associated with baptism (cf. Bammel 1971–72, 100).

Q 7:18–35

It is in 7:18–35 that the conflicting views of John, to which I earlier referred, are found. On the one hand, the portrait of John painted in 3:7b–9, 16–17 is continued and refined. On the other, statements are made in 7:18–35 that especially oppose the subservient status otherwise assigned to John by Q's redaction. It is these statements, specifically, the sayings in 7:24b–26, 28a, 33, that will most require our attention. But, first, a quick review of what is said in 7:18–23 and 7:31–35.

Q 7:18–23. In 7:18–23, Jesus is magnified at John's expense. John's importance in the pericope is simply to provide a prominent point of departure. John through his disciples is made to ask whether Jesus is indeed "the Coming One" or whether they should "expect someone else." The self-put-down begun by John in 3:16 is here continued.

In 7:22–23, Jesus' plate is immediately heaped with choice morsels of Isaianic prophecy, suggestive of its present fulfillment in his person, followed by a beatitude that vaguely threatens all who would be scandalized by such self-aggrandizement. As for John, he has already quickly faded into the background — so much so, in fact, that the abrupt transition in 7:24a to the question of John's own proper characterization seems forced and inadequately motivated.[20]

Q 7:31–35. At the other end of the discourse, in 7:31–35, neither John nor Jesus is the main concern. Rather, the primary interest has here become how best to characterize "this generation." In contrasting ways, John and Jesus are both important at this point (7:33–34) merely to highlight the feckless folly of Q's inattentive contemporaries.[21]

In 7:33–34, nonetheless, striking characterizations of both John and Jesus are recorded. John is said to have come neither eating nor drinking, as though he were demon-possessed, while the reputation of Jesus, who came eating and drinking, is that of a drunkard and a glutton, a friend of tax collectors and sinners.[22]

Regarding the figure of Jesus, in 7:34 we are suddenly light-years away from the previous portrait painted of him in 7:18–23. Instead of the messianic aura surrounding the man in 7:18–23, it is now the fog of a hangover that in 7:33 envelopes the fearless feaster. Any scandal provoked by Jesus' person in 7:34 will not be due to eschatological surprise and wonder, but the direct result of his low-life associations.[23]

John is his equal.[24] At least, in 7:33 John stands on a par with Jesus, though at the opposite end of the moral spectrum. There is no hint of inferior ranking. Between them, the two define a social style that, whether eating and drinking or not, was consistently liable to denigration as perverse and in bad taste, not to mention, in Jesus' case, frequently "out-to-lunch."[25]

It is difficult, indeed impossible, to imagine that the hand responsible for creating the exchange between John and Jesus in 7:18–23 also produced or even would have welcomed the saying in 7:33–34. The contrast is simply too great in the way that John and Jesus are both depicted in these two respective units. Granted that in 7:33–34 we read what others said about John and Jesus and not presumably what they and their early followers likely would have said about themselves.[26] Nonetheless, the rhetoric in 7:33–34 is so strong, aggressive, and inconsistent regarding the reciprocal status of John and Jesus as depicted in 7:18–23 that what is said in 7:33–34 cannot be taken merely as a different perspective, supporting, as it were, *a la chiaroscuro* the initial presentation of John and Jesus in 7:18–23.[27]

In fact, the image given in 7:33–34 of the relation between John and Jesus and the moral character each embodied is just not the same as the one promoted in 7:18–23. It is therefore most unlikely that both 7:18–23 and 7:33–34 were first introduced into the Synoptic Sayings Source as part of the same literary stratum. If, then, as Kloppenborg and others have argued (and I agree), 7:18–23 is properly to be assigned to Q's redaction, for reasons that I have developed elsewhere, I conclude that 7:33–34 was originally part of Q's formative stratum.[28]

Q 7:33. As already noted, the saying in 7:33 has John "neither eating nor drinking" and being "demon-possessed" (*daimonion echei*). The first description essentially corresponds to what we otherwise might know about the man's personal habits.[29] The second characterization of John, however, as being "demon-possessed" is routinely ignored or shunted aside by scholars,[30] even when the statements regarding both John and Jesus in 7:33–34 are otherwise thought to be essentially true historically.[31] It is also frequently thought necessary either to qualify or simply to deny the obvious "asceticism" here attributed to John.[32]

In fact, however, both descriptions of John depict him precisely

as an ancient "ascetic" and, furthermore, have analogies in the
history of Cynicism. The spare diet of many Cynics, restricting
themselves to water and a few mean vegetables, is common knowledge.[33] And the accusation that John was "demon-possessed" is
equivalent to Plato's well-known calumny of Diogenes, whom
Plato accused of being simply "Socrates gone mad."[34] At the level
of Q's formative stratum, John was remembered as one more of
those "doggone" philosophers.

Q 7:24–28. Regarding the sayings in 7:24–28, these four verses
together constitute an ever-tighter jumble of alternating points of
view on John, roughly divisible into the following four segments:
(*a*) 7:24ab–26; (*b*) 7:27; (*c*) 7:28a; and (*d*) 7:28b. Overall, the
unit (7:24–28) is usually understood to focus particularly on John,
given the explicit introduction to the sayings in terms of John in
7:24a and the reiterated use of John's name in 7:28. Recently,
however, some scholars have drawn attention to the fact that the
parallel saying to 7:24–25 in *Gos. Thom.* 78 does not mention
John at all; formally, moreover, it is clear that the introductory
statement in 7:24a was not originally part of the interrogative sequence that follows; hence the sayings in 7:24b–26, 27 cannot
simply be assumed to describe John (see Cameron 1990, 44). But
is there really an alternative? To whom else would these utterances
refer?[35]

Q 7:24b–26/Gos. Thom. 78. On the assumption that, at least
in Q, the sayings in 7:24b–26 were originally about John, the
image of him developed here through a series of leading questions is glossy indeed. In the end, the man emerges as someone
"even greater than a prophet" (7:26b) — a statement once more
extremely difficult, if not impossible, to reconcile with John's subordinate inquiry of Jesus in 7:19 regarding whether or not Jesus
is "the Coming One" predicted by prophetic literature.[36] Does
someone truly "greater than a prophet" look elsewhere for another "stronger than he, who is coming" (3:16) as the prophets
foretold?[37]

Or is this merely a coy ploy on Jesus' behalf, that is, by the
redactor of Q, further to enhance the superior status of Jesus as
already displayed in 7:18–23, by now elevating the value of his
supporting cast, namely, John, as much as possible?[38] If so, it
would quickly be a counterproductive move, for the kind of person
evoked in 7:24b–26 might easily "steal the show."[39]

Nothing said in 7:24b–26 is guaranteed to keep John in his

place. Indeed, the *via negationis* by means of which equivocal characterizations of John are consistently surmounted in the text only serves to encourage a sense of John's superlative character. Words simply cannot be found to describe him (unlike Jesus, whose basic being has just been summarized in 7:22 with a few snippets of Scripture). At the same time, as I have argued elsewhere, by virtue of the "negative" nature of the sayings in 7:24b–26, a specific profile is implied for John, not unlike the relationship between a shadow and its owner. Cynic parallels especially to 7:25, the "linchpin" in this progressive characterization of John through contrast, help, then, to visualize concretely the type of person we should finally imagine.[40]

> The suggestion is made here [in 7:25] that perhaps those who went out into the desert to John thought that they would see the sort of person otherwise excoriated by the popular philosophers for lurid living, the sort especially prone to gather in the royal court like flies at a banquet. Perhaps they thought for some strange reason that John too would be dressed like one of these sycophants, arrayed in cloth as purple as their prose, though John in the desert could hardly have been farther away from and more inimical to the official center of power and influence than he was. (Vaage 1994, 100)

> Unlike the classical (canonical) prophets of Israel, whose identity resided especially in their opposition to the erosion and ignorance of traditional values by the developing and decadent monarchy, John appears, at least in 7:25, to have defined himself as a Cynic through opposition to the reigning culture as such. The royal dwellings with their palatial life symbolized, both for John and for the Cynics, the dominant aspirations and pitfalls of advancing "civilization."
>
> At the formative stage of Q, it was not the call to repentance or renewal of the religious patrimony of Abraham that especially distinguished John but, rather, his stance in the desert. Beyond the circuit of conventional society in an altogether different orbit from the one that united ancient kings and their customary critics, John stood apart, in fundamental disagreement with the current order of things — at whose margin, nonetheless, if barely, he could still be found.[41]

Again, it is difficult, if not impossible, to suppose that such a person would have been so emphatically lauded by the same editorial mind-set that otherwise considered John to be unworthy to untie the sandal-straps of his anticipated successor. Moreover, it is

hardly probable that John's forced self-diminution in 3:16; 17:18–
23 would subsequently and, as it were, "naturally" have given
way to the exuberant exaltation of his person in 7:24b–26. Quite
the contrary! It is much more likely that 7:24b–26 (together with
7:33–34) already existed in Q prior to the introduction of 7:18–
23, 31–32, 35 into the document.[42] For the same reason, as already
discussed, the memory of John preserved in these sayings (7:24b–
26, 33) is also more likely to recall the "historical" John "wie er
eigentlich gewesen war."[43]

Q 7:27. Virtually all scholars agree that 7:27 has been secondarily added to 7:24b–26. Many would also agree that 7:27
was inserted at its present location in the Synoptic Sayings Source
between 7:26 and 7:28 after 7:28a(b) was first appended to 7:24b–
26. The view of John in 7:27 as a precursor or forerunner to
Jesus certainly coheres with the similar place assigned to John by
Q's redaction both in 3:16 and in 7:18–23. With some certainty,
therefore, we may conclude that, at the earliest, 7:27 was first introduced into Q when the two sayings-complexes regarding John
in 3:7b–9, 16–17 and 7:18–35 were created (see Vaage 1994, 184
n. 76). In fact, it may have been even later.[44]

Q 7:28ab. The "prehistory" of 7:28 remains uncertain.[45] If,
as some scholars think, the first half of the verse was once an
"independent" saying, subsequently appended to 7:26 before the
intervention of 7:27 and the addition of 7:28b, its view of John
would reflect the same uncompromising memory of the man otherwise found in Q 7:24b–26, 33.[46] According to 7:28a, in John one
could see "the greatest man ever born,"[47] not unlike Alexander the
Great, the ancient world's supreme example of a kingly conqueror,
who is reputed to have said after meeting Diogenes, "Had I not
been born Alexander first, I would have been Diogenes."[48] Diogenes himself was wont to say that there was likely no one more
content than he. So, too, John was thought to have achieved a
similarly superior status.

Conclusion

Q presents us overall with two quite different views of John. One
is the work of Q's redaction; the other, the memory tradition of
Q's formative stratum. At the level of Q's redaction, John appears
as the well-known eschatological prophet, announcing God's imminent judgment on an impenitent generation and looking for "the

Coming One" whose precursor John thereby becomes. Only at this (redactional) stage is baptism ever mentioned in Q regarding John, and even then it remains, at most, a minor feature of his characterization. Stratigraphically, the image of John promoted by Q's redaction is a secondary fabrication and, therefore, less likely to recall the actual features of the "historical" figure "wie er eigentlich gewesen war."

As depicted by Q's formative stratum in 7:24b–26, 28a, 33, the "historical" John was rather like a Cynic. As Jesus, so John, too, struck a peculiar and probably disturbing pose on the social margins of first-century C.E. southern (Roman) Syria. While nothing is said explicitly in Q about John's appearance (cf. Mark 1:6), what we read in 7:25, 33 makes clear that John would hardly have conformed to the ancient Mediterranean world's image of the ideal well-dressed man. John was much too roughly hewn — and extremely skinny, if, in fact, he ate and drank so little.

According to Q's formative stratum, John provoked sufficient intrigue that many went out to see him in the wilderness, eager to discern just what it was that John was up to out there, the less kind among them claiming that the man was simply mad. Seen by some as "more than a prophet" and "the greatest man that ever was," for others the only thing divine about John was the demon in him. May his howling bones rest in peace.

NOTES

1. The same is apparently true for early "mainline" Jewish literature. According to Neuman (1950–51, 139): "There is no reference to John the Baptist under any aspect in Tannaitic or Talmudic literature."

2. See Kraeling (1951, 183–84): "It is interesting to note that during the whole of the second and third centuries, while the forces of syncretism were thus apparently capitalizing upon the Baptist rite, Christian legend and the Christian Church Fathers have very little to say about John." Only in the fourth century, that is, after the imposition of imperially sanctioned orthodoxy, does there eventually emerge "a great body of Baptist legend that soon spreads over the entire eastern Christian world," whose historical usefulness, however, Kraeling quickly discounts. See, further, Ernst 1989, 242.

3. Bammel (1971–72, 115) refers as well (though unconvincingly) to *Gos. Thom.* 52 and observes that *Gos. Thom.* 78 "contains the saying of Matt. xi. 7b–8, but without any reference to John, so to speak, in a debaptizisted form." See, further, *Acts of Thomas* 36. In addition, Ernst

(1989, 227) discusses (again unconvincingly) *Gos. Thom.* 104 (in this regard referring [227 n. 46] misleadingly to the preceding statement by Bammel, which only concerns *Gos. Thom.* 78).

4. At least, *Ap. Jas.* 4:2 provides no new information about John's death. In fact, the passage does not seem to be especially interested in John at all, but rather in the topic of prophecy and its cessation. See Ernst (1989, 228): "Whether through the image of cutting off (= ending) a positive statement is also made about the role of the Baptist as head and representative of prophecy, is hard to say."

5. Koester 1982, 71. As Koester himself has frequently urged, however, after reviewing the canonical writings, including Q, researchers would do well to reconsider certain aspects of this other "apocryphal stuff." Possible sources beyond those already mentioned (before 320) include: (1) *Gospel of the Nazarenes;* (2) *Gospel of the Ebionites;* (3) *Gospel of the Hebrews;* (4) *Protevangelium of James* (22–24); (5) Pseudo-Clementines; (6) Justin Martyr (*Dial.* 49, 51); (7) *Exegesis on the Soul* (NH 2, 6.135.23); (8) *Gospel of the Egyptians* (NH 3, 2.65.23ff.); (9) *Second Treatise of the Great Seth* (NH 7, 2.63.34); (10) *Testimony of Truth* (NH 9, 3.30.24; 31.3; 39.24; 45.6, 12); (11) *Valentinian Exposition* (NH 11, 2b.41; 2c.42.11); (12) *Pistis Sophia* (7.7, 62, 133, 135); (13) *Opus imperfectum in Matthaeum.* Other possible sources (after 320) include: (14) Slavonic Josephus; see Eisler 1931; further, Kraeling (1951, 210 n. 16): "The 'Slavonic' Josephus is probably a Russian version of a Byzantine form of the extant Greek Jewish War enriched with materials from the Hebrew Josippon, Hegesippus and pious imagination"; Ernst 1989, 258–63; (15) Mandean Book of John or *Sidra d'Yahha;* see Mead 1924, 35–70; further, Webb 1991, 45; (16) Syriac *Life of John;* see Mingana 1927; (17) Zacharias apocrypha. See, further, Ernst 1989, 242–52.

6. For John the Baptist in Matthew (3:1–12, 13–17; 4:12; 9:14–17; 11:2–19; 14:3–12; 17:10–13; 21:23–27, 28–32), see Trilling 1959, 271–89; Wink 1968, 27–41; Bammel 1971–72, 101–4; Meier 1980; Ernst 1989, 155–85. For John the Baptist in Luke (1:5ff.; 3:1–18, 19–20; 4:25–26; 7:18–35; 9:54; 11:1; 16:16)-Acts (1:5, 22; 10:37; 11:16; 13:24–25; 18:24–28; 19:1–7), see Wink 1968, 42–86; Böcher 1979; Bachmann 1980; Ernst 1989, 81–154.

7. It would hardly be a sufficient response to invoke the specter of ongoing "oral" tradition or "other sources" in order to redeem from the creative fires of authorial invention the "special material" about John in either Matthew or Luke, as though in this fashion one could somehow alchemically convert such matter back into primary memory substance. By affirming the validity of the two-source hypothesis as the best available solution to the Synoptic problem, we necessarily acknowledge, it seems to me, that Matthew and Luke were certainly capable of and, indeed, in-

clined to create a larger narrative, on the basis of whatever they found before them, replete with enhanced cast and characters, including the figure of "John the Baptist."

8. If the Gospel of John is dependent in some fashion on the Synoptic Gospels, at least in this regard, the number of independent witnesses regarding John is reduced even further. See, for example, Crossan 1991, 234. Everything taken by Mason (1992, 167) to indicate the independence of the Fourth Gospel from the Synoptic traditions seems to me to support the opposite point of view (except for the reference to Jesus also baptizing). The controverted passage in Josephus is *Ant.* 18.116–19. Beyond the text-critical question whether or not the passage is a later Christian interpolation, the historical adequacy of its portrait of John is often doubted, though for reasons that tend primarily to betray the view of John otherwise held by the interpreter. See, for example, Koester (1982, 71): "Josephus suppresses the eschatological component of John's preaching"; Mason (1992, 179): "Josephus has a well-known tendency to suppress apocalyptic themes that he finds in his sources; inasmuch as those themes implied the end of the Roman order they were singularly unsuited to his readership and patrons." In addition to Josephus, Bammel (1971–72, 95) mentions Hegesippus (the early medieval Latin version of Josephus) and *Josippon* (the medieval Hebrew version of Josephus) as further sources, both of which are furthermore said by Bammel to be unhandicapped historically in portraying John through their lack of any association of him with the figure of Jesus. For an English translation of the text regarding John in *Josippon,* see Neuman 1950–51, 137–38. In the manuscript tradition of *Josippon,* John is variously called "John the High Priest," a rabbi, and, on one occasion, Rabban. In some texts, there is no mention of John having baptized. Neuman (1950–51, 143) argues against any direct dependence of *Josippon* where John is concerned on either Josephus or the New Testament, positing instead "the existence of a Jewish source common to both and to Josephus as well as the author of Hegesippus, each writing utilizing the account according to his pattern of thought."

9. For John the Baptist in Mark, see Wink 1968, 1–17; Bammel 1971–72, 96–99; Ernst 1989, 4–38. For John in John, see Glasson 1955–56; Boismard 1963; Wink 1968, 87–106; Payot 1969; Bammel 1971–72, 109–13; Linnemann 1973; Trocmé 1980; Ernst 1989, 186–96.

10. See Mark 6:25; 8:28; also 6:14; 11:30–33. This differs from both Q and the Gospel of John, neither of which ever refers to John as "the Baptist." Matthew (11:11, 12) and Luke (7:20, 33) both refer to John twice as the Baptist in Q contexts but never agree in doing so at the same place. The Gospel of John (1:25, 26, 28, 31, 33; 3:23; 10:40) does describe John as baptizing.

11. The reference in Mark 1:4 to John's "baptism of repentance for

forgiveness of sins" also contrasts notably with Paul's (lack of) discussion of these themes. Paul seldom speaks of repentance, and when he does, it is almost exclusively as the remorse felt after fraternal conflict (2 Cor 7:9, 10; 12:21; Rom 2:4) and never in relation to baptism. Paul never speaks of "forgiveness" (*aphesis*) of sins.

12. A few additional place-names are mentioned in connection with John. In John 1:28, John is said to have been baptizing in Bethany beyond the Jordan, and in 3:23 at Aenon near Salim. It is only regarding Jesus in relation to John that the Gospel of John (3:26; 4:1–2) provides the distinct recollection of Jesus also baptizing.

13. See Bammel (1971–72, 100): "For this reason the question posed by the disciples (Luke vii.18ff.) does not, in the eyes of the Q author, imply a doubt on the side of the master. It is to be taken as the normal form of inquiry with which someone who appears likely to be the *erchomenos* is faced. John figures therefore as the one who was not only able to sort out and comprehend Jesus but who was qualified to pose such a question. The Samuel motif is appearing in Q."

14. Mark 1:7–8; John 1:15, 26–27, 30–31, 32–33; Acts 1:4–5; 11:16; 13:25; 19:4; also *Pistis Sophia* 133. Though Crossan (1991, 440), an ardent advocate of this approach to the problem of the historical Jesus, sees only two instances of independent attestation in the present case, namely, Q 3:16–17 (including John and Acts) and Mark 1:7–8.

15. See the essay by Wendy Cotter, in this volume, p. 136.

16. Clear and perspicacious, but fundamentally flawed, is Mason's effort (1992, 170–74) to suggest that Q (3:16) spoke only of a coming baptism by fire. Cf. Moreland and Robinson 1993, 502.

17. The structural symmetry between 3:7b–9 and 3:16–17 (see below) could also be seen as a secondary redundancy, due to the conjunction of two originally independent units. On the other hand, such close symmetry is unlikely to have developed independently.

18. The only other possible mention of baptism would occur in 3:7a. Cf. Moreland and Robinson 1993, 501: *e[ip]en tois e[rch]omeno<i>s [ochlois] [epi to] baptis[ma] autou*, though I find this reconstruction unconvincing.

19. It would clearly be unreasonable to insist here on strictly botanical grounds that while a tree may preponderantly produce good or bad fruit, there is always inevitably a mixture of "wheat" and "chaff" on every stalk of grain.

20. Also observed by Jacobson 1992, 114.

21. In 7:18–23, though John is mentioned in 7:18 and a potentially hostile audience is implied in 7:23, it is nonetheless clearly the question of Jesus' specific identity that is of primary interest. In 7:24–28, though Jesus is presumably the speaker and a new group of "politically correct" persons associated with the kingdom of God is referred to in 7:28b, how

properly to characterize John is plainly the main concern. In 7:31–35, though both John and Jesus are described in some detail in the middle verses of this passage (7:33–34), the principal problem, as indicated in 7:31, is determining the best comparison for "this generation" (cf. Kloppenborg 1987a, 112). Hence the people of "this generation" are said to be first like children in the agora (7:32) and, then, to be unlike "children of Wisdom," by whom alone the paragon of true understanding is ultimately vindicated (7:35). The censured lot are, presumably, the same "brood of vipers" (*gennēmata echidnōn*) inveighed against in 3:7b, who falsely seek security in their inherited status as children of Abraham (3:8).

22. The form-critical debate about whether or not every *ēlthon* saying must be seen as an early Christian (church) creation versus being one of the *ipsissima verba Jesu* is irrelevant here, if only because in the present instance the historical Jesus' view of John is not in question but, rather, the shifting memory tradition of Q in this regard. For the "authenticity" of 7:33–34, see Backhaus 1991, 74–77. Strange, nonetheless, is the statement by Backhaus (1991, 76): "The *Deutewort* [7:33–34] as found in Q — versus the Lukan formulation of the saying — in no way implies a history-of-salvation look backward over the total work of John and Jesus but, rather, only illustrates an aspect of their work. Against this, one cannot refer to the retrospective view of the Q community, since it is possible that the Q community changed the original understanding of the saying without changing its wording."

23. Backhaus (1991, 81) refers to the description of Jesus in 7:34b as a *stereotype[r] Vorwurf* (stereotypical change), invoking Deut 21:18–21; Prov 23:20–21. This, however, is not an accurate characterization.

24. See Backhaus (1991, 80): "Characteristically, Jesus is understood on the basis of his difference from the Baptist: John is the measure whereby Jesus is evaluated, insofar as the *Deutewort* positively ascribes to Jesus the behavior that the Baptist renounced." Backhaus is mistaken, however, when he then writes: "The pair of participles [*esthion kai pinon*] that in itself is fully void of content, gains a certain contour only against the background of the Baptist's activity." For the moral connotations of "eating and drinking" in antiquity, see Malherbe 1989, 84–85.

25. See Backhaus (1991, 81): Jesus "is seen against the background of the Baptist movement; though not, in fact, as a member of it or as someone who earlier belonged to the Baptist circle but, rather, as an autonomous prophet alongside John; the parallel formulation with *erchestai* already attests to this. Both divine messengers are interpreted in terms of contrast, not dependence. They are active for the same cause and in the same mission, but with respect to their message and their appearance they are *ex origine* completely different."

26. See Witherington (1988, 240): "Now of course this is to a degree a caricature. John did eat and drink some things, and we have no evidence

that Jesus was famous for over-indulgence." The final statement, however, is itself also a caricature. For Jesus is remembered throughout the Synoptic tradition as having been quite a banqueter, a practice regularly celebrated by New Testament scholars as "the eschatological wedding joy of Jesus" (Backhaus 1991, 81) or some such inclusive virtue.

27. See Vassiliadis 1975, 407. Vassiliadis contrasts the egalitarian view of John and Jesus in 7:31–35 with their ranked description in 7:18–30.

28. For a more detailed analysis of the composition history of 7:31–35, in which 7:33–34 would constitute the primary unit of the passage and 7:31–32 and 7:35 would be both redactional "frames" together enveloping the contrasting characterizations of John and Jesus in 7:33–34, a construction developed at the same time that 7:18–35 was first composed, see Vaage 1991b, 109–13; further, Vaage 1994, 187 n. 13. I disagree at this point with Kloppenborg 1987a, 111–12, 115–17.

29. See Mark 1:6; 2:18. Backhaus (1991, 80) speaks of John's "penitential fasting," but there is no indication in Q that the (stratigraphically later) demand by John to produce "fruit worthy of repentance" (3:8) was in any way supposed to be achieved through his (earlier) restricted diet.

30. *Pace* Backhaus 1991, 80 n. 362, Foerster in his article on *daimon* (1964) never once cites this passage. Scobie (1964, 47) associates John's choice of the wilderness as the scene of his ministry with the charge laid against him that "he has a demon," noting that "the wilderness was looked upon as the home of evil spirits by some people" (see Leviticus 16; 4 Macc 18:8; Matt 12:43). On the basis of a reading of Mark 3:22 and the statement that Jesus "has Beelzebul" as meaning "actually has him under his power so that he can make him do as he wishes," Kraeling (1951, 12) claims: "The thought is not that John is possessed by a demon but that he has a demon under his control who must do as John tells him . . . to bring him food whenever he wished, quite as Aladdin could order the genie of the lamp to spread a meal before him at his pleasure."

31. See, for example, Bammel (1971–72, 126): "According to Luke vii.33 the Baptist was characterized by *daimonion echei*. In fact, it was against Jesus that such an accusation was raised [Mark 3:21ff.]. It is therefore difficult to understand the phrase as being just a derivation from historical data." In his entire book, Ernst never once even notes that such a thing was said of John, despite affirming in a (limited) discussion of Q 7:33: "It may be that historical remembrances are in play: there is evidence for the ascetical lifestyle of the Baptist in the Markan tradition (1:6; 2:18–20)" (see Ernst 1989, 76). Further, Schüling (1991, 87): "The trademark of the Baptist was elaborated [by the reference to his having a demon], in order to document the rejection of the eschatological proclamation by this generation." Cf. Lupieri (1988, 75 n. 53): "The antithetical contrast between the Baptist and the Nazarene is thereby complete, and the two phrases [7:33–34] are in perfect equilibrium with one

another; the accusation against both is a false charge. To the defamatory remarks about Jesus, however, a true statement has been added: 'friend of tax-collectors and sinners.' "

32. See, for example, Ernst 1989, 286–88. Scobie (1964, 134–41) provides a discussion of the nature of John's "asceticism," understood primarily as a question of fasting, but concludes: "While we do not rule out these possibilities, much the likeliest explanation is that John's motives must principally be understood in the light of the prevailing Jewish conception of fasting, namely that it expressed humiliation before God and symbolized repentance for sin" (pp. 139–40); further: "Neither John's rite of baptism, nor his practice of asceticism could be properly understood of themselves; they only made sense when they were related to his message" (p. 209).

33. For references, see Vaage 1994, 178 n. 6. One might also compare the description in Mark 1:6 of what John ostensibly did eat — "locusts and wild honey" — to the other well-known Cynic habit of ingesting uncooked or socially repugnant food. See, for example, Diog. Laert. 6.73, 77; Lucian, *Vit. auc.* 10.

34. See Diog. Laert. 6.54: *Sōkratēs mainomenos.* Cf. John 10:20: *Daimonion echei kai mainetai.*

35. Regarding *Gos. Thom.* 78=Q 7:24b–25, Cameron (1990, 44) writes: "It is Jesus who is the speaker; conceivably he or his followers are implicitly being characterized." According to Bammel (1971–72, 123 n. 2): "The Q speech [7:24bff.] is only loosely linked with the question of the Baptist (especially in sys of Matt. xi. 7). The speech, at least the beginning of it, with its allusions to the pilgrimage into the desert, would find its most natural location on the occasion of a similar event. Did the compiler of Q have such a location in mind?"

36. Whether or not the title "the Coming One" enjoyed messianic status in contemporary Judaism (see Uro 1991, 11), it is clearly employed in Q (3:16; 7:19) as an indicator of superlative status and in 7:22–23 is thought to be adequately confirmed by citing selected phrases from the book of Isaiah. Cf. Mal 3:1; Zech 9:9.

37. The final statement in 7:26b regarding John, *nai lego hymin kai perissoteron prophetou,* is regularly "underinterpreted" by scholars, whose primary model for characterizing John is otherwise precisely that of a prophet. See, for example, Backhaus (1991, 59): "Jesus...emphasizes agreement with his audience when he characterizes the Baptist as 'a prophet of a truly prophetic sort' [citing Heinz Schürmann] (Matt 11:9/ Luke 7:26; N.B. '*nai*')....At the same time, however, Jesus goes beyond this common judgment when he adds a '*maius*' to the dignity that has thus been affirmed. This '*maius*' must reside in the fact that for Jesus, the Baptist is the definitive end-time messenger, and his call to repentance the only message needed;...the Baptist breaks open the typical patterns

of thought of the Old Testament prophetic tradition; and if indeed Jesus here carries forward the people's judgment, the 'maius' can only be clarified in the light of the message of the *basileia*"; Ernst (1989, 62): "The saying [7:26] seeks to make clear that the Baptist cannot be made to fit into any existing category," only to conclude that "John understood himself as a prophet in the general sense, viz., God's prophet at the end of time" (p. 300); Witherington (1988, 235–36): "Jesus did not view John as just another in the long line of OT prophets, though he was certainly a prophet. He puts John not only in the prophetic category but in a higher one as well. This perhaps suggests that Jesus saw him as the last and great eschatological prophet.... In short, he saw him as having a definitive role unlike any previous prophet, for John was to have the task of preparing the people for the Coming One and his activity." One of the reasons for this curiously ambivalent and recurring interpretation is the continuing translation of the Greek particle *nai* in *nai lego hymin* as simply an affirmative reply to the preceding question, that is, as a declarative "yes," ignoring the problem created by its use here as part of the emphatic introductory formula, *nai lego hymin*. In Luke 11:51; 12:5, for example, the same particle in the same construction plainly has no independent meaning. See, further, Berger 1970, 9–12, esp. 10 n. 3; Weiss 1907, 313–15. Together with the immediately subsequent *kai* + the comparative, the rhetorical effect is essentially equivalent to the contestatory reply *nai alla* ("yes, but") found elsewhere in Greek literature.

38. Cf. Cameron (1990, 55–56): "The questions addressed by Jesus in Q 7:24–26 function as the statement of the opposite" in the chreia elaboration that Cameron proposes as the underlying logic of 7:18–35.

39. Hence the evident "containment strategies" in 7:27, 28b.

40. See Vaage 1994, 96–101. In 7:25, the opposition of John to Herod Antipas, as narrated in Mark 6:17–29, is sometimes thought to be implied. It was this conflict that especially marked the memory of John for many in antiquity. See, for example, Josephus (*Ant.* 18.116–19); further, *Josippon*, where John's execution is associated with Herod's killing of many of the sages of Israel. According to Neuman (1950–51, 140): "[T]he linking of John with the Jewish sages is attested by all the recensions of *Josippon*."

41. Vaage 1994, 101; further, Kraeling (1951, 16): "For John to live as he did and where he did, meant to separate himself from the normal, the safeguarded, the planned life of men. Such separation implies a profound disregard of and simultaneously also a deep revulsion against the established cultural order. For this reason, it cannot be casual in origin, but must have its roots in some bitter experience that turned him permanently aside from the normal course of human life."

42. Cf. Ernst (1989, 79): "The second set of sayings (Matt 11:2–6, 7–11 [12–13] par.) can hardly be unlocked with a single master key.

Recollections of historical occurrences, authentic sayings of Jesus on the greatness of the Baptist, and scribal elaborations and theological commentaries on the basis of subsequent experiences stand next to one another, and only with difficulty might they be reduced to a common denominator."

43. See above, p. 182. Backhaus (1991, 58) argues for the "authenticity" of 7:24b–26 (for other scholars who think similarly, see ibid., n. 205).

44. Together with 11:42c and 16:17, there are reasons to think that 7:27 may, in fact, be due to Q's tertiary redaction, that is, the same compositional stratum of the document responsible for the temptation narrative in Q (4:1–13), principally because of the use in this verse (7:27) of the citation formula, *gegraptai,* otherwise found in Q only in the temptation narrative (4:4, 8, 10), as well as the explicit citation of the LXX — actually, a conflation of Mal 3:1 and Exod 23:20 — again otherwise occurring only in Q 4:1–13. Cf. Cameron 1990, 56–57.

45. Its eventual meaning at the level of Q's redaction has already been discussed. See above, p. 191.

46. For the scholarly literature, see Vaage 1994, 184 n. 78; further, Backhaus 1991, 56 nn. 195, 200; also Witherington 1988, 235. Backhaus (1991, 56–57) thinks that both halves of 7:28 must always have formed a unity, and presents four main arguments, the last two of which identify non sequiturs in the tradition-historical reasoning opposed to his position, both of which objections have a certain validity. His first two arguments, however, beg the question. Most dubious is the statement: "Mt 11:11a/ Luke 7:28a can hardly have been transmitted alone, since without the second half of the saying it is just an all-too-trivial compliment without kerygmatic depth."

47. Cf. the descriptions of Enoch and Joseph in Sir 49:14–25.

48. See Ps-Diogenes, ep. 32; further, Diog. Laert. 6.32; Juvenal, *Sat.* 14.311–14.

Abbreviations

AB	Anchor Bible
BA	*Biblical Archaeologist*
BAGD	Bauer, Arndt, Gingrich, and Danker, *Greek-English Lexicon of the NT*
BASP	*Bulletin of the American Society of Papyrologists*
BBB	Bonner biblishe Beiträge
BETL	Bibliotheca ephemeridum theologicarum lovaniensium
Bib	*Biblica*
BJRL	*Bulletin of the John Rylands University Library*
BZ	*Biblische Zeitschrift*
BZNW	Beihefte zur Zeitschrift für die neutestamentliche Wissenschaft
ConBNT	Coniectanea biblica, New Testament
EKKNT	Evangelisch-katholischer Kommentar zum Neuen Testament
ExpT	*Expository Times*
FRLANT	Forschungen zur Religion und Literatur des Alten und Neuen Testaments
FzB	Forschung zur Bibel
G&R	*Greece and Rome*
GRBS	*Greek, Roman, and Byzantine Studies*
HSCP	*Harvard Studies in Classical Philology*
HTKNT	Herders theologischer Kommentar zum Neuen Testament
HTR	*Harvard Theological Review*
HTS	Harvard Theological Studies

HUCA	*Hebrew Union College Annual*
ICC	International Critical Commentary
IDB	*Interpreter's Dictionary of the Bible*
IDBSup	*Interpreter's Dictionary of the Bible, Supplement*
INJ	*Israel Numismatic Journal*
Int	*Interpretation*
JAAR	*Journal of the American Academy of Religion*
JBL	*Journal of Biblical Literature*
JJS	*Journal of Jewish Studies*
JR	*Journal of Religion*
JRS	*Journal of Roman Studies*
JSNTSup	Journal for the Study of the New Testament, Supplement series
JTS	*Journal of Theological Studies*
NovT	*Novum Testamentum*
NovTSup	Novum Testamentum, Supplements
NTAbh	Neutestamentliche Abhandlungen
NTS	*New Testament Studies*
QD	Quaestiones disputatae
RB	*Revue biblique*
RHPR	*Revue d'histoire et de philosophie religieuses*
SBLASP	Society of Biblical Literature Abstracts and Seminar Papers
SBLDS	Society of Biblical Literature Dissertation Series
SBLSBS	Society of Biblical Literature Sources for Biblical Study
SBLTT	Society of Biblical Literature Texts and Translations
SBS	Stuttgarter Bibelstudien
SBT	Studies in Biblical Theology
SJLA	Studies in Judaism in Late Antiquity
SNTSMS	Society for New Testament Studies Monograph Series

SNTU/A	*Studien zum Neuen Testament und seiner Umwelt, series A*
SR	*Studies in Religion/Sciences religieuses*
TDNT	*Theological Dictionary of the New Testament*
WMANT	Wissenschaftliche Monographien zum Alten und Neuen Testament
WUNT	Wissenschaftliche Untersuchungen zum Neuen Testament
ZDPV	*Zeitschrift des deutschen Palästina-Vereins*
ZNW	*Zeitschrift für die neutestamentliche Wissenschaft*
ZPE	*Zeitschrift für Papyrologie und Epigraphik*
ZTK	*Zeitschrift für Theologie und Kirche*

Works Cited

Aitken, Ellen B.
1992   "The Covenant Formulary in Q 6:20b–49." Paper presented
          at the one hundred twenty-eighth annual meeting of the
          Society of Biblical Literature, San Francisco, California.

Attridge, Harold W.
1989   *The Epistle to the Hebrews: A Commentary on the Epistle to
          the Hebrews.* Hermeneia. Philadelphia: Fortress.

Bachmann, M.
1980   "Johannes der Täufer bei Lukas: Nachzügler oder Vor-
          läufer?" Pp. 123–55 in *Wort in der Zeit: Festschrift K. H.
          Rengstorf.* Ed. W. Haubeck and M. Bachmann. Leiden:
          E. J. Brill.

Backhaus, Knut
1991   *Die "Jüngerkreise" des Täufers Johannes: Eine Studie zu
          den religionsgeschichtlichen Ursprüngen des Christentums.*
          Paderborner theologische Studien 19. Paderborn: Ferdinand
          Schöningh.

Bagnall, Roger S.
1989   "Official and Private Violence in Roman Egypt." *BASP*
          26:201–16.

Bain, David
1977   "Conventional Entrances." In *Actors and Audience: A Study
          of Asides and Related Conventions in Greek Drama.* Oxford
          Classical and Philosophical Monographs. Oxford: Oxford
          University Press.

Bammel, Ernst
1965   "John Did No Miracle: John 10:41." Pp. 179–202 in *Mira-
          cles.* Ed. C. F. D. Moule. London: A. R. Mowbray.
1971–72   "The Baptist in Early Christian Tradition." *NTS* 18:95–128.

Barley, Nigel
1972   "A Structural Approach to the Proverb." *Proverbium* 20:
          737–50.

Baroja, Julio Caro
1965   "A Historical Account of Several Conflicts." Pp. 79–137 in Peristiany 1965b.

Beardslee, William A.
1970   *Literary Criticism of the New Testament.* Guides to Biblical Scholarship. Philadelphia: Fortress.

Beare, F. W.
1962   *The Earliest Records of Jesus.* Oxford: Basil Blackwell.

Benveniste, Emile
1971   *Problems in General Linguistics.* Miami Linguistics Series 8. Coral Gables, Fla.: University of Miami Press.

Bergemann, Thomas
1993   *Q auf dem Prüfstand: Die Zuordnung des Mt/Lk-Stoffes zu Q am Beispiel der Bergpredigt.* FRLANT 158. Göttingen: Vandenhoeck & Ruprecht.

Berger, Klaus
1970   *Die Amen-Worte Jesu: Eine Untersuchungen zum Problem der Legitimation in apokalyptischen Rede.* BZNW 39. Berlin: Walter de Gruyter.
1984   "Hellenistische Gattungen im Neuen Testament." Pp. 1031–1432 in *Aufstieg und Niedergang der römischen Welt.* Teil 2: *Principat.* Ed. Hildegard Temporini and Wolfgang Haase. Vol. 25.2. Berlin and New York: Walter de Gruyter.

Betz, Hans Dieter
1979   *Galatians: A Commentary on Paul's Letter to the Churches in Galatia.* Hermeneia. Philadelphia: Fortress.
1985a   "The Beatitudes of the Sermon on the Mount (Matt. 5:3–12): Observations on Their Literary Form and Theological Significance." Pp. 17–39 in Betz 1985c.
1985b   "Eschatology in the Sermon on the Mount and the Sermon on the Plain." Pp. 343–50 in *Society of Biblical Literature 1985 Seminar Papers.* Ed. Kent H. Richards. SBLASP 24. Atlanta: Scholars Press.
1985c   *Essays on the Sermon on the Mount.* Philadelphia: Fortress.
1990   "The Sermon on the Mount and Q: Some Aspects of the Problem." Pp. 19–34 in *Gospel Origins and Christian Beginnings: In Honor of James M. Robinson.* Ed. James E. Goehring et al. Sonoma, Calif.: Polebridge.

Bieber, Margarete
1961   *The History of the Greek and Roman Theater.* 2d ed.
         Princeton, N.J.: Princeton University Press.

Bitzer, Lloyd F.
1968   "The Rhetorical Situation." *Philosophy and Rhetoric* 1:1–14.

Bjorndahl, Sterling G.
1988   "Promoting the Undivided: A Chreia Elaboration in *Thomas*
         61–67." Paper presented at the one hundred twenty-fourth
         annual meeting of the Society of Biblical Literature (Nag
         Hammadi Section), Chicago.

Böcher, O.
1979   "Lukas und Johannes der Täufer." *SNTU/A* 4:27–44.

Boismard, Marie-Emile
1963   "Les traditions johanniques concernant le Baptiste." *RB*
         70:5–42.

Booth, Alan D.
1980   "Aspects of the *Circulator* by Persius and Horace." *G&R*
         26:166–69.

Bornkamm, Günther, Heinz Joachim Held, and Gerhard Barth
1960   *Überlieferung und Auslegung im Matthäusevangelium.*
         WMANT 1. Neukirchen-Vluyn: Neukirchener Verlag.

Bourdieu, Pierre
1965   "The Sentiment of Honour in Kabyle Society." Pp. 191–241
         in Peristiany 1965b.

Brown, Peter
1971   "The Rise and Function of the Holy Man in Late Antiquity."
         JRS 61:80–100.
1976   "Town, Village and Holy Man: The Case of Syria." Pp. 213–
         20 in *Assimilation et résistance à la culture gréco-romaine
         dans le monde ancien.* Ed. D. M. Pippidi. Bucharest: Editura
         Acadeimi.
1982   *Society and the Holy in Late Antiquity.* Berkeley: University
         of California Press.

Bultmann, Rudolf K.
1962   "The Study of the Synoptic Gospels." Pp. 11–76 in *Form
         Criticism: Two Essays on New Testament Research.* Ed. Ru-
         dolf K. Bultmann and Karl Kundsin. New York: Harper
         & Row.

1968   *The History of the Synoptic Tradition.* Rev. ed. Oxford: Basil Blackwell.

Bultmann, Rudolf K., and Karl Kundsin
1962   *Form Criticism.* New York: Harper & Bros.

Butts, James R.
1987   "The Voyage of Discipleship: Narrative, Chreia, and Call Story." Pp. 199–219 in *Early Jewish and Christian Exegesis: Studies in Memory of William Hugh Brownlee.* Ed. Craig A. Evans and William F. Stinespring. Atlanta: Scholars Press.

Cairns, Francis
1972   *Generic Composition in Greek and Roman Poetry.* Edinburgh: Edinburgh University Press.

Cameron, Ron
1984   *Sayings Traditions in the Apocryphon of James.* HTS 34. Philadelphia: Fortress.
1990   " 'What Have You Come Out to See?' Characterizations of John and Jesus in the Gospels." Pp. 35–69 in *The Apocryphal Jesus and Christian Origins* = *Semeia* 49. Ed. Ron Cameron. Atlanta: Scholars Press.

Campbell, J. K.
1965   "Honour and the Devil." Pp. 139–70 in Peristiany 1965b.

Castor, George DeWitt
1912   *Matthew's Sayings of Jesus: The Non-Marcan Common Source of Matthew and Luke.* Chicago: University of Chicago Press.

Catchpole, David R.
1993   *The Quest for Q.* Edinburgh: T. & T. Clark.

Cohen, D.
1991   "Sexuality, Violence, and the Athenian Law of *Hubris.*" *G&R* 38:171–88.

Collins, Adela Yarbro
1989   "The Son of Man Sayings in the Sayings Source." Pp. 369–89 in *To Touch the Text: Biblical and Related Studies in Honor of Joseph A. Fitzmyer, S.J.* Ed. Morna P. Horgan and Paul J. Kobelski. New York: Crossroad.

Collins, John J.
1993   "Wisdom, Apocalypticism, and Generic Compatibility." Pp. 165–85 in *In Search of Wisdom: Essays in Memory of John G. Gammie.* Ed. Leo G. Perdue et al. Louisville: Westminster/John Knox.

Cotter, Wendy
  1987   "The Parable of the Children in the Market Place, Q (Lk) 7:31–35: An Examination of the Parable's Image and Significance." *NovT* 29:289–304.
  1989   "Children Sitting in the Agora: Q (Luke) 7:31–35." *Forum* 5/2:63–82.
  1995   "Prestige, Protection and Promise: A Proposal for the Apologetics of Q2." Pp. 117–38 in Piper 1995.

Crossan, John Dominic
  1983   *In Fragments: The Aphorisms of Jesus.* San Francisco: Harper & Row.
  1987   "Tradition in the Formation of Q." Paper presented at the one hundred twenty-third annual meeting of the Society of Biblical Literature (Q Seminar), Boston.
  1991   *The Historical Jesus: The Life of a Mediterranean Jewish Peasant.* San Francisco: Harper & Row.

Crum, J. M. C.
  1927   *The Original Jerusalem Gospel: Being Essays on the Document Q.* London: Constable & Constable.

Dalman, Gustaf Hermann
  1924   *Orte und Wege Jesu.* 3d ed. Gütersloh: Bertelsmann.

Davies, William D., and Dale C. Allison
  1988   *A Critical and Exegetical Commentary on Matthew I–VII.* ICC. Edinburgh: T. & T. Clark.

Deatrick, Eugene P.
  1962   "Salt, Soil, Savior." *BA* 25:41–48.

Delobel, Joël, ed.
  1982   *Logia: Les paroles de Jésus — The Sayings of Jesus: Mémorial Joseph Coppens.* BETL 59. Leuven: Uitgeverij Peeters and Leuven University Press.

Denich, B. S.
  1974   "Sex and Power in the Balkans." Pp. 243–62 in *Woman, Culture, and Society.* Ed. Michelle Zimbalist Rosaldo et al. Stanford, Calif.: Stanford University Press.

Derrett, J. Duncan M.
  1982   "Law and Society in Jesus' World." Pp. 477–564 in *Aufstieg und Niedergang der römischen Welt.* Teil 2: *Principat.* Ed. Hildegard Temporini and Wolfgang Haase. Vol. 25.1. Berlin and New York: Walter de Gruyter.

Dibelius, Martin
1935   *From Tradition to Gospel.* New York: Charles Scribner's Sons.

Downing, F. Gerald
1985   "Ears to Hear." Pp. 97–121 in *Alternative Approaches to New Testament Study.* Ed. A. E. Harvey. London: SPCK.
1988a   *Christ and the Cynics: Jesus and Other Radical Preachers in First-Century Tradition.* JSOT Manuals 4. Sheffield, England: JSOT Press.
1988b   "Quite Like Q: A Genre for 'Q': The 'Lives' of Cynic Philosophers." *Bib* 69:196–225.

Downs, Roger M., and James T. Meyer
1978   "Geography and the Mind: An Exploration of Perceptual Geography." *American Behavioral Scientist* 22:59–77.

Downs, Roger M., and David Stea
1973   "Cognitive Maps and Spatial Behavior: Process and Products." Pp. 8–26 in *Image and Environment: Cognitive Mapping and Spatial Behavior.* Ed. Roger M. Downs and David Stea. Chicago: Aldine.

Draper, Jonathan A.
1995   "Social Ambiguity and the Production of Text: Prophets, Teachers, Bishops, and Deacons and the Tradition of the Community of the 'Didache.'" Pp. 284–312 in *The "Didache" in Context: Essays on Its Text, History, and Transmission.* Ed. Clayton N. Jefford. NovTSup 57. Leiden: E. J. Brill.

DuBoulay, J., and R. Williams
1987   "Amoral Familism and the Image of Limited Good: A Critique from a European Perspective." *Anthropological Quarterly* 60:12–21.

Duckworth, George E.
1952   *The Nature of Roman Comedy: A Study in Popular Entertainment.* Princeton, N.J.: Princeton University Press.

Edwards, Douglas R.
1988   "First Century Urban/Rural Relations in Lower Galilee: Exploring the Archaeological and Literary Evidence." Pp. 169–82 in *Society of Biblical Literature 1988 Seminar Papers.* Ed. David Lull. SBLASP 27. Atlanta: Scholars Press.
1992   "The Socio-Economic and Cultural Ethos of the Lower Galilee in the First Century: Implications for the Nascent Jesus Movement." Pp. 53–74 in *The Galilee in Late Antiquity.*

Ed. Lee I. Levine. New York: Jewish Theological Seminary of America.

Edwards, Richard A.
1976   *A Theology of Q.* Philadelphia: Fortress.

Eisler, Robert
1931   *The Messiah Jesus and John the Baptist.* London: Methuen.

Ernst, Josef
1989   *Johannes der Täufer: Interpretation — Geschichte — Wirkungsgeschichte.* BZNW 53. Berlin: Walter de Gruyter.

Farmer, William R.
1962   "John the Baptist." *IDB* 2:955–62.

Fischel, Henry A.
1968   "Studies in Cynicism and the Ancient Near East: The Transformation of a Chreia." Pp. 372–411 in *Religions in Antiquity: Essays in Memory of Erwin Ransdall Goodenough.* Ed. Jacob Neusner. Leiden: E. J. Brill.

Fish, Stanley
1990   "Rhetoric." Pp. 203–22 in *Critical Terms for Literary Study.* Ed. Frank Lentricchia and Thomas McLaughlin. Chicago: University of Chicago Press.

Fisher, Nicholas R. E.
1976   "Hybris and Dishonour I." *G&R* 23:177–93.
1979   "Hybris and Dishonour II." *G&R* 26:32–47.

Fitzmyer, Joseph A.
1981   *The Gospel according to Luke I–IX.* AB 28. Garden City, N.Y.: Doubleday.

Foerster, Werner
1964   "*Daimōn, Daimonion.*" TDNT 2:1–20.

Foster, George M.
1965   "Peasant Society and the Image of Limited Good." *American Anthropologist* 67:293–315.
1975   "Response to 'Image of Limited Good, or Expectation of Reciprocity?'" *Current Anthropology* 16:86–87.

Freyne, Sean
1980   *Galilee from Alexander the Great to Hadrian, 323 B.C.E. to 135 C.E.: A Study of Second Temple Judaism.* Wilmington, Del.: Michael Glazier.

Gagarin, D.
1979   "The Athenian Law against *Hybris.*" Pp. 229–36 in *Ark-touros: Hellenic Studies Presented to Bernard M. W. Knox on the Occasion of His 65th Birthday.* Ed. G. W. Bowersock et al. Berlin and New York: Walter de Gruyter.

Gal, Zvi
1992   *Lower Galilee during the Iron Age.* Dissertation series, American Schools of Oriental Research 8. Winona Lake, Ind.: Eisenbrauns.

Garnsey, Peter
1988   *Famine and Food Supply in the Graeco-Roman World: Responses to Risk and Crisis.* Cambridge: Cambridge University Press.

Gilmore, David D., ed.
1987   *Honor and Shame and the Unity of the Mediterranean.* A Special Publication of the American Anthropological Association 22. Washington, D.C.: American Anthropological Association.

Glasson, Thomas F.
1955–56 "John the Baptist in the Fourth Gospel." *ExpT* 67:245–46.

Goodman, Martin
1983   "The First Jewish Revolt: Social Conflict and the Problem of Debt." Pp. 417–27 in *Essays in Honour of Yigael Yadin.* Ed. G. Vermes and Jacob Neusner = *JJS* 33 (1982). Totawa, N.J.: Allanheld Osmus.

Goody, Jack
1986   *The Logic of Writing and the Organization of Society.* Studies in Literacy, Family, Culture, and the State. Cambridge and New York: Cambridge University Press.

Gould, Peter R., and Rodney White
1974   *Mental Maps.* Pelican Geography and Environmental Studies. Harmondsworth, England: Penguin.

Gregory, James R.
1975   "Image of Limited Good, or Expectation of Reciprocity?" *Current Anthropology* 16:73–92.

Guéraud, Octave
1931   *Enteuxeis: Requêtes et plaintes addressées au roi d'Égypte au IIIe siècle avant J. C.* Publications de la Société Royal Égyptienne de Payrologie. Textes et document 1. Cairo: Imprimerie de l'institut français d'archéologie orientale.

Gundry, Robert H.
1982   *Matthew: A Commentary on His Literary and Theological Art.* Grand Rapids, Mich.: Wm. B. Eerdmans.

Harnack, Adolf von
1907   *Sprüche und Reden Jesu: Die zweite Quelle des Matthäus und Lukas.* Beiträge zur Einleitung in das Neue Testament 2. Leipzig: J. C. Hinrichs.
1908   *The Sayings of Jesus: The Second Source of St. Matthew and St. Luke.* New Testament Studies 2. London: Williams & Norgate; New York: G. P. Putnam's Sons.

Harris, William V.
1989   *Ancient Literacy.* Cambridge, Mass.: Harvard University Press.

Hartin, Patrick J.
1991   *James and the "Q" Sayings of Jesus.* JSNTSup 47. Sheffield, England: Sheffield Academic Press.

Havener, Ivan
1987   *Q: The Sayings of Jesus.* Good News Studies 19. Wilmington, Del.: Michael Glazier.

Hengel, Martin
1968   "Das Gleichnis von den bösen Weingärtnern, Mc 12:1–12 im Lichte des Zenonpapyri und der rabbinischen Gleichnisse." *ZNW* 59:1–39.

Herntrich, Volkmar
1965   "*Krinō.*" *TDNT* 3:923–32.

Hock, Ronald F., and Edward N. O'Neil
1986   *The Chreia in Ancient Rhetoric.* Vol. 1: *The Progymnasmata.* SBLTT 27; Graeco-Roman Religion Series 9. Atlanta: Scholars Press.

Hoffmann, Paul
1969a   "Die Anfänge der Theologie in der Logienquelle." Pp. 134–52 in *Gestalt und Anspruch des Neuen Testaments.* Ed. Josef Schreiner. Würzburg: Echter.
1969b   "Die Versuchungsgeschichte in der Logienquelle." *BZ,* n.s. 13:207–23.
1970a   "Jesusverkündigung in der Logienquelle." Pp. 50–70 in *Jesus in den Evangelien.* Ed. Josef Blinzler and Wilhelm Pesch. SBS 45. Stuttgart: Verlag Katholisches Bibelwerk.
1970b   "Die Offenbarung des Sohnes: Die apokalyptischen Voraussetzungen und ihre Verarbeitung im Q-Logion Mt 11, 27 par Lk 10, 22." *Kairos* 12:270–88.

1971   "Lk 10, 5–11 in der Instruktionsreden der Logienquelle."
        Pp. 37–53 in *Evangelisch-Katholisches Kommentar zum
        Neuen Testament*. Vorarbeiten 3. Zurich: Benziger Verlag;
        Neukirchen-Vluyn: Neukirchener Verlag.

1972   *Studien zur Theologie der Logienquelle*. NTAbh, NF 8.
        Münster: Verlag Aschendorff.

1984   "Tradition und Situation: Zur 'Verbindlichkeit' des Gebots
        der Feindesliebe in der synoptischen Überlieferung und in der
        gegenwärtigen Friedensdiskussion." Pp. 50–117 in *Ethik im
        Neuen Testament*. Ed. Karl Kertelge. QD 102. Freiburg im
        Breisgau: Herder.

Horsley, Richard A.

1985   "Ethics and Exegesis: 'Love Your Enemies' and the Doctrine
        of Non-violence." *JAAR* 54:3–31.

1987   *Jesus and the Spiral of Violence: Popular Jewish Resistance in
        Roman Palestine*. San Francisco: Harper & Row.

1989a   "Questions about Redactional Strata and the Social Relations
        Reflected in Q." Pp. 186–203 in *Society of Biblical Literature
        1989 Seminar Papers*. Ed. David Lull. SBLASP 28. Atlanta:
        Scholars Press.

1989b   *Sociology and the Jesus Movement*. New York: Crossroad.

1991a   "Logoi Prophētōn: Reflections on the Genre of Q." Pp. 195–
        209 in *The Future of Early Christianity: Essays in Honor of
        Helmut Koester*. Ed. Birger Pearson. Minneapolis: Fortress.

1991b   "Q and Jesus: Assumptions, Approaches, and Analyses."
        Pp. 175–209 in *Early Christianity, Q and Jesus = Semeia
        55*. Ed. John S. Kloppenborg with Leif E. Vaage. Atlanta:
        Scholars Press.

1991c   "The Q People: Renovation, not Radicalism." *Continuum*
        1:49–63.

1992   "Response to Walter Wink: 'Neither Passivity nor Violence:
        Jesus' Third Way.'" Pp. 126–32 in Swartley 1992.

Jacobson, Arland D.

1978   "Wisdom Christology in Q." Ph.D. diss., Claremont Gradu-
        ate School.

1982   "The Literary Unity of Q." *JBL* 101:365–89.

1990   "Proverbs and Social Control: A New Paradigm for Wisdom
        Studies." Pp. 75–88 in *Gnosticism and the Early Chris-
        tian World: In Honor of James M. Robinson*. Ed. James E.
        Goehring et al. Sonoma, Calif.: Polebridge.

1992   *The First Gospel: An Introduction to Q*. Foundations and
        Facets: Reference series. Sonoma, Calif.: Polebridge.

Jeremias, Joachim
1958   *Jesus' Promise to the Nations.* SBT 1/24. London: SCM.
1966   *Abba.* Göttingen: Vandenhoeck & Ruprecht.

Kelber, Werner H.
1983   *The Oral and the Written Gospel: The Hermeneutics of Speaking and Writing in the Synoptic Tradition, Mark, Paul, and Q.* Philadelphia: Fortress.

Kennedy, George A.
1984   *New Testament Interpretation through Rhetorical Criticism.* Chapel Hill: University of North Carolina Press.

Kindermann, Heinz
1979   *Das Theaterpublikum der Antike.* Salzburg: Otto Müller.

Klassen, William
1992   " 'Love Your Enemies': Some Reflections on the Current Status of Research." Pp. 1–31 in Swartley 1992.

Kloppenborg, John S.
1987a   *The Formation of Q: Trajectories in Ancient Wisdom Collections.* Studies in Antiquity and Christianity. Philadelphia: Fortress.
1987b   "Symbolic Eschatology and the Apocalypticism of Q." *HTR* 80:287–306.
1988   *Q Parallels: Synopsis, Critical Notes, & Concordance.* Foundations and Facets: New Testament. Sonoma, Calif.: Polebridge.
1989   "*The Formation of Q* Revisited: A Response to Richard Horsley." Pp. 204–15 in *Society of Biblical Literature 1989 Seminar Papers.* Ed. David E. Lull. SBLASP 28. Atlanta: Scholars Press.
1990a   "City and Wasteland: Narrative World and the Beginning of the Sayings Gospel (Q)." Pp. 145–60 in *How Gospels Begin* = *Semeia* 52. Ed. Dennis E. Smith. Atlanta: Scholars Press.
1990b   " 'Easter Faith' and the Sayings Gospel Q." Pp. 71–99 in *The Apocryphal Jesus and Christian Origins* = *Semeia* 49. Ed. Ron Cameron. Atlanta: Scholars Press.
1990c   "Nomos and Ethos in Q." Pp. 35–48 in *Gospel Origins and Christian Beginnings: In Honor of James M. Robinson.* Ed. James E. Goehring et al. Sonoma, Calif.: Polebridge.
1990d   "The Sayings Gospel Q: Translation and Notes." Pp. 35–74 in John S. Kloppenborg et al., *Q Thomas Reader.* Sonoma, Calif.: Polebridge.
1991   "Literary Convention, Self-Evidence, and the Social History of the Q People." Pp. 77–102 in *Early Christianity, Q and*

Jesus = Semeia 55. Ed. John S. Kloppenborg with Leif E. Vaage. Atlanta: Scholars Press.

1993   "The Sayings Gospel Q: Recent Opinion on the People behind the Document." *Currents in Research: Biblical Studies* 1:9–34.

1994   Ed. *The Shape of Q: Signal Essays on the Sayings Gospel.* Minneapolis: Fortress.

1995a   "Jesus and the Parables of Jesus in Q." Pp. 275–319 in Piper 1995.

1995b   "The Sayings Gospel Q: Literary and Stratigraphic Problems." Forthcoming in *Aufstieg und Niedergang der römischen Welt.* Teil 2: *Principat.* Ed. Hildegard Temporini and Wolfgang Haase. Vol. 25.6. Berlin and New York: Walter de Gruyter.

Koester, Helmut

1982   *Introduction to the New Testament.* Vol. 2: *History and Literature of Early Christianity.* Hermeneia: Foundations & Facets. Philadelphia: Fortress.

1990   *Ancient Christian Gospels: Their History and Development.* Philadelphia: Trinity Press International; London: SCM.

Kraeling, Carl H.

1951   *John the Baptist.* New York: Charles Scribner's Sons.

Laufen, Rudolf

1980   *Die Doppelüberlieferungen der Logienquelle und des Markusevangeliums.* BBB 54. Konigstein: Peter Hanstein.

Lausberg, Heinrich

1973   *Handbuch der literarischen Rhetorik: Eine Grundlegung der Literaturwissenschaft.* 2d ed. Munich: Max Hueber.

Layton, Bentley

1968   "The Sources, Date and Transmission of *Didache* 1.3b–2.1." *HTR* 61:343–83.

Linnemann, Eta

1973   "Jesus und der Täufer." Pp. 219–36 in *Festschrift für Ernst Fuchs.* Tübingen: J. C. B. Mohr (Paul Siebeck).

Llewelyn, S. R.

1992   *New Documents Illustrating Early Christianity.* Vol. 6: *Inscriptions and Papyri First Published in 1980–81.* North Ryde, Australia: Macquarie University.

Lowenthal, David, and Martyn John Bowden, ed.
1976   *Geographies of the Mind: Essays in Historical Geosophy in Honor of John Kirtland Wright.* New York: Oxford University Press.

Lucas, F. L.
1923   *Euripides and His Influence.* Boston: Marshall Jones.

Lührmann, Dieter
1969   *Die Redaktion der Logienquelle.* WMANT 33. Neukirchen-Vluyn: Neukirchener Verlag.
1972   "Liebet eure Feinde (Lk 6, 27–36/Mt 5, 39–48)." *ZTK* 69:412–38.
1994   "Q in the History of Early Christianity." Pp. 59–73 in Kloppenborg 1994.

Lupieri, Edmondo
1988   *Giovanni Battista fra storia e leggenda.* Brescia: Paideia.

Luz, Ulrich
1985–90 *Das Evangelium nach Matthäus.* EKKNT 1/1–2. Zurich: Benziger Verlag; Neukirchen-Vluyn: Neukirchener Verlag.
1989   *Matthew 1–7.* Minneapolis: Augsburg.

Lynch, Kevin
1960   *The Image of the City.* Publications of the Joint Center for Urban Studies. Cambridge, Mass.: Technology Press.
1973   "Some References to Orientation." Pp. 300–315 in *Image and Environment: Cognitive Mapping and Spatial Behavior.* Ed. Roger M. Downs and David Stea. Chicago: Aldine.

McCloskey, Donald N.
1982   *The Rhetoric of Economics.* Rhetoric of the Human Sciences. Canberra, Australia: Australian National University.

McCown, C. C.
1938   "The Geography of Luke's Central Section." *JBL* 57:51–66.
1940   "The Scene of John's Ministry and Its Relation to the Purpose and Outcome of His Mission." *JBL* 59:113–31.
1941   "Gospel Geography: Fiction, Fact, and Truth." *JBL* 60:1–25.

MacDowell, D.
1976   "*Hybris* in Athens." *G&R* 23:14–31.

Mack, Burton L.
1970   "Wisdom Myth and Myth-ology: An Essay in Understanding a Theological Tradition." *Int* 24:46–60.

1987   *Anecdotes and Arguments: The Chreia in Antiquity and Early Christianity.* Institute for Antiquity and Christianity: Occasional Papers. Claremont, Calif.: Institute for Antiquity and Christianity.

1988a   "The Kingdom That Didn't Come: A Social History of the Q Tradents." Pp. 608–35 in *Society of Biblical Literature 1988 Seminar Papers.* Ed. David J. Lull. SBLASP 27. Atlanta: Scholars Press.

1988b   *A Myth of Innocence: Mark and Christian Origins.* Philadelphia: Fortress.

1990   *Rhetoric and the New Testament.* Guides to Biblical Scholarship. Minneapolis: Fortress.

1993   *The Lost Gospel: The Book of Q & Christian Origins.* San Francisco: HarperSanFrancisco.

Mack, Burton L., and Edward N. O'Neil
1986   "The Chreia Discussion of Hermogenes of Tarsus." Pp. 153–81 in *The Chreia in Ancient Rhetoric.* Vol. 1: *The Progymnasmata.* Ed. Ronald F. Hock and Edward N. O'Neil. SBLTT 27; Graeco-Roman Religion Series 9. Atlanta: Scholars Press.

Mack, Burton L., and Vernon K. Robbins
1989   *Patterns of Persuasion in the Gospels.* Foundations & Facets: Literary Facets. Sonoma, Calif.: Polebridge.

MacMullen, Ramsay
1974   *Roman Social Relations, 50 B.C. to A.D. 284.* New Haven: Yale University Press.

Malbon, Elizabeth Struthers
1986   *Narrative Space and Mythic Meaning in Mark.* San Francisco: Harper & Row.

Malherbe, Abraham J.
1986   *Moral Exhortation: A Greco-Roman Sourcebook.* Library of Early Christianity 4. Philadelphia: Westminster.

1989   *Paul and the Popular Philosophers.* Minneapolis: Fortress.

Malina, Bruce J.
1981   *The New Testament World: Insights from Cultural Anthropology.* Atlanta: John Knox.

Manson, T. W.
1949   *The Sayings of Jesus.* London: SCM.

März, Claus-Peter
1985   " 'Feuer auf die Erde zu werfen bin ich gekommen': Zum Verständnis und zur Entstehung von Lk 12, 49." Pp. 479–

511 in *A cause de l'évangile: Mélanges offerts à Dom Jacques Dupont*. Lectio divina 123. Paris: Editions du Cerf.

Mason, Steve N.
1992   "Fire, Water, and Spirit: John the Baptist and the Tyranny of Canon." *SR* 21:163–80.

Mead, George R. S.
1924   *The Gnostic, John the Baptizer*. London: Watkins.

Meier, John P.
1980   "John the Baptist in Matthew's Gospel." *JBL* 99:383–405.

Meshorer, Ya'akov
1986   "The Lead Weight." *BA* 49:16–17.

Mingana, Alphonse
1927   "Woodbrooke Studies." *BJRL* 11:438–89.

Moessner, David P.
1989   *Lord of the Banquet: The Literary and Theological Significance of the Lukan Travel Narrative*. Minneapolis: Fortress.

Moreland, Milton C., and James M. Robinson
1993   "The International Q Project Work Sessions 31 July–2 August, 20 November 1992." *JBL* 112:500–506.

Moulton, James Hope, with Wilbert Francis Howard and Nigel Turner
1963–85 *A Grammar of New Testament Greek*. 4 vols. Edinburgh: T. & T. Clark.

Mullins, Terrence Y.
1980   "Topos as a NT Form." *JBL* 99:541–47.

Neirynck, Frans
1982   "Recent Developments in the Study of Q." Pp. 29–75 in Delobel 1982.

Neuman, Abraham A.
1950–51 "A Note on John the Baptist and Jesus in *Josippon*." *HUCA* 23:137–49.

Neusner, Jacob
1976   " 'First Cleanse the Inside': The Halakic Background of a Controversy Saying." *NTS* 22:486–95.

Oakman, Douglas E.
1991   "The Countryside in Luke-Acts." Pp. 151–79 in *The Social World of Luke-Acts: Models for Interpretation*. Ed. Jerome H. Neyrey. Peabody, Mass.: Hendrickson.

Payot, C.
1969   "L'interprétation johannique du ministère de Jean Baptiste."
         Foi et Vie 68:21–37.

Percy, Ernst
1953   *Die Botschaft Jesu.* Lunds Universitets Arsskrift, NF 1/49,
         no. 5. Lund: C. W. K. Gleerup.

Perdue, Leo G.
1986   "The Wisdom Sayings of Jesus." *Forum* 2/3:3–35.

Perelman, Chaim, and Lucie Olbrechts-Tyteca
1969   *The New Rhetoric: A Treatise on Argumentation.* Notre
         Dame, Ind.: University of Notre Dame Press.

Peristiany, Jean G.
1965a   "Honour and Shame in a Cypriot Highland Village."
         Pp. 171–90 in Peristiany 1965b.
1965b   Ed. *Honour and Shame: The Values of Mediterranean Society.*
         London: Weidenfeld & Nicholson.
1965c   "Introduction." Pp. 9–18 in Peristiany 1965b.

Piper, John
1979   *Love Your Enemies: Jesus' Love Command in the Synoptic
         Gospels and in the Early Christian Paraenesis.* SNTSMS 38.
         Cambridge: Cambridge University Press.

Piper, Ronald A.
1982   "Matthew 7, 7–11 Par. Lk 11, 9–13: Evidence of Design and
         Argument in the Collection of Jesus' Sayings." Pp. 411–18 in
         Delobel 1982.
1989   *Wisdom in the Q-Tradition: The Aphoristic Teaching of
         Jesus.* SNTSMS 61. Cambridge and New York: Cambridge
         University Press.
1994   "Matthew 7:7–11 par. Luke 11:9–13: Evidence of Design and
         Argument in the Collection of Jesus' Sayings." Pp. 131–37 in
         Kloppenborg 1994.
1995   Ed. *The Gospel behind the Gospels: Current Studies on Q.*
         Leiden: E. J. Brill.

Pitt-Rivers, Julian Alfred
1965   "Honour and Social Status." Pp. 21–77 in Peristiany 1965b.

Polag, Athanasius
1979   *Fragmenta Q: Textheft zur Logienquelle.* Neukirchen-Vluyn:
         Neukirchener Verlag.

Potter, Jack M., May N. Dias, and George M. Foster, eds.
1967   *Peasant Society: A Reader.* Boston: Little, Brown & Co.

Qedar, S.
1986–87 "Two Lead Weights of Herod Antipas and Agrippa II and the Early History of Tiberias." *INJ* 9:29–35, plates 4–5.

Redfield, Robert
1965   *Peasant Society and Culture: An Anthropological Approach to Civilization.* Chicago: University of Chicago Press.

Reed, Jonathan
1992   *The Population of Capernaum.* Institute for Antiquity and Christianity, Occasional Papers 24. Claremont, Calif.: Institute for Antiquity and Christianity.
1994a   "Places in Early Christianity: Galilee, Archaeology, Urbanization, and Q." Ph.D. diss., Claremont Graduate School.
1994b   "Populations, Numbers, Urbanization, and Economics: Galilean Archaeology and the Historical Jesus." Pp. 203–19 in *Society of Biblical Literature 1994 Seminar Papers.* Ed. Eugene H. Lovering. SBLASP 34. Atlanta: Scholars Press.

Rhoads, David M., and Donald M. Michie
1982   *Mark as Story: An Introduction to the Narrative of a Gospel.* Philadelphia: Fortress.

Robbins, Vernon K.
1985   "Pragmatic Relations as a Criterion for Authentic Sayings." *Forum* 1/3:35–63.
1988   "The Chreia." Pp. 1–23 in *Greco-Roman Literature and the New Testament: Selected Forms and Genres.* Ed. David E. Aune. SBLSBS 21. Atlanta: Scholars Press.

Robertson, Archibald T.
1914   *A Grammar of the Greek New Testament in the Light of Historical Research.* New York: Hodder & Stoughton.

Robinson, James M.
1964   "LOGOI SOPHŌN: Zur Gattung der Spruchquelle Q." Pp. 77–96 in *Zeit und Geschichte: Dankesgabe an Rudolf Bultmann.* Ed. Erich Dinkler. Tübingen: J. C. B. Mohr (Paul Siebeck).
1971   "LOGOI SOPHŌN: On the Gattung of Q." Pp. 71–113 in *Trajectories through Early Christianity.* James M. Robinson and Helmut Koester. Philadelphia: Fortress.
1975   "Jesus as Sophos and Sophia." Pp. 1–16 in *Aspects of Wisdom in Judaism and Early Christianity.* Ed. R. L. Wilken. Notre Dame, Ind.: University of Notre Dame Press.

1982   "Early Collections of Jesus' Sayings." Pp. 389–94 in Delobel 1982.
1990   "The International Q Project Work Session 17 November 1989." *JBL* 109:499–501.
1991   "The International Q Project Work Session 16 November 1990." *JBL* 110:494–98.
1992a   "The International Q Project Work Session 16 November 1991." *JBL* 111:500–508.
1992b   "The Sayings Gospel Q." Pp. 361–88 in *The Four Gospels 1992: Festschrift Frans Neirynck.* Ed. Frans Van Segbroeck et al. BETL 100. Leuven: Leuven University Press and Uitgeverij Peeters.
1995   "The Jesus of Q as Liberation Theologian." Pp. 259–74 in Piper 1995.

Romm, James S.
1992   *The Edges of the Earth in Ancient Thought: Geography, Exploration, and Fiction.* Princeton, N.J.: Princeton University Press.

Saldarini, Anthony J.
1988   *Pharisees, Scribes and Sadducees in Palestinian Society: A Sociological Approach.* Wilmington, Del.: Michael Glazier.

Sato, Migaku
1988   *Q und Prophetie: Studien zur Gattungs- und Traditionsgeschichte der Quelle Q.* WUNT 2/29. Tübingen: J. C. B. Mohr (Paul Siebeck).

Schenk, Wolfgang
1981   *Synopse zur Redenquelle der Evangelien: Q-Synopse und Rekonstruktion in deutscher übersetzung.* Düsseldorf: Patmos.

Schmidt, Karl Ludwig
1919   *Der Rahmen der Geschichte Jesu: Literarkritische Untersuchungen zur ältesten Jesus-Überlieferung.* Berlin: Trowitsch & Sohn.

Schneider, Jane
1971   "On Vigilance and Virgins: Honor, Shame, and Access to Resources in Mediterranean Society." *Ethnology* 10:1–24.

Scholer, David M.
1989   "Q Bibliography 1981–1989." Pp. 23–56 in *Society of Biblical Literature 1989 Seminar Papers.* Ed. David J. Lull. SBLASP 28. Atlanta: Scholars Press.

1990   "Q Bibliography Supplement I: 1990." Pp. 11–13 in *Society of Biblical Literature 1990 Seminar Papers*. Ed. David J. Lull. SBLASP 29. Atlanta: Scholars Press.

1991   "Q Bibliography Supplement II: 1991." Pp. 1–7 in *Society of Biblical Literature 1991 Seminar Papers*. Ed. Eugene H. Lovering. SBLASP 30. Atlanta: Scholars Press.

1992   "Q Bibliography Supplement III: 1992." Pp. 1–4 in *Society of Biblical Literature 1992 Seminar Papers*. Ed. Eugene H. Lovering. SBLASP 31. Atlanta: Scholars Press.

1993   "Q Bibliography Supplement IV: 1993." Pp. 1–5 in *Society of Biblical Literature 1993 Seminar Papers*. Ed. Eugene H. Lovering. SBLASP 32. Atlanta: Scholars Press.

Schottroff, Luise
1978   "Non-violence and the Love of One's Enemies." Pp. 9–39 in *Essays on the Love Commandment*. Ed. Luise Schottroff et al. Philadelphia: Fortress.

Schüling, Joachim
1991   *Studien zum Verhältnis von Logienquelle und Markusevangelium*. FzB 65. Würzburg: Echter.

Schulz, Siegfried
1972   *Q: Die Spruchquelle der Evangelisten*. Zurich: Theologischer Verlag.

Schürmann, Heinz
1969   *Das Lukasevangelium*. HTKNT 3/1. Freiburg im Breisgau: Herder.
1982   "Das Zeugnis der Redenquelle für die Basileia-Verkündigung Jesu." Pp. 121–200 in Delobel 1982.
1991   "Zur Kompositionsgeschichte der Redenquelle: Beobachtungen an der lukanischen Q-Vorlage." Pp. 326–42 in *Der Treue Gottes trauen: Beiträge zum Werk des Lukas: Für Gerhard Schneider*. Ed. Claus Bussmann and Walter Radl. Freiburg im Breisgau, Basel, and Wien: Herder.

Scobie, Alexander
1969   *Aspects of the Ancient Romance and Its Heritage: Essays on Apuleius, Petronius, and the Greek Romances*. Beiträge zur klassischen Philologie 30. Meisenheim am Glan: Hain.

Scobie, Charles H. H.
1964   *John the Baptist*. London: SCM.

Scott, Bernard Brandon
1989   *Hear Then the Parable: A Commentary on the Parables of Jesus*. Minneapolis: Fortress.

Sellew, Philip
1986   "Early Collections of Jesus' Words: The Development of Dominical Discourses." Th.D. diss., Harvard Divinity School.

Sevenich-Bax, Elisabeth
1993   *Israels Konfrontation mit den letzten Boten der Weisheit: Form, Funktion und Interdependenz der Weisheitselemente in der Logienquelle.* Münsteraner theologische Abhandlungen 21. Altenberge: Oros.

Smith, Jonathan Z.
1978   *Map Is Not Territory: Studies in the History of Religions.* SJLA 23. Leiden: E. J. Brill.
1986   "Jerusalem: The City as Place." Pp. 25–38 in *Civitas: Religious Interpretations of the City.* Ed. Peter S. Hawkins. Atlanta: Scholars Press.
1987   *To Take Place: Toward Theory in Ritual.* Chicago: University of Chicago Press.

Stambaugh, John E.
1988   *The Ancient Roman City.* Ancient Society and History. Baltimore: Johns Hopkins University Press.

Steck, Odil H.
1967   *Israel und das gewaltsame Geschick der Propheten.* WMANT 23. Neukirchen-Vluyn: Neukirchener Verlag.

Stein, Robert H.
1987   *The Synoptic Problem: An Introduction.* Grand Rapids, Mich.: Baker Book House.

Steinhauser, Michael G.
1981   *Doppelbildworte in den synoptischen Evangelien: Eine form- und traditionskritische Studie.* FzB 44. Würzburg: Echter.

Streeter, B. H.
1924   *The Four Gospels: A Study of Origins, Treating of the Manuscript Tradition, Sources, Authorship, and Dates.* London: Macmillan.

Swartley, Willard M., ed.
1992   *The Love of Enemy and Nonretaliation in the New Testament.* Studies in Peace and Scripture. Louisville: Westminster/ John Knox.

Tannehill, Robert C.
1970   "The 'Focal Instance' as a Form of New Testament Speech: A Study of Matthew 5:39b–42." *JR* 50:372–85.

1975   *The Sword of His Mouth.* Semeia Supplements 1. Philadel-
            phia: Fortress.

Taylor, Vincent
1953   "The Order of Q." *JTS* 4:27–31.
1959   "The Original Order of Q." Pp. 246–69 in *New Testament
            Essays: Studies in Memory of T. W. Manson.* Ed. A. J. B.
            Higgins. Manchester: Manchester University Press.
1970   *New Testament Essays.* London: Epworth.

Theissen, Gerd
1973   "Wanderradikalismus: Literatur-soziologische Aspekte der
            Überlieferung von Worten Jesu im Urchristentum." *ZTK*
            70:245–71.
1977   " 'Wir Haben alles verlassen' (Mc. X, 28). Nachfolge und
            soziale Entwurzelung in der jüdisch-palästinischen Gesell-
            schaft des 1. Jahrhunderts n.Chr." *NovT* 19:161–96.
1978   *Sociology of Early Palestinian Christianity.* Philadelphia: For-
            tress.
1979a   "Gewaltverzicht und Feindesliebe." Pp. 160–97 in Theissen
            1979b.
1979b   *Studien zur Soziologie des Urchristentums.* WUNT 19. Tü-
            bingen: J. C. B. Mohr (Paul Siebeck).
1979c   "Wanderradikalismus: Literatursoziologische Aspekte der
            Überlieferung von Worten Jesu im Urchristentum." Pp. 79–
            105 in Theissen 1979b.
1979d   " 'Wir Haben alles verlassen' (Mc. X, 28): Nachfolge und
            soziale Entwurzelung in der jüdisch-palästinischen Gesell-
            schaft des 1. Jahrhunderts n.Chr." Pp. 106–41 in Theissen
            1979b.
1985   "Das 'schwankende Rohr' (Mt 11, 7) und die Grüngungs-
            münzen von Tiberias." *ZDPV* 101:43–55.
1991   *The Gospels in Context: Social and Political History in the
            Synoptic Tradition.* Minneapolis: Fortress.

Tödt, Heinz Eduard
1959   *Der Menschensohn in der synoptischen Überlieferung.* Gü-
            tersloh: Gerd Mohn.
1965   *The Son of Man in the Synoptic Tradition.* London: SCM.

Trilling, Wolfgang
1959   "Die Täufertradition bei Matthäus." *BZ*, n.s. 3:271–89.

Trocmé, Etienne
1980   "Jean-Baptiste dans le quatrième évangile." *RHPR* 60:129–
            51.

Trowbridge, C. C.
1913   "On Fundamental Methods of Orientation and Imaginary Maps." *Science* 38:888–97.

Tuan, Y.-F.
1978   "Literature and Geography: Implications for Geographical Research." Pp. 194–206 in *Humanistic Geography: Prospects and Problems*. Ed. David Ley and Marwyn S. Samuels. Chicago: Maaroufa.

Tuckett, Christopher M.
1983   *The Revival of the Griesbach Hypothesis: An Analysis and Appraisal*. SNTSMS 44. Cambridge and New York: Cambridge University Press.
1989   "A Cynic Q?" *Bib* 70:349–76.
1991   "On the Stratification of Q." Pp. 213–22 in *Early Christianity, Q and Jesus = Semeia 55*. Ed. John S. Kloppenborg, with Leif E. Vaage. Atlanta: Scholars Press.

Übelacker, Walter G.
1989   *Der Hebräerbrief als Appell: Untersuchungen zu Exordium, Narratio und Postscriptum (Hebr 1–2 und 13, 22–25)*. ConBNT 21. Stockholm: Almqvist & Wiksell.

Uro, Risto
1987   *Sheep among the Wolves: A Study on the Mission Instructions of Q*. Annales Academiae Scientiarum Fennicae. Dissertationes humanarum litterarum 47. Helsinki: Suomalainen Tiedeakatemia.
1991   "John the Baptist and the Jesus Movement: What Does Q Tell Us?" Paper presented at the one hundred twenty-seventh annual meeting of the Society of Biblical Literature (Q Seminar), Kansas City, Missouri.

Vaage, Leif E.
1988a   "An Archeological Approach to the Work of the Jesus Seminar." Paper presented to the spring meeting of the Jesus Seminar, Sonoma, California.
1988b   "The Woes in Q (and Matthew and Luke): Deciphering the Rhetoric of Criticism." Pp. 582–607 in *Society of Biblical Literature 1988 Seminar Papers*. Ed. David Lull. SBLASP 27. Atlanta: Scholars Press.
1991a   "The Composition of Q: A Response to Papers by John S. Kloppenborg, Dieter Lührmann, and Arland Jacobson." Paper presented at the fall 1991 meeting of the Westar Institute, Edmonton, Alberta, October 24–27.

1991b   "The Son of Man Sayings in Q: Stratigraphical Location and
         Significance." Pp. 103–29 in *Early Christianity, Q and Jesus*
         = *Semeia 55*. Ed. John S. Kloppenborg, with Leif E. Vaage.
         Atlanta: Scholars Press.
1994   *Galilean Upstarts: Jesus' First Followers according to Q.*
         Valley Forge, Pa.: Trinity Press International.
1995   "Q and Cynicism: On Comparison and Social Identity." Pp.
         199–229 in Piper 1995.

van Unnik, W. C.
1954   "The Teaching of Good Works in I Peter." *NTS* 1:92–110.
1966   "Die Motivierung der Feindesliebe in Lk 6.32–35." *NovT* 8:
         284–300.

Vassiliadis, Petros
1975   "The Function of John the Baptist in Q and Mark." *Theolo-
         gia* 46:405–13.

Vermes, Geza
1983   *Jesus the Jew: A Historian's Reading of the Gospels.* 2d ed.
         London: SCM.

Walz, Christian, ed.
1832–36 *Rhetores Graeci.* 9 vols. Stuttgart: J. G. Cotta.

Wanke, Joachim
1980   "Kommentarworte: Älteste Kommentierung von Herren-
         worten." *BZ*, NF 24:208–333.

Watson, Duane F.
1989   "1 Cor 10:23–11:1 in the Light of Greco-Roman Rhetoric:
         The Role of Rhetorical Questions." *JBL* 108:301–18.
1991   *Persuasive Artistry: Studies in New Testament Rhetoric in
         Honor of George A. Kennedy.* JSNTSup 50. Sheffield, Eng-
         land: Sheffield Academic Press.

Weaver, Dorothy Jean
1992   "Transforming Nonresistance: From *Lex Talionis* to 'Do Not
         Resist the Evil One.'" Pp. 32–71 in Swartley 1992.

Webb, Robert L.
1991   *John the Baptizer: A Socio-Historical Study.* JSNTSup 62.
         Sheffield, England: Sheffield Academic Press.

Wegner, Uwe
1985   *Der Hauptmann von Kafarnaum.* WUNT 2/14. Tübingen:
         J. C. B. Mohr (Paul Siebeck).

Weiss, Johannes
1907   Die Schriften des Neuen Testaments. 2d ed. Göttingen: Van-
          denhoeck & Ruprecht.

Westermann, Claus
1967   Basic Forms of Prophetic Speech. Philadelphia: Westminster.

White, John Lee
1972   The Form and Function of the Body of the Greek Letter: A
          Study of the Letter-body in the Non-literary Papyri and in
          Paul the Apostle. 2d ed. SBLDS 2. Missoula, Mont.: Scholars
          Press.

Whybray, R. N.
1965   Wisdom in Proverbs: The Concept of Wisdom in Proverbs
          1–9. SBT 1/45. Naperville, Ill.: A. R. Allenson.

Williams, James G.
1981   Those Who Ponder Proverbs: Aphoristic Thinking and Bib-
          lical Literature. Bible and Literature Series 2. Sheffield, Eng-
          land: Almond.

Wilson, Walter T.
1991   Love without Pretense: Romans 12.9–21 and Hellenistic-
          Jewish Wisdom Literature. WUNT 2/46. Tübingen: J. C. B.
          Mohr (Paul Siebeck).

Wink, Walter
1968   John the Baptist in the Gospel Tradition. SNTSMS 7. Cam-
          bridge: Cambridge University Press.
1976   "John the Baptist." IDBSup: 487–88.
1992a   "Counterresponse to Richard Horsley." Pp. 133–36 in Swart-
          ley 1992.
1992b   "Neither Passivity nor Violence: Jesus' Third Way (Matt.
          5:38–42 Par.)." Pp. 101–25 in Swartley 1992.

Witherington, Ben
1988   "Jesus and the Baptist: Two of a Kind?" Pp. 225–44 in Soci-
          ety of Biblical Literature 1988 Seminar Papers. Ed. David J.
          Lull. SBLASP 27. Atlanta: Scholars Press.

Wolff, Hans Julius
1970   "Some Observations on Praxis." Pp. 526–35 in Proceed-
          ings of the Twelfth International Congress of Papyrology. Ed.
          Deborah Hobson Samuel. American Studies in Papyrology 7.
          Toronto: A. M. Hakkert.

Wrege, Hans-Theo
1968   *Die Überlieferungsgeschichte der Bergpredigt.* WUNT 9. Tübingen: J. C. B. Mohr (Paul Siebeck).

Youtie, Herbert C.
1971a   "AGRAMMATOS: An Aspect of Greek Society in Egypt." *HSCP* 75:161–75.
1971b   "*Bradeōs graphōn:* Between Literacy and Illiteracy." *GRBS* 12:239–61.
1973–75 *Scriptiunculae.* 3 vols. Amsterdam: Adolf M. Hakkert.
1975a   "*Hypographeus:* The Social Impact of Illiteracy in Graeco-Roman Egypt." *ZPE* 17:201–21.
1975b   " 'Because They Do Not Know Letters.' " *ZPE* 19:101–8.
1981–82 *Scriptiunculae Posteriores.* 2 vols. Bonn: Rudolf Habelt.

Zeid, Abou A. M.
1965   "Honour and Shame among the Bedouin of Egypt." Pp. 243–59 in Peristiany 1965b.

Zeller, Dieter
1977   *Die weisheitlichen Mahnsprüche bei den Synoptikern.* FzB 17. Würzburg: Echter.
1982   "Redaktionsprozesse und wechselnder 'Sitz im Leben' beim Q-Material." Pp. 395–409 in Delobel 1982.
1984   *Kommentar zur Logienquelle.* Stuttgarter kleiner Kommentar, Neues Testament 21. Stuttgart: Verlag Katholisches Bibelwerk.
1993   "Redactional Processes and Changing Settings in the Q Material." Pp. 116–30 in Kloppenborg 1994.

Index of Modern Authors

Aitken, E., 52n. 10
Allison, D., 177nn. 7, 12
Arnal, W., 7, 8, 11
Attridge, H., 127n. 1

Bachmann, M., 195n. 6
Backhaus, K., 198nn. 22, 23, 24, 25;
    200n. 37, 201n. 43, 202n. 46
Bagnall, R., 5
Bain, D., 149n. 9
Bammel, E., 138, 184, 188, 194n. 3,
    195n. 6, 196n. 8, 197n. 13,
    199n. 31, 200n. 35
Barley, N., 114n. 24
Baroja, J., 129n. 33
Beardslee, W., 114n. 29, 115n. 30
Beare, F., 177n. 7
Benveniste, E., 112n. 10
Bergemann, T., 8
Berger, K., 117, 201n. 37
Betz, H., 8, 94n. 3, 103, 113n. 18;
    115nn. 30, 32; 127n. 1
Bieber, M., 150n. 10
Bitzer, L., 13
Bjorndahl, S., 127n. 1
Böcher, O., 195n. 6
Boismard, M., 196n. 9
Booth, A., 36n. 50
Bornkamm, G., 1
Bourdieu, P., 130nn. 33, 34
Bowden, M., 30n. 2
Brown, P., 129n. 26
Bultmann, R., 22, 32nn. 16, 17;
    51n. 2, 67n. 8, 90, 114n. 29, 170,
    171, 176n. 4, 177n. 10
Butts, J., 127n. 1

Cairns, F., 117
Cameron, R., 7, 10, 149nn. 6, 7;
    150n. 12, 154, 163n. 13, 191,
    200n. 35, 201n. 38
Campbell, J., 129n. 32
Carruth, S., 7, 8, 9, 10, 31n. 9
Castor, G., 1
Catchpole, D., 68nn. 8, 14, 15;
    69nn. 23, 24; 71n. 41

Cohen, D., 130n. 37
Collins, A., 51n. 4
Collins, J., 51n. 4
Cotter, W., 8, 10, 36n. 49, 49,
    149n. 2, 150n. 15, 163nn. 12,
    17; 177n. 10, 178n. 15, 179n. 20,
    180nn. 22, 23; 197n. 15
Crossan, J., 96n. 17, 114n. 24, 154,
    177n. 8, 196n. 8, 197n. 14
Crum, J., 1, 35n. 39, 36n. 55

Dalman, G., 31n. 5
Davies, W., 177nn. 7, 12
Deatrick, E., 35n. 42
Denich, B., 130n. 34
Derrett, J., 70n. 33
Dibelius, M., 176n. 4
Douglas, R., 5, 7, 8, 10, 30n. 1
Downing, F., 115n. 30, 122, 128n. 23
Downs, R., 18, 19, 30n. 2
DuBoulay, J., 124, 129n. 29
Duckworth, G., 150n. 9

Edwards, D., 25
Edwards, R., 114n. 29
Eisler, R., 195n. 5
Ernst, J., 183, 186, 194n. 2, 195n. 6,
    199n. 31, 200n. 37, 201n. 42

Farmer, W., 176n. 3
Fischel, H., 127n. 1
Fisher, N., 130n. 37
Fish, S., 162n. 9
Fitzmyer, J., 68n. 16, 177n. 8
Foerster, W., 199n. 30
Foster, G., 122, 129nn. 29, 30;
    130n. 38
Freyne, S., 128n. 20

Gagarin, D., 130n. 37
Gal, Z., 34n. 33
Garnsey, P., 35n. 41
Gilmore, D., 129n. 31
Glasson, T., 196n. 9
Goodman, M., 128n. 20
Goody, J., 129n. 27

Gould, P., 19, 31n. 3
Gregory, J., 129nn. 29, 30
Guéraud, O., 5
Gundry, R., 32nn. 11, 12, 15

Harnack, A., 1, 35n. 39, 150n. 13,
   166, 177n. 9
Harris, W., 36n. 50, 129n. 27
Hartin, P., 8, 10, 95n. 8, 155, 156,
   159
Havener, I., 98, 149nn. 1, 3, 8; 165
Hengel, M., 70n. 33
Herntrich, V., 38
Hock, R., 127n. 8
Hoffmann, P., 1, 2, 3, 69n. 21, 119,
   150n. 13, 155, 164n. 20, 176n. 4
Horsley, R., 4, 5, 7, 12, 30n. 1,
   34nn. 29, 32; 51nn. 1, 4, 6;
   52nn. 7, 9, 10, 11, 13; 53, 63,
   66nn. 1, 2; 69n. 20, 71nn. 39, 44;
   120, 122, 164nn. 20, 22, 24

Jacobson, A., 6, 9, 12, 33n. 21, 41,
   51n. 4, 114n. 28, 150n. 13, 153,
   159, 162n. 11, 165, 172, 176n. 2,
   177nn. 8, 12; 184, 197n. 20
Jeremias, J., 35n. 36, 51n. 2

Kelber, W., 90, 91, 92
Kennedy, G., 100, 115n. 31, 127n. 1
Kindermann, K., 138, 149n. 9
Klassen, W., 66n. 3
Kloppenborg, J., 5, 6, 7, 8, 9,
   10, 13, 14n. 1, 19, 20, 30n. 1,
   31n. 8, 34nn. 27, 28, 34; 35n. 35,
   36nn. 52, 55; 41, 46, 49, 51nn. 3,
   4, 5; 52nn. 12, 15; 53, 62, 64,
   66, 66n. 2, 69n. 28, 70n. 37,
   71n. 39, 75, 76, 80, 81, 82, 83,
   84, 85, 86, 87, 88, 89, 90, 92,
   94nn. 1, 2; 113n. 17, 114n. 29,
   115nn. 30, 32; 128n. 22, 129n. 28,
   135, 140, 150n. 14, 157, 162n. 8,
   163n. 12, 164n. 26, 166, 169, 170,
   172, 173, 176n. 2, 177nn. 8, 12;
   180n. 21, 184, 187, 188, 198n. 21,
   199n. 28
Koester, H., 7, 181, 195n. 5, 196n. 8
Kraeling, C., 176n. 3, 194n. 2,
   199n. 30, 201n. 41

Laufen, R., 79
Lausberg, H., 101, 113nn. 11, 21;
   114n. 26

Layton, B., 97n. 29
Linnemann, E., 196n. 9
Llewelyn, S., 61, 69n. 27, 70n. 33
Lowenthal, D., 30n. 2
Lucas, F., 138, 149n. 9
Lührmann, D., 1, 6, 12, 14, 32n. 17,
   33n. 20, 34n. 30, 51n. 3, 71n. 41,
   131n. 42, 150n. 13, 159, 163n. 12,
   177n. 5
Lupieri, E., 199n. 31
Luz, U., 35n. 36, 57, 66n. 5, 68n. 15,
   69nn. 18, 25; 71n. 41
Lynch, K., 18, 19, 31n. 3

MacDowell, D., 130n. 37
Mack, B., 13, 30n. 1, 112n. 1,
   113n. 20, 118, 119, 120, 121,
   122, 127nn. 1, 8; 129nn. 24, 25;
   131n. 43, 149n. 1, 152, 162n. 5,
   180n. 23
MacMullen, R., 35n. 41
Malbon, E., 31n. 5
Malherbe, A., 102, 113n. 13,
   198n. 24
Malina, B., 57, 65, 129n. 31
Manson, T., 1, 165, 177n. 7
März, C., 7, 177n. 6, 178n. 14
Mason, S., 196n. 8
McCloskey, D., 162n. 9
McCown, C., 31nn. 6, 8
Mead, G., 195n. 5
Meier, J., 195n. 6
Meshorer, Y., 25
Meyer, J., 18, 19, 30n. 2
Michie, D., 31n. 5
Mingana, A., 195n. 5
Moessner, D., 31n. 5
Moreland, M., 113n. 15, 197n. 16
Moulton, J., 26
Mullins, T., 116, 117, 118

Neirynck, F., 176n. 4
Neuman, J., 194n. 1, 196n. 8
Neusner, J., 52n. 14

Oakman, D., 55
Olbrechts-Tyteca, L., 103, 110,
   111
O'Neil, E., 127n. 8

Payot, C., 196n. 9
Percy, E., 150n. 13
Perdue, L., 105

Perelman, J., 103, 110, 111
Peristiany, J., 123, 129n. 31,
    130nn. 33, 35
Piper, J., 68nn. 11, 14
Piper, R., 4, 5, 10, 13, 27, 68n. 11,
    70n. 35, 71n. 42, 82, 96n. 21, 109,
    117, 118, 127nn. 5, 6; 159, 160,
    162nn. 1, 3, 7
Pitt-Rivers, J., 123, 129n. 33,
    130n. 34
Polag, A., 177n. 8

Qedar, S., 25

Redfield, R., 6
Reed, J., 4, 13, 25, 36nn. 58, 59;
    129n. 28
Rhoads, D., 31n. 5
Robbins, V., 3, 107, 112n. 10,
    115nn. 30, 32; 118, 127n. 1,
    131n. 43
Robertson, A., 26
Robinson, J., 1, 7, 35n. 42, 66,
    66n. 7, 76, 93, 96nn. 28, 29;
    97n. 29, 112nn. 8, 9; 113n. 15,
    114n. 22, 166, 197n. 6
Romm, J., 34n. 32

Saldarini, A., 42
Sato, M., 6, 21, 32n. 17, 33nn. 20,
    22, 24
Schenk, W., 150n. 13
Schmidt, K., 31n. 5
Schneider, J., 123
Scholer, D., 2
Schottroff, L., 66n. 3, 69n. 25,
    70n. 38, 71nn. 40, 45
Schüling, J., 79, 199n. 31
Schulz, S., 6, 67n. 8, 71n. 41, 149n. 6,
    163n. 12
Schürmann, H., 7, 9, 82, 84, 127n. 9
Scobie, A., 36n. 50
Scobie, C., 176n. 3, 177n. 9, 200n. 32
Scott, B., 47
Sellew, P., 79
Sevenich-Bax, E., 7
Smith, J., 30n. 2
Stambaugh, J., 36n. 56
Stea, D., 18
Steck, O., 33n. 23, 34n. 26, 135,
    164n. 23

Stein, R., 170, 171
Steinhauser, M., 163n. 12
Streeter, B., 177n. 8
Swartley, W., 66n. 3

Tannehill, R., 96n. 13, 120
Taylor, V., 94n. 5
Theissen, G., 3, 28, 96n. 14, 119,
    121, 122, 128nn. 16, 17, 18
Tödt, H., 1
Trilling, W., 195n. 6
Trocmé, E., 196n. 9
Trowbridge, C., 30nn. 2, 3
Tuan, Y., 19
Tuckett, C., 53, 72n. 45, 164n. 23
Übelacker, W., 127n. 1
Uro, R., 32n. 17, 33nn. 19, 20;
    200n. 36

Vaage, L., 7, 8, 11, 72n. 45,
    96nn. 11, 13, 14, 20, 25; 163n. 14,
    179n. 19, 185, 199n. 28, 200n. 33,
    201nn. 40, 41; 202n. 46
van Unnik, W., 130n. 41
Vassiliadis, P., 199n. 27
Vermes, G., 35nn. 39, 44

Wanke, J., 96n. 18
Watson, D., 113n. 21, 127n. 1
Weaver, D., 56, 66n. 2, 69n. 22
Webb, R., 195n. 5
Wegner, U., 32n. 13, 34n. 31
Weiss, J., 201n. 37
Westermann, C., 149n. 6
White, R., 19, 31n. 3
Whybray, R., 152
Williams, J., 114n. 24
Williams, R., 124, 129n. 29
Wilson, R., 8
Wink, W., 57, 63, 66nn. 4, 5; 166,
    176n. 3, 184, 195n. 6
Witherington, B., 198n. 26, 201n. 37,
    202n. 46
Wolff, H., 61
Wrege, H., 94n. 3

Youtie, H., 5, 129n. 27

Zeid, A., 130n. 33
Zeller, D., 7, 67n. 8, 128n. 22,
    150n. 13

Index of Ancient Texts

HEBREW BIBLE AND APOCRYPHA

Exodus
22:24–26	57
23:20	136, 144
23:30	202n. 44

Leviticus
16	199n. 30

Deuteronomy
19:15–21	69n. 22
19:17	69n. 22
19:18	69n. 22
24:10–13	57
24:17	57
32:11	46

2 Kings
1:8	183

Job
28	162n. 5

Psalms
9	38
10:18	38
72:4	38
76:9	38
82:1–3	38
103:6	38
117:26	34n. 27, 149n. 3, 173
140:12	38
146:7	38

Proverbs
1–9	151, 152
8:22	151
9:4	152
22:17–24:34	103

Isaiah
8:6–8	149n. 6
14:13a, 15	149n. 3
29:18–19	136, 141
29:18	149n. 3
30:12–14	149n. 6
35:5–6	136, 141, 149n. 3
42:6–7	149n. 3
61:1–2	149n. 3

Jeremiah
7:25–34	50
22:1–9	46
22:5	149n. 3
25:4–14	50

Daniel
7:13	173
9:4b–19	50

Hosea
2:5–7	149n. 6
4:1	48
12:7	48

Micah
3:1–2, 4	149n. 6
6:8	48
7:6	44, 149n. 3

Nehemiah
9:5–37	50

Amos
4:1–2	149n. 6

Zechariah
7:9	48
9:9	200n. 36

Malachi
3:1–2	173
3:1	136, 144, 200n. 36, 202n. 44

1 Esdras
4:30	56

Wisdom

7:27	154, 157
10:1–4	156
10:19	152

Sirach

1:8–9	152
1:10	152
4:11	154
24:19–20	152
49:14–25	202n. 47

4 Maccabees

18:8	199n. 30

Psalms of Solomon

17:28–32	38

Jubilees

1:7–26	50

SECOND TEMPLE JEWISH LITERATURE

Josephus, *Antiquities*

6.300–309	47
13.318	42
13.332	35n. 38
18.5.2	169
18.116–19	196n. 8, 201n. 40
18.117	183

1QS (Manual of Discipline)

8:1–4	38

RABBINIC LITERATURE

Mishnah
'Abot

3:18	97n. 28

B.Qam.

8:6	56

Sukk.

3.9	34n. 27

'Abot R. Nathan [A]

24	97n. 28

Lam. Rab.

Proem 31	49

SAYINGS GOSPEL Q
(*Boldface numbers indicate an entire section devoted to a text.*)

3:2–4	153, 177n. 8
3:2	28
3:3	19, 20
3:7–7:35	184
3:7–17	184
3:7–9	11, 13, 40, 53, 135, **136–40**, 142, 153, **165–80**, 185, **186–88**
3:7	28, 168
3:7a	167
3:7b–9	183, 184, 186, 188, 189
3:7b	186, 187
3:8–9	24, 138
3:8	136, 168, 171, 186, 188, 198n. 21
3:8a	187
3:9	168, 172, 188
3:9b	174
3:16–17	40, 135, **136–40**, 142, 153, **165–80**, 184, **186–88**
3:16	167, 168, 169, 170, 174, 185, 187, 188, 193, 200n. 36
3:16a	188
3:17	24, 168, 169, 187, 188
4:1–13	94n. 2, 202n. 44
4:1	20
4:5–8	2
4:9	20, 29
4:16	20
6:20–49	8, 11, 43, 44, **75–97**, **98–115**, 153, 156
6:20–23	80
6:20b–23	81
6:20b–23b	140
6:20–21	45
6:20b–21	81
6:20	78, 79
6:20b	77, 95n. 10, 108, 111
6:21	77, 78
6:21a	108
6:21b	108
6:22–23	50, 53, 58, 60, 65, 77, 78, 79
6:22–23b	80
6:23	9, 102, 161
6:24–26	45
6:27–38	113n. 15

6:27–36	*5, 27, 52n. 9,* **53–72,** **116–31**
6:27–35	*58, 80, 140*
6:27–31	*103*
6:27–30	*79*
6:27–29	*78*
6:27–28	*78, 79*
6:27	*56, 103, 113n. 12*
6:27a	*55, 117*
6:28b	*117*
6:29–30	*58, 59, 63, 65, 78*
6:29	*58*
6:29b	*58*
6:30	*58, 59, 63, 71n. 40,* *77, 78*
6:31–33	*104, 111*
6:31	*69n. 24, 77, 78, 94n. 6,* *118*
6:32–45	*103*
6:32–36	*78*
6:32–34	*118*
6:32–33	*65, 79*
6:35	*65, 111, 118*
6:35a	*80*
6:35b	*80*
6:36–45	*140*
6:36	*65, 95n. 8*
6:37–42	*127n. 4*
6:37–38	*58, 60, 79, 80*
6:38	*5, 24, 78*
6:39–45	*80*
6:39–42	*9*
6:39	*77, 78, 94n. 6, 105,* *114n. 22*
6:40	*78, 79, 114n. 22*
6:41–42	*9, 26, 77, 78, 94n. 6,* *101, 110, 111, 113n. 15*
6:43–45	*78, 107, 109, 114n. 22,* *127n. 4*
6:43–44	*24, 77, 78, 79, 174*
6:44	*26, 29, 105*
6:45	*77, 78*
6:46–49	*78, 140*
6:46	*9, 26, 101, 102, 105*
6:47–49	*43*
6:47	*102*
6:48	*29*
6:49	*102*
7:1–10	*12, 33n. 21, 40, 141,* *163n. 11*
7:1	*20*
7:3	*34n. 31*
7:6	*29*
7:9	*23, 141, 171*
7:18–35	*12, 40, 135,* **144–48,** *154, 180n. 21, 184,* **189–93**
7:18–27	*144*
7:18–23	*10, 39, 40,* **140–42,** *154, 171, 185, 189, 190*
7:19	*21, 140, 168, 173,* *200n. 36*
7:22–23	*141*
7:22	*136, 141, 142*
7:23	*96n. 25*
7:24–28	*40, 140,* **142–44,** *148, 191*
7:24–26	*11, 28, 143, 163n. 11,* *183, 191*
7:24	*21, 32n. 13*
7:26b–27	*144*
7:27	*136, 173, 183, 185, 193*
7:28	*144, 148, 165, 166,* *181, 193*
7:28a	*11, 183, 186*
7:28b	*185, 186*
7:31–35	*27, 40, 49,* **145–47,** *151,* **153–56,** *189*
7:31–34	*137, 146*
7:31	*34n. 30, 40, 49, 186*
7:32	*26, 27, 186*
7:33–34	*11, 145, 183, 186*
7:33	*186, 199n. 31*
7:35	*6, 146, 154, 159, 165,* *172, 183, 186*
9:57–10:16	*87, 88*
9:57–62	*87, 89, 131n. 43*
9:57–60	*11, 87, 89*
9:57	*21*
9:58	*29, 162n. 3*
9:59–60	*89*
9:62	*24*
10:2–16	*87*
10:2–11	*11, 89*
10:2	*24, 172*
10:3–16	*87*
10:3–4	*89*
10:4–6	*89*
10:5–11	*44*
10:6	*2*
10:6b	*89*
10:8–11	*27*
10:9	*40, 96n. 25*
10:10–15	*171*
10:10–11	*89*
10:10	*35n. 45*
10:11	*40*
10:12	*7, 21, 173*

SAYINGS GOSPEL Q (continued)

10:13–15	*32n. 17, 44*
10:13–14	*21, 22, 53*
10:13	*21, 32n. 18, 172*
10:15	*21, 149n. 3*
10:16	*11, 89*
10:21–24	*39, 87*
10:21–22	*151, 158, 159, 161*
10:21	*159*
10:23	*96n. 25*
11:2–13	*88*
11:2–4	*62, 87, 89*
11:2	*96n. 25*
11:4	*45*
11:4a	*89*
11:8	*26*
11:9–13	*61, 62, 87, 89,*
	127n. 4, 178n. 16
11:10	*90*
11:11–12	*90, 125*
11:11	*26*
11:13	*172*
11:14–26	*40*
11:14–20	*39, 52n. 15*
11:17	*29*
11:19	*137*
11:20	*40, 96n. 25*
11:21–22	*29*
11:29–35	*131n. 43*
11:29–33	*172*
11:29–32	*40, 49, 137, 171*
11:29–30	*34n. 29*
11:29	*34n. 30, 49*
11:30	*149n. 4*
11:31–32	*13, 24, 40, 137, 161*
11:31	*33n. 21, 34n. 29, 149n. 4,*
	151, 158, 159
11:32	*21, 34n. 30, 149n. 4, 172*
11:33	*24*
11:39–52	*4, 13, 38, 40, 46,*
	47, 50, 53
11:39–48	*89*
11:39–41	*27, 47, 48*
11:39–40	*29*
11:39	*137*
11:39a	*136*
11:39b–44	*172*
11:40–41	*137*
11:41	*136*
11:42	*25, 27, 47, 136, 137*
11:42c	*94n. 2, 202n. 44*
11:43	*26, 48, 137*
11:44	*47, 48, 137, 172*
11:46–52	*172*
11:46	*27, 48, 136, 137*
11:47–52	*51*
11:47–51	*51*
11:47–48	*137, 157*
11:47	*48*
11:48	*29*
11:49–51	*6, 12, 49, 53, 137,*
	*151, **156–58**, 159, 161*
11:50–51	*40, 49*
11:51	*34nn. 28, 29; 149n. 4,*
	157
11:51b	*158*
11:52	*48, 89, 157*
12:2–34	*87, 88*
12:2–12	*43, 45, 87, 90*
12:2–9	*127n. 4*
12:2–7	*87*
12:2–3	*62*
12:4–7	*28, 61, 71n. 40, 87, 89*
12:8–9	*28, 62*
12:10	*28, 62*
12:11–12	*28, 61, 87, 89*
12:11	*45*
12:22–34	*88*
12:22–32	*29, 119*
12:22–31	*62, 87, 89, 90, 120,*
	127n. 4
12:23	*90*
12:24–26	*90*
12:24	*25*
12:27–28	*90*
12:27	*9, 34n. 29, 136*
12:28	*25, 172*
12:30	*33n. 21, 125*
12:31	*96n. 25*
12:33–34	*89*
12:39–59	*40*
12:39–40	*66n. 6, 172*
12:42–46	*13*
12:43	*96n. 25*
12:49–59	*43, 44*
12:49	*171, 177n. 6*
12:51–53	*39, 53*
12:52–53	*149n. 3*
12:54–56	*29*
12:56	*172*
12:57–59	*26, 28, 45, 89, 172*
12:58–59	*5, 58, 60*
12:59	*28*
13:18–19	*29, 89*
13:18	*25, 96n. 25*
13:19	*25*
13:20–21	*89*
13:20	*96n. 25*

13:24–14:35	88
13:24	26, 46, 88
13:25–27	96n. 23
13:26	35n. 45, 46
13:28–30	33n. 21, 96n. 23
13:28–29	38, 39, 46, 47
13:28	34n. 29, 136, 137
13:29	33n. 21
13:34–35	18, 34n. 26, 38, 46, 53, 96n. 23, 136, 137, 138, 141, 147, 151, 158, 160, 161, 171, 173
13:34–35a	46
13:34–35b	50, 51
13:34	21, 22, 172
13:34a	33n. 25
13:35	7, 168, 173
14:16–24	26, 28, 46, 47, 89, 96n. 23
14:18	25
14:21	28, 35n. 45
14:23	28
14:26–27	89
14:26	88
14:27	88, 89
14:34–35	88
14:35	25, 172
15:4–7	89
16:13	64, 89
16:16	96n. 25, 140, **144**, 163n. 11, 166, 180n. 21, 184, 186
16:17	202n. 44
16:18	5, 94n. 2
17:1–4	44
17:2	25, 172
17:6	25
17:18–23	193
17:22–37	43
17:22–27	137
17:23–37	13, 40
17:23	142
17:24	142
17:26–27	34n. 29, 142, 149n. 4
17:28–30	142, 173
17:28	149n. 4
17:31–37	137
17:33	26, 88, 89
17:34–35	142
17:35	25
17:37	142
19:12–27	13, 137
19:12–20	89
19:21	172
19:23	26
22:28–30	12, 34n. 30, 38, 39, 71n. 39, 137, 142
22:30	23

NEW TESTAMENT

Matthew
3:1–12	195n. 6
3:1	31n. 8
3:13–17	195n. 6
4:12	195n. 6
4:13	20
5:25–26	70n. 31
5:29–30	68n. 15
5:38–42	71n. 45
5:39	68n. 15
5:39b	58
5:40	58
5:41	58, 66n. 4
5:42	58
5:46–47	119
8:1–4	32n. 13
8:1	32n. 13
8:5–10	32n. 13
8:11–12	38, 46
8:28	32n. 13
9:14–17	195n. 6
10:17	36n. 51
11:2–19	195n. 6
11:7b–8	194n. 3
11:19	155
12:23	34n. 29
12:24	52n. 15
12:38	49
12:43	199n. 30
14:3–12	195n. 6
17:10–13	195n. 6
18:8–9	68n. 15
18:12	35n. 43
19:28	38
20:3	35n. 41
21:23–27	195n. 6
21:28–32	195n. 6
26:67	56
27:51b–53	32n. 11

Mark
1:2–3	183
1:2	150n. 12, 173, 182, 183
1:4	31n. 8, 182, 183
1:5–6	167
1:5	182

Mark (continued)

1:6	*183, 200n. 33*
1:7–8	*168, 170, 197n. 14*
1:7	*168, 182*
1:8	*182*
1:9	*182*
1:10	*182*
1:12	*182*
1:23–28	*182*
1:24	*182*
1:40–45	*32n. 13*
2:1	*32n. 13*
2:16	*145*
2:18–20	*183*
2:18	*145, 199n. 29*
3:11	*182*
3:22	*50, 199n. 30*
3:30	*182*
4:24	*79*
5:1–18	*182*
6:7	*182*
6:14–16	*182*
6:15	*183*
6:17–29	*182*
6:20	*182*
6:27–28	*181*
6:30–32	*182*
6:45	*32n. 18*
7:1–2	*50*
7:24–30	*182*
8:12	*49*
8:22–23	*32n. 18*
8:38	*49*
9:11–13	*183*
9:14–27	*182*
9:19	*49*
12:1–9	*47*
13:9	*45*
13:30	*49*
13:31	*93*
14:65	*68n. 12*

Luke

3:1–18	*195n. 6*
3:2	*31n. 8*
3:14	*68n. 9*
3:19–20	*195n. 6*
4:16	*20*
4:25–26	*195n. 6*
6:20–49	*76*
6:24–26	*56*
6:29	*119*
6:34	*59*
6:47	*76*

7:18–35	*195n. 6*
7:35	*155*
8:22	*31n. 10*
9:10–12	*32n. 18*
9:54	*195n. 6*
9:57	*32n. 16*
9:61–62	*35n. 35*
10:30	*55*
11:1	*195n. 6*
11:15	*52n. 15*
12:39	*55*
13:28–29	*46*
15:4	*35n. 43*
16:9–13	*127n. 4*
16:16	*195n. 6*
17:20–37	*93*
18:1–8	*69n. 29*
22:28–30	*38*
22:36–38	*55*
22:49–52	*55*
23:19	*55*
23:32	*55*
23:39–43	*55*

John

1:6–8	*184*
1:7	*184*
1:15	*197n. 14*
1:19–34	*184*
1:26–27	*197n. 14*
1:27	*179n. 18*
1:28	*184*
1:29	*184*
1:30–31	*197n. 14*
1:32–33	*197n. 14*
1:34	*184*
1:36	*184*
1:44	*32n. 18*
3:26	*184, 197n. 12*
3:28	*184*
4:1–2	*197n. 12*
10:20	*200n. 34*
10:41	*184*
12:21	*32n. 18*
13:16	*79*
15:20	*79*
20:31	*184*

Acts

1:4–5	*197n. 14*
1:5	*195n. 6*
1:22	*195n. 6*
5:36–37	*55*
10:37	*195n. 6*

11:16	195n. 6, 197n. 14
13:24–35	195n. 6
13:25	197n. 14
15:28	95n. 9
18:24–28	195n. 6
19:1–7	195n. 6
19:4	197n. 14

Romans

2:1	79
2:4	197n. 11
12:14	79

2 Corinthians

7:9	197n. 11
7:10	197n. 11
12:21	197n. 11

James

3:12	79
4:11–12	79

1 Peter

2:18–25	71n. 40
3:14	79
4:13–14	79

EARLY CHRISTIAN LITERATURE

Acts of Thomas

36	194n. 3

1 Clement

13:1–2	95n. 9
13:2	83, 93

2 Clement

13:4	78, 79

Didache

1:3–6	93
1:3	78, 79
1:4–5	78
11:8	79

Justin *Dialogue*

49	195n. 5
51	195n. 5

P. Egerton 2

fr. 2 recto	95n. 9

P. Oxyrhynchus 1

1–4	95n. 9

P. Oxyrhynchus 1224

fr. 2 recto col. 1	95n. 9

Polycarp *To the Philippians*

2:3	78, 79
12:3	78, 79

NAG HAMMADI AND RELATED LITERATURE

Apocryphon of James

4.2	181

Apocalypse of Peter (NHC VII,3)

76.4–8	95n. 9

Book of Thomas (NHC II,7)

145.3–8	95n. 9

Dialogue of the Savior

53	95n. 9

Exegesis of the Soul (NHC II,6)

135.23	195n. 5

Gospel of the Egyptians (NH III,2)

65.23–25	195n. 5

Gospel of Thomas

6	77, 78, 94n. 6
26	77, 78, 94n. 6, 96n. 17
34	77, 78, 94n. 6, 96n. 17
43	77, 78, 94n. 6
45	77, 78, 94n. 6
46	181
52	194n. 3
54	77, 78, 94n. 6
68–69a	77, 78
68	77
69	78
69b	77, 78
78	191, 194n. 3
95	77, 78
104	195n. 3

Pistis Sophia

7.7	195n. 5
7.62	195n. 5
7.133	195n. 5
7.135	195n. 5
133	197n. 14

Testimony of Truth (NHC IX,3)

30.24	*195n. 5*
31.3	*195n. 5*
39.24	*195n. 5*
45.6	*195n. 5*

Valentinian Exposition
(NHC XI,2)

b.41	*195n. 5*
c.42.11	*195n. 5*

Second Treatise of the Great Seth
(NHC VII,2)

63.64	*195n. 5*

CLASSICAL AUTHORS

Aphthonius *Progymnasmata*

3.4	*115n. 34*
3	*114n. 24, 127n. 8*
4	*106*

Aristotle *Rhetoric*

1.2.3–5	*112n. 2*
1.2.3	*99*
1.2.4	*99, 100*
2.1.5	*112n. 3*
2.18.4–5	*115n. 33*
2.21.2	*106*
2.21.3–6	*114n. 25*
2.21.9	*107*
2.21.11	*107*
2.21.13–14	*107*
2.21.16	*106*
3.12.4	*108*
3.14.12	*112n. 6*

Cicero
De inventione

2.22.68	*114n. 26*

De oratore

2.9.35	*99*
2.42.182	*99*
2.43.184	*100*
2.81.333	*100*

Part. Or.

6.22	*100*
15.53	*108*

Demetrius *De elocutione*

5.279	*104*

Dio Chrysostom

32.11	*102*
77/78.37–45	*113n. 13*

Diogenes Laertius

6.32	*202n. 48*
6.54	*200n. 34*
6.73	*200n. 33*
6.77	*200n. 33*
8.17–18	*113n. 19*
10.139–154	*113n. 18*

Epictetus *Diss.*

3.23.23–38	*113n. 13*

Epicurus

Kyriai Doxai	*103*

Euripides *Medea*

1.1–11	*139*
1.36–46	*139*

Hermogenes *Progymnasmata*

3–4	*115n. 34*
4	*106*
7.1	*114n. 24*

Isocrates
Antidosis

278–280	*99*

Nicocles or the Cyprians

48–62	*113n. 16*

To Nicocles

17–40	*113n. 16*

Juvenal *Sat.*

14.311–14	*202n. 48*

Longinus *On the Sublime*

12.2	*115n. 33*
25.1	*110*
26.3	*127n. 9*

Lucian *Vit. auc.*	*200n. 33*

Nicolaus of Myra

162–184	*127n. 8*

Seneca *De Ira*

2.34.1	*70n. 38*

Sophocles *Oedipus Rex*

1.82–84	*139*
1.85–91	*143*

Plutarch
De liberis educandis
  12.17   *113n. 19*
Demetrius
  33   *35n. 36*
Quomodo adulator ab amico
  internoscatur
  73C–74E   *113n. 13*

Quintilian
  1.9.3–5   *114n. 24*
  2.15.34   *99*
  3.8.12   *112n. 4*
  3.8.36   *99*
  3.8   *122*
  4.1.7   *112n. 5*
  4.1.78   *99*
  5.11.36   *115n. 34*
  5.11.37   *106, 107*
  5.11.44   *114n. 28*
  8.3.71   *105*
  8.4.1–29   *115n. 33*
  8.5.3   *106*
  8.5.4   *114n. 25*
  8.5.5–7   *106*
  8.5.6   *105*
  8.5.7–8   *107*
  8.5.9   *109*
  8.5.10–11   *110*
  8.5.10   *114n. 26*
  8.5.13   *107*

  8.5.32   *114n. 27*
  9.2.6–7   *113n. 21*
  9.2.10–11   *105*
  9.2.15   *104*
  9.2.28   *104*
  9.2.29   *113n. 11*
  9.3.50   *108*

Rhetorica ad Alexandrum
  1   *115n. 34*
  7   *114n. 26*
  11   *106*
  15   *112n. 4, 110*
  29   *112n. 5*

Rhetorica ad Herennium
  2.13.19   *114n. 26*
  2.29.46   *115n. 34*
  4.17.24   *114n. 25*
  4.18.26   *109*
  4.23.33   *104*
  4.30.41   *108*
  4.36.48–49   *113n. 11*
  4.37.49   *101*
  4.43.56–44.58   *127n. 8*

Theon *Progymnasmata*
  202.5   *114n. 24*

Xenophon *Anabasis*
  2.6.1   *31n. 10*